STONEWALL
IN THE
VALLEY

STONEWALL
IN THE
VALLEY

Thomas J. "Stonewall" Jackson's
Shenandoah Valley Campaign
Spring 1862

ROBERT G. TANNER

DOUBLEDAY & COMPANY, INC.
Garden City, New York

Grateful acknowledgment is made to the following for permission to use previously copyrighted material:

David McKay Company, Inc.–DESTRUCTION AND RECONSTRUCTION by Richard Taylor, copyright © 1955 by Richard Taylor. Published by Longmans Green and Company. STONEWALL JACKSON AND THE CIVIL WAR by G. F. R. Henderson, copyright © 1961 by Longmans Green and Co. Published 1936 by Longmans Green and Co. Reprinted by permission of David McKay Company, Inc.

University of North Carolina Press–THE VALLEY OF VIRGINIA IN THE AMERICAN REVOLUTION by Freeman H. Hart and NOTES ON THE STATE OF VIRGINIA edited by William Peden. Published for the Institute of Early American History and Culture.

University of Pittsburgh Press–A BORDERLAND CONFEDERATE by William L. Wilson, copyright © 1962 by the University of Pittsburgh Press. Reprinted by permission.

Library of Congress Cataloging in Publication Data

Tanner, Robert G
Stonewall in the valley.

Bibliography: p. 410
Includes index.
1. Shenandoah Valley Campaign, Mar.-Sept., 1862.
2. Jackson, Thomas Jonathan, 1824–1863. I. Title.
E473.74.T36   973.7′32
ISBN 0-385-12148-2
Library of Congress Catalog Card Number 76–3002

FOR MY PARENTS

CONTENTS

PART III

LIST OF ILLUSTRATIONS

Following page 316

MAPS

ACKNOWLEDGMENTS

Historical writing, at least as it pertains to the War Between the States, is often a process of elimination, and the historian's hardest decisions may concern what to delete. During the past decade this author examined a vast amount of original source material, and for their aid in the difficult task of deletion, I am grateful to the following:

Dr. William G. Bean, a scholar for almost half a century at Washington and Lee University, Lexington, Virginia, who shared the as yet unpublished diaries of John Apperson and Harry Morrison and the unpublished manuscript of John Lyle, all veterans of the Stonewall Brigade and of the "Liberty Hall Volunteers"; Colonel Campbell Brown, who granted use of the reminiscences of his grandfather Captain Campbell Brown, chief of staff of R. S. Ewell's division; Dr. Percy G. Hamlin, who authorized citations from his important volume of General Ewell's personal letters, *The Making of a Soldier;* Dr. James A. Miller of Winchester, Virginia, who allowed me to reproduce here passages from the letters of his grandfather Dr. Abraham Miller, a surgeon with the Valley Army; Mrs. C. O. Phillips of Philippi, West Virginia, who graciously consented to our quoting from the wartime diary of her grandfather, the 31st Virginia's Jim Hall; and Dr. Charles Turner, professor of history at Washington and Lee University, who thoughtfully provided copies of and authority to cite from the letters of two Stonewall Brigade veterans, Theodore Barclay and James K. Edmondson. (The Barclay and Edmondson collections are found in "The Castle," headquarters of the Rockbridge County Historical Society in Lexington, Virginia.)

A great deal of the research for this book was undertaken at university libraries and other research centers. In this realm, Lieutenant Colonel George B. Davis and his outstanding staff at Preston Library of the Virginia Military Institute, Lexington, deserve particular thanks for the assistance given throughout the four years of my cadetship at V.M.I. I am also grateful to Colonel Davis for his role in securing the permission of the Stonewall Jackson Foundation to use its John Garibaldi and T. J. Jackson Papers. The following librarians and archivists have provided additional guidance and permission to extract from original material: B. E. Powell, Duke University, Durham, North Carolina; Margaret Cook, College of William and Mary, Williamsburg, Virginia; Mrs. R. O. La Follette, Handley Library, Winchester, Virginia; Kurt E. Brandenburg, Museum of the Confederacy, Richmond, Virginia; Mrs. Joseph Waggener, Tennessee State Library and Archives, Nashville; Wilbur E. Meneray, Tulane University Library, New Orleans, Louisiana; Carolyn A. Wallace, University of North Carolina at Chapel Hill; Edmund Berkeley, Jr., University of Virginia, Charlottesville; and John Melville Jennings and William M. E. Rachal, Virginia Historical Society, Richmond. Much valuable work has also been accomplished in the National Archives and Library of Congress, Washington, D.C.; State of Georgia Department of Archives and History, Atlanta; Virginia State Library, Richmond; Atlanta Historical Society; Atlanta Public Library; and the libraries of Bridgewater College, Bridgewater, Virginia; Emory University, Atlanta, Georgia; and Wake Forest University, Winston-Salem, North Carolina.

Several scholars have read drafts of this work, and their patience and instructive criticism entitles them to more than my thanks here can express. In this group are Dr. James I. Robertson, Jr., Virginia Polytechnic Institute, Blacksburg, Virginia; Professor Theodore Ropp, Duke University; Dr. Frank Yearns, Wake Forest University; and Dr. John Barrett, Virginia Military Institute. Special appreciation is due to Dr. Barrett, my teacher and adviser at V.M.I., and much of whatever may be worthwhile in this book will stem from an effort to emulate the attention to detail and analytic precision with which he teaches American history.

Thanks must also go to Mr. James Geary, director of the New Market Battlefield Memorial in New Market, Virginia. Mr. Geary made the Battlefield Park's facilities available for a summer retreat during which several difficult chapters were completed. My very real debt to Mr. Geary, and to all of his staff, for much encouragement and assistance is hereby happily acknowledged.

Mr. William C. Davis, editor of the *Civil War Times Illustrated* and the author of several outstanding books on the war, was kind enough to review the last draft of this work. Even at that relatively late stage he was able to make several valuable suggestions, and his aid is much appreciated.

Working under considerable pressure, Mrs. Lucy Sheffield and her assistants at the Emory Typing Service skillfully prepared the manuscript, and their many helpful suggestions and consistent good humor merit special recognition.

For support and advice along the way I am indebted to Harry Butler, Harold Neale, Henry L'Orange, and Thomas Thompson, Jr., none of whom despaired about this manuscript in its early stages.

Pat Edison did a splendid job of transforming the author's notions into many of the maps appearing herein. It was originally planned to reproduce the Jedediah Hotchkiss maps of the Battles of Kernstown, McDowell, Winchester, and Port Republic, but technical problems made reproduction impossible, and these maps have been redrawn for inclusion. A few of the details sketched by Hotchkiss have been eliminated, and some details have been added, but in the significant respects these redrawings are true to the originals.

Finally, my sincere thanks go to Miss Jean Anne Vincent, Mr. Joseph Gonzalez, and Miss Georgiana Remer, Doubleday and Company, for an adventurous spirit willing to take on this book and for the hard work which brought it into final form. Virtually every page has benefited from their thoughtful comments, and the author could not have received better or more patient editorial guidance.

Robert G. Tanner

Atlanta,
January 1, 1976

INTRODUCTION

On June 21, 1863, Colonel James Fremantle of Her Majesty's Coldstream Guards trotted down into the Shenandoah Valley of Virginia and overtook Robert E. Lee's army on its march to Gettysburg. Fremantle had come to America as a military observer of the great Civil War, then in its third summer; a painstaking diarist who recorded all he learned, Fremantle was the perfect officer for this task, and on that June day he made a significant notation. Upon entering the Valley, Confederate soldiers who knew almost nothing about it began to boast of "Stonewall" Jackson's "celebrated" Valley Campaign, and that evening Fremantle wrote: "'Stonewall' Jackson is considered a regular demigod in this country."[1] Only a year after its close, the Valley Campaign of 1862—Jackson's Valley Campaign as it is now known—was in the hands of the romanticizers.

As a result, the actual Campaign is perhaps as little known today as it was to the rebels who bragged about it to Fremantle. Confederate blunders (and there were Confederate blunders in the Valley Campaign of 1862) were either never understood as errors or simply forgotten. Each Southern movement has become, in romantic retrospect, an integral step in a brilliantly conceived strategy, and to suggest that Stonewall operated for several crucial weeks within a command system so nebulous that two general officers were at one time issuing him contradictory orders would seem absurd, although this was actually the case. Skirmishes of the advance and rear guards have been escalated into battles; Federal demidivisions encountered by the rebels have grown into separate armies. Worst of all, the generally calm Union reaction to news from the Shenandoah has been distorted into a panic for the safety of Washington that supposedly paralyzed cities like Boston and New York after the Battle of Winchester on May 25, 1862.

That the Battle of Winchester should be credited with stampeding the North is attributable to two additional misconceptions that seem welded to the Campaign. First is the view that Jackson, pursuing the inspiration of General Robert E. Lee, maneuvered throughout the spring of 1862 to offer the Valley Army as a standing threat to President Abraham Lincoln. Even Jackson's great military biographer, Colonel G. F. R. Henderson, could not disabuse himself of this idea: "It was at Lincoln that Lee was about to strike, at Lincoln and the Northern people, and an effective blow at the point which people and President deemed vital [i.e., Washington, D.C.] might arrest the progress of their armies as surely as if the Confederates had been reinforced by a hundred thousand men."[2]

A second misconception is a logical extension of the first. It holds that Lee and Jackson's feint succeeded and that Lincoln twice scrambled Union troop movements for fear the Valley Army was about to overrun Washington. Colonel William Allan, who served as a Confederate ordnance officer throughout the Campaign and who in 1880 published the only history of it, credited Jackson with causing "to be detained, for the defense of Washington and Maryland, forces in the aggregate four or five times as numerous as his own. . . ."[3] Describing the impact of the Battle of Kernstown on the Union high command, Allan asserted that "the sensitiveness of the Federal government to the danger of Washington, excited by Jackson, led to the detachment of McDowell's corps from McClellan. . . ."[4] Major Robert Dabney, Jackson's chief of staff during the Campaign, wrote of Lincoln's reaction to the Battle of Winchester: ". . . the terror inspired by Jackson caused the President to refuse his consent [to General McDowell's march from Fredericksburg to Richmond]; he was unwilling to expose his Capital to a sudden blow from this ubiquitous leader; and instead of sending McDowell forward, he commanded him to retire nearer to Washington."[5] Colonel Allan joined Dabney in this view.[6] And yet a careful reading of the correspondence reveals that Jackson was not dispatched to harass Washington via the Shenandoah and that Lincoln's fateful decisions in the spring of 1862 did not result from fear of the Valley Army.

This is not to suggest that everything written about the Campaign is hyperbole. The Shenandoah Valley Campaign of 1862 was an extraordinary episode of our Civil War. Men did extend themselves in magnificent and memorable ways, and for that reason alone it is imperative that romance not cloud this chapter of the war. There is need, in short, for a new history of the Valley Campaign.

Similarly, the Campaign as a military operation has not been presented since 1880 to the growing corps of military historians. This is particularly unfortunate, for as a victory over adverse odds it has few equals. Confederate efforts in the Shenandoah began with a warning that means would be small, and the rebels achieved all they did despite an enemy force which outnumbered them at least two to one. The Union on occasion mustered three and even five times the Confederate strength, yet the Valley Army triumphed. There is rich reward for the student of military operations in a study of this Campaign: ". . . to the student of military art," noted Colonel Allan, "it affords an admirable example of an aggressive-defensive campaign, and one of the best instances in modern times of the degree to which skill and daring may neutralize superiority of numbers and resources."[7]

And the Campaign offers still more than this, for it is both a lesson in the value of time—time occasionally measured only in hours—and a distillation of the elements of successful strategy. The Valley Campaign was waged by men constrained to make every day count, and the military historian will find no better example of an army operating so successfully under the tyranny of waning time. The Campaign also brings into focus the reasoned application of principles of war too often dismissed as incidental to the "instinctive brilliance" and "strategic genius" of a commander. Such vague attributes can imply that strategic success is somehow beyond the reader's understanding, that it is a thing reserved for a select company of the great captains alone. The Valley Army's outstanding strategy, however, becomes readily comprehensible when analyzed in terms of objectives, terrain, and what Jackson knew or may reasonably be assumed to have known of the enemy situation. Examples of this point are the Confederate march to McDowell in early May, the operations of May 24, and the subsequent retreat through Strasburg at the end of May. At each of these junctures the rebels were pursuing the only logical course available. The Campaign ultimately is an illustration that strategic brilliance springs from hard work and common sense in the application of fundamental principles of war.

A recounting of the Valley Campaign of 1862 thus appears a useful contribution in several areas. But a question arises, one posed by Jackson himself. Had Stonewall been an actor, his popularity at the box office would have been counterbalanced by the resentment he sparked among his colleagues, all of whom he invariably upstaged. Douglas Southall Freeman once observed that the saga of Robert E. Lee's Army of Northern Virginia from the Battle of Cedar Mountain to Chancellorsville was essentially Jackson's military biography, and this is true. Is it, then, not inescapably true that a history of the Valley Campaign, Jackson's greatest strategic accomplishment, must profile his achievements to the exclusion of others? *Stonewall in the Valley* was the only title which seemed to fit this volume, yet that title unquestionably stresses the man over the events. Must this history retrace the exhaustive researches of Jackson's many biographers?

The answer is no. This is not a biography of Jackson, not even a military biography. Much of the Campaign must be narrated from his side, and Jackson's development as a commander is traced because it is a significant aspect of the Campaign. But more basically, Jackson provides a contrast which sharpens depiction of Valley Army rank and file, and it is these men who hold center stage here. These civilians were forged into veteran fighters of awesome reputation within six months. No Confederate in the Shenandoah escaped the crucible of those months, and the struggle of Valley Army men to overcome adversity at all levels is a unifying theme of these pages. The struggle is told whenever possible in the rebels' own words, eyewitness accounts fully as compelling as a historical chronicle or strategic study of the Campaign. As much as it is a historical and military work, this volume is also the record left by men enduring boredom, hunger, exhaustion, and fear as they grew from volunteers to veterans.

Implicit in the foregoing is a decision to emphasize the Confederate view of the Campaign. This is done without apology, for that story is more engrossing by far than that of the Federals, who squandered their opportunities in the Valley. Nevertheless, if this work is to be useful to the military historian there must be greater attention to Union strategy than otherwise might be the case. Chapters 5, 6, and 12 accordingly probe Union planning and mistakes. Appendix B and several lengthy footnotes also develop Union strategy. The goal is to present a study sufficiently detailed to elaborate the Confederacy's remarkable achievements in the Valley, yet general enough so that the military historian may evaluate the strategy of both sides.

In summary, *Stonewall in the Valley* is offered to provide a readable account of the South's largely unknown Valley Campaign of 1862, to analyze a classic of the warrior's art, and to trace the forging of an army which, at its peak in the spring of 1862, was dreaded as invincible.

PROLOGUE

The Stonewall Brigade was going home. Sergeants were in the camp now, bellowing to strike tents. That guaranteed it. The brigade was leaving the Confederate Army camped at Centreville, Virginia, and going home to the Shenandoah Valley. Private John Opie of the 5th Virginia began to fantasize about a furlough; the E Company Irishmen of the 33d Virginia celebrated with another barrel of stolen whiskey. Rarely did the entire brigade agree on anything, but every man was happy about this shift. The transfer to Winchester, Virginia, would get them out of General Joseph E. Johnston's soggy camps and into the army of their former commander, Major General "Stonewall" Jackson. And it would return them to the Valley most knew as home.

On November 9, 1861, an eager rebel swarm in the guise of an infantry brigade descended on the depot at Manassas Junction, Virginia. An assortment of wheezing locomotives, discards from the roundhouses of the North, awaited to transport them to the Valley. Cars to accommodate five regiments had been ordered; enough for only three had come. Forced to await space on the return trains, the 4th and 33d Virginia shuffled aside, grunting about army boondoggles. The 2d, 5th, and 27th Virginia tossed up their gear and packed in around it: soldiers clambered atop the cars, wedged between them, hung to brakes, ladders, vents, cracks, or anything they could grasp.

An eight-hour journey bounced these Virginians across sections of their state which history would make famous. They rumbled westward through Thoroughfare Gap of the Bull Run Mountains. During the summer of 1862 they would come back over this gap on one of the toughest marches they ever knew, and at the end of

that march, they would pillage the station they had just left and
crush the Union army of Major General John Pope. Beyond the
mountains came endless stands of cedar and slippery elm and
hickory. By 1864, when the last trappings of adventure, even of
purpose, were stripped from the war, these forests became the
lair of the rebel raider Colonel John Mosby, and men would stalk
one another here with a fury no one harbored in the autumn of
1861.

Farther on, in Manassas Gap of the Blue Ridge, cedar and
hickory gave way to mountain laurel, and steam yielded to mus-
cle. Several grades here were too sharp for the gorged trains, so
everyone walked, creating a scene which was vintage Confederacy
—hundreds of foulmouthed infantry kicking up dust and flinging
bits of gravel at the lumbering baggage cars beside them. Eventually they gained the summit and entered the Shenandoah Valley.
Wags such as Private Jim Frazier of the 5th Virginia immediately
warned that it was not uncommon for the couplings between an
engine and its cars to snap on the downgrade. The show that followed, with the locomotive straining to keep clear of the butting
cars, was spectacular, they said. The suddenly uneasy men re-
boarded and enjoyed the ride less until the tracks leveled off outside Front Royal and struck westward across the Valley floor
to Strasburg, where the convoy halted soon after dark. The troops
were hungry, parched, and ready for a bung knocking. They
plunged off the trains and made for town in roaring good spirits.

Next morning, November 10, many men were too drunk to
make reveille. Roll callers tallied scores absent. In the 27th Virginia only Captain James Edmondson's Company H answered up
all present, and it totaled fully a third of the regiment.[1] Other
rebels were already heading home on self-granted holidays. John
Opie was thinking about it as the regiments marched for Winchester, Stonewall Jackson's headquarters, but a rumor circulated
during the day that kept him in ranks. Winchester's civilians were
said to have volunteered to shelter the regiments for the night.
This was welcome news: tents had been left at Strasburg because
there were no wagons to haul them, and there was promise of a
rainstorm from the northwest. The rebel pace quickened. A real
bed awaited.

Abruptly, just outside Winchester, the column halted, stood silent under a brisk rain shower, then exploded with profanity as orders came to countermarch several miles to an unsheltered bivouac. Jackson, who knew his soldiers would carouse all night once they got inside Winchester, was determined to keep them out. Stonewall's rock-ribbed discipline—"He would have a man shot at the drop of a hat, and drop it himself," grumbled one rebel[2]— would not permit a single night's relaxation. He had belted Winchester with local militia under instructions that no one was to be admitted without a pass signed by himself.

The Stonewall Brigade nearly mutinied as a result. When Colonel William Harman of the 5th Virginia motioned for a countermarch, his own brother, captain of the regiment's lead company, refused to obey. A lieutenant and then a sergeant balked, until the irate colonel spurred toward the sergeant threatening to saber him. At that, Captain Harman drew his sword and promised revenge. The brothers glared at each other for long, wet minutes, before, slowly, orders prevailed.[3]

Or so it seemed. In fact, the indomitable Stonewall Jackson was about to be outflanked and overrun. As John Opie's company sloshed away, Opie broke ranks and announced that anyone who wanted to go into town could follow him. Three men did, and they darted off, part of a mob that numbered officers and enlisted men alike. Lieutenant Henry Kyd Douglas of the 2d Virginia reached the official campground as the last officer with his regiment, which had shrunk to one fifth its size.[4] Douglas' comrades were on the road to Winchester, and the militia they met on the way never had a chance. Forged passes abounded. When John Opie's group was stopped, they weighed the alternative of going back to a tentless camp beneath the heavy rain, then blared that "Jackson and all hell" could not keep them out of Winchester, fixed bayonets, and charged. The terrified militiamen fled.[5] Another pack of invaders chased a militia detail into the center of town before letting it escape.[6]

The 5th Virginia's Jim Frazier masterminded the most ingenious break-in that evening. He collected 50 or 60 men from different regiments and marched them to a guard post. Halting his command, Frazier stepped forward with an explanation that General Jackson had summoned his "company" to Winchester to arrest unauthorized men there. The militia promptly opened the way. A few hundred yards down the road, the "company" disbanded, and each man found friends and a warm bed. "I think it safe," chuckled one of Frazier's company, "to say that fully half the brigade visited Winchester that night."[7]

The men in ranks had had their way: theirs was a homecoming not even Stonewall Jackson could deny.

Part I

1

THE SHENANDOAH

We spent ye best part of ye
Day in admiring ye Trees and
richness of ye land.

—GEORGE WASHINGTON

Between the river-laced Piedmont Region and the matted Allegheny Mountains of the Middle Atlantic States there is a corridor. That corridor, in Virginia, is the Shenandoah Valley. The Valley runs southwestward from the Potomac River more than one hundred fifty miles to the James. It is flanked on the east by the Blue Ridge and on the west by the Alleghenies, but the passage between these boundaries is a generally smooth path of clover and blue grass. Indian tribes which followed migrating herds up and down this corridor did not realize that it was one of the great early highways of the New World; they were content to regard it simply as a gift of the stars.

The Valley spans geologic time as well. The northern fringes touch or are near two eastward flowing rivers which are among the oldest of North America, the Potomac and the Susquehanna. From the Valley's southern fringes, it is a short journey to the New and Kanawha rivers, younger streams which flow westward to the Ohio River Valley. Many who traveled between the Atlantic Ocean and the Ohio followed the easy water routes that curled around the Shenandoah, and for them this Valley was more portage than corridor.

It was at the same time a sally port, a staging area for those who had no patience or no time for river detours and chose instead to strike due west to the heartland of the Ohio River Valley.

The western margin of the Shenandoah was little more than one hundred miles from the Ohio Valley, but the way was treacherous. It was walled by the highest mountains east of the Mississippi and by forests of tangled hardwoods. Dead trees lay like abatis among the living; the forest floor, where air never stirred, was spiked with brambles that could shred a man's flesh. Yet there were wind passes and stream beds through this wilderness. With his pack filled from the abundant game which grazed in the Shenandoah, a hearty man could survive a trek across the high mountains.

Corridor, portage, and sally port, the Shenandoah touched many sections of America, and its early history was the clash of people in motion.

The Indians warred here first. Delawares paddled up the Susquehanna, then traveled south to the Valley on foot. Ferocious and arrogant Shawnees were hardened by the march over the Alleghenies from the west. Cherokees pushed northward from Tennessee and Catawbas, from the banks of their river homeland in the Carolinas. Why they warred is not known; there was buffalo and elk and red-tailed deer for all, and still the Indians clashed.[1]

Every fall, when hunters stalked their game in the Valley, the war arrows also flew. The Catawbas and Delawares were the bitterest rivals. Though neither tribe claimed the region, neither could tolerate the other in it. They skirmished continually, and there were outbreaks of full-scale carnage, as when a Delaware war party snatched some prisoners deep within the Catawba homeland. A vengeful Catawba band tracked them for two hundred miles, eventually overtaking the raiders just west of the Shenandoah at the Hanging Rock, a jutting limestone cliff that left only a narrow ledge between it and a stream. The Delawares had foolishly halted on this ledge. The Catawbas flung themselves across the stream and behind their prey. Years later, a visitor identified a seventy-yard trench of Delaware graves near the battleground.[2]

Who the first white man was to enter the Valley is a matter of debate. As early as 1670 German John Lederer was poking around some passes of the Blue Ridge. "A pretty scholar" according to one contemporary, Lederer wrote an account of travels to the Valley in Latin, but the truth of some statements is doubtful: his imagination probably exceeded his skill in Latin.[3] An expedition led by Thomas Batts and Robert Fallam may have traversed the southern Shenandoah during 1671. Batts and Fallam certainly reached the New River and claimed it and the unknown river into which it fed, the Ohio, for England, thereby lodging Britain's foot in the trans-Allegheny door.[4]

Royal Governor Alexander Spotswood's popularly accepted claim to discovery of the Shenandoah probably rests more on his skill as a host and a promoter than on his prowess as an explorer. Spotswood came to the New World as governor of Virginia Colony in 1710. He whet a thirst for expansion with good rum and fast talk and drove the frontier steadily westward toward the Blue Ridge. Superstitious colonists dreaded that barrier as a haunt of sundry monsters; Spotswood had an idea the Great Lakes, discovered the previous century, were on the other side. In 1716 he persuaded thirty of the local gentry to join him in an expedition to find the answer.

Spotswood's answer was the Valley, a land of great charm with its smooth vistas, supple contours, and gentle name: Shenandoah, daughter of the stars. Spotswood first saw it from the crown of the Blue Ridge on September 7, 1716, and the governor marked the occasion royally, ordering his wine steward to unstrap saddlebags bulging with champagne and other suitable potions. Spotswood claimed the Valley for King George I of England and led a toast to his sovereign's health with champagne. The explorers fired a volley and pledged the health of the Princess Royal with burgundy. Another volley, and Spotswood led a salute to the remainder of the royal family with claret. A ragged volley followed. Next came a toast to the governor, by which time no one recalled what beverage was sampled. Before dark, a comely little stream meandering across the Valley had grown grand enough to be styled the Euphrates.[5]

For all Spotswood's bibulous enthusiasm to entice Virginians beyond the Blue Ridge, it was the Pennsylvania Germans and the Dutch who pioneered this frontier. Eager to increase its population at the expense of other colonies, Virginia retained professional promoters. By 1730 the colony had granted John and Isaac Van Meter a tract of 40,000 Valley acres on condition that they settle one non-Virginia family per thousand acres on it. The Van Meters had two years in which to satisfy this requirement, a con-

dition imposed with most subsequent large grants. The result was
a frantic pace in early Valley settlement. One promoter, threatened with forfeit of his land for insufficient population, supposedly
met his quota by representing every cow of his herd as a family
head.[6] Germans and Dutch from Pennsylvania were recruited for
the Valley before they were in any way inured to the hardships of
frontier life, and particularly to frontier warfare.[7] Sometimes
pathetically unarmed, they moved south from counties like Lan-
caster, Lebanon, and Berks, forded the Potomac and raised villages
in the northern Shenandoah such as Mecklenburg (later Shepherds-
town), Stephensburg (Newtown), Staufferstadt (Strasburg), and
Muellerstadt (Woodstock).

Behind the Germans and Dutch came Scotch-Irish pioneers,
who first nestled between them and the Potomac. The outcome of
this arrangement was recorded by an early historian:

> The national prejudices which existed between the Dutch and Irish
> produced much disorder and many riots. It was customary for the
> Dutch on St. Patrick's Day to exhibit the effigy of the saint, with a
> string of Irish potatoes around his neck, and his wife Sheeley with
> her apron loaded also with potatoes. This was always followed by a
> riot. The Irish resented the indignity to their saint and his holy
> spouse, and a battle followed. On St. Michael's Day the Irish would
> retort and exhibit the saint with a rope of sour krout [*sic*] about his
> neck. Then the Dutch, like the Yankee, "felt chock full of fight"
> and at it they went pell-mell. . . .[8]

The Scotch-Irish trekked on into the southern Shenandoah, where
they were reinforced by Englishmen migrating from east of the
Blue Ridge. Counties named Rockbridge and Botetout and villages named Lexington and Fincastle sprang up to rival the
unpronounceable German communities.

These hamlet toeholds were possible only because the Indians
initially ignored the whites to pursue tribal wars. But by the mid-
1700s this had changed. Braves of all tribes saw their game
preserve vanishing, as farms, many laid out by a teenage surveyor
named George Washington, cluttered the bison trails. Indians saw
the passing of their world and began to fear the white farmers as
the true enemy.

Indian fears were exploited by France, which at that time embodied the very devil to the English-speaking world. France and England asserted conflicting titles to much of the North American continent west of the Shenandoah. England had chartered Virginia Colony to extend from the Atlantic to the Pacific, and the claim this charter gave to the Ohio River Valley was buttressed by Batts and Fallam's discovery of the New River. As early as 1745 Virginia was granting tracts of land located along the Ohio River. France claimed the same region by reason of Sieur de La Salle's explorations and, more practically, by occupation. French trappers and traders based in Canada carried the fleur-de-lis throughout the Ohio River region, but their sway was tenuous and would snap if fence-loving English farmers penetrated the Alleghenies. It thus became urgent to dam the westward spread of English colonies, and in this struggle, aroused Indians became France's major weapon.

Vicious Indian raids began to threaten the colonies from New York to the Carolinas. Virginia's long and open frontier along the Shenandoah made it especially vulnerable, and the massacre of George Painter's family near Muellerstadt was typical of the violence that engulfed the Valley in the 1750s. Painter and his wife were ambushed and killed and their bodies thrown into the burning house. His babies were strapped to branches for target practice; rescuers found four riddled corpses swaying with the wind. White captives were herded to Indian villages, where drunken savages jabbed blazing pine needles into their prisoners' eyes or poured gunpowder into gaping wounds and touched off the powder.[9]

Virginia's royal governor at this time, Robert Dinwiddie, was not slow to link these atrocities to French possession of the Ohio Valley. The French had to be driven out and the governor selected surveyor George Washington to convey the message. Born as the first whites were settling the Shenandoah, Washington spent his youth surveying the Valley. He had pocketed enough from his frugal dealings to purchase 1,459 acres of Valley real estate before his nineteenth birthday, and that purchase sealed his commitment to a region he found surpassingly beautiful. He did not hesitate to serve as Dinwiddie's courier. The French were certain to reject the governor's demand, but diplomacy required that it be delivered anyway; Washington understood the task was a necessary first step in halting Indian depredations. He made an arduous journey which carried him almost to Lake Erie in midwinter and brought back to Williamsburg an unequivocal "No."

Washington's reward was command of a small body of troops on the Shenandoah frontier. Displaying a sure grasp of military geography, he attempted to shield the Valley by fortifying a strategic river junction *west* of the Alleghenies. The conception was foresighted, but Washington was denied adequate support. The attempt ended with his Virginians being thrown back into the Valley, where they learned they had ignited a conflict known in America as the French and Indian War and in Europe as the Seven Years' War.

King George II of England, who had succeeded his father in 1727, dispatched professionals to fight this war in the New World. Seventeen-fifty-five saw the arrival of Major General Edward Braddock, who wisely attached Washington to his otherwise ill-starred expedition. Unfortunately, Braddock ignored Washington's advice. Marshaling his army in the northern Shenandoah, Braddock bored through the Alleghenies toward Fort Duquesne, at the confluence of the Allegheny and Monongahela rivers, where marauding Indians swapped Valley scalps for French rum and gunpowder. Braddock's Redcoats methodically widened a trail all the way to Duquesne to accommodate wagons and heavy artillery. Washington protested this blind application of textbook tactics to forest warfare—Braddock halted "to level every Mole Hill," he fumed[10]—and augured the disaster that came. The British were annihilated within sight of their objective by an outnumbered band of Indian warriors and French soldiers employing surprise and good cover. Washington, who extracted the survivors almost single-handedly, was left to contend with two immediate consequences of defeat: the Shenandoah was stripped of army protection and the Indians had won a new highway into the Valley.

Slaughter of colonists in the Valley peaked with sudden fury, and twenty-three-year-old Washington was promoted to commander of Virginia's entire armed establishment and charged with defense of the Shenandoah. It was not a promising assignment. Washington reconnoitered the Valley frontier, to discover farms whose owners had fled leaving dishes on the table and livestock straying in the field. He also related stumbling across the grave of one man killed by Indians, hastily buried by neighbors, then dug up and gnawed by wolves.[11]

At this stage of his career, Washington lacked both the magnetism to restore public confidence with a grand gesture and the means to end Indian depredations through action. As a result, he was criticized mercilessly. Foreshadowing his behavior during the colonies' struggle for independence from England, Washington replied with silence. He established headquarters in the northern Shenandoah town of Winchester and fortified it as best he could. He shuffled his ragged militia companies from one stopgap post to another, and he continued to urge the project which had sparked this war, a system of frontier defenses *west* of the Valley. Washington realized the impossibility of garrisoning every mile of this elongated frontier. He knew, on the other hand, that the Shenandoah was a natural sally port, that it was possible to recruit and provision here, to rest, refit, and prepare expeditions into the defiles of the Alleghenies, and Washington believed active garrisons in those defiles could protect the Valley.

Washington was heeded, and Governor Dinwiddie entrusted him with construction of bristling defenses from the Potomac to the James. Strongpoints were planned in the gaps and along streams plunging out of the Alleghenies. These defenses generally were of three types: two-story log cabins with the second story projecting over the first, palisaded stockades, and large, rectangular forts capable of sheltering several hundred men.[12] Washington devoted the year 1756 to these fortifications, beginning work at the northern and southern ends of his line and hammering toward the middle. He mastered every conceivable difficulty to construct twenty-two strongpoints, only to realize that their completion aggravated another problem. He had never intended that log ramparts would replace vigilance; he had envisioned the Shenandoah's forward redoubts as shelters for active garrisons. He thus was appalled to discover his Valley militiamen adopting the sedentary theory of garrison duty. Washington toured the line during November and confided to Dinwiddie:

> I found them [the garrisons] very weak for want of men, but more so by indolence and irregularity. None I saw in a posture of defense, and few that might not be surprised with the greatest of ease.

An instance of this appeared at Dickinson's Fort, where the Indians ran down, caught several children playing under the walls, and had got to the gate before they were discovered. . . . They [the militia garrisons] keep no guard, but just when the enemy is about; and are under fearful apprehensions of them; nor even stir out of the forts. . . .[13]

Until Valley militiamen could be taught to stalk, ambush, and harry the Indians, Washington's line remained a partial barrier. Such lessons took time, time which meant the loss of Valley lives. Late in 1757, after Washington had contemplated forcing all Valley families to group themselves permanently near the largest forts, he wrote Dinwiddie that unless more powerful garrisons were mustered or a major expedition mounted against Fort Duquesne, there would hardly be "one soul living on this side of the Blue Ridge the ensuing autumn."[14]

Again displaying a sure grasp of military reality, Washington had realized that the key to the war was Fort Duquesne. George II's advisers had similar ideas and in 1758 sent General John Forbes to take it. Forbes assembled a large expedition, followed a wiser route to Duquesne than had Braddock and succeeded in almost anticlimactic fashion. The French razed their fortress and fled as Forbes approached. England's prize was control of the Ohio River Valley. Washington's prize, after treating the electorate to almost a half gallon of spirits per man,[15] was a seat from the Shenandoah in Virginia's House of Burgesses.

Throughout most of the world, the Seven Years' War sputtered to a conclusion in 1763 with the Treaty of Paris, by which France ceded its Ohio Valley possessions to England. And though peace ostensibly returned to North America, the Shenandoah remained in a state of turmoil. Whites were now eager to settle the newly won land beyond the Alleghenies. Indians, having been swept back onto those lands, resisted all the more fiercely. During the summer of 1763 the fabled Chief Pontiac assembled an Indian confederacy to continue the war without the French. Chief Cornstalk and his Shawnee braves pledged to carry this war to the Shenandoah.[16] Atrocities on both sides spawned revenge and greater horrors: soon Indians and whites alike fattened their dogs with the flesh of their prisoners.

New massacres finally jolted the Valley into the strong defensive posture Washington had advocated. His chain of Allegheny forts was strengthened, and Valley militiamen began to harry the Indians from those forts with increasing might. The frontier was never sealed, but breakthroughs became rarer and more costly for the Indians. By 1774 the Shenandoah was able to spearhead an awesome counterattack. An army drawn from the southern Shenandoah knifed westward into Shawnee territory via the Kanawha River that autumn, and Shawnee scouts reeled back with word that the indolent militia of earlier years was no more. Now came a compact, mobile striking force. Protected in the column's center were 500 pack horses carrying thousands of pounds of fresh provisions; the marching column itself was surrounded by a swarm of skirmishers. Officers were able and the men were superbly armed. All in all, it was probably the best-planned and -led American expedition ever fielded to that time. At the junction of the Kanawha and Ohio rivers, the Valley army found its enemy.

One of the great pitched battles of the American West ensued. Each side numbered approximately 1,000, including, under the leadership of Chief Cornstalk, Shawnees, Delawares, Mingoes, and Ottawas. The Valley army was encamped on a peninsula between the Kanawha and Ohio. Before dawn on October 9, 1774, Cornstalk led his braves across the Ohio to this peninsula and advanced toward the white camp through a wooded bottom entangled with vines and creepers. Other braves waited on the far banks of the Ohio and Kanawha to slaughter whites who attempted to swim the rivers. The ambush was nearly complete when Cornstalk's scouts foolishly sprang at two Shenandoah men foraging for wild turkeys. One of these foragers escaped to report: ". . . five acres of ground covered with Indians as thick as they [can] stand one beside another."[17]

Valley men probed outside their camp and found Cornstalk in the tangled bottom land, where the battle exploded. Both sides fought from behind trees, rocks, or whatever cover they could find. The lines often surged to within twenty paces of each other, and every Valley army field officer was soon killed or wounded. The fight lasted six to eight hours, until Valley frontiersmen repulsed an Indian flank attack and pursued to gain commanding ground on the Indian flank. The stampede that followed broke the Shawnees forever, and Cornstalk begged for peace before year's end.[18]

The struggle for American independence erupted within another year, and in this war the Shenandoah proved a vital corridor linking northern and southern colonies. The Continental Congress' first troop requisition from Virginia was filled by two companies of Shenandoah marksmen,[19] who marched northeastward along the Valley, crossed the Potomac, and continued through to Philadelphia and Boston. These marksmen were followed along the Shenandoah corridor by hundreds more. The corridor led southward as well, and Valley men moved that way in 1776 to help repel a British landing at Charleston, South Carolina. Their equipment—long rifles, tomahawks, and scalping knives—bore witness to the Valley's readiness for war. Major General Charles Lee is reported to have said of the Valley regiment which joined him at Charleston: "[It] was not only the most complete of the province, but, I believe, of the whole continent. It was not only the most complete in number, but the best armed, clothed and equipped for immediate service. Its soldiers were alert, zealous and spirited."[20]

At home, the Valley successfully fielded its militia reserves against Indians, who were now sponsored by the English rather than the French. The reserves held. The Valley's western bulwarks were too strong to be breached, its garrisons too alert to be bypassed. The very existence of these outworks had nudged the frontier into the Alleghenies, and the new frontier in turn flung its garrisons farther west; Virginia's defenses soon rested on the Ohio River. The frontier struggle would grind on under its own bloody momentum throughout the Revolution and for a decade thereafter, but it would grind toward an outcome made inevitable by Washington's first bold step into the Alleghenies.

When the man who had spent his youth surveying the Shenandoah and his early manhood defending it took his first presidential oath, the Valley, after two generations of war, had conquered peace on its own terms.

II

The seven decades between Washington's first inauguration in 1789 and John Brown's raid on Harper's Ferry in 1859 witnessed enormous material and economic progress throughout the Shenandoah. Valley men and women of this period fervently believed that the blessings of peace, resown throughout the land, would prove longlasting,[21] but that was not to be: these decades of growth actually molded the Shenandoah into a region that neither Union nor Confederacy could ignore during the stark years 1861–1865.

Near the northern edge of this vast battleground was Winchester, first city of the Valley. Winchester was founded in 1743 by one of the earliest Englishmen to pioneer the Shenandoah, and British influence adhered in many ways, including street names such as Piccadilly, Loudoun, Kent, and Cork. As British tradition dictated, Winchester also boasted a courthouse complete with whipping post and ducking stool. The latter was a broad plank balanced on a pivot; offenders were strapped on the plank and dunked into a murky stone-lined pit. Unruly females and town drunks kept the stool busy during frontier days.[22]

During the era of ducking stools and Indian raids, Winchester remained a crossroads village of sixty log cabins lining streets which, despite tidy English names, were mires.[23] Only with the close of the Revolution and the dawn of sustained peace did Winchester come of age. The easiest route to market for much of the Shenandoah's crops and manufactured goods was northeastward along the Valley corridor to Winchester, thence to Washington, Baltimore, or Pennsylvania. Economically, the Valley was tied as closely to the North as to Tidewater Virginia, and Winchester was a conduit for much of a rapidly expanding trade.

Tavern keepers were first to tap the new wealth. On the corner of Loudoun and Cork streets, Peter Lauck raised the sign of his Red Lion Inn. William Van Horne announced fine accommodations on the corner of Loudoun and Fairfax; Henry Marsh was in competition across the street. Stables, wagon yards, and warehouses sprouted to accommodate the traffic such inns attracted.[24]

Local entrepreneurs joined the boom. Charles Welch and George Legg established a mill on Market Street and shipped their flour northward. George Barnhard opened a coach factory. George Ginn manufactured stoves, plows, and mill machinery and amassed, in the quaint phrase of an early writer, "a snug property."[25]

The log courthouse on Loudoun Street grew into an imposing

courthouse square with a plastered court building crowned by a town clock. Taverns were within walking distance of the square, and on their way down Loudoun Street to refresh themselves, city fathers watched the construction of a new jail, market house, tobacco warehouse, and fire station. In the laissez-faire spirit of the age, the fire station was a private enterprise operated by the Star Fire Company. Some things, however, do not change: court days found the public vying with judges for room at hitching posts on the square, and soon new posts appeared marked JUDGES' HORSES ONLY.[26]

By the 1840s Winchester was thriving. The city welcomed a medical school and installed gas street lights along raised sidewalks that replaced boards strewn atop the mud. The population was affluent enough to support three drama societies, a library, and corset factory.[27] There were numerous private schools. Some, like Miss Marie Smith's Dresden Embroidery School or Lucinda Morrow's Girls' School—the latter charged a regal tuition of three dollars per quarter—polished the city's young ladies. Others, like Winchester Academy, honed its young men with classes in chemistry, civil engineering, higher mathematics, Italian, German, and Hebrew.[28] Graduates of Winchester's schools officered the banks, newspapers, courts, and churches that flourished in this community of comfortable red brick homes.

South of Winchester stood the villages of Staufferstadt and Muellerstadt, which bowed to popular desire after the Revolution and substituted the more euphonious names of Strasburg and Woodstock respectively. But some elements of German tradition lingered. Strasburg had a German-language weekly well into the 1800s. Enriched by limestone strata, the pastures around these villages provided lush grazing, and Valley men of German and Dutch extraction displayed their ancestral talent for breeding livestock. The Valley had sustained Washington's army at the siege of Yorktown with 500,000 pounds of dressed beef and large herds on the hoof[29]—this at a time when the Shenandoah was supplying its own militia forces as well—and by the mid-1800s, Valley dairies and ranches were among America's best.

As a prime horse and mule region, the Valley was rivaled only by middle Tennessee and Kentucky. Horses especially were a mania in the Shenandoah. The Valley's young men searched the bloodlines of their steeds as reverently as their elders traced family genealogies, and, finding too little challenge on the hunt, they revived the medieval style tournament they had read of in Sir Walter Scott's novels. Youths presented themselves at these spectacles as plumed and armored knights. Lances at the ready, they charged toward a target of three rings spaced thirty yards apart. The rings dangled from bars by thin wires and decreased in diameter from two inches to a barely visible half inch, but many a rider was steady enough of seat and hand to collect all three on his lance during a single charge.[30]

Most Valley riders were carried on the rolls of Virginia's militia, yet tournaments were the most martial exercises they knew. All able-bodied Virginians between the ages of eighteen and forty-five were supposedly enrolled in militia units from their county of residence. In 1861 a 140,000-man paper army of five infantry divisions and five regiments each of cavalry and artillery existed; Shenandoah counties were assigned to provide one infantry division and much of the cavalry.[31] A general staff, chaplains, surgeons, and even musicians were also authorized, but, in truth, this militia had atrophied following the Revolution. Poor muster rolls left at least 60,000 men unaccounted for. Senior militia commanders tended to be prominent citizens with proper State House connections but without military experience. Equipment was inadequate or nonexistent: as late as 1861 none of Virginia's cavalry regiments were armed.[32] Quarterly militia drills were required by law[33] but rarely took place that frequently. When held, these drills mingled the atmosphere of county fair, family reunion, and revival meeting, and in the Shenandoah, they were the only social events to rival the tournament.

This neglect of military matters was perhaps explained by the fact that many Valley men had little time to spare from their fields. Between 1800 and 1820, the iron plow replaced the wooden plow, and fertilizers came into widespread use in the Shenandoah, with accompanying increased yields of barley, flax, beans, and root crops. Orchards of bright-flowering apple trees began to grace the land. Corn, oats, rye, and above all wheat burgeoned into major industries. Wheat yields of twelve bushels per acre, nearly twice the average from other sections of Virginia, were common during the 1830s; the Valley average was fifteen bushels by the 1850s. Careful harvesters gleaned crops of thirty and even forty bushels per acre, and all Valley farmers were overworked with the bounty of their fields.[34]

It was not by chance, then, that the first mechanical reaper, Cyrus McCormick's "Virginia Reaper," was wired together in the Valley. McCormick, Rockbridge County-born, came to manhood watching a sea of grain toss around him. He toiled long hours with a scythe, and the ache of his arms prompted an idea. In 1831 he demonstrated the first machine to incorporate the principal components of the modern grain harvester: straight reciprocating knife, guards, platform, main wheel, side-moving cutter, and divider at the outer end of the cutter bar. This product of a Valley man's imagination revolutionized world agriculture and made possible the endless grain fields of America's Midwest.

McCormick's reaper also highlighted the Shenandoah as one of the more industrial regions of the South. Iron forges had been glowing here since the Revolution and had given impetus to other industries. Woolen factories and flour and lumber mills abounded. J. Meixell and Company began production of a sophisticated threshing machine at its Harrisonburg plant by 1839; C. S. Weaver was in competition by 1844. Nine years later Henry Miller of Harrisonburg patented a corn harvester. Miller's neighbor J. G. Sprinkel patented a novel steam engine, and by 1861 his engines were powering the presses of the *Rockingham Register*.[35]

During their early years, towns like Harrisonburg and Staunton, which lay in the southern Valley and were not convenient to Winchester by road, shipped their goods to market by river, which explains names such as Port Republic among the inland hamlets of the southern Shenandoah. There were few roads worthy of the name between those hamlets and Northern markets, so gundalows, or barges, measuring nine by ninety feet funneled Valley flour and pig iron down the Shenandoah to the Potomac.[36] River trade even became dominant enough to shape the Valley's language with a curious idiom. Shenandoah streams drain generally northward to the Potomac, and to go *downstream* is thus to go *northward,* to go *upstream* is to go *southward*. The Valley's *northern* region accordingly became known as the *lower* Shenandoah and the *southern* region, as the *upper*. Similarly, to travel *northward* is to go *down* the Valley, while to travel *southward* is to go *up* it. When turnpikes and railroads supplanted river highways, this seemingly backwards terminology* persisted. The idiom remains common usage in the Shenandoah today, and it is observed throughout this work.

Water transport was so much a part of early life around the Shenandoah that when its rivers could no longer bear the expanding commerce the solution was a better river. The same era which saw New York's Erie Canal saw two major waterways projected across the Valley's northern and southern fringes. The most important was the Chesapeake & Ohio (C & O) Canal, which was to link the Atlantic with the Ohio River Valley. Though never completed, the canal was nevertheless an outstanding achievement of its time. By 1850 it had pushed its sixty-foot-wide channel along Maryland's Potomac shore from Washington as far as Cumberland. Barges of one hundred tons' burden plied its waters, and it steadily grew into a major artery for Allegheny coal fueling the East Coast. The mirror image of the C & O was the James River Canal; its promoters hoped to mingle the waters of the James and the Kanawha. Financial difficulties stopped work on it near Buchanan, in the upper Shenandoah, where, despite disappointment for the backers, it opened Valley commerce to Richmond and eastern Virginia on a truly competitive basis.

Between these canals flowed the Shenandoah River, which was unsuited to canalization. The middle Valley therefore faced potential isolation by poor roads and crowded rivers, and its solution was a superhighway for the horse and wagon. In 1834 the Virginia legislature chartered the Valley Turnpike Company to lay a road from Winchester south to Staunton. Engineers of the Valley Turnpike—or simply the Pike as it was known locally—made a then uncommon effort to keep the right of way straight, so that travelers were sometimes astonished by a clear view ahead for two or even three miles. The Pike was bedded with cement and buttressed on either side with limestone shoulders; its smooth surface was supported by layers of compacted gravel piled atop the cement bed.[37]

---

* In normal usage, because the top of a map always represents the northernmost portion of the area depicted, to go *up* is to go *north*, and, conversely, because the bottom of a map represents the southernmost portion of the area depicted, to go *down* is to go *south*.

The Pike, completed by 1840, was a superb paved, or macadamized, highway, impervious to rains which dissolved other Valley
roads. This trunkline encouraged other parallel and intersecting
pikes, some also macadamized, although the typical Shenandoah
road of the 1860s remained a dirt track. A hard-swearing corps of
teamsters toiled over these routes. Among the foulest of mouth
was John Harman, who, as Army quartermaster, later accomplished apparent miracles of transportation for the Confederate
Army during the Valley Campaign. There was, however, nothing
miraculous about his success; it was grounded on the many years
John Harman spent overseeing a Valley stage line.

Accelerating communication demands brought railroads into
the Valley during the 1840s and 50s. The Baltimore & Ohio
(B & O) Railroad came first with a right of way stretching from
Baltimore to Harper's Ferry, Virginia. There the line bridged the
Potomac and hurried through the lower Valley. It entered Martinsburg, veered north to hug the Potomac's south bank until it
crossed the river to Cumberland, Maryland, and ran from there
southwestward to the Ohio River Valley, a route which capitalized
on the Valley's central location in the eastern states. The line both
tapped Shenandoah resources for the Atlantic seaboard and utilized its best routes to and through the Alleghenies to the Ohio
heartland. Harper's Ferry and Martinsburg became thriving depot
towns as the line made the Valley's lower exits more attractive to
Northern merchants. Winchester quickly ran a thirty-two-mile
spur to Harper's Ferry to link itself with the B & O and retain its
position as the transportation hub of the southern Valley.

The B & O was one of America's major railroads by the 1860s.
It was also one of the longest, totaling 513 miles of track exclusive
of numerous sidings. Its assets reached the then staggering sum of
$30 million and included 236 locomotives and more than 3,400
freight cars. Both sides would claim the B & O when war came,
but it was the Union which acted first to secure its terminals in
Baltimore, Maryland, and Wheeling, Virginia (now West Virginia). Thereafter the Confederacy sought to cripple it, and the
South would damage this line more frequently and more exten-
sively than any other.[38]

Impressive as were B & O facilities, the prewar Valley required
even additional rail outlets. Had the Shenandoah been a garrison

state like Prussia, it would have planned these new lines according to military contingencies, but here economic factors governed. The Valley's second right of way was surveyed in the 1850s from Strasburg to Manassas Junction, thirty miles southwest of Washington, where the route could join an existing roadbed leading north into Washington and south to Gordonsville and eventually to Richmond. A Prussian would have been disgusted, because if a conflict did arise the new line inevitably would be severed as Northern forces advanced to protect Washington by occupying Manassas Junction. Nevertheless, work commenced and progressed rapidly. The Manassas Gap Railroad built westward across Piedmont, Virginia, climbed the Blue Ridge at the gap which shares its name, and descended to span the Shenandoah River by an impressive 450-foot wooden trestle at Front Royal. From Strasburg the line swung south and into trouble. Stage owners, wagoneers, and bargemen opposed it, as did one prominent farmer who feared the iron horse would frighten his milch cows.[39]

Adverse interests could not throttle the Manassas Gap Railroad, although they did delay it. By 1861 the railhead lay at the village of Mount Jackson, and a forty-mile gap yawned between it and the Virginia Central Railroad. That line extended west from Richmond to Gordonsville, thence across the Blue Ridge and upper Shenandoah. Its principal Valley depot was Staunton. To travel by rail from Strasburg to Staunton it was necessary to follow a two hundred-mile semicircle east through Manassas Junction, south to Gordonsville and west across the Blue Ridge again. And there was still another gap in the Valley's rail net: a projected track between Strasburg and Winchester was not even surveyed by 1861.

Nor did the two Virginia lines serving the Shenandoah match the capabilities of the B & O. The Manassas Gap was a mere seventy-seven miles long, and it was so deficient in sidings that for many hours each day it was a one-way railroad. The Virginia Central owned only 27 locomotives and 188 box- and flatcars. Its only repair shops were located in Richmond and were so small that maintenance had to be performed outdoors.[40] If there was any single area in which the Valley was at a decided disadvantage as civil war neared, it was in its rail net.

In the field of education, on the other hand, the Valley surpassed many areas North and South. The Shenandoah's college tradition began when George Washington richly endowed a promising academy in the late 1700s. This institution thereafter renamed itself Washington College (today, Washington and Lee University) and moved to Lexington in the upper Valley. Seeking to prepare its students for peace with a curriculum of ancient and modern languages, mathematics, and philosophy, Washington College actually groomed a generation of warrior historians prior to the 1860s. When war came to the Shenandoah, hundreds of the college's students and alumni joined the South, among them Alexander "Sandie" Pendleton, Hugh White, Edward Moore, John Apperson, and James Langhorne. These were bright young men who observed as well as fought the war, and their observations, contained in lucid diaries and letters, are an invaluable source on the Valley Campaign of 1862.

Lexington became a two-college town with the founding of the Virginia Military Institute in 1839. Conceived by a distinguished group of educators and soldiers, including a veteran of Napoleon's 1812 Russian campaign, V.M.I. evolved during the next two decades into an incomparable Southern tradition: a college modeled on West Point but designed to prepare young men for the civilian as well as military life. The appeal of that goal was quickly demonstrated. President Zachary Taylor personally supervised additions to the Institute's arsenal, the State of Virginia expanded its barracks, and the original faculty of West Pointers was strengthened by Institute graduates. Those instructors coupled scientific and military education with rigorous discipline, and on the eve of war, the V.M.I. alumni and Corps of Cadets provided the South with an invaluable reserve of officers. Throughout the Valley Campaign of 1862, V.M.I. was well represented: at various times the Confederate cavalry and many Southern batteries and infantry regiments were commanded by V.M.I. men.

For those aspiring to college, there were numerous Shenandoah preparatory academies, such as the institutions of Winchester. Also typical of both the number and excellence of Valley schools were those clustered around Martinsburg, where no less than a dozen educational ventures prospered in a county of only a few thousand inhabitants. As was true of Valley colleges, these academies trained many who, though they were little more than boys, left eloquent accounts of their wartime experiences. John Opie and John Casler were outstanding among this number.

Valley academies were the personal achievements of no-nonsense schoolmasters such as New York-born Jedediah Hotchkiss. Hotchkiss came to love the Shenandoah on a walking tour in 1847, and it became his home for the next fifty years. He achieved such initial success with a variety of tutoring jobs that Augusta County farmers subscribed his Mossy Creek Academy, near Staunton. A few years later he founded a second school. Both ventures flourished, probably because Hotchkiss typified his adopted neighbors. He was a sincere Christian, a family man, serious, and thrifty. Even his hobby, map making, distinguished him as a solid and sensible citizen. He was self-taught as a map maker, but he became a recognized expert, and his hobby was to serve the Confederacy well.

Hotchkiss was representative of the Shenandoah in two other respects: he abhorred slavery and stoutly opposed secession. Slavery had long been declining throughout the Valley, and what few slaves remained were among the best treated of the South. Concerning disruption of the Union, the Shenandoah consistently opposed it. When the Union began to fragment, the people of Staunton pledged their loyalty to it en masse.[41] Every county of the Valley rejected disunion with a majority of votes for the southern moderates John C. Breckinridge or John Bell in the presidential election of 1860. Even so, the Valley never doubted that it belonged to Virginia, and Virginia, to the South. The South, commented the Winchester *Virginian,* was "one family . . , and if South Carolina secedes, and thus inaugurates a final issue with the North, we are necessarily forced to stand in defense of our homes, interests and people."[42]

Valley residents nodded in anguished agreement with that comment, all the while hoping that a war which grew more certain with increasingly strident debate over slavery might somehow spare them. But this was a pipe dream. The Shenandoah's very location, combined with an abundance of almost all things, made it a battlefield in the years 1861–65. The Valley was a natural corridor between North and South. Its farms could both sustain armies and swell their ranks with literate recruits. Here were iron foundries, machine shops, and textile mills. Here was a military academy already renowned as the West Point of the South. And here was an arsenal, the United States Arsenal at Harper's Ferry.

At the northeast corner of the Valley, the Shenandoah and Potomac rivers converge in turbulent splendor. Thomas Jefferson described the scene as a "riot and tumult roaring" and wrote: "You stand on a very high point of land. On your right comes up the Shenandoah, having ranged along the foot of the [Blue Ridge] mountain a hundred miles to seek a vent. On your left approaches the Potomac, in quest of a passage also. In the moment of their junction they rush together against the mountain, rend it asunder, and pass off to the sea. . . . This scene is worth a voyage across the Atlantic."[43]

This mighty rush of rivers swept the town of Harper's Ferry into existence. In 1747 Robert Harper, an English architect commissioned to design a meeting house for Winchester's Quakers, passed this way. Like Jefferson later, he was awed by the natural beauty here. With an architect's practical eye, he also saw need for a ferry, and Harper's Ferry was born.

Years later, a fledgling United States Government harnessed the waters at Harper's Ferry to power an arms factory. The quality and variety of weapons produced in this armory grew, and a storage place became necessary. A government complex arose at the Virginia end of the B & O's Potomac bridge. Two storage buildings were built for an arsenal near the bridge; located west of the arsenal, across the intersection of Potomac and Shenandoah streets, was a sturdy brick fire-engine house. The armory itself lay west of the fire station. It was within a walled enclosure, although it was by no means well secured: its low walls were manned at night by only one watchman.

It was this complex which John Brown, "Osawatomie" Brown of Bleeding Kansas, coveted. In Brown's fanatic mind the key to ending slavery was guns. If he could provide even a few thousand arms, he had no doubt that slaves across the South would explode in bloody revolt. And it made no matter to Brown that there were few slaves in the Valley to be armed—the Lord, he must have believed, would raise up an army somehow for the holy work of butchering slaveholders.[44]

On the evening of Sunday, October 16, 1859, after several months spent making furtive reconnaissances of the Harper's Ferry area from his headquarters in an old farmhouse across the Potomac in Maryland, Brown launched his now famous raid. His "army" consisted of a handful of followers. Beneath the cover of a hard rainstorm, he slashed all telegraph wires into Harper's Ferry and stationed several men to obstruct the B & O bridge. Things continued to go according to plan when Brown approached the armory. The night watchman refused him entrance, but he easily broke inside the walls. Brown's eyes blazed with a wilder light as he saw rows of newly made muskets, and he immediately dispatched runners to spread the word of liberation among local slaves.

Harper's Ferry discovered itself at war the next morning. Workers reporting for the armory's morning shift were herded inside its walls under leveled rifles. Raiders opened fire on the town, and several townspeople, including the mayor, a grocer, and a Negro porter, fell.

A snarling posse of Harper's Ferry men and county militia, many of them the worse for drink, counterattacked that afternoon. They first shattered the detail on the B & O bridge. One abolitionist there tried to escape by swimming the Potomac but was wounded and drifted to a rock; Valley men swarmed over the rock and knifed him to death. The mob flung its one prisoner off the bridge and used him for target practice as he bobbed helplessly down the Potomac.

Brown, meanwhile, concentrated his men in the brick engine house on Potomac Street, and the fighting continued throughout the day and night. The abolitionists had provisioned themselves well; townspeople helped themselves from the arsenal across the street from Brown's fort, and the gunfire grew deafening. There were more dead and wounded on both sides.

Mercifully, this slaughter was ended on Tuesday morning. Eighty Marines under the command of United States Army Colonel Robert E. Lee arrived to quell the insurrection. Lee deployed his troops and demanded Brown's surrender; when the crazed man hollered "No," the Marines finished the affair. They battered their way inside the engine house and disarmed Brown, who lay wounded on the floor with his bleeding sons. Only then did Brown have time to consider that not a slave had joined him.[45]

During Brown's subsequent trial on charges of treason and conspiracy to commit murder, numerous affidavits were offered to support the defense contention that Brown was insane,[46] but the prosecution prevailed. On December 2, 1859, he was hanged amid extraordinary precautions. Two thousand Valley militia, buttressed by the Virginia Military Institute Corps of Cadets, formed a square around Brown's gallows. Loaded howitzers studded the array to devastate an oft-rumored rescue attempt which never came. Before thousands of relieved onlookers, John Brown kicked out the final seconds of his life.[47]

For the Valley, the terror at Harper's Ferry kindled bitter memories. Save that white had preyed on white, John Brown's raid was little different from Indian strikes of a century earlier: the surprise attack, the killing and the counterattack had all unfolded in a hideously familiar sequence.

For the nation, Brown's raid was the omen of horrors never known before, or since, in America. Events moved rapidly after October 16, 1859: Abraham Lincoln was elected President within one year; South Carolina seceded from the Union within fourteen months. Fort Sumter was bombarded into submission in another four months. Lincoln mobilized 75,000 volunteers in April 1861 to suppress the rebellion, and the Shenandoah confronted a new war.

2

A NEW WAR

*The exposed condition of the Virginia frontier
between the Blue Ridge and the
Allegheny Mountains has excited the
deepest solicitude of the government.*

—JUDAH P. BENJAMIN

The Shenandoah's most tragic conflict began as a romp. Valley volunteers and militia by the hundreds mustered in Winchester as Virginia's Secession Convention met. Bombardment of Fort Sumter on April 12–13, 1861, made the outcome of this convention certain, and the majority of Virginians were ready to embrace the Southern cause. Most Valley men were in accord. And Shenandoah men knew they could not demonstrate their loyalty better than by securing the Harper's Ferry arsenal. They waited fitfully for word of a secession vote and crowed about easy victories they would win. Since Harper's Ferry was guarded by only fifty Federal troops, this was safe talk; there was heady assurance in the companionship of overwhelming numbers.

When Virginia voted itself out of the Union on April 17, the novice army fidgeting in Winchester instinctively swarmed northward. Captain John Imboden's men trundled along hauling a horseless battery of 6 cannons. As the guns seemed to gain weight with every mile, Imboden stopped to hire some horses. The farmer he approached, however, thought the rebel horde a poor risk and refused, whereupon Imboden took the animals he needed by force. As Imboden moved on, the red-faced farmer shook his clenched fist and promised an indictment from the next county grand jury.[1]

On the evening of April 18 the rebel mob swarmed into
Harper's Ferry. Some men had been here before to snipe at John
Brown and led the surge along High Street, glowing with the thrill
of a short-lived chase. The arsenal in front of them suddenly
erupted, and the streets were flayed with whizzing triggers, bolts,
and stocks. The defenders had fled, igniting powder trains which
sparked into the warehouse. The attackers, now a fire brigade,
swerved into the armory enclosure. They saved the priceless arms-
making machinery there by working through the night without regard for repeated explosions from the crackling arsenal, which was
just dangerous enough to spice this first conquest. War, the rebels
decided, was exhilarating.

Other Virginians were frantic to join this advance guard, because Harper's Ferry lay far enough north to generate hope that it
might see at least one gallant battle before the Yankees surrendered. It was the front, and men who would fight to reach
Winchester in November did not tarry there for food or shelter in
April. Striking heroic poses, they disdained the comforts of
Winchester and scampered off like boys on a spring outing who,
distracted by a scuffle, desert the picnic table. "As we marched out
of town the brass bands were playing, the drums beating, colors
flying, and the fair ladies waving their handkerchiefs and cheering
us on to 'victory or death.' Oh! how nice to be a soldier," wrote
one.[2]

As if by order, each new arrival at Harper's Ferry placed himself on full alert. His days passed in relentless vigilance demanded
by the conviction that a Northern army would attack momen-
tarily. If one man was detailed as night sentry, his entire company
was apt to join him voluntarily. Since officers supposed the Federals planned to storm the town by train and debark at the depot,
many sentinels spent hours faithfully staring at B & O track.[3] Even
the enemy's refusal to deliver such a shrewd blow did not dampen
Confederate zeal.

The Yankees, after all, were to be thrashed with ease. One
grand victory should finish the war, and it would not do to miss
any of this romantic adventure. Nor should one attend in less than
immaculate dress. Many Valley men reported for duty wearing
garish buff and yellow uniforms.[4] Captain Jim Edmondson sent
home from Harper's Ferry for striped calico shirts; white ones got

dirty too fast. He also required a pair of pants in a shade he specified as blue caramel.[5] One rebel wrote: "[M]any of the privates brought with them their personal servants, while the officers were equipped with all that was necessary for elaborate entertainment."[6] John Imboden believed the "fuss and feathers" displayed around Harper's Ferry could match the Champs Élysées on a pleasant afternoon.[7] It was a splendid frolic and confirmed the universal opinion that the soldier's whole duty was to posture heroically.

On April 30 a colonel of Virginia volunteers arrived to correct that opinion. He was Thomas J. Jackson, an obscure retired United States Army brevet major whose advent went unnoticed because, according to notions of the day, he hardly looked like a soldier. He wore a plain, ill-fitting U. S. Army uniform. He was cursed with absurdly big feet and hands, and his speech was as ungainly as his movements. The only notable thing about him was the lemon he sucked incessantly; his expressionless look struck some as "wooden,"[8] some as "sleepy,"[9] and no one as inspiring. After meeting Jackson one group of officers despaired: ". . . there must be some mistake about him; if he was an able man he showed it less than any of us had ever seen."[10]

But Jackson was an able man, and he had instructions from Governor John Letcher of Virginia to take command at Harper's Ferry. His first care was to sort out the troops thronging his camps. These he found to be of two types. One consisted of the burgeoning Virginia volunteer force, of which Jackson was an officer; the other was the militia. Volunteers were enrolling in newly authorized statewide units which would soon join regiments from sister states in a true Confederate army. The county-based militiamen, on the other hand, were local defense forces entangled by politics and of little value on the battlefield. The perfectionist Jackson had no use for this militia system and lured the militiamen into the volunteer forces whenever possible.

Volunteers were obliged to enlist for either a one-year term or for the duration of the war.[11] The majority of gallants at Harper's Ferry assumed one year was ample time to whip the North. Jackson was less certain and encouraged enlistment "for the duration," but there were few men willing to commit themselves to such an

indefinite future. Most signed on only for twelve months. (In the
spring of 1862 Confederate armies almost disappeared as a consequence.)

Volunteer or militiaman, enrolled for the duration or not, all of
Jackson's men were set to drill, target practice, guard duty, and
more drill. Reveille blared at 5 A.M. every day,[12] and Jackson
kept his men busy for the next seventeen hours. Much of that time
was spent evacuating captured arms-making machinery, all of
which found its way to Richmond or Columbia, South Carolina.[13]
To arm his own troops, Jackson offered to purchase private weapons at a tempting five dollars apiece.[14] When that did not work, he
took the responsibility of ordering 1,000 flintlocks from the state
arsenal at Lexington.[15] There were no horses to pull his wagons,
so Jackson dispatched his quartermasters to buy them on credit.
When credit was refused, he simply impressed the animals.[16] Artillerist Imboden, who had left Harper's Ferry prior to Jackson's
arrival, returned a few days later: "What a revolution three or
four days had wrought! I could scarcely realize the change. . . .
The presence of a mastermind was visible in the changed conditions of the camp."[17]

Imboden also returned in time to see Jackson swing into action on another front. By some unwritten détente, the Baltimore &
Ohio Railroad had been allowed to continue its service across the
Valley's tip to the Allegheny coal fields. The railroad was shuttling
coal to Washington at capacity along this route, and Jackson decided to stop it. From Point of Rocks, some miles east of Harper's
Ferry on Maryland's Potomac shore, to Martinsburg the B & O
was double tracked, that is, had separate lines allowing traffic to
pass in opposite directions. Both tracks crossed the Potomac at
Harper's Ferry. Jackson, making a veiled threat, warned company
officials that racket from the never-ending trains disturbed his
camps and must cease. The railroad agreed to his demand to funnel its traffic through Harper's Ferry between 11 A.M. and 1 P.M.
When the B & O timetable was readjusted to give the town the
busiest railroad in America two hours a day, Jackson pounced. At
11 A.M. he began barricading the eastbound lane at Point of
Rocks while permitting westerly traffic as usual. He had the
reverse done at Martinsburg. At 1 P.M. Jackson tore up all ends
of the double track and stranded more than 400 locomotives and
cars.[18]

This man Jackson got things done. In three weeks he had hammered a mob into the rudiments of an army and hoodwinked one of the Union's major railroads out of the war. He soon gave his volunteers something else to scrawl home. Anticipating the upcoming transfer of forces raised by Virginia to Confederate command, the Confederate Government dispatched Brigadier General Joseph E. Johnston to take control at Harper's Ferry. Johnston arrived before Jackson received official notice of his mission, and the latter declined to turn over command until he was shown proper authorization. Jackson knew Johnston at least by reputation, and he knew it would serve Virginia's best interest to integrate her forces as speedily as possible into the Confederate army. Nevertheless, he required the necessary paperwork and would have arrested Johnston had he insisted on taking charge without it. Before he assumed command, Johnston had to dig through his saddlebags until he found a letter which established his authority.[19]

Few other colonels, especially those who knew something of Joe Johnston, would have sent him back to his saddlebags for orders. An autocratic, petulant man, Johnston did not tolerate any trespass on his authority. He regarded civilian as well as military superiors with a certain mistrust and tended to be curt in his dealings with them. Johnston was the highest ranking former U. S. Army officer to join the South, and he would become one of its five full generals—only to take offense at the fact that he ranked fourth in seniority. He was, however, a generous superior—his men came to know him simply as "Old Joe"—and because he treasured his own prerogatives, he respected the correctness of Jackson's stand. He also was impressed by Jackson's groundwork: militia who had refused to volunteer had been weeded out, those who had volunteered had been grouped into Virginia regiments which in turn were ready to come under Confederate authority. Jackson's reward was promotion to brigadier general in the Confederate army and command of one of three infantry brigades Johnston organized at Harper's Ferry.[20]

The new brigade consisted of the 2d, 4th, 5th, 27th, and 33d Virginia regiments. Every man was a volunteer. They were drawn largely from the Shenandoah, and a contingent of Allegheny and Blue Ridge mountaineers added strength. Jackson thought it a "promising" unit and went to work on it.[21] He saw that each man got a musket and drilled them until they could barely hobble. Extraordinary attention to every paragraph in the manual of arms won him the respect of his soldiers and Johnston's greater confidence.

Jackson hoped to bloody his brigade quickly. In this he differed from Johnston, who was to prove himself an apostle of strategic retreat. Before the war's end Johnston would back to the gates of the South's two most important cities, Richmond and Atlanta. His premise was that territory lost could be regained, but the casualties of a great battle could not.

Accordingly, when a Union army forded the Potomac upstream from Harper's Ferry on June 15 Johnston withdrew to Winchester, and his troops had their first lesson in massive destruction as they evacuated Harper's Ferry. B & O bridges over the Potomac were blown up; captured locomotives were derailed into the river. At other points across the lower Valley, water towers were destroyed, bridges blown up, a hundred miles of telegraph wire torn down, and captured trains, loot from Jackson's great train robbery, put to the torch. Many of the cars burned were 20-ton coal gondolas with full loads; they glowed for weeks.[22]

A month of sporadic skirmishing occupied the Valley, until, on July 18, the news every volunteer craved reached Winchester. A Federal army from Washington, under the command of Brigadier General Irvin McDowell, was advancing on Manassas Junction and the Southern army of Brigadier General Pierre Beauregard, conqueror of Fort Sumter and the Confederacy's earliest folk hero. The battle everyone assumed would decide the war was at hand, and Johnston was summoned to evade the enemy opposite him and reinforce Beauregard. When the destination was announced, Jackson's brigade bolted forward into a sprint. Equally jubilant citizens packed the sidewalks when the rebels paraded through Winchester, and everyone beamed with the knowledge that war was a glorious, romantic adventure. It was magnificent, wrote Mrs. Cornelia McDonald, "the Confederate banners waving, the bands playing, and the bayonets gleaming in the sun. . . . Many of the companies were made up of mere boys, but their earnest and joyous faces were fully as reassuring as the martial music was inspiriting."[23]

The ensuing Southern victory at the First Battle of Manassas (known in the North as the First Battle of Bull Run) was a classic bit of Americana. Johnston eluded the Federal army facing him and reached Manassas Junction at the eleventh hour. Jackson's brigade entered the fight swiftly, withstood a fierce artillery barrage and fiercer infantry attacks, to win itself and its general the title "Stonewall." Those who cherish a romantic tale insist the name was given by Brigadier General Barnard Bee, who, with his own brigade shattered and fleeing, spotted Jackson's firm lines and called to his men: "There is Jackson standing like a stone wall! Rally behind the Virginians!" Revisionists might claim Bee was hollering in disgust over Jackson's refusal to advance to the more exposed position Bee held,[24] but in the rosy glow of victory, connotations of the name "Stonewall" were only good. From that day on Jackson was known as "Stonewall" and his men were the "Stonewall Brigade."

Jackson, normally silent to the point of rudeness,[25] boasted that his brigade was to the Southern army what the Imperial Guard had been to Napoleon.[26] He wrote to his wife that his command "was the first to meet and pass our retreating forces—to push on with no other aid than the smiles of God; to boldly take its position with the artillery that was under my command—to arrest the victorious foe in his onward progress—to hold him in check until reinforcements arrived—and finally to charge bayonets, and, thus advancing, pierce the enemy's center." In reply to her anger at the small mention of him in newspaper accounts of the triumph, Jackson added a thought which disclosed a crack in his Christian armor—ambition: ". . . I am thankful to my ever kind Heavenly Father that he makes me content to await His own good time and pleasure for commendation. . . ."[27] Jackson did not even consider that commendation might not come at all; it was, he seemed to assert, cached in Heaven anticipating efforts he would not fail to give.

With the battle that swept Jackson to write of Napoleon's Imperial Guard and inspired his men to don the title "Stonewall," the spirit of romantic adventure crested. The next weeks showed Valley volunteers some less exhilarating facets of army life. The rebel victors were as disorganized by their success as the vanquished and they remained near the battlefield to regroup. The only stream through the Stonewall Brigade's camp tasted of decaying corpses.[28] Southern railroads faltered under the burden of supplying the army at Manassas Junction and by August the rebels knew hunger. To alleviate the situation, a great camp was established at Centreville, but autumn came early with a chilling rain. Even Jackson could not drill in ankle deep mud, and his troops were left to cope with an ever-increasing boredom.[29]

The romance of war had begun to fade for the Confederacy. Forts Hatteras and Clark, in North Carolina, were smashed by a Union fleet that summer, and the coastal sounds of North Carolina were shut to blockade runners. Confederate forces occupied a few cities in neutral Kentucky during September, but the occupation only heightened Union sentiment among Kentuckians, who helped Federal armies secure the most strategic points. In November, Port Royal Sound, South Carolina, was lost to overwhelming Union naval power.

In Virginia the Southern position was eroding. Stories of dissension in the high command were carried like a serial by the Richmond newspapers. General Beauregard had fallen into an embarrassing wrangle with Confederate President Jefferson Davis over his plans for the battle at Manassas. Piqued at standing second after General Johnston in command of the combined forces around Centreville, Beauregard tried to wield his brigades as a semiautonomous force, until Secretary of War Judah P. Benjamin cautioned him that he was not "first in command of half the army."[30] The warning did no good, and Beauregard was shunted off to Tennessee with his reputation as a folk hero beclouded. Senior only to Beauregard when the Confederacy promoted five men to the rank of full general, Johnston griped about seniority bitterly enough to poison his relations with President Davis forever.

Northwest of Staunton, Union columns stabbed deep into the Alleghenies of western Virginia. Having followed Virginia in her secession and become a full general in the Confederate Army, Robert E. Lee mobilized a small force, the Army of the Northwest, to reclaim this territory, but first-rate men were betrayed by second-rate equipment. Poor Confederate logistics slashed rations to four biscuits per day per man[31]; lack of medical support left some regiments at one-quarter strength.[32] Wrote one rebel:

We had the most awful march up here through the mud and cold. When we came here we had to lie on the frozen ground without any fire. We have now built a fireplace in our tent, but we have no straw, and a continual vapor is rising from the frozen but now thawing ground. . . . Many times the mud has been shoe-top deep in and out of our tents. . . . It is evidently a condition in which God never intended any human being to be placed.[33]

The Confederate drive to free the Alleghenies was a failure that buried Lee in the public mind for a year. It also cost Virginia fifty of her doggedly antislavery mountain counties, which, on October 24, voted to secede from the Old Dominion and began to organize the new state of West Virginia.

By autumn of 1861 Virginia was awakening to the reality that it had slipped back a hundred years. The Shenandoah was once again Virginia's frontier, and beyond the Valley the Alleghenies were suddenly alien, infested with an enemy more powerful than even the Shawnees.

II

Union strikes against the fringes of the Shenandoah grew more serious throughout the autumn. Federals were particularly active among the many Union sympathizers of the fertile South Branch Valley (in what is now West Virginia), to the west of Winchester, and there were persistent rumors of an impending effort to capture Romney. That village dominated the South Branch Valley (named for the South Branch River, a tributary of the Potomac) and lay only two days' march from Winchester.

As had been the case when Washington headquartered in Winchester a century earlier, the Shenandoah Valley was virtually undefended. Three brigades of quibbling militia, perhaps 1,500 men, were in the field.[34] These men bore ancient flintlocks for which there was insufficient ammunition, or none at all.[35] Although militia ranks had thinned as many men volunteered, militia officers remained plentiful. These peacocks refused to vacate their ceremonial posts or to combine their understrength units, so that brigadier generals headed regiments, colonels headed companies, and captains led squads.[36] The two pieces of heavy artillery in the Shenandoah could not be used because no one knew how to load them.[37] The Valley's only cavalry was a semiguerrilla outfit headed by sixty-year-old Colonel Angus McDonald and a younger but wholly inexperienced Lieutenant Colonel Turner Ashby.

Shenandoah defenses were crumbling by October. The enemy struck swiftly and in force against Romney, capturing the village, 300 rifles, and 100 horses and mules of Colonel McDonald's command.[38] As the Confederate grasp west of the Valley faltered, B & O crews pushed reconstruction on segments of the line destroyed earlier by rebel raiders; after the fall of Romney, Northern crews were free to concentrate on the important Big Cacapon River bridge thirty miles northeast of the village. On the Valley's opposite flank, Federals seized Harper's Ferry and rifled local wheat bins for a week before Turner Ashby could muster 300 militia with their antiquated muskets, some cavalry companies, and a light cannon mounted on a converted wagon. A ragtag skirmish ensued during which Ashby's cannon collapsed and the enemy safely recrossed the Potomac while militia officers tried to pull rank on Ashby, who had been the only real fighter on the field.[39]

Word of these debacles reached the Confederate capital at Richmond more quickly by agitated letters from prominent Valley citizens than through official channels. James L. Ranson depicted conditions near Harper's Ferry directly to President Davis: "Last night a lady swam the Shenandoah to let us know that the enemy were being re-enforced, and the first aim would be to destroy our woolen factories along the Shenandoah; also our large flouring mill. . . . This done, our whole county must be devastated, and, to say nothing of mills, slaves and other valuable property, all the grain in stock or garner will be burned up."[40] The Valley's representative in the Confederate Congress, Alexander R. Boteler, warned the Secretary of State: "The condition of our border is becoming more alarming every day. No night passes without some infamous outrage upon our loyal citizens."[41] Another prominent Virginian, Andrew Hunter, pleaded the problem as one of command to Secretary of War Benjamin: "The feeling is becoming very general among our people that while we have men ready and willing to protect the border against these incursions of the enemy, yet that we are suffering needlessly for want of competent officers. . . . I beg leave to submit whether it be not practical and expedient to send here . . . some competent regular or experi-

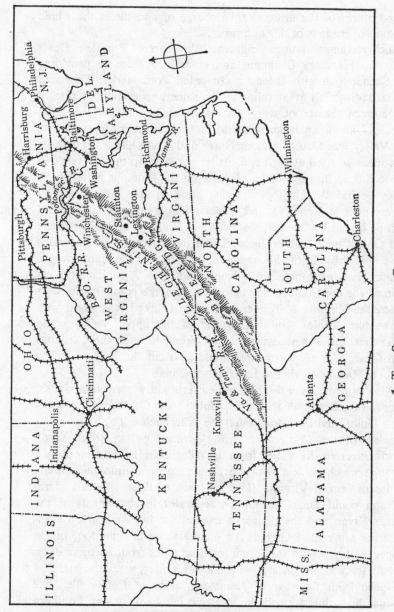

1. THE SHENANDOAH CORRIDOR.

Note especially the strategic rail routes crossing the Valley's northern and southern reaches.

enced officer of the army to take charge of and direct the whole
military operations of this quarter . . ."[42]

Such recommendations heightened the fears of President Davis
and War Secretary Benjamin and committed them to providing
the Shenandoah with at least a competent commander. They recognized Virginia's great valley as the salient geographic feature of
the eastern theater of war—the entire region east of the Alleghenies—and knew it must be held. In terms of military geography,
the Valley was thrust between North and South like a giant spear
—a spear whetted at each end. At its northern tip the Shenandoah
plunged deep into the Union. Rebels on the Potomac stood thirty
miles behind Washington and one hundred fifty miles north of
enemy lines in Kentucky and Illinois. Those Federal wings could
best be linked by the Baltimore & Ohio Railroad and Chesapeake
and Ohio Canal, but as Jackson had demonstrated, these routes
were vulnerable in the Shenandoah, constraining the Yankees to a
lengthy detour through Pennsylvania and Ohio. A similar problem
loomed for the Confederacy across the Valley's southern tip, near
which the Virginia & Tennessee Railroad linked Richmond with
its western armies. Union conquest of the upper Valley could
sever that link and necessitate a rail circuit through the Carolinas
and Georgia. Such a conquest could also cut the flow of Valley
grain to Richmond via the James River Canal.

Also strategic were the Valley's eastern and western boundaries;
here too the Shenandoah divided Union from Confederacy. To the
west Union divisions dominated the Alleghenies. To the east was
the lair of the Confederate army protecting Richmond. Good
roads traversed the Valley from the Alleghenies to the Blue Ridge,
through which no less than eleven gaps opened onto the alluvial
plains of central Virginia. Through each of these gaps a Federal
column could lunge behind Confederates located north of the
James River, and the danger worsened the farther north a Confederate army maneuvered. An enemy force at Staunton, in the
upper Valley, would stand one hundred miles from Richmond; an
enemy force at Winchester, in the lower Valley, would be half that
distance from the rear of Johnston's army at Centreville. The
Shenandoah thus formed the strategic left flank of any Southern
defensive line in Virginia. Jackson, perhaps the Confederacy's

ablest student of military geography, firmly believed that "if this Valley is lost, Virginia is lost."[43]

The reverse was also true: so long as the South controlled the Valley, it could maintain a war in Virginia. An army inferior in numbers must exploit secrecy and surprise, and the forested Blue Ridge passes offered the rebels excellent opportunities for cloaked maneuver. The Shenandoah remained the corridor that Valley men reinforcing George Washington during the Revolution had shown it to be. Lee invaded Pennsylvania in 1863 behind the cover of the Blue Ridge. The Confederate raider Lieutenant General Jubal Early came this way during 1864 to threaten Washington, and rebel guerrilla John Mosby fought for months using the byways of the Valley.

Further, a poor army with at best just sufficient transportation, like the rebels defending the Old Dominion, required ready rations in any area of extended operations, and the Shenandoah was one long wheatfield. Its farms alone could sustain Confederate armies in Virginia for many months. "[The Shenandoah] is a perfect stomachic Elysium," marveled one rebel. "[H]ot batter cakes and good coffee, butter and molasses, eggs, two sorts of preserves, milk, hot loaf bread, mush, boiled ham was the bill of fare this morning. . . . For dinner we have canned tomatoes and corn and beans, and everything in as great abundance as at breakfast, only more so."[44] Not until 1864 did the North see that rebels continued to sally from the Shenandoah because they could eat as they marched there, and then Major General Philip Sheridan was loosed with 50,000 men to ravage Valley farms. In the process he annihilated the Confederates who opposed him, though he might have spared himself this effort. Once Sheridan scorched the Valley's agricultural base, no sizable Confederate force could ever operate there again.

But Sheridan was three years away and would not descend upon the Valley until the North grasped its total significance. In 1861 Federal concern focused on the lower Valley between the Manassas Gap Railroad and the Potomac. Two things made this sector of immediate importance. First, the lower Shenandoah flanked Washington. Anywhere north of Strasburg was north of Washington, and anywhere north of Martinsburg was north of Baltimore. The headquarters of Confederate Valley forces at

Winchester was a scant sixty miles northwest of the Union capital.
Also critical were the B & O and C & O links between Washington
and the Midwest. Despite Union progress in rebuilding the B & O's
Allegheny trackage, full east–west service was impossible because of destruction of the Potomac bridges at Harper's Ferry,
while the C & O Canal was subject to harassment by Turner
Ashby's cavalrymen. President Davis and Secretary Benjamin
knew all of this, and when they spun their map around to study
the Valley from the viewpoint of their Northern counterparts, they
feared that it was only a matter of time until the enemy moved
against it in force. Clearly the Union could not permit the Shenandoah to prick at Washington and gash its vital communications
much longer.

So Davis and Benjamin marked Union progress toward the Valley like a slow blue stain on their war map and decided they
must act. Though they had no troops to spare, they could provide
the leader that Valley citizens had requested. They hoped at the
same time to end turmoil in the Southern command structure.
Their solution was the creation, on October 22, of a department
of war embracing Virginia north of the Rappahannock River;
General Johnston was entrusted with over-all command.[45] The
Shenandoah was designated a separate district within Johnston's
department. The Valley District was bounded by the Blue Ridge
and Alleghenies and extended south from the Potomac to the vicinity of Staunton, an area of roughly 5,000 square miles. The
District was to have its own army and its own commander, and,
largely because his exploits at the head of a Shenandoah-raised
brigade had made him something of a local idol, Jackson was
chosen as chief of the Valley District.[46]

Under the new organization Johnston would continue as Jackson's superior and synchronize Valley operations with those of the
main army at Centreville. Beyond that, Jackson, now a major general, was largely independent. His immediate task was to gather
an army to shield the Valley. How he accomplished this was his
problem; he was advised only that he would have to succeed with
little help. Secretary Benjamin bluntly cautioned Jackson that his
initial force would be small, mostly the militia already in the field,
and that Richmond could promise nothing more than reinforcements when available. In the meantime, the Valley militia might

provide some additional help, and Richmond hoped Jackson's popularity in the area might also stimulate an outpouring of volunteers.[47]

The Confederate Government waged much of the war by fielding commanders without armies; such posts connoted either desperation or supreme confidence. In this case the government expressed its faith in Jackson, yet he was disappointed. Ironically, he would have preferred not to return to the Valley, the field of his greatest triumphs, but to the Alleghenies, mountains which had frustrated no less a man than Robert E. Lee.[48] Western Virginia was Jackson's boyhood home, and he was troubled by Union advances there. As early as his tour of duty at Harper's Ferry, he had lobbied for an Allegheny command.[49] He realized, as had Washington before him, that the Valley's best defense was occupation of western Virginia. Yet Jackson accepted the Valley assignment without pressing his personal desires.

Jackson left Centreville to assume command of the Valley Army on November 4, 1861, with a staff of two men. One was Colonel J. T. L. Preston, a founder of the Virginia Military Institute and Jackson's principal administrative officer in his capacity as assistant adjutant general. Soon Preston would vacate this post to return to V.M.I. The second aide was twenty-one-year-old Lieutenant Sandie Pendleton, who would remain with Stonewall until the General's death. Sandie was the son of Brigadier General William N. Pendleton, soon to be Robert E. Lee's artillery chief, and both father and son called Jackson friend. Jackson knew full well the extraordinary talents of this young lieutenant, that he had entered Washington College at age thirteen and instructed some classes before graduation. What Jackson could not have known was that Pendleton's delightful letters home, letters treasured by the Pendleton family long after the war, would constitute an invaluable account of the Campaign this journey to the Valley began.

Despite a fatiguing train ride that carried him only to Strasburg by dark, Jackson pushed his party on to Winchester before midnight.[50] Early next morning, without ceremony, he assumed command of the Valley District.

Jackson's first task was to study the strategic situation, and here one thing was readily apparent: the Shenandoah was threatened on two fronts. On the west an estimated 4,000 Union troops around Romney were stripping the South Branch Valley, and those Federals were just two days west of Winchester by an all but undefended road.⁵¹ The Valley's western border was equally exposed for fifty miles south of Winchester, and, for the present at least, Jackson was most concerned with this front. The Union divisions of Major General N. P. Banks dominated western Maryland to form the northern front. Banks massed a heavier force to the north, but, excepting the foray against Harper's Ferry, he had remained relatively inert and had made little effort to co-ordinate activity on his front with Allegheny-based operations.

If the enemy fronts did converge on the Valley, Jackson could guess how they would come. He foresaw one Northern column driving east from Romney to Martinsburg, another column sweeping south from Maryland to Martinsburg, and the two forces uniting there to advance on Winchester. If that happened, there would be nothing Jackson could do; the combined Union host would outnumber him beyond hope. Fortunately, the Federals were divided by command as well as geography. Those to the west belonged to the Department of Western Virginia, which was headquartered in the Allegheny wilderness at a flyspeck called Camp Gauley Mountain. Banks's divisions belonged to the Army of the Potomac, which was headquartered at Washington. Co-operation between separate military commands would be difficult, giving Jackson that much aid from his opponents. Nevertheless, Jackson had drawn the most difficult task Richmond had to allot that autumn—defense of a long frontier exposed from not one direction but two. From the first, he understood that his Valley Army must play a desperate game: operate between larger enemy concentrations so as to keep them apart.

If his Army failed in this game, it could not expect rescue. A demidivision of infantry, the closest Southern forces, faced heavy odds forty miles east of Winchester at Leesburg. Johnston was farther away, at Centreville. To complicate matters, there was no direct steam communication between Centreville and Winchester. The Manassas Gap Railroad, it will be recalled, swung south at Strasburg. From that city a trip to Winchester would have to be completed over the macadamized Valley Pike.

The Pike ran up the Shenandoah from Winchester to Staunton, and the line of that highway on his map beckoned Jackson's eye to

the southwest. Here his thoughts lingered. He knew Robert E.
Lee's Army of the Northwest was recovering near Huntersville,
West Virginia, from its unsuccessful Allegheny offensive. Lee had
been transferred to defend the Confederacy's Atlantic seaboard,
leaving Brigadier General William W. Loring in charge at Huntersville. Brigadier General Edward Johnson (not to be confused
with General Joseph E. Johnston, who commanded at Centreville)
screened Allegheny passes northwest of Staunton with part of this
army, but the bulk of it was idle. As boredom was the worst sequel to the punishment these men had endured, Stonewall determined to offer them a taste of victory.

Before his first day at Winchester ended, Jackson dispatched
Colonel Preston to Richmond with a candid message that the Valley was "defenseless" and that part or all of Loring's army must
be redeployed to it. The need was great: "It is very important that
disciplined troops not only of infantry, but also of artillery and
cavalry be ordered here. It appears to me that there should be at
least twenty pieces of field artillery, with their complement of
horses, harness, implements, etc., assigned to this command."[52]
Richmond had nothing like those reinforcements on hand, but the
dismal state of Valley District defenses, worse now, (because of
Romney's fall) than when the District was created, compelled War
Department action. Probably before Colonel Preston arrived, Secretary Benjamin had decided to shift the Stonewall Brigade and
Captain William McLaughlin's first-rate Rockbridge Artillery
back to the Valley from Joe Johnston's army at Centreville.[53] He
realized Jackson needed more, and the Secretary hinted that Loring's command might be made available.[54]

Johnston howled so loudly about losing the Stonewall Brigade
that Benjamin had to placate Old Joe with double its numbers in
replacements, explaining: "The Valley District is entirely defenseless and will fall into the hands of the enemy unless General
Jackson has troops sent to him immediately."[55] Excited by rumors
of a transfer, Jackson's former command leapt when it got the
word. The 2d, 5th, and 27th Virginia swarmed ahead by train to
make a surprise visit to Winchester on the evening of November
10. The 4th and 33d Virginia waited behind at Manassas Junction
for the return trains. Since no one knew when these trains would
return, the men were not permitted to pitch their tents, even after

a steady rain began, and Private John Casler of the 33d recollected: ". . . we had a glorious night in the rain and mud."[56] Casler, however, was squatting in the wrong mudhole. The E Company Irishmen of his regiment swilled a barrel of whiskey and grew so jolly their last officer deserted the Army in despair.[57] A long night followed before the trains appeared and the last of the Stonewall Brigade bounced home to the Shenandoah.

3

THE MANNER OF MEN

I burned fencerails when cold, stole
when hungry, drank when thirsty,
swore when angry, and was
oftentimes insubordinate.

—JOHN OPIE

Mrs. Cornelia McDonald, who depicted the "joyous" boys parading through Winchester on their way to Manassas in July, wrote of those who returned in November: "All the glory seemed to have departed from the eager and enthusiastic army of the summer before."[1] It was true. The rebels now felt much as they looked: patience, like boot leather, was thinning, and thoughts of war's romance were as faded as their uniforms. Conditions around Winchester did not brighten this outlook. The autumn was unusually severe. Storms screamed down from the Alleghenies bringing days of rain. Frigid winds slashed the cotton tents of the Stonewall Brigade; rebels sometimes battled for hours merely to hold tent poles in place.[2] Mumps, fever, and diphtheria swept the ranks.[3]

The boys pined for home, but there were no furloughs. Instead, entire regiments were detailed to begin a ring of fortifications around Winchester. Telegraph lines were repaired, strung to new points, and maintained with regularity. Gun crews were taught to serve the heavy artillery at Winchester. Winter uniforms were issued.[4] The War Department was delighted with progress in the Valley.[5]

The Stonewall Brigade's volunteers were not. Their thoughts were of home, or, until they could pry furloughs from Jackson, of Winchester's female population. The boys were in such a state that many of them saw "every woman" as a beauty who deserved attention accordingly.[6] Jackson, of course, sought to restrain such unmilitary endeavors. Declaring Winchester off limits, he isolated the Stonewall Brigade in a camp four miles north of the city, but this only challenged the ingenuity of his men. Jackson's old regiments also considered the new camp unfair since the militia remained near Winchester to guard it. Volunteers harbored a collective grudge against the "melish," whose sole function appeared to be blocking their fun. They supposed the militiamen enjoyed an easy life in the city while they languished in rural exile, and, with no hope of furloughs, the volunteers could not be denied escapes to clean, warm Winchester.

Private John Opie of the 5th Virginia devised a three-stage plan for outwitting the "melish." He first learned their password by eavesdropping on a militia post barring the road to Winchester. Next, he used chalk to decorate his jacket with officer's shoulder straps which were indistinguishable at night from the real item. Finally, he "obtained" a sword, and when dark fell, "there was a full fledged lieutenant—sword, shoulder straps and countersign. The objective point, Winchester; the attraction, the beautiful girls of the town."[7]

Private George Baylor of the 2d Virginia resorted to impersonation of another sort. He decamped with three friends and headed for the nearest checkpoint, with one truant howling like a madman. The others pretended to be his escort to Winchester's mental ward. When the militia hesitated to pass them, the "lunatic" flung himself at the guards, and the way was immediately opened.[8]

Winchester was a reward worth such imaginative efforts. A favorite pastime there was eating, and every family welcomed soldiers to the table. One girl remembered that the table was never set at her house "without a large addition to the family circle. This is always prepared for, morning, noon and night, as it is a matter of course that soldiers will be brought in just at the right time and so cordially received that they feel they have perfect right to come again whenever it is convenient to them."[9] These meals were a prelude to what rebels called the "social campaign of Winchester."[10] There were frequent dances. Bees were organized in which girls knitted for soldiers while the soldiers entertained them.

The fun was splendid, although the knitting accomplished by thirty girls at one bee was assessed by private Lanty Blackford of the Rockbridge Artillery as insufficient to put a single Confederate in socks.[11] In some cases the fun went too far, and militia doctor Abraham Miller would soon diagnose "a number of girls in the different neighborhoods in an interesting way, so the war has done something for the increase of the army."[12]

The troops also waged a campaign against Jackson's ban on liquor. At Stonewall's order, spirits were authorized to soldiers for medical purposes only. Local taverns were supposed to sell only to the bearer of a prescription signed by a surgeon, endorsed by the colonel of his regiment, and endorsed again by his brigade commander, but this was a simple obstacle for the thirsty to hurdle. Three tipplers forged the appropriate names on a bogus prescription and sent another to Winchester in the guise of hospital orderly, who inevitably returned with a fifth of pain killer.[13]

Officers too broke the prohibition. Captain Albert Pendleton of the 4th Virginia received a package from home containing liquid refreshment. He shared his good fortune at lunch one day, and his fellow officers departed to conduct afternoon drill in a haze of joyous anticipation.[14] The L Company officers of the 5th Virginia received three kegs of rye from home and invited other officers of the regiment to join them. Private Opie was not included, which he regarded as an oversight to be corrected:

> Securing two tin buckets, we left for the rear of the tent, which was crowded with officers who were compelled to stand up for the want of space. We pulled up two or three tent pins, rolled out a keg, filled our two buckets with the old rye, and then rolled back the keg and replaced the tent pins. We then made a campfire that resembled Vesuvius and raised Cain; but as the officers of the regiment were engaged in the same meritorious business, we escaped punishment. The next morning the regimental colors were found lashed to the tallest tree in the camp.[15]

Opie did not relate, probably could not remember, whether officers or enlisted men raised the colors.

While lashed above the 5th Virginia's camp, the regimental battle flag meant that the troops had won a round in an unceasing clash between themselves and Stonewall. Jackson always sought to pound his men into the mold of the thoroughly obedient professional soldier, but he never succeeded. An assertive independence was virtually built into the Valley Army. Its companies were drawn from neighborhoods of a few hundred, sometimes a few dozen, families, and privates found it difficult to accept a cousin or boyhood friend as a superior. Further, the Confederate practice of selecting company officers by company election tended to exclude strict disciplinarians from positions of command.

Straggling (leaving the marching column without permission) was the most common means by which Jackson's soldiers ignored discipline. Men were constantly leaving ranks for a hot meal or a comfortable place to rest for the night. They were often tempted to drop out by well-meaning Southern women who inevitably had food ready for passing troops or were forced to straggle when they outran their wagons and had nothing to eat. Jackson's relentless marches worsened the problem by literally walking the boots off his men. The barefooted drifted to the rear, where, with the exhausted and the malingerers, their numbers were sometimes considerable. Jackson's columns were never the compact surging mass portrayed by his admirers; they tended to be, rather, a weary corps surrounded by hundreds of roving panhandlers.

Marches led eventually to battlefields, and there too an ingrained individuality marked these men. They could not be arrayed in the shoulder-to-shoulder formations prescribed by military textbooks of the day. They were quick-witted and self-reliant, "more of a freelance than a machine," said one of their generals.[16] In attack, each rebel aligned on himself, dodging forward and firing as he saw fit. In defense, each judged the strength of his position for himself and left when he thought it useless to remain. John Opie was to state later, without a twinge of guilt: "In war, I ran when it was necessary, fought when there was a fighting chance. . . ."[17]

But the most persistent obstacle to rigid discipline in the Valley Army proved to be its very youth. John Casler, who was destined to become one of the Army's best anecdoters, was hardly beyond his twenty-first year when the war started. Typical also was John Opie, who was seventeen on the eve of war and welcomed it as salvation from his classes in analytical geometry. Junior officers were scarcely older. Thirty-seven-year-old Jackson was an antique to these youngsters, who called him "Old Jack" as often as they did "Stonewall" and who did not appreciate his regulations any more than youth enjoys restrictions of any kind. "The truth is," asserted one of these young warriors, "we were soldier boys, and the boy was sometimes more in evidence than the soldier."[18]

The commander of these soldier boys was of different, more rigid stuff. Major General Thomas J. Jackson was utterly serious in all things. The early death of both parents and a hard youth in the mountains of western Virginia had already made him a humorless young man when he entered the United States Military Academy at West Point in 1842. Ill-prepared academically, Jackson had to devote more time to his studies than most of his classmates. He did so without complaint and stood seventeenth in a graduating class of forty-two. He earned two promotions for gallantry during the Mexican War and rose to the rank of brevet major before he left the U. S. Army in 1851, after, portentously, a bitter feud with a fellow officer.

During the next ten years Jackson taught at the Virginia Military Institute, where he worked as diligently as ever, but received little appreciation. When cadets gathered to laugh and gossip about their teachers, they came down hardest on him. He became the butt of the roughest cadet humor. Upperclassmen once strapped a gagged "rat" (the V.M.I. term for a freshman) to a chair, tilted it against Jackson's door and disappeared. When Jackson opened the door, the helpless rat plopped at his feet.[19]

Despite harassment, Jackson slowly garnered a measure of respect. He became the man at V.M.I. who got the call where there was serious work to be done. He commanded the V.M.I. detachment at John Brown's execution, and he marched the Corps of Cadets to Richmond to serve as drill instructors when the war began. After a brief scare by an assignment to the map-making department, Jackson secured his first command at Harper's Ferry.

In his personal habits Jackson was a strange man. He impressed many as incapable of laughter; jokes seemed a mystery to him. He sat bolt upright at his desk and never touched the back of his chair. When thinking, Jackson stared ahead fixedly, totally absorbed by his business.[20] He often rode beside his marching columns, raising alternate arms heavenward. Some said Jackson was praying, others claimed that Jackson supposed this peculiar practice relieved weight in the hand by draining blood back to the heart. Such oddities of behavior, coupled with his religious fervor, gave rise to talk that Jackson was insane.

This talk of lunacy was a recurring irritant in Jackson's life, especially until the talkers grew accustomed to him. Many V.M.I. cadets found that three or four years were insufficient to adjust and dismissed him as a "hell of a fool." During the spring of 1862, when their commands merged with the Valley Army, Generals Taylor, Ewell, and Whiting all questioned Jackson's sanity, doubts which gave way to admiration as victories followed. According to the measure of victories gained, Jackson was sane enough.

One measure of Jackson's sanity was his silence. He never shared his thoughts if there was an alternative, and if there was no other way, he said no more than absolutely essential. "If silence be golden, he was a 'bonanza,'" reflected one observer.[21] This silence implemented Jackson's desire to "mystify, mislead, and surprise," not only the enemy but his own forces as well.[22] His marching orders, for example, invariably specified a move "in the direction of" a place which was not the goal. He veiled his intentions so consistently that Major General Richard Ewell, who came to admire Stonewall, nevertheless admitted that he never received a message from Jackson without dreading orders to march on the North Pole.[23]

Like his speech, Jackson strove to make his discipline the tightest in the Confederacy. He had a mania for enforcement of regulations, and he probably court-martialed more offenders than any other officer of the Confederate Army. In July 1862 Jackson unquestionably set some sort of record by keeping every general of his command busy with court-martial duty.[24] He expected everyone to follow orders without delay, question, or comment. "Arrest," he tersely instructed the commander of one disorderly regiment, "any man who leaves his post, and prefer charges and specifications against him that he may be Court-Martialed. It will not do to say that your men cannot be induced to perform their duty. They *must be made to do it*" (italics Jackson's).[25]

Enormous ambition fueled this devotion to duty. When Dr.

Hunter McGuire, a member of his staff, asked Jackson about his emotions the first time he came under enemy fire during the Mexican War, the General confided he was afraid the battle would not be severe enough to allow him to win distinction. McGuire thereafter observed an intense earthly ambition in his chief: "Ambition? Yes, far beyond what ordinary men possess."[26] Nothing less than the conquest of a continent could slake that ambition. Jackson once visited Quebec, and there he stood before the Wolfe Memorial on the Plains of Abraham and read aloud Wolfe's last words, "I die content." In a rare show of emotion, Jackson exclaimed: "To die as he died, who would not die content."[27]

A craving for distinction, for the delayed commendation Jackson wrote of to his wife after the First Battle of Manassas, flowed in the blood of this man. It conflicted mightily with a genuine Christian humility. The vigor with which Jackson practiced Christian discipleship—before the war he would neither read nor write a letter on Sunday—sprang partially from this conflict, but he never quieted his ambition. Shrewd Brigadier General Richard Taylor once glimpsed this compulsion: "It was but a glimpse. The curtain closed, and he was absorbed in prayer. Yet in that moment I saw an ambition as boundless as Cromwell's and as merciless. . . . [H]is ambition was vast, all absorbing. Like the unhappy wretch from whose shoulders sprang the foul serpent, he loathed it, perhaps feared it; but he could not escape it—it was himself. . . ."[28]

Once, when he was unable to obtain sufficient rifles for his command, Jackson requested twelve-foot pikes as substitutes.[29] The requisition has appeared comical over the years, but Jackson meant no jest. Stonewall intended that all those so armed would fight until he gave the word to stop, and he would have court-martialed the shirkers. Jackson gave his best effort under every circumstance and demanded no less from others. One perceptive rebel touched the essence of Jackson when he wrote: "In truth the great soldier was an altogether earnest man. . . ."[30]

In his earnest way, Jackson did not see the boy in any of his soldiers, and he reacted sternly to their escapades around Winchester. Many of those who broke into town on the evening of November 10 were promptly arrested, and Old Jack's restrictions grew harsher as his troops continued to evade them. When he discovered that visiting relatives were smuggling liquor to his men, he ransacked every civilian vehicle entering his camps. All spirits found were poured on the ground, and the wagon and team were confiscated.[31] Stonewall issued orders requiring all officers to obtain passes from his office before they left their camps.[32] One soldier, a father of four, was executed by firing squad for assaulting an officer.[33]

Despite such efforts, Old Jack never forged a professional army. His troops became unbelievably tough fighters, but professional obedience he could not instill. Declared one of Jackson's rebels: "The Confederate soldier was peculiar in that he was ever ready to fight, but never ready to submit to the routine duty and discipline of the camp or the march. The soldiers were determined to be soldiers after their own notion and do their duty for the love of it, as they thought best. The officers saw the necessity for doing otherwise, and so the conflict was commenced and maintained to the end."[34]

From this clash of volunteers and a rigid professional soldier emerged an immortal compromise, Jackson's "Foot Cavalry."

II

Even more pressing than Jackson's concern with discipline during November and December of 1861 was the weakness of the Army of the Valley District (already called simply the Valley Army), and Jackson sought reinforcements with a special urgency. He reminded Secretary Benjamin that the Army needed Loring's command. He ordered his militia commanders, Brigadier Generals Boggs, J. H. Carson, and G. S. Meem, to concentrate their brigades at Winchester, and he assembled and armed all other militia units from the northern Shenandoah.[35]

The Valley Army's first reinforcement came in the person of one man, Brigadier General Richard B. Garnett, a new commander for the Stonewall Brigade. Garnett bore the name of a distinguished family which had already given an able son (Brigadier General Robert Garnett) to the Confederate cause. A West Pointer, Richard Garnett had seen twenty years' duty on the western frontier. He had battled Indians from Texas to the Dakotas and served in California in the raucous days after gold was discovered on John Sutter's land. His trim, agile appearance bespoke a strenuous life in the open, and he was browned until he resembled the rancheros of California. Brooding eyes set in a narrow, almost pinched face added something of the conquistador image.

Despite his qualifications, Garnett reached the Shenandoah with two handicaps: he was replacing the brigade's first and very successful commander, Jackson, and, second, Jackson did not want him. The Stonewall Brigade eyed Garnett skeptically, a challenge he overcame with time. He was as direct and unpretentious as Jackson, and, unlike the latter, he was willing to hear grievances. Excepting Jackson, Garnett proved the most popular of the brigade's seven commanders, and it became as much Garnett's Brigade as it was the Stonewall Brigade.* The second problem he could not master. Jackson believed Garnett's assignment to the Valley was due to political influence, which immediately tainted Garnett in Jackson's opinion. When his discipline proved milder than Jackson's, the latter's doubts mounted.[36]

Old Jack was better pleased by his own efforts to organize artillery batteries for the Army. His U. S. Army career had been with the artillery, and he appreciated the uses of cannon. Fortunately, the Army had many excellent gunners, many of whom had learned gunnery from Jackson on the V.M.I. drill field. The General found an idle section (2 guns) and assigned it to a former student, Lieutenant W. E. Cutshaw. To man his guns, Cutshaw got the Irishmen of the 33d Virginia, whose antics had driven their last officer to desert from Manassas Junction while the regiment awaited its return to the Valley. The section grew mildly proficient in a few days, and Jackson planted it at Hanging Rock,[37] a strongpoint on the road to Romney which had once witnessed a massacre of Delaware Indians.

The governor of Virginia scraped together 5 guns for the Valley District. They were odd looking things—"alleged cannons," someone quipped[38]—but they could do good work under an efficient

---

* Traditionally, Civil War brigades, both North and South, were identified simply by the surname of their commanders. A nickname such as Stonewall was an exception resulting from unusual unit courage. Hence, Jackson's original command was known both as the Stonewall Brigade and as Garnett's—later Winder's—Brigade.

officer. Jackson thought of dependable Joe Carpenter, who cap-
tained Company A of the 27th Virginia. Like Cutshaw, Carpenter had been one of Jackson's promising gunnery pupils, and the
student now received a new task from his former professor. Jackson transferred Carpenter to lead the new battery; the infantrymen of Company A went along to become cannoneers.[39] A similar
transfer converted Captain James Waters' Company L of the 5th
Virginia to Waters' West Augusta battery.

The finest battery in the Shenandoah, and one of the very best
of the Confederacy, was Captain William McLaughlin's Rockbridge Artillery. Its ranks were crowded with well-educated young
men: twenty-eight college graduates, twenty-five theology students, and seven men with master's degrees.[40] From its rosters
rose leaders such as Sandie Pendleton's famous father, Brigadier
General William N. Pendleton. These gunners hailed from the
Lexington area, and Jackson knew many of them by name. He
was therefore especially concerned to hear that some had picked
up the Stonewall Brigade's drinking habits. The battery's march to
Winchester from Centreville had included an unscheduled halt at
a wayside distillery, after which it ingloriously entered Winchester
with a wagonload of dead-drunk gunners.[41]

Another battery emerged from the cavalry operating around the
Valley. Three young cavalrymen, all of them Jackson's students six
months earlier, had ventured beyond their lessons. Captain Robert
Chew, nineteen, and Lieutenants Milton Rose, seventeen, and
Jamie Thomson, eighteen, sold Turner Ashby and Secretary Benjamin the idea of a battery of horse artillery. Unlike conventional
artillery units in which gunners trailed the cannons on foot, each
of Chew's men would ride his own mount. The battery would go
where the cavalry went, as fast as it went. The idea stressed mobility; guns must be lightweight and a large contingent of spare
horses was essential. Benjamin was particularly enthusiastic about
the concept and provided the first horse artillery in America since
the Mexican War with a flexible complement of 3 guns: a stubby
12-pounder howitzer deadly at short range, a medium-range
3-inch rifled piece, and a long-range English Blakely gun.[42]

Chew's battery was to serve under Lieutenant Colonel Turner
Ashby, a man born for combat. Three generations of Ashby's
forebears had fought America's battles. A great-grandfather had

served through the French and Indian War; a grandfather was wounded when George Washington attempted to surprise the British at Germantown, Pennsylvania. His father, John Ashby, was a Virginia hero of the War of 1812, and Turner Ashby was worthy of his stock. He had been in the saddle since his boyhood in Fauquier County, east of the Blue Ridge, and he could do anything on a horse. At thirty-four years of age, he was a paladin, respected by all he met as a natural leader. When rowdy construction gangs were pushing the Manassas Gap Railroad through Fauquier during the 1850s, Turner had organized a company of mounted citizens and enforced order. Upon hearing of John Brown's raid at Harper's Ferry, Turner had gathered his company for action. He had arrived too late to see Brown captured, but for the next eight weeks his riders patrolled the Potomac to blunt any abolitionist effort to free Brown.

After Virginia seceded in April 1861 Turner Ashby's company resumed its Potomac patrols near Harper's Ferry, where tragedy struck. His younger brother fell in an ambush, and there were rumors he was sabered without mercy after begging to surrender. Those close to Turner felt he believed the story and became obsessed with revenge.[43] He ambushed and harassed the Federals constantly. He temporarily shut down the B & O by expertly blasting a boulder onto its tracks.[44] He borrowed a farmer's homespun suit and swayback plow horse and ambled across the Potomac, passing himself off as a horse doctor. The disguise made him welcome in Northern camps all the way to Pennsylvania, and he returned with valuable information.[45]

Such intense energy made Ashby the ideal company commander; only later, when his fame attracted too many riders to his command for him to manage, did his command deteriorate. In the beginning he won much praise. An inspector general from Richmond visited Harper's Ferry in May, found Ashby to be "an excellent officer,"[46] and added: "I am quite confident that, with the vigilance which is exercised by Captain Ashby, no enemy can pass the point which he is directed to observe."[47] Even perfectionist Jackson felt secure at Harper's Ferry with Ashby on patrol.[48]

By the time Colonel Angus McDonald organized a regiment of Shenandoah cavalry, Ashby was the unquestioned choice for his second in command, as lieutenant colonel,[49] and it was a wise

choice. Ashby's already growing reputation helped attract companies led by captains like John Winfield, John Fletcher, and
George Sheetz. These men were not soldiers by profession, but
they were resolved to learn; Sheetz, for example, was seen squint-
ing over *The Cavalry Officer's Manual* at many a fireside.[50] Even
without experience, McDonald's regiment provided most of what
defense the Valley had from July to November 1861. Sixty-year-
old McDonald was unable to meet the strain of active campaigning for long, and when Jackson assumed command of the Valley
District, Ashby headed the entire contingent of Shenandoah cavalry. He had deployed his men on a picket line that stretched
eighty miles, from Harper's Ferry west to Moorefield.

Ashby galloped between these outposts on a huge white horse
which accented his swarthy complexion and beard. He was short
but very strong; his endurance seemed eternal. Unfortunately, his
correspondence (official and private) was sketchy, so it is difficult
today to know the real man.

One thing is certain: Ashby did not know fear. He once remained under enemy fire with complete indifference while he
munched his breakfast; when cautioned, he merely replied:
"Never mind that . . . I am very hungry."[51] He believed a leader
should take his men to the front and take risks in order to inspire
his troopers.[52] His infectious courage heartened ordinary men
to follow wherever he rode, and hundreds refused to join rebel
ranks without assurances they could serve under Ashby.[53]

Unfortunately, courage was often counterbalanced by another
Ashby trait, his seeming unwillingness (or his inability) to effectively discipline his troopers. He did not share the concern of able
captains like Sheetz for the details of camp administration or regimental organization. A farmer, Ashby had enjoyed little formal
and no military education, and he naïvely saw the boundless patri-
otism of his men as a substitute for any real discipline.[54] His riders
were perfect shots. Their tall, blooded mounts were superb. What
more was necessary to make a cavalryman? Ashby asked.

That question foreshadowed disaster. Romantic dreams had encased the thoughts of those who became the Valley cavalry long
before the war, and it was for this reason that the region's social
highlight had been the medieval-style tournament copied from the
novels of Scott. (Rumor had it that Ashby, a frequent contestant,
entered one tournament dressed as an Indian. He rode Indian

fashion without saddle or bridle and won his event.) But now a "band of brothers" mentality acquired before the war did more than the enemy to hurt Ashby's regiment. It remained deficient in organization, training, and discipline. It had only one other field-grade officer, Major Oliver Funsten, who had shown commendable zeal as a recruiter but who had no military training.[55] Some companies lacked officers and even noncommissioned officers.[56] With a roll of extra clothes dangling from his saddle, a boy trotted off to join Ashby's cavalry. When he got tired or the weather turned unpleasant, he strayed home. "Every private was a general and needed no guidance or direction from his officer," vowed one trooper.[57] Without benefit of discipline, Ashby troopers, and some of his officers, greeted the war as a jolly new tournament.

Lack of clear-cut jurisdiction obliged Jackson to tolerate such ragged discipline, for Ashby's regiment enjoyed a vague autonomy which sheltered it from Stonewall's direct control. The Valley cavalry was recruited under special War Department authorization and reported to Richmond, not Winchester.[58] (Likewise, authorization and equipment for Chew's battery came from Secretary Benjamin, not Jackson.) Ashby was willing to co-operate with Stonewall for the most part, but on matters such as discipline he showed little promise.

There came a time when Ashby did not know how many men he could field, but that was later; in November he told Jackson that he had 34 officers and 508 men. Stonewall listed those figures with his first monthly report. He also showed 4,000 effective infantry and artillerymen. There were approximately 20 pieces in his batteries and roughly 1,000 militia in his training camps.[59] It would have pleased Jackson to learn that news of better discipline among the militia had already reached Richmond.[60]

At the headquarters of this little host, Jackson was collecting a staff which matched his own devotion to hard work. He was so determined to have capable aides that he investigated all prospects to the point of discovering whether they got up early, a mark of diligence Jackson esteemed.[61] And the General usually got good men for Headquarters whether they wished to be there or not. Major John Harman, the Shenandoah's renowned stage operator, had been trying to resign since the General talked him into being quartermaster of the Stonewall Brigade.[62] Harman wanted to get back to his stage line, but Jackson snatched him again during No-

vember and named him Valley Army quartermaster. Frustration
stoked the incredibly foul language with which John Harman
brilliantly managed the Army's wagon trains. Such language also
earned him several lectures from the pious Jackson.[63]

Like Harman, many on the staff of the Valley Army had served
Jackson when he headed the Stonewall Brigade. Sandie Pendleton
had been Jackson's chief of ordnance then and served now as
aide-de-camp, a position which allowed him to deal with every aspect of Army administration. Doctor Hunter McGuire was Valley
District medical director. An inspired student, McGuire had
taught medicine in Philadelphia at age twenty-two. When the war
started, Richmond posted young McGuire to Harper's Ferry while
Jackson was in command. The latter kept him waiting for a week
while he checked him out, then never let him go. McGuire was
graced with an innovative mind, and he assembled an ambulance
corps and the Confederacy's first system of reserve hospitals for
the Valley Army.[64]

To guard Headquarters, Jackson chose Captain Harry Morrison's Company I, the Liberty Hall Volunteers of the 4th Virginia. This remarkable company was initially recruited from
Washington College, and it ranked among the best educated units
of the war, North or South. One fourth of its men had been preparing for the ministry. The unusual concentration of intelligence
and devotion attracted Jackson, although he never favored his
guard. The Liberty Hall Volunteers were often in the front rank
of their regiment during battles. Quieter times saw these rebels
stationed near Headquarters with four sentries at the General's
door, where they learned to step lightly. "Not that he was cross,"
recalled Lieutenant John Lyle, "but anywhere in his neighborhood
was a proper place to put on your dignity."[65] Only once did that
dignity falter. Late one evening a sentry started a whistling bee,
and things grew jolly until Jackson stepped from his office and
"squelched it."[66]

III

His army improving steadily, Jackson moved to seize the initiative in the Valley District. On November 20 he offered General
Johnston and Secretary Benjamin his first essay in strategy, a

strategy which proved very similar to that urged by George Washington one hundred years earlier. Jackson argued, in essence, that the Valley must be defended at its western frontier; the Shenandoah could best serve as a sally port from which to catapult an aggressive garrison into the Alleghenies around Romney. If reinforced by Loring's Army of the Northwest, Jackson wrote, he would attempt to surprise and recapture this strategic town.

Jackson believed the chance of success was good because an offense from the recently defenseless Valley would not be expected, and the fruits of success would be significant. The unlooked-for surrender of the Federal garrison at Romney would be a sobering demonstration of Southern power to the many Union sympathizers of the fertile South Branch Valley. Several good roads crossed this valley toward the Shenandoah; a vigilant Southern force at Romney could deny the enemy these passages and thus prevent the junction of Union fronts around Martinsburg which Jackson had dreaded since his first day as Valley District commander. Indeed, to Jackson the most important reason for plunging into the Alleghenies was that territory taken there would be a buffer between enemy fronts to the north and west. Jackson did not divulge details of how the Yankees at Romney were to be trapped, but he stressed the need for surprise and capture. He visualized a swoop, not a gradual build-up culminating with a Braddock-like advance. Care had to be taken to conceal Confederate intentions.

Jackson packaged something for everyone in his scheme. He knew Johnston anticipated an attack at Centreville, so he argued that the Romney thrust would give the impression that Johnston had been weakened; this should precipitate a Northern offensive; if not, nothing could, and Johnston could stop worrying about Centreville. Jackson promised to reach Johnston in time to help if the enemy did advance. He also knew Loring, at Huntersville, was worried about Union moves toward Staunton if Loring left the upper Valley; for him, Jackson noted that any such advance would expose the enemy rear to Confederates at Romney. For Secretary of War Benjamin, Jackson suggested that capture of the Romney garrison would enable the Valley Army to guard the Shenandoah against remaining Federal forces without additional reinforcements. Speed and capture were essential; let Loring come at once, Jackson concluded.[67]

Conceived in urgency, Jackson's offensive materialized slowly. Johnston did not welcome the prospect of Jackson drawing enemy attention toward Centreville.[68] Benjamin merely informed Loring of the plan and allowed him to decide if he would join it.[69] Loring waited almost until December to agree to the effort. When he did, it was with a promise his men would cheerfully endure every hardship, but at the same time he pleaded the necessity of delaying his march for Winchester until transportation could be assembled to move a large baggage train with him. This might take two or even three weeks. Nor did Loring commit his entire force. Elements of the Army of the Northwest under Brigadier General Edward Johnson were to remain on station west of Staunton. Loring would bring only three brigades totaling approximately 6,000 men to the Valley District.[70]

Jackson had premised his operation upon immediate action with every available man and was disappointed by Loring's response. By mid-December his impatience was mounting. The Union reportedly bolstered its Romney garrison to a strength of 7,000 during a break in the squally weather.[71] The rebels were not as swift. By mid-month only one brigade from the army of the Northwest was encamped at Winchester. The other two dawdled with supplies around Staunton. Jackson implored Benjamin to get Loring moving, but nothing happened.[72]

Stonewall at length resolved to occupy his troops with a raid on the C & O Canal. An ingenious series of dams along the Valley's northern border kept the canal at a roughly constant depth. One of these dams, No. 5, fed a particularly long stretch directly below Martinsburg. With the B & O Railroad dismantled, the Union was making maximum use of the canal to amass coal reserves inside Washington, and Jackson determined to sever this flow.

Stonewall planned a raid in force. Carson's militia brigade, Garnett's brigade, and the Rockbridge Artillery prepared to march. The orders, typically, were silent about destination. Lieutenant Jim Langhorne of the Headquarters Guard wrote his father: *"We as usual,* do not know . . . which direction we are to go. . . . No one but Old Jack himself knows where, or for what purpose we are going."[73]

Reveille sounded at 4 A.M. on December 16. Rebels downed as

much breakfast as they could hold and lined up; before dawn they were headed toward the Potomac.[74] The fatiguing march was enlivened only by speculation about some flatboats Jackson was hauling northward.[75] On the seventeenth the column picked up Ashby's cavalry at Martinsburg and pressed on to Dam No. 5. Darkness was falling as the Confederates approached the Potomac undetected by Union pickets on the far bank.[76]

No time was lost. Since ammunition shortages barred the rebels from bombarding the dam with artillery, a hole would have to be opened with pick and crowbar.[77] Jackson enjoined absolute silence on his regiments, banned campfires,[78] and gathered 30 hearty Irishmen from the 27th Virginia, whom he dispatched down to the Potomac's south shore to erect a brush screen; at dawn the Irishmen were back, leaving behind them a protected area where Confederates could work at night.[79]

Northern artillery discovered the rebels soon after dawn and began to shell the Virginia shore. Their aim was poor, and many Confederates were attracted to a hilltop to take a peek at the enemy. Among them was Private George Neese of New Market. A recent volunteer with Chew's horse battery, Neese was a typical rebel: young, quick-witted, and blessed with a feeling for the comical. One wild shell sailed over him and exploded some distance to his rear. Any veteran would have ignored it as harmless, but that shell was Neese's first hostile fire, and he recorded in a diary destined to become a classic of the war: "Though oblivion may blot all else from my memory, its darkest waters can never erase the fear that rushed all over me, and crept into every little corner of me . . . when I heard the frightful screaming whiz of the first shell. . . . I laid so close to the ground that it seemed to me I flattened out a little, yearning for a leave of absence."[80]

To Neese's right, Captains McLaughlin and Chew each rolled a gun onto a hill above the dam to drive off annoying Federal sharpshooters. A few rounds finished this job, and the rebels were jeering the fleeing enemy when a concealed Union battery opened on them with frightening accuracy. McLaughlin yelled for everyone to take cover in trees fifty yards to the right and sent Lieutenant William Poague to fetch the rest of the Rockbridge Artillery.

Poague never forgot the scene which greeted his return to the rebel artillery near the dam. Officers and men alike were snake-dancing from one side of a big pine tree to the other as Yankee shells burst around them. Jackson was there, standing in the open, trying to talk the gunners back to their pieces. No one responded, and even Jackson was seen to duck an occasional incoming shell. There was only one man present who did not bow his head. With arms folded across his chest, Turner Ashby strolled quietly back and forth before the abandoned cannons. Poague decided right there that Ashby was the bravest man he ever saw, a thought which Poague admitted came to him hunched as low in his saddle as the pommel would allow. As fresh Confederate guns arrived, the enemy ceased firing and the Southerners did not reopen.[81]

The 4th Virginia supplied that night's fatigue party, which was to begin chipping a hole in the dam itself. Grumbling that it was a "dam detail,"[82] the troops crept down to the river, where Jackson had their equipment waiting: crowbars, axes, picks, and a barrel of whiskey. This time the spirits were authorized, and each man quaffed a pint.[83] Thus fortified, they completed their assignment in relative happiness.

Word spread of how Stonewall braced those who toiled on the dam—Old Jack had personally ladled out the whiskey to assure none went astray[84]—and the work detail for the next night eagerly anticipated its special ration. But these hopes were dashed as Union gunners shelled a mill near the river bank. It blazed so brightly the fatigue party could not approach the Potomac without being picked off by enemy riflemen. The night was lost.[85]

Federals could make torches of other nearby buildings on succeeding nights, forcing Stonewall to a strategy as simple as it proved effective. He feinted an invasion. Carson's militia brigade and the flatboats Jackson had brought along moved up the Potomac under orders to be as obvious as possible. When the enemy hurried upstream as expected, Captains Frederick Holliday of the 33d Virginia and Henry Robinson of the 27th Virginia led volunteers to finish work on the dam. The structure was constructed in such a way that a breach could only be completed by men working from the river, and the rebels endured hours in the numbing water before they battered through and left this segment of canal a muddy trough.[86]

The breach was small, but there was no more time for this enterprise. The rebels marched southward. Their swift pace was interrupted by only one incident, an escapade involving none other than Jackson. Long after Stonewall was dead, his staff relished this tale:

> . . . after riding along some distance, the General spied a tree hanging heavy with persimmons, a peculiar fruit of which he was very fond. Dismounting, he was in a short time seated aloft among the branches, in the midst of abundance. He ate in silence and when satisfied started to descend, but found that it was not so easy as the ascent had been. Attempting to swing himself from a limb to the main fork of the tree, he got so completely entangled that he could move neither up nor down and was compelled to call for help. He remained suspended in that attitude until his staff, convulsed with laughter, brought some rails from a fence near by and made a pair of skids to slide him to the earth.[87]

If this episode amused Jackson, which is unlikely, it was his last laugh for some time. He had returned to Winchester by December 23 and learned that Loring still had not arrived. Worse, fresh intelligence from Romney numbered the enemy there at 10,000 men, with additional reinforcements expected.[88]

Yet the offensive had to be launched, for two reasons. First, Jackson was literally losing the attention of his men, who yearned more intensely than ever for furloughs. Most of them were confronting their first Christmas away from their families, and homesickness was reaching epidemic proportions. On Christmas Day the troops flocked to their surrogate families in Winchester, but this only heightened their longing for home. One rebel sighed: "Many who spent last Christmas with wife and children at home will be missing this time—perhaps to join the happy group in merry Christmas never again."[89] Jim Langhorne was awash in melancholy as he thought: "How different will be the year approaching . . . to those of the few years of my short life. Instead of being at home with those I love so dearly, exchanging bright hopes for the future . . . I will be on a hostile march against those who at this time last year I called 'brothers, countrymen and friends.'"[90] Jackson rightly sought to jerk his men from such reveries.

Second, not to move on Romney was tantamount to surrendering the lower Shenandoah. By December 16 B & O crews had finished repairing the bridge on the Big Cacapon River northeast of Romney, and now the road was fully rebuilt except across the Valley's narrow tip. That alone would rivet Union attention to the area. Federals west and north of Winchester eventually must realize the superiority of their position and unite around Martinsburg. Jackson emphasized this danger in a Christmas Eve letter to Johnston: ". . . our true policy is to attack the enemy in his present position [at Romney] before he receives additional re-enforcements, and especially never to permit a junction of their forces at or near Martinsburg."[91] The delay in undertaking this operation had caused Jackson to drop the word "capture" and use "attack," but he did not think the mission a forlorn one. When joined by Loring's command, the Valley Army would number 7,500 volunteers, 2,200 militia, and 650 cavalry, a force equal to the enemy in Romney. Jackson closed his message to Johnston with a promise to march against Romney at the "earliest practicable moment."[92]

This moment depended on Loring, and that did not promise an early start. Loring had delayed his redeployment to Winchester until December while he assembled stores and baggage, and as he moved, the first severe storm of the winter broke around Huntersville. The Army of the Northwest slid out of the Alleghenies along gullies of snow and mud, and much of its stores were lost. "The wagoneers were forced to throw out tents, blankets, etc., all of which were burnt; they also abandoned broken wagons and horses who would step off the road and roll many feet down the mountain," wrote Lieutenant Lavender Ray of the 1st Georgia.[93] This trek sparked hopeful rumors that the Northwesterners were heading for comfortable winter quarters at Winchester, and some jubilant men threw away their weapons en route.[94]

Loring's column was delayed further by Shenandoah men and women who proved too generous. The passing regiments were fed and fed again. Lieutenant Ray recalled slogging into the little village of Bridgewater during a snowstorm to be welcomed by the ever-smiling women with milk, bread, and other good things.[95] Sergeant Ham Chamberlayne met one Valley man passing out invitations to soldiers to join him for supper; after supper the host insisted Chamberlayne drop in at his brother-in-law's home, where he was entertained so royally he forgot to rejoin his regi-

ment. Next morning, Chamberlayne escorted his host's three
daughters to watch the column march off, then returned with them
for still another meal. "Our march thro [sic] the Valley will be altogether one of the pleasant remembrances of my life . . ," he
wrote.[96] This sort of attention did not encourage haste, and Loring's force was not completely assembled at Winchester until the
day after Christmas.[97]

The Army of the Northwest—Loring's command was to retain
its separate identity even while a part of the Valley Army—was
an incomplete division of three brigades. The first to reach
Winchester was that of Colonel William B. Taliaferro and
consisted of the 1st Georgia, 3d Arkansas, and 23d and 37th Virginia regiments. Taliaferro was a Tidewater aristocrat commissioned captain during the Mexican War and mustered out in 1848
as an infantry major. He served afterwards in the Virginia legislature, where he formed political alliances beneficial to his rise to
commander of the entire Virginia militia by 1859; Jackson would
soon discover Taliaferro had not lost the habit of wielding political clout in military matters. At the same time, Taliaferro's severe
and often pointless regulations had stirred talk among his men
that the enemy would be spared the trouble of shooting him. One
Georgian had gotten drunk on the march to Winchester and assaulted Taliaferro, then managed to vanish from the guardhouse
the night before his court-martial.[98]

Conditions in Loring's other units were much the same. Like
Jackson's, Loring's men had grown tired of the war and intended
to seize what pleasure they could regardless of officers. The second of Loring's brigades, Brigadier General S. R. Anderson's, was
an all-Tennessee unit—the 1st, 7th, and 14th regiments. Christmas
Day found these regiments camped around Strasburg, where, like
the Stonewall Brigade on its return to the Valley, they had gone
on a spree. When orders came to hurry immediately to Winchester, the Tennesseans balked until they downed their fortified
eggnog, and some of them promptly passed out on the road.[99]
Colonel William Gilham commanded the third of Loring's brigades, consisting of the 21st, 42d, and 48th Virginia regiments
and 1st Regular Battalion (a unit one half the size of a regular
regiment). Gilham had been a professor of infantry tactics at
V.M.I. before the war and had known Jackson well. Finally, two

good batteries were attached to Loring, Captain L. M. Shumaker's
and Captain L. S. Marye's, with four guns each.

As commander of these units General Loring was now also second in command of the Valley Army. Loring had done a man's
work while still a boy during the Seminole War in Florida during
the 1830s; he had lost an arm in the Mexican War at the battle of
Chapultepec. Despite this wound, Loring had remained in the
U. S. Army, to fight Indians on the frontier and gain a colonelcy by
1856, making him the youngest line colonel of the old army.
There was no question of his courage, yet he had displayed little
aptitude for high command. His redeployment to Winchester had
been inexcusably slow. Worse, he seemed powerless to prevent his
troops, who had admittedly suffered severely in the Alleghenies,
from slipping close to serious demoralization.

Eager or disillusioned, the Northwesterners were all going on
Jackson's expedition to Romney, as was every other man he could
muster. He armed the last of his militia units. All furlough
requests were rejected. Richmond hinted that it might have some
Choctaw Indians available; send them at once, Jackson replied.[100]

The weather moderated as year's end approached. By December 31 three mild days convinced Jackson the "earliest practicable
moment" for his offensive was at hand, and he moved. Several
companies of Garnett's brigade joined Ashby in a new raid against
Dam No. 5.[101] Artillery batteries filled their limber chests. All
units were ordered to march at 6 A.M. the next day, January 1,
1862.[102]

The destination, as usual, was kept secret from the troops,
which prompted the inevitable speculation. Hospital Orderly John
Apperson of the 4th Virginia noted in a well-kept diary that some
men assumed they would move toward Romney, some thought toward Hanging Rock, and others, he wryly added, hoped they
would shift into more comfortable quarters.[103] Lieutenant Langhorne assessed the bits of information he gathered during his sentry
duties at Headquarters and concluded the Army would make another comparatively easy strike at the C & O Canal.[104] A wiser
Captain John Graybill of the 33d Virginia ventured no guesses,
reflecting in his diary only that Jackson's orders "indicated something more than a march."[105]

4

THE ROMNEY WINTER

In all the war I never . . . endured
such physical and mental suffering.

—WILLIAM T. POAGUE

January 1, 1862, began a winter ordeal for the Valley Army. Taliaferro's brigade of Loring's command did not begin its march until noon; militia units scheduled to move at 6 A.M. started ten hours late.[1] The morning was unseasonably warm, tempting hundreds of men to ignore orders and stuff greatcoats into their company wagons—then temperatures dropped. The wind whipped down from the northwest, a sign of bad weather, and soon it was freezing.[2] Major Harman was hospitalized and unable to lead the supply trains, and his profane energy was missed. The wagons lagged, and rebels could not retrieve their overcoats.[3] By evening the Army's van had trudged only eight miles northwest of Winchester to Pughtown, and its wagons were strewn over each of those miles.

Rebels were compelled to improvise against the cold that night. Messmates pooled blankets and bedded down en masse—"hog fashion," John Casler called it.[4] Some men risked breaching the Army's most inflexible standing regulation, that banned the use of fence rails from surrounding fields for firewood, to be punished by icy gusts that sprayed them with sparks. At the camp of the Rockbridge Artillery, flames jumped into dry grass and raced the gunners for their cannons; only at the last minute were the pieces saved.[5]

Jackson too was a victim of the confusion that bedeviled the Army. That morning a Valley citizen had presented Stonewall a bottle of fine, rare whiskey. Jackson expressed his thanks hurriedly, imagined he saw a decanter of wine, and set it aside for safekeeping. The afternoon's cold prompted a drink, and Jackson quaffed several fingers' worth of his present. If the "wine" tasted strong to him, he said nothing of it as he passed the flask to his staff, which, emboldened by the General's example, emptied it. Shortly the brew's true nature became apparent. Old Jack began to talk, freely ranging over a variety of topics. He complained of the heat and unbuttoned his overcoat. "The truth is," wrote one of the staffers, "General Jackson was incipiently tight."[6]

Though he spoke of many things that evening, Jackson let no hint of the destination escape him. The first day's march had led the Army off the direct highway from Winchester to Romney and northwestward toward mountainous Morgan County, West Virginia, and the Potomac; no one knew why. Silent again by morning, Jackson led deeper into the Alleghenies. The weather deteriorated all day. The wagon ruts that served as a road kept the supply trains spread out for miles.[7] Breakdowns repeatedly stalled the trains and kept them far behind the infantry. The column began to cross a half-frozen bog about dusk, and here most of Loring's regiments became completely entangled with each other.[8] Many men had exhausted their rations and had begun to scavenge as the Army halted a scant eight miles beyond Pughtown, at Unger's Store.[9]

If this camp offered any comfort, it was to those few who were more concerned with guessing their mission than eating. They noted that Carson's militia brigade and several cavalry companies reached Unger's Store from Martinsburg that evening.[10] (Ashby was still opposite Dam No. 5 and did not rejoin the Army until January 5.) Jackson had now concentrated every available man, which meant serious work awaited, and where this work lay would be revealed by the route taken the next day. If the Army marched due north tomorrow, it would move on the resort village of Bath and, six miles beyond it, the town of Hancock, Maryland, on the Potomac's far bank. Or, the Army might follow a westward road from Unger's Store through Bloomery Gap to Romney.

When Old Jack motioned to push northward on January 3,

many saw his goal but few his purpose. A Union force of 1,400 held Bath. This bridgehead could be expanded from across the Potomac and thus endangered the right flank of any Confederate advance on Romney. Jackson intended to wipe out the Federal bridgehead, cross the Potomac, and destroy valuable supply depots around Hancock. Rail and telegraph links between Union forces in western Maryland and at Romney also passed through this area, and Jackson wished to disrupt them to render concerted enemy action more difficult when he did descend upon Romney.

The first thing was to take Bath. Jackson quizzed soldiers who lived thereabouts and learned that the village stood at the eastern foot of a ridge called Warm Spring Mountain. The road by which the Army was traveling paralleled the eastern base of this ridge through Bath and continued straight on to the Potomac. Another road traversed the ridge from Bath to join a route at the mountain's western base. This combined highway led northward to a depot on the Baltimore & Ohio Railroad, thence through a gorge to the Potomac. To shut this potential escape route, Stonewall planned for his militia to cross the mountain some miles south of Bath and push along its western fringe. Simultaneously, Loring was to storm directly into Bath on the main road east of Warm Spring Mountain and herd the enemy northward toward the Potomac or westward into the militia. Though it would require a strenuous march, Jackson planned to fight this action on January 3 and demanded haste of his officers.[11]

The plan was simple but realistic, and only Confederate dawdling on the third defeated it. Taliaferro's brigade started the march by backtracking to its wagons through the bog it had painfully traversed the previous night. By the time his men had struggled across that swamp and eaten, Taliaferro was forced to rest them for two hours.[12] When its wagons overtook the Stonewall Brigade during the day, Garnett allowed his famished men to prepare a meal. Jackson soon encountered the Stonewall Brigade and demanded an explanation.

"I have halted to let the men cook their rations," offered Garnett.

Stonewall glowered: "There is no time for that."

"But it is impossible for the men to march farther without them," the brigadier objected.

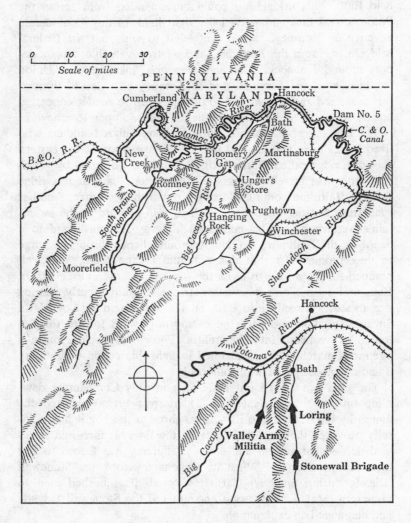

2. AREA OF OPERATIONS AGAINST ROMNEY, JANUARY 1862.
Inset: Action of January 4.

Stonewall repeated his orders and growled: "I never found any-thing impossible with this brigade."[13]

It moved immediately, and Jackson spurred on, angry that his men could think it more important to eat than march.

The expedition neared Bath at dusk with its collective mind someplace else. The militia column moving west of Warm Spring Mountain gave up its advance when it found the road obstructed with a few trees felled by the enemy.[14] Colonel Gilham, at the head of Loring's infantry, stumbled into Federal pickets; Gilham deployed cautiously and began an inconclusive skirmish. With surprise vanishing, Jackson ordered him to charge, but Loring countermanded the order and told Gilham to bivouac for the night.[15]

That countermand worsened already cool relations between Loring and Jackson. Six years Jackson's senior, Loring had antici-pated having some part in mapping the offensive when he reached Winchester. Instead, he was asked and told nothing,[16] and his atti-tude soured. Handed a dispatch from Jackson to keep moving, Loring reportedly exploded with words to the effect: "By God, this is the damnest outrage ever perpetrated in the annals of his-tory, keeping my men here in the cold without food."[17] Jackson, in turn, was frustrated by the inert spirit of Loring's command. He blamed it for the new night the Confederates now faced in the open. With wagons far to the rear there was little food or shelter against a snowfall that commenced after dark: "I nessled as close to a tree as I could and tried to sleep . . . ," wrote Lavender Ray.[18]

The next day, January 4, was worse. A renewed militia drive was promptly stopped by the enemy. Attempting to sideslip this obstacle, the militia was surprised and several militia regiments panicked, neutralizing the entire column.[19] With his skirmishers often losing contact with the enemy, Gilham proceeded lethar-gically toward Bath, halting a half mile outside it when he spotted Federals atop Warm Spring Mountain. Unaccountably, he took no further action.[20] Loring did nothing.

The morning and early afternoon passed. Finally, Jackson, fear-ful of exposing his army to another night outside Bath, took over Loring's task. He brought forward the 1st Tennessee and sent it swarming up Warm Spring Mountain; he threw Gilham's command directly toward Bath. Gilham's regiments double-timed through town and converged with the Tennesseans near the mountain's crown only to spot one Federal column streaming northward to the Potomac, while another disappeared to the west. The escape route of those fleeing westward had been cleared by the earlier panic of the Valley militia.[21]

There was no time for Jackson to join in as his men loosed obscenities on the militia. He instructed Gilham to overtake the Federals retiring west of Warm Spring Mountain. He dispatched the 3d Arkansas farther west to demolish the newly rebuilt B & O trestle over the Big Cacapon River. The balance of Loring's command was to follow several companies of cavalry, which had already thundered down the main highway toward the Potomac. Garnett was to occupy Bath and stand ready to support these missions. Hoping to salvage something from the day, Jackson dashed for Hancock.[22]

Nothing came of this pursuit. Gilham trailed the enemy into a narrow defile. Here the Union rear guard took a blocking position which he found unassailable, and Gilham abandoned the chase. Without bothering to inform Jackson, he camped for the night.[23] The Arkansas detachment moving on Big Cacapon River met determined resistance and was unable to reach its target. Approaching the Potomac, Jackson was nearly trampled by cavalrymen fleeing an ambush. Somehow he rallied them and thrust almost to Hancock before a second ambush stalled his advance. He hustled up two guns, blasted out the enemy, and prodded his riders forward again. The rebels finally reined on a bluff overlooking Maryland, but twilight made it impossible to ford the Potomac. Perhaps as a gesture of defiance to a day in which nothing went right, Jackson had his gunners lob several shells across the river.[24]

Had other officers and men shown Jackson's energy, they might have won warm quarters and abundant rations in Hancock. As it was, only Garnett's brigade shared the meager stores remaining at Bath.[25] Loring's men, spread over the countryside on an arctic night, suffered terribly.[26]

The following days saw the expedition's first solid achievements. The Arkansans burned the Big Cacapon railroad bridge and tore up miles of track and telegraph wire.[27] Under fire from enemy sharpshooters, cavalrymen dodged into a bulging B & O warehouse. They seized everything they could carry and burned the rest.[28] Jackson dispatched Ashby, who was just in from Dam No. 5, across the river under a flag of truce with a message for Hancock's commandant: evacuate within one hour or the town would be shelled. When the enemy refused, Southern artillery opened. The bombardment was in retaliation for past Northern shellings along Virginia's Potomac shore.[29]

Union batteries replied, but the deadliest hazard during these operations came from the weather. Mountain folk spoke of this as the cruelest winter in decades.[30] Snow fell again on January 5, deepening the layer in which the Confederates huddled to six inches.[31] It was too bitter even to cut firewood, and Jackson actually suspended regulations and allowed his men to burn fence rails—it was the only way to keep them alive. Pickets were not allowed fires and were literally near death after a few hours on duty.[32] Recalled one: "If I should use the army parlance and say [I] stood picket . . . I should have missed it. I ran picket for hours around and around a big tree; I had to do it to keep from freezing."[33]

Northern reinforcements, meanwhile, massed around Hancock, forcing Jackson to abandon his idea of crossing the Potomac. The alluring Union warehouses on the far bank had to be forgotten. Yet Jackson was not entirely dissatisfied with progress to date. Communications between the Alleghenies and the Potomac were severed, and the Federals were probably misled as to the true Southern objective. The Army had achieved everything it could along the Potomac; on January 7, it marched southward.[34]

Jackson's hope of now reaching Romney seemed to die with the anguish of the next days. Beneath dark, somber skies the temperature plunged below zero; one estimate claimed 20 degrees below.[35] Pulling his overcoat tighter, Lieutenant Henry Douglas saw ice frozen into the matted beards of his comrades. He made these observations in glances, because the road was caked with an unbroken sheet of ice and it was dangerous to take eyes off it for long. Despite careful stepping, Douglas sat down three times "with emphasis."[36] John Lyle remembered the roar of men's rumps "hitting the road with a thud like that of a pile driver."[37] Legs were broken as men went down and bowled over those around

them.[38] Loring's attitude was not improved when his horse fell
and rolled over on him.[39]

The plight of the supply train was appalling. Overturned
wagons littered the road. The horses had not been roughshod
prior to leaving Winchester and could barely stand, so four infantrymen were detailed to assist each wagon. John Casler of the 33d
Virginia toiled in one of these fatigue parties. Everytime his vehicle rounded a curve, Casler and friends strained mightily to keep
the horses upright and the wheels on the road. Casler once
glanced up to see Old Jack throw his shoulder into a stalled
wagon as hard as any private.

Ahead lay a hillock which tore Casler's attention from the General. Slight inclines were tedious work, and this knoll proved an
agony. Casler's animals repeatedly smashed to the ground. At
least one horse was on its side or belly throughout the upward
shove. No sooner could that one be coaxed up than another
slammed down, and sometimes all four collapsed at once.[40] Not
far away Private Clem Fishburne of the Rockbridge Artillery was
struggling with his gun. Descents were Fishburne's greatest trial.
Brakes were useless on icy slopes, and the heavy cannon behind
the team often lurched out of control and rammed the horses into
a thrashing heap. Icicles of blood dangling from their knees almost to the ground bore silent testimony to the torment of these
animals.[41]

The greatcoated Confederates lumbered on through a wilderness of snow. Eddying blasts swirled round them on every side.
Their twisting and climbing road disappeared in places; at others,
the wind had scooped and piled snow to bar the way. Men survived by filching raw corn from the horses or by gnawing roots of
sassafras plants.[42] Pneumonia and yellow jaundice disabled hundreds.[43] Many were severely frostbitten and the flesh on their feet
and hands peeled off like onion skin.[44] Jackson continued to permit
the use of fence rails for fires,[45] around which his men packed
until their uniforms smoked.[46] Fearful of what new ventures
awaited, the Valley Army crept southward.

In the forest surrounding Unger's Store, a brawny officer squat-
ted in the snow fumbling with pen and paper. He was Major
Elisha Paxton of the 27th Virginia, a man whose immense

strength had won him the nickname "Bull." His hand numb, Bull could manage only a few lines to his wife, including the observation: "I take it for granted the General will come to the conclusion from this experiment that a winter campaign won't pay and will put us into winter quarters."[47] Though Paxton did not know it, Jackson had been forced to think of winter quarters—or worse.

On January 7 Jackson had received news which sent slivers of ice through him: Federals had surprised and routed the outpost at Hanging Rock, the only rebel strongpoint on the direct road from Romney to Winchester. It was there that Lieutenant Cutshaw's rowdy Irish gunners had been deployed, but they had lost both their pieces during the melee without a chance to fire.[48] For the next forty-eight hours, while his brigades staggered into Unger's Store, Jackson worried about this raid. His latest intelligence estimated there were as many as 18,000 Federals in Romney.[49] If the Hanging Rock attack indicated Union fronts from west and north were preparing to move toward each other, the rebels might be trapped in a fatal position halfway between Winchester and Romney. The only precaution Stonewall could take against this danger was to stitch together a few hundred infantry and hurry them south to watch the enemy at Hanging Rock.[50] The Yankees then mysteriously abandoned their incursion and withdrew to Romney as those rebels approached.

Jackson did not pursue. Thankful for a reprieve, he dispatched Meem's militia brigade to Moorefield, forty miles southwest of Winchester, and ordered Carson's militia brigade to reoccupy Bath. These shifts stripped 800 men from the main column[51] and meant but one thing: the Valley Army was going over to the defense. Jackson had culled the Shenandoah to bring every possible man into ranks before he left Winchester; scattering them now would have been unthinkable if he still proposed to attack 18,000 Federals at Romney.[52]

Indeed, Jackson had little choice about halting. Weary Hospital Orderly John Apperson noted in his diary that the Army was being crippled from sickness.[53] One of Loring's brigades carried 300 men on its sick list, another, more than 500.[54] Dr. McGuire had 1,300 sick in Winchester. (Compared to the sick, the 4 killed and 28 wounded the Army had suffered in combat seemed trifling.[55]) The sick overflowed Winchester's hospitals and had to be carted to other cities.[56] Subtracting hospitalized and redeployed men, the Valley Army near Unger's Store numbered at best 7,000 effectives.

Jackson's offensive had ground to a halt; at this point he could not have planned realistically to do more than parry the next enemy move.[57] In the meantime, he organized an essential cleanup. He put every farrier in the Army to work roughshodding the horses. Huge kettles were brought to a boil and the troops were ordered to bathe. Few of them had washed since December, and now they uncovered booming colonies of lice in their flannel underwear. It was a grisly experience for Jackson's teenagers; the snow hissed by their fires, pools of slush crept under their feet, and they stood naked in the cold to pick the "graybacks" off one another.[58]

In the midst of this cleanup, startling news arrived from Ashby. The Yankees had evacuated Romney![59] They had fled suddenly, leaving tents standing and precious medical supplies untouched. Ashby's scouts were already in the abandoned city. To Jackson it seemed a miracle, a blessing from the Almighty. Less devout men correctly surmised the Romney garrison had not been as strong as Southern sources indicated. The force which had first ousted the rebels during October was 2,500,[60] and this force had increased only to 5,000 or 6,000 by January.[61] The raid on Hanging Rock had been a sham designed to draw the rebels from the Potomac, where the Union dreaded a major operation.[62] The enemy had never planned to defend Romney against Jackson, whose strength they had overestimated as much as he had theirs,[63] and had left the place after receiving a false report that the rebels were approaching.[64] The enemy had given Jackson a prize he no longer thought he could take.

Stonewall's response was good news to every soldier of the Army: he began signing a ream of furlough petitions. Several high-ranking officers, including Colonel Gilham, were permitted to return to teaching duties at the Virginia Military Institute.[65] Jackson might as well have announced by general orders that the expedition's hard work had ended. The rebels now needed only to occupy Romney and secure the blessing of the Almighty. The Army resumed its march on January 13. Garnett headed the column so that no further time would be squandered by Loring's indifferent marchers.[66]

When the Confederates broke camp at Unger's the sun was actually shining.[67] It seemed a good omen, until a thaw made slush of the road. Garnett's brigade outpaced its trains and suffered through another night without canvas.[68] Loring's regiments were hopelessly mixed with their trains. The 21st Virginia was held to a day's march of two hundred yards by wagons ahead of it. The wind quickened during the afternoon, and the sun vanished behind slate-colored clouds.[69] That night it snowed two inches.[70] The next day alternated rain and sleet.[71] The fifteenth was among the most miserable days ever known in the Alleghenies; sleet fell for hours, covering everyone with ice.[72] Loring's command floundered beneath this inclement pounding. One regiment inched five hundred yards and counted it a triumph.[73] Taught in a sterner school, Garnett's brigade slogged into Romney by dark on the fifteenth. Jim Langhorne reported home with obvious pride: ". . . our brigade can beat them [Loring's brigades] marching badly. . . ."[74]

The distance separating Garnett's and Loring's brigades was more than the result of swift movement. Unused to Jackson's demands, Loring's men could not believe he had not retreated to Winchester days ago. Like most newcomers to Jackson's command, they equated his tenacity with insanity. They talked mutiny and swore to follow Jackson no longer. They booed and hissed him when he passed. "Lunatic," they shouted.[75] The resentful, disorganized Northwesterners did not begin filtering into Romney until January 17.[76]

By then, Jackson was advocating virtually a new expedition. His scouts reported that the Maryland village of Cumberland, twenty miles northwest of Romney, contained valuable enemy stores. Strategic B & O bridges were close by. Jackson asked Secretary of War Benjamin to dispatch him 4,000 additional infantrymen for an attempt to capture the Federal garrison and depots at Cumberland and to hit the B & O again.[77] The reinforcements were not available, which nullified all prospect for a successful advance. But possession of Romney had aroused Old Jack's ambition, and he drew up another plan for the men he did have. He decided to strike the gigantic New Creek railroad bridge

west of Cumberland. Jackson calculated its destruction would
sharply cut the flow of supplies into Cumberland. The enemy
force there should wither like poison ivy snipped at the root, leaving Romney that much more secure. Stonewall alerted the first
two brigades to enter Romney, Garnett's and Taliaferro's, to
prepare for another march.[78]

These orders were probably the worst Jackson ever issued, particularly considering the many furloughs already granted. Jackson
had reports that Cumberland was girded with 12,000 Federal
troops,[79] yet he planned to march into their vicinity with two
shrunken brigades. The Stonewall Brigade was now in effect a
reinforced regiment. Its 4th Virginia was led by two captains and
a handful of lieutenants; John Apperson thought two thirds of his
regiment was either on furlough or the sick list, now grimly called
the "broken book."[80] No more than one third of the brigade appeared fit for action to Jim Langhorne.[81] Taliaferro's command
was decimated. His 23d Virginia Regiment was smaller than a
company; its Company C had fifteen men able to walk.[82] Jackson's newest orders required too much, and Taliaferro's brigade
seethed on the edge of open rebellion. Stonewall quickly saw in its
attitude that hope of a renewed advance was fanciful. He abandoned the Cumberland raid.[83]

The Valley Army now moved into winter quarters to guard the
Shenandoah. Carson's militia brigade concentrated at Bath;
Meem's militia brigade held Moorefield.[84] Boggs's militia picketed
the environs of Romney, and Loring's command held the village
itself. Garnett's Stonewall Brigade, which had proven the most dependable marching unit of the Army, was to take station at
Winchester where it would be within supporting distance of all
fronts. Ashby's cavalry would rove the frontier and provide early
warning of Union threats.[85] In taking these positions, the Army
was repeating the forward defensive strategy employed by George
Washington one century earlier.

The focal point of these dispositions was the garrison at Romney, the post of greatest danger. The Federals were only twenty
miles away at Cumberland, and the South Branch Valley road system offered several routes by which they could launch a surprise
attack. Jackson feared such a strike above all else. To lessen this
danger, he deployed squads of relay couriers, sought extra cav-

alry, and commenced a telegraph line to Winchester.[86] Like Washington, he also expected his men to defend their western bulwark actively. They would need to reconnoiter, ambush, and harry the enemy, and these mountain battles would hold the Valley.[87]

Unfortunately, conditions at Romney thwarted vigilance from the start. "Of all the miserable holes in creation, Romney takes the lead . . . a hog pen . . . ," protested Private Ted Barclay of the Headquarters Guard.[88] It rained daily. Every street was an open sewer thanks to indiscriminate dumping by the Yankees, who had also left the courthouse building stacked high with rotten meat.[89] The streets decayed into slimy pools so deep even horses could hardly move.[90] Some regiments were quartered in cotton tents amid this muck; others lived in such poor buildings as had survived Yankee conquest. Private Dick Waldrop of the 21st Virginia, a young Richmonder who learned on this trip how much he missed his home in a proper city, lodged in a room with glassless windows on three sides and almost no wall on the fourth: "Altogether, it is so uncomfortable that *loafers* can't be prevailed upon to come near us."[91]

Hallelujahs erupted from Garnett's brigade when it was ordered out of Romney.[92] As it departed for Winchester, it was watched by a surly Army of the Northwest. "Jackson's Lambs," screamed some, thinking Jackson showed favoritism to his old command with a comfortable assignment near Winchester. The Stonewall Brigade hurled obscenities back and left a garrison smoldering with resentment.[93]

Garnett's march to Winchester took three days along a road lined for miles by gutted houses; they were the result of the Northern raid on Hanging Rock. The Yankees had looted and slaughtered freely; cows, hogs, and even chickens lay decomposing along the way. For men who did not know it yet, this carnage was a blunt definition of "civil war." Garnett's men entered Winchester on January 25 and slumped exhausted and disillusioned around their campfires.[94] Bull Paxton's first letter home might have been written for all of them: "I think I am dirtier than I ever was before, and may be lousy besides. I have not changed clothes for two weeks, and my pants have a hole in each leg nearly big enough for a dog to creep through. . . . I am afraid the dirt is

striking in, as I am somewhat afflicted with the baby's complaint
—a pain under the apron. . . ."[95]

Jackson had sloshed ahead of Garnett to reach Winchester on
the evening of January 23. It was an entry more gratifying than
that of almost three months ago. On November 4, 1861, he had
arrived with two aides to assume a defenseless command. He had
quickly identified the probable enemy threat and fashioned a reasonable plan to counteract it.[96] Admittedly, that plan had not succeeded completely. The enemy had suffered few casualties, and
Confederate ranks were severely thinned from illness, although
when Jackson returned to Winchester patients were leaving the
hospitals there at a rate of 30 to 100 men per day.[97] But more important, Jackson had achieved what he had set out to achieve with
his winter expedition. Romney was again Southern, and Union
fronts to the west and north had been shoved farther apart. Some
needed stores had been captured and additional damage inflicted
on the Baltimore & Ohio Railroad. With earnest hard work, Jackson had dragged the Valley Army through its first offensive.

II

Within a week the Valley Army was stripped of its achievements. The flinty prospect of finishing the winter at Romney
whipped Loring's men into an insubordinate frenzy. Officers of
one regiment refused to leave their quarters during foul weather.[98]
Soldiers of all ranks utilized a new grant of furloughs to hasten to
Richmond. There they manufactured tales of Jackson's insanity
and besieged government officials with demands to evacuate Romney.[99]

In Romney, Loring did little to quiet the discontent. Eleven
brigade and regimental officers signed and handed a petition to
Loring condemning the occupation of Romney:

> Instead of finding, as expected, a little repose during midwinter, we
> are ordered to remain at this place. Our position at and near Rom-
> ney is one of the most disagreeable and unfavorable that could well
> be imagined. We can only get an encampment upon the worst of
> wet, spouty land, much of which when it rains is naught but one

sheet of water and a consequent corresponding depth of mud, and this, too, without the advantage of sufficient wood, the men having to drag that indispensable article down from high up on the mountain side.

Another consideration we would endeavor to impress upon your mind: All must be profoundly impressed with the paramount importance of raising an army for the next summer's campaign. When we left Winchester, a very large proportion of your army, with the benefit of a short furlough, would have enlisted for the war, but now, with the present prospect before them, we doubt if one single man would re-enlist. But if they are yet removed to a position where their spirits could be revived, many, we think, will go for the war.

The petition concluded by urging Loring to appeal to the War Department, if necessary, to secure relief. Endorsing the petition as expressing "the united feeling of the army," Loring dispatched it to Secretary Benjamin by way of Jackson. The latter sent it on with a four-word comment: "Respectfully forwarded, but disapproved."[100]

Colonel Samuel Fulkerson of Loring's 37th Virginia sought the support of a friend in the Confederate Congress with this description of Romney:

This place is of no importance in a strategic point of view; the country around it has been exhausted by the enemy, and its proximity to the enemy and the Baltimore and Ohio Railroad will wear us away (already greatly reduced) by heavy picket and guard duty. Besides this, there is no suitable ground and not sufficient wood here upon and by which men can be made comfortable. We have not been in as uncomfortable a place since we entered the service.

With the benefit of a short furlough for the men, I am satisfied that at Winchester I could have enlisted 500 of my regiment for the war. With the present prospect before them, I do not know that I could get a single man.[101]

Colonel Taliaferro saw this letter and added a malevolent postscript: "The best army I ever saw of its strength has been destroyed by bad marches and bad management. . . . Not one [man] will re-enlist, not one of the whole army. It will be suicidal for the Government to keep the command here."[102]

Not content with this, Taliaferro skulked to Richmond and lobbied among his political friends for Loring's withdrawal. Taliaferro later claimed President Davis gave him a friendly hearing and concluded that Jackson had made a mistake.[103]

The horror stories from Romney converged on Richmond with rumors of an enemy stab into the lower Shenandoah. From his post at Leesburg, Brigadier General Daniel H. Hill spied increased activity across the Potomac and relayed word of it to Johnston.[104] The latter agreed that the Valley Army might be in trouble if the Federals were moving on Harper's Ferry or Winchester.[105] Warnings of such a thrust reached Stonewall from Secretary Benjamin on January 24.[106] Two days later an alarmed President Davis suggested that Benjamin have Johnston review the Valley's defenses.[107]

Rumor moved more swiftly than Johnston. On January 29 he had his inspector general en route to the Valley,[108] but Richmond was already stirred up by additional speculation that Northern forces were closing on Loring.[109] The substance of these rumors has not survived, but they evidently forecast a Union advance into the area between Romney and Winchester.[110] At any rate, the stories were accepted. "It will be necessary to act promptly," Davis wrote Benjamin on the twenty-ninth.[111] Action came the next day. Without awaiting Johnston's evaluation or consulting either him or Jackson, Davis instructed Benjamin to send the following telegram to Jackson at Winchester: "Our news indicates that a movement is being made to cut off General Loring's command. Order him back to Winchester immediately."[112]

That order both ignored Jackson's authority and questioned his ability. Jackson attributed any unusual enemy activity north of the Potomac to B & O rebuilding efforts near Hancock,[113] and he was correct in this judgment. Benjamin's order demanded that he act on a different explanation, a precedent which rendered Jackson a puppet to tabletop strategists in Richmond. Neither the supposedly imminent Federal attack nor the adverse conditions complained of by Loring's army justified such an intrusion into Jackson's sphere of command. There was, in fact, no Union drive under way against Romney, and even had there been, to sacrifice Jackson's positions at the first enemy threat implied a fatal want of confidence in him. It also left Richmond looking foolish, be-

cause the government had tacitly approved defense of Romney
when it sent Loring to join the Valley Army in order to take the
place.

Jackson immediately issued the necessary orders for Loring's
withdrawal to Winchester, a move which forced Jackson to abandon most of the positions held by his militia in the South Branch
Valley as well. Three months of planning and hard work ruined,
Jackson then sent a taciturn message by way of Johnston to Benjamin:

                                    Headquarters Valley District
                                    Winchester, Va. January 31, 1862

Hon. J. P. Benjamin, Secretary of War:

   Sir: Your order requiring me to direct General Loring to return
with his command to Winchester immediately has been received
and promptly complied with.
   With such interference in my command I cannot expect to be of
much service in the field, and accordingly respectfully request to be
ordered to report for duty to the superintendent of the Virginia
Military Institute at Lexington, as has been done in the case of
other professors. Should this application not be granted, I
respectfully request that the President will accept my resignation
from the Army.
   I am, sir, very respectfully, your obedient servant,

                                    T. J. Jackson,
                                    Major-General, P.A.C.S.[114]

Stonewall had quit the Valley Army, perhaps the war.

Jackson had not quit working. He knew that his resignation would require some days for approval, and during that inter-
val Jackson tried energetically to salvage something for whoever
succeeded him. He assured Johnston there was no Union drive
under way against Romney and urged him to prevent Loring's
withdrawal.[115] (This Johnston could not do.) Davis was primarily
responsible for the evacuation order, but Jackson cannily re-
frained from attacking the President while he made his point. He
told his own political friends, among them Virginia's Governor
Letcher, that his action was a protest against the Secretary of

War's interference with a commander in the field. He grew almost eloquent in his rationale of this point: ". . . if the Secretary persists in the ruinous policy complained of, I feel that no officer can serve his country better than by making his strongest possible protest against it, which, in my opinion, is done by tendering his resignation, rather than be a willing instrument in prosecuting the war upon a ruinous principle."[116]

The consequences of that ruinous principle worked back up the Confederate chain of command. Johnston felt the slight implied by the order of January 30 as keenly as Jackson. The former had no news of the order until he opened Jackson's letter of resignation. Johnston understood Jackson's frustration; he had experienced the same thing through Richmond's meddling with his army at Centreville. He therefore delayed Jackson's letter and made a friendly appeal to him suggesting that they join to reason with the government on the matter and, failing a satisfactory reply, that both ask to be relieved.[117] Johnston also sent a bitter complaint about the Secretary of War to Davis. Davis replied with an equally caustic letter about Johnston.[118]

In Winchester Jackson found it more difficult than he had supposed to leave the Valley Army. Friends throughout the Shenandoah and across the state implored him not to do so. Governor Letcher sent Congressman Alexander Boteler, one of Jackson's closest friends, to Winchester with a personal letter hammering on the theme of duty. Letcher's letter and an exhaustive interview with Boteler finally changed Jackson's mind. On February 15 Letcher received Jackson's written authorization to withdraw the resignation, which Johnston had forwarded to Richmond on the seventh, and by acting immediately, the governor soon had the resignation returned to Jackson.[119]

This trouble was followed by other unhappy incidents. The Army of the Northwest, which evacuated Romney at a pace never known on the march toward it, was elated by the first rumors of Jackson's resignation and intended to celebrate by pummeling the Stonewall Brigade. A huge riot loomed as the Northwesterners straggled into Winchester. Though they were more a collection of individuals than fighting units[120] and though complaining of a hard march, Loring's men possessed abundant energy for bloody fights whenever they collided with Jackson's Lambs.[121]

Jackson took a written jab at Loring. He readied court-martial charges against him on two counts, neglect of duty and conduct subversive of good discipline, and submitted them for Johnston's approval. Johnston concurred and asked Richmond to assemble a tribunal of sufficiently high-ranking officers.[122] But someone in the government objected, and the serious charges were never brought on for a hearing. Loring was soon promoted to major general and transferred to the deep South, where an evil star pursued him. Lieutenant General John C. Pemberton, the defender of Vicksburg, in Mississippi, blamed him for the Southern defeat at the Battle of Champion's Hill, which made Vicksburg's fall inevitable. Loring led a division and later a corps without distinction during the apocalyptic struggle for Atlanta in 1864, and he was second in command of the Army of Tennessee at its humiliations outside Franklin and Nashville in the same year. Court-martial charges preferred by Jackson against Colonel Gilham were also ignored in Richmond.

Next, Secretary Benjamin, observing every link in the chain of command, informed Johnston that President Davis believed Loring's units must be removed from the Valley. Loring's Virginia regiments and batteries should join the main army at Centreville; all other regiments should reinforce the collapsing Southern army in Tennessee.[123] Johnston published these orders but allowed Jackson to arrange all details of the redeployment. (Jackson had won his point, and no one ever interfered with the internal workings of his Valley District again.) Overprotective now, Jackson briefly refused to expose his unhappy regiments to the elements. On February 18 he explained to Johnston: "The 1st Tennessee leaves for Knoxville at dawn tomorrow; it would have left this morning, but I thought it best not to move until something could be heard respecting the time when the cars would receive them, as the weather has been very bad and the troops are comfortable in the present condition."[124]

It rained briskly the next day, but there was no more time for delay. Jackson sent the Tennessee regiments on their way. The Stonewall Brigade had burst into Winchester on a day much like this, except the rain then was a thick November stream. Today the Tennesseans disappeared beneath a lighter, almost springlike rain. Those rebels who remained must have thought that only the rain

had changed in the Shenandoah, for with Romney's evacuation
and the expected loss of Loring's brigades the District would be
almost as naked as it had been during the previous November.
Affairs had come full circle in the Valley for many reasons.
Poor roads, supply train breakdowns, and awful weather occa-
sioned much of the misery on the expedition against Romney. Exposure to the cruel weather was a product of Loring's dawdling.
Had he assembled his forces at Winchester by the end of the
three-week estimate he gave on November 29, that is, by December 20, the Valley Army could have held Romney before the January snows. Loring also bore responsibility for an ill will that
abetted the surliness of his command. Yet these were the
superficial causes. The rains during February may have given the
Valley Army an opportunity to reflect on more fundamental explanations for its failure to achieve permanent results.

III

If Jackson analyzed his conduct of the winter expedition, he
could not have concluded that he met his own rigid standards. His
generalship was uneven, his strategy and tactics wavering from
good to less than adequate, his decisions sometimes deftly gauging
the limits of the possible and sometimes sweeping far beyond
them—illustrating that even great generals have formative pe-
riods. Jackson obviously had not mastered every detail of the leap
from brigade to army commander.

Jackson marched from Winchester with a grossly exaggerated
impression of Union strength. This was initially the fault of his intelligence sources, but ultimately the fault of Jackson for believing
those sources. Even with his erroneous information, however,
Jackson was correct to launch his offensive. Notwithstanding the
risk of a Union surprise attack and the somewhat scattered
deployment necessitated by a rebel garrison in the South Branch
Valley, Romney's occupation was wise and showed Stonewall was
alert to possibilities the enemy overlooked. Jackson lay between
two Northern fronts, and every mile he could wedge between them
lessened the opportunity for enemy co-operation and increased

the Valley Army's chance—its only chance—to deal separately with each Union front.

Jackson's decision to march on Romney via Bath was also sound. The Bath attack disrupted vital communications and masked the true Southern objective. And an incidental benefit of the attack should have become clear to Jackson on the way to Bath: capture of its garrison would have done much to re-energize Loring's faltering brigades. But clumsy tactics squandered this opportunity. Stonewall entrusted the critical task of blocking the western escape route from Bath on January 3 and 4 to his inexperienced militia, and he was disappointed. One of the militia regiments which panicked and allowed the enemy to escape Bath on the fourth was seeing its first action. It had been issued muskets less than two weeks earlier.[125] There seems no reason why more reliable units were not assigned the kingpin position given the militia.

Faulty deployment might have been corrected by pushing Loring into Bath early on the morning of January 4. By that time Jackson was aware of Loring's slowness. Why then did Stonewall himself not prod the Army of the Northwest forward at first light? Gilham's brigade spent the night of January 3 barely two miles outside Bath but did not enter it until approximately 2 P.M. the next afternoon. The records do not explain why Jackson permitted the morning hours to be lost, thereby incurring an uncomfortable share of responsibility for at least part of the Union garrison's escape.[126]

By his retreat from Bath and his halt at Unger's Store on the ninth, Jackson demonstrated that he knew when to quit; reported Northern strength in both instances made it unwise to continue. And he was flexible enough to change plans and occupy Romney when the enemy handed it to him. Jackson erred when he issued orders to launch what was in effect a new expedition against Cumberland after reinforcements were denied him. That strike would have offered 3,000 exhausted rebels as prey to 12,000 enemy. Federals were on the alert for Confederate thrusts from Romney, and bad roads and weather were at work to prevent a quick Southern retreat. It is more than likely that Jackson's raiding column would have been trounced, leaving only two of Loring's unhappy brigades and the militia to defend the Shenandoah. With his plan for this raid, Jackson highlighted one of his major flaws as a commander: ambition sometimes clouded his objectivity.

Two more Jackson traits emerged during the Romney winter, and each would mark him until his death. First, in everything he did, from massing troops to throwing his shoulder into a stalled wagon, Old Jack showed a formidable drive; "go-aheaditiveness," one eyewitness called it. Few men could have pushed the Valley Army as far as the Potomac, but Jackson had pushed on from there, had freed large areas from the enemy and established workable defenses with grumbling troops pounded by savage weather. It was a magnificent personal achievement displaying explosive energy. Yet within a week this success was undone because of a second trait, Jackson's inability to work skillfully with his fellow officers and soldiers. He might, for example, have told Loring a little of his plans; he might have explained to Loring's regiments the purpose in holding Romney. Such gestures could have helped preserve the gains made, but they were beyond Jackson. From his soldiers he did not expect and probably did not want understanding of orders—what he wanted was unquestioning obedience. The Romney winter revealed Jackson was without sympathy for the confusion or low spirits of others, and this gruffness, which seemed so harsh to his citizen soldiers, only grew coarser as the war progressed.

If Old Jack's inexperience hurt the Valley Army, the attitude of its rank and file was equally damaging. When those boys had crowded Southern recruiting camps during April 1861, they had imagined war as a pageant of heroic deeds performed on spotless battlefields. Eight months of army life had blunted that illusion and turned thoughts to home and mother.

Instead of furloughs, the Valley Army was given a lesson in the school of the soldier more terrible than anything it had encountered.[127] That lesson taught Private John Green of the 21st Virginia what it meant to march sixteen hours a day through gales of sleet, bed down in a snowstorm, and push on the next morning with nothing to eat. Green admitted: "I had read something of the suffering of our forefathers [in 1776] but never realized them until we came on this tour."[128] Private George Harlow of the 23d Virginia found that war was a comrade dreading whether he

would lose two toes or his entire foot from frostbite.[129] Lieutenant
Henry Douglas of the 2d Virginia recognized war for what it was
as he watched ambulances packed with human wreckage file into
Winchester: "Sentimentalists who imagine there is no way to die
in war would be shocked at the sight of those who are expiring
without a wound. . . ."[130] No, there were no spotless battlefields
in war. "Ma," wrote Lieutenant Jim Langhorne of the Headquarters Guard, "the romance of the thing is entirely worn off, not
only with myself but with the whole army."[131]

The Valley Army had needed men who were alert and resolved
on the march against Romney, not boys dazed by lost illusions.
Soon these rebels would master hunger and cold, but on this
march they had buckled under the shock of hard lessons. Many
had merely shuffled along with little interest in the outcome; theirs
was a mood of men in whom the eagerness of volunteers was
spent and the endurance of veterans unforged. These soldiers had
discovered that war, no matter how brightly begun, really means
little bands of gaunt men toiling over roads that have no end.
They had grasped what it means to be a soldier, but they had yet
to adjust their lives to that stark realization. The Romney winter
produced a short-lived and too expensive Confederate success;
given the mood and inexperience of the Southern soldiers and
their General, it could hardly have been otherwise.

The immediate result of the Romney expedition was to intensify
the longing of "Loring men" and "Jackson men" alike to escape
the army, and letters from Winchester now reflected an ominous
clock watching. "If I live this twelve months out, I intend to try
mighty hard to keep out of [the army]. . . . I don't think I could
stand it out another year . . ," wailed George Harlow.[132] Private
John Garibaldi of the 4th Virginia determined not to volunteer
again: "I shall belong to the militia myself, for I see that the militia don't have so much hardship to go thru as the volunteers have,
and they are getting the same wages and the same kind of rations,
and they have more liberty than us."[133] But the militiamen too
were weary. Militia surgeon Abraham Miller resolved: "I am getting tired of soldiering. . . . I will hold on to my commission until
after the draft, and then I will resign and try it at home for a
while."[134]

The draft Miller wrote of was Virginia's answer to the most serious problem facing the South. The initial one-year enlistment of virtually the entire Confederate Army would be expiring soon, and Southern soldiers elsewhere were little more disposed to reenlist than those in the Valley. The Virginia legislature therefore ratified, on February 8, a bill under which all Virginia males between age eighteen and forty-five not serving with the army would be entered in a militia pool from which they could be conscripted to fill state "volunteer" units.[135]

A plan enacted by the Confederate Congress the previous December had offered Virginian volunteers temporary escape from both the Confederate army and the Old Dominion's draft. Designed to insure re-enlistment of volunteers already in ranks, the law granted a generous bounty and a sixty-day furlough to all volunteer privates and noncommissioned officers who signed on for the duration of the war. In addition, re-enlistees were guaranteed the right to reorganize themselves into new companies, elect new officers, and even change their branch of service.[136]

This well-intentioned law, known as the Furlough and Bounty Act, nearly wiped out the Valley Army. Thousands of men signed their re-enlistment papers and vanished on leave. As February drifted toward March, regiments waned into companies, companies into squads. On February 28 Captain Graybill of the 33d Virginia rostered 41 men present in his company; by March 17 Graybill listed 24.[137] Many of those who remained with the Army were arranging transfers to the cavalry. This preoccupation with the cavalry extended to Jackson's own doorstep, where his Headquarters Guard was aching to form a mounted outfit.[138]

Tales of the carefree life with Ashby's cavalry were especially delicious after the Romney experience. Private George Baylor joined the cavalry and happily recalled: "On horseback I felt like a new man and contemplated the war from a much more favorable standpoint."[139] As if to invite a rush, Secretary Benjamin authorized Ashby during February to add ten companies to the ten already under his command.[140] The cavalry chief reported the muster of eight new companies in less than a month.[141] To supervise this horde there was only Ashby, Major Funsten, and five or six novice staff officers.[142]

But even service under Ashby was not sufficient lure for some men. Dick Waldrop's company of the 21st Virginia was canvassed and not a man said he would re-enlist; one of Waldrop's comrades muttered that the entire regiment had "gone to the dogs and will soon go to pieces."[143] Jackson was compelled to grant several hundred additional furloughs for men to go home as recruiters.[144] Other difficulties arose: capable Colonel Preston left Jackson's staff to return to the Virginia Military Institute; the Federals renewed their onslaughts along the Valley frontier; the militia deserted by scores.[145] On the last day of February the Valley Army boasted a paper strength of 13,759, of whom only 5,400 were present and effective[146] and that remnant was shrinking by several hundred per week. Listening one afternoon to the rain that heralded spring, Hospital Orderly Apperson admitted in his diary that the Southern cause was getting "dark and doubtful."[147]

Part II

MARCH 1862

*It requires a vast amount of faith
to be cheerful amid the general gloom.*

—HARRY MORRISON

In Winchester, diarist John Apperson wrote of "dark and doubtful" Southern hopes. In Richmond, President Jefferson Davis, unopposed during a recent election to select a permanent Confederate President, echoed Apperson's fears in his February inaugural address. "Disasters" was the word Davis chose to review the war's recent months: "At the darkest hour of our struggle, the Provisional gives place to the Permanent Government. After a series of successes and victories . . , we have recently met with serious disasters."[1]

It was true. On the North Carolina coast Union Major General Ambrose E. Burnside captured Roanoke Island, 30 cannons, and 2,500 prisoners two weeks before Davis spoke. Burnside's victory primed him for forays into the Tarheel State's interior, buoyed Union sympathizers in the state, and threw open a backdoor approach to Richmond. Soon after Burnside struck, the Confederacy's hopes for its ironclad *Virginia* faded with news of its drawn battle against the Union's ironclad *Monitor*.

West of the Alleghenies, Southern armies were retreating along a four-hundred-mile front. The Confederates had been routed at the battle of Mill Springs, Kentucky, during January. In Tennessee, Forts Henry and Donelson had surrendered to Union Major General Ulysses S. Grant by mid-February, and the defense of

Tennessee collapsed with the loss of 14,000 prisoners. Irreplaceable foundries and rolling mills fell with Nashville to Union Brigadier General Don Carlos Buell. Missouri and northern Arkansas were lost forever when a Confederate army was mauled at the Battle of Pea Ridge in early March.

The situation in Virginia was critical. Effective communication between General Johnston and Richmond had ceased partly as a result of caustic letters exchanged during the crises over Jackson's resignation. Faced by overpowering enemy numbers, Johnston began to withdraw on March 5 from the Manassas-Centreville area without even informing President Davis. The evacuation was badly managed in other respects as well. Some heavy guns in working order were left for the enemy. Unable to empty an army packing plant, Johnston consigned a million pounds of beef to the flames, and his ill-fed retreating columns were tormented by the aroma of sizzling steak.[2] The Federals seized Manassas Junction, and Johnston could not field a corporal's guard to harass them. "This army," he warned on February 16, "is far weaker now than it has ever been since July 20, 1861. . . . The law granting furloughs and bounty for re-enlistment has done much to disorganize it, and [other] furloughs given under the orders of the War Department have greatly reduced its numerical strength."[3] He added a few days later: "The army is crippled and its discipline greatly impaired by the want of general officers; . . . a division of five brigades is without generals; and at least half the field officers are absent—generally sick."[4]

At winter's end, many people, in both North and South, looked for one final Union victory in Virginia to end the faltering Confederacy.

North of the Potomac, sprawled around Washington and across Maryland, lay the presumed victor of that coming Armageddon, the Army of the Potomac. It numbered more than 150,000 fresh volunteers. For months these men had been drilled and polished by the approved European textbooks. They paraded like professionals. They were superbly equipped by the factories of the North, and anything not available at home was purchased abroad in prodigal quantities. "There never was an army in the world that began to be supplied as well as ours . . ," huffed one Union general. "The amount of waste is fearful. . . . I have seen loaves of bread thrown away that had not even been broken open. Our men will not use it if it is a little stale."[5]

The leader of this well-appointed colossus was hailed as the savior of his country, as a "Young Napoleon," and his dossier was outstanding. Major General George B. McClellan had matriculated at West Point by special permission at age fifteen and graduated far ahead of his struggling Virginian classmate Thomas Jackson. He had been promoted twice during the Mexican War, had instructed at West Point, and had served as official United States observer during the Crimean War. He had directed the Union's drive across Virginia's Allegheny frontier in the spring of 1861, and though success lost nothing by his telling, he had demonstrated undeniable skill. After the Union's Manassas debacle, McClellan was given command of the Department of the Potomac, an area of operations including Washington, Northern Virginia, and parts of Maryland (including Banks's command). McClellan proceeded to hammer these far-flung fragments into the magnificent Army of the Potomac, and by March 1862 he was prepared to lead that host to war.

McClellan intended to march on Richmond. Only one hundred miles from Washington, Richmond housed some of the most valuable munitions and industrial works remaining to the Confederacy. Here were boiler factories, mills, and shipyards. Richmond was the hub of Virginia's rail and canal net. It was the seat of the Confederate Government, and the spirit of a fledgling nation could not survive the loss of such a symbol. McClellan believed that if he lunged toward Richmond, Johnston would be compelled to interpose, which would, he hoped, position Johnston's army to receive the final blow.

McClellan's problem was how to approach Richmond. The direct way was a march south from Washington through Manassas Junction and Fredericksburg. But McClellan had misgivings about this route. He had watched British divisions erode before Russian defenses during the Crimean conflict, and he knew the Russian positions were ditches compared to the rivers that barred the one hundred miles between his army and Richmond. McClellan esteemed Johnston as a master of defensive warfare, who would wait in deadly traps behind those rivers. McClellan also realized that the farther he pushed from Washington over the miserable roads of eastern Virginia, the more dependent he became for supplies on the bridge-studded Richmond, Fredericksburg & Potomac Railroad—an open invitation for rebel cavalry to strand him with one well-directed raid. Long before March, the Young Napoleon had begun to seek an alternate route.

McClellan's search for another way ended with one of the most ingenious amphibious proposals of military history. Instead of tramping overland from Washington to Richmond, McClellan decided to skirt Johnston by sailing his 150,000 men down Chesapeake Bay from Washington to Fortress Monroe. Already firmly garrisoned by Northern troops, Fortress Monroe dominated the tip of a peninsula formed by the York and James rivers (which gave McClellan's operation its name, the Peninsula Campaign). Richmond stood only sixty miles to the west. The Union bastion and a powerful navy guaranteed McClellan's communications and freed him to sweep westward toward the Confederate capital. On the way he expected to fight Johnston on his own terms. McClellan envisioned a frantic rebel effort to redeploy Johnston from northern Virginia to the Peninsula. He foresaw Southern units losing cohesion along clogged roadways, batteries streaming onto the Peninsula without ammunition, brigades arriving without commanders, the enemy driven to sacrifice divisions in costly stopgap attacks and, ultimately, abandonment of Richmond by a shattered opponent.

McClellan's vast and in many ways admirable scheme eventually was submitted to the scrutiny of United States Secretary of War Edwin L. Stanton. With an outstanding career as a courtroom lawyer behind him, Stanton tended to direct the Union's war effort much like a barrister prosecuting his client's case. True to form, he decided that before McClellan sailed for the Peninsula to try the main issue, he should resolve a pending matter: the lower Shenandoah must be secured for the Baltimore & Ohio Railroad. McClellan amiably consented to this, for it did not require much reshuffling of his plan. The Young Napoleon contemplated shifting the right wing of his army, General Banks's corps in western Maryland, to cover the Washington area while the Army of the Potomac was on the Peninsula, but there was no reason Banks could not first clear the lower Valley. McClellan launched him

1. Major General Thomas J. "Stonewall" Jackson, commander of the Valley Army. (Courtesy of the Library of Congress)

2. Brigadier General Turner Ashby, commander of the Valley Army's cavalry. Embodiment of the Southern ideal of chivalry, Ashby proved as lax a disciplinarian as Jackson was severe. In the climactic hour of the Valley Campaign his riders forfeited their dream of dashing, romantic adventure. (Courtesy of the Library of Congress)

3. Jackson and his staff. A wartime composite featuring rare photographs of some principal Valley Army staff members; missing are Major John Harman, the Army's indefatigable quartermaster, and Colonel Stapleton Crutchfield, chief of artillery. (Courtesy of the Library of Congress)

4. *above left:* Major General Richard S. Ewell, second in command of the Valley Army during the decisive months of May and June 1862. He later admitted that he never saw a courier from Stonewall approach without anticipating orders to attack the North Pole. (Courtesy of the Library of Congress)

5. *above right:* Brigadier General William W. Loring, second in command of the Valley Army during its disastrous march against Romney. He was the first of nearly a dozen officers with whom Jackson clashed violently during the Valley Campaign. (Courtesy of the Library of Congress)

6. *below:* The Shenandoah Valley from Maryland Heights. A wartime sketch by Alfred R. Waud. (Courtesy of the Library of Congress)

into the Shenandoah during the last week of February with orders to oust the Confederates from Winchester, to plant a small garrison there for the protection of rail and canal communications, and to shift the majority of his command eastward to Manassas Junction. Explaining that pacification of the Shenandoah would set in motion the Peninsula Campaign, McClellan assigned Banks the over-all task of securing the Washington area.[6]

Strategically, McClellan's Peninsula Campaign was grounded on two assumptions: one, that the rebels would mass around Richmond rather than counterattack Washington while the Army of the Potomac was steaming down Chesapeake Bay; and, two, that if the enemy did counterattack, Banks could handle it after he reached Manassas. Thinking only in military terms, McClellan accepted these assumptions as facts and assured everyone that Washington faced no danger; Johnston was certain to concentrate on the Peninsula, he said. Should the rebels do the unexpected, the capital was well fortified, and there were thousands of militia in Pennsylvania and New York to succor the city. McClellan insisted that a standing force of 30,000 men was ample shield for the capital and its environs.

McClellan convinced many that his strategy was sound, even brilliant. There remained, however, one doubter, President Abraham Lincoln. And Lincoln, with final control over Union strategy, was the one man who had to be satisfied about the Peninsula offensive. McClellan never devoted the time he should have to convincing Lincoln about his plan, perhaps because the latter had so far wielded his constitutional powers as Commander-in-Chief sparingly. But if McClellan had any question about Lincoln's willingness to intervene and plot the course of armies when he thought it necessary, the general was destined for a shock.

Lincoln approved the goal of seizing Richmond, but he preferred a march against it by way of Manassas and Fredericksburg so as to keep McClellan between the rebels and Washington. Lincoln's ambassadors had doubtless cautioned him that Europeans might equate surrender of the national capital with the collapse of the Union; if Washington fell, foreign recognition of the Confederacy was a likely result. The loss of Washington would also shatter morale on the home front. Lincoln, in short, did not like McClellan's plan.

McClellan, however, clung to his turning movement, and in March Lincoln finally acquiesced in return for a promise, or at least what he thought was a promise. The President demanded that Washington should be left entirely secure when the Army of the Potomac sailed, and Lincoln ordered McClellan and his corps commanders to determine the force necessary to provide this security,[7] an indirect means of requiring that McClellan's subordinates approve his dispositions. McClellan would have been justified in resigning over those demeaning orders (Jackson had done so for less cause) but instead chose the less forthright approach of acquiescing to the results of Lincoln's intrusion while secretly resolving to maintain the integrity of his strategy by any means. At a proper council of war a majority of corps commanders decided that complete security for Washington translated into 25,000 men at Manassas Junction and 30,000 within the city itself.[8] McClellan could agree to this because he was still counting on Banks's forces from the lower Valley to provide an ample garrison for Manassas, but it would shortly become evident that McClellan regarded this commitment as one to be met if all went according to plan and not, as Lincoln conceived it, as a precondition to the Peninsula offense. A still uneasy Lincoln ordered Secretary Stanton to emphasize that he would hold McClellan to this pledge: "The President, having considered the plan of operations agreed upon by yourself and the commanders of army corps, makes no objection to the same, but gives the following direction as to its execution: 1st. Leave such force at Manassas Junction as shall make it entirely certain that the enemy shall not repossess himself of that position and line of communication. 2nd. Leave Washington entirely secure."[9]

Lincoln thus had what he regarded as a promise of Washington's absolute security, while McClellan had what he regarded as a warranty of freedom from interference with his Peninsula Campaign; neither man actually understood the other's assumption, the worst possible circumstance under which to conduct a difficult sea–land offensive.

Lincoln and McClellan might have discovered and perhaps resolved their differences given time, but they had run out of time in March 1862. Banks had entered Winchester by midmonth. Even before this news, 400 ships had begun embarkation of McClellan's

lead divisions. It was a glorious sight, the largest army ever arrayed on the American continent boarding the largest fleet ever
seen in these waters. The Army of the Potomac numbered
150,000 men, with 15,000 horses and mules, 1,100 wagons, 60
batteries of field artillery, and every accouterment of modern warfare: siege equipment, field telegraphs, even hydrogen balloons for
aerial reconnaissance.[10] European observers were much impressed
with the power and efficiency of the army, a fact not overlooked
by the peacockish McClellan. "Rely upon it," he wrote Secretary
Stanton jauntily, "I will carry this thing through handsomely."[11]

II

Under the spreading pall of McClellan's vast maneuvers in the
east, the Shenandoah reverted to the sidelines. Johnston outlined
what he wanted from the Valley District on March 1. Unaware of
McClellan's impending sea movement, Johnston expected the
Army of the Potomac to march directly south and planned to retire in front of it toward Richmond. The Valley Army must fall
back on line with the main army, protect its flank, secure the Blue
Ridge passes and slow or stop enemy progress up the Shenandoah. Johnston especially needed Jackson to prevent Banks from
reinforcing McClellan, who, Johnston knew, substantially outnumbered him.[12]

Johnston's instructions typified his concept of strategy: retreat
so as to preserve the main army and allow only a diversionary detachment to immobilize greatly superior enemy forces. The Valley
Army was only to be a sideshow in that retreat—if it was equal
even to this minor task. Johnston had already permitted Jackson
to retain the Virginia regiments and batteries of Loring's command previously ordered to Centreville[13]; in addition, the Army
of the Northwest had been broken up (with the exception of a
remnant under Edward Johnson west of Staunton) and largely absorbed by the Valley Army. Yet even with these reinforcements,
the Valley Army could only muster eleven skeleton regiments and
its militia.

The term "Valley Army" itself was a misnomer for a force that
numbered barely 3,600 infantry by mid-March. Garnett's com-

mand, the 1st (Stonewall) Brigade, was its backbone. Colonel Jesse Burks commanded the 2d Brigade; this was Gilham's former unit, composed of the 21st, 42d, and 48th Virginia and the 1st Regular Battalion (nicknamed the Irish Battalion). Only the 23d and 37th Virginia remained from Taliaferro's command to form the 3d Brigade. Taliaferro had left the Shenandoah and his brigade was now headed by Colonel Fulkerson of the 37th Virginia. To Garnett's brigade were attached Captain McLaughlin's Rockbridge Artillery and Captain Carpenter's battery; Captains Waters' and Marye's batteries served with Burks's brigade, and Captain Shumaker's battery served with Fulkerson's brigade. The total artillery muster was 27 small guns, including Captain Chew's mounted battery. Valley militia regiments were too weak now to be useful on the battlefield and had been assigned sentry and picket missions. Colonel Ashby's cavalry carried out similar duties with a paper strength of 600 riders but rarely fielded that number. The entire Army did not exceed 4,600 men.[14]

If its army mirrored the weakness of Confederate units everywhere, the Valley District also had its share of the disasters rocking the South. Federals had reoccupied Romney on February 7. Five days later they drove Shenandoah militia from Moorefield. Southern militia guarding Bloomery Gap were routed with the loss of 17 officers and 50 men on the fourteenth. Union Brigadier General James Shields was gathering 12,000 men at Paw Paw, a scant ten miles west of Bloomery Gap. On the northern front Banks's 28,000 men had spilled over the Potomac into Harper's Ferry on February 24. By March 6 Banks held Bunker Hill, only twelve miles north of Winchester on the Martinsburg road,[15] and Jackson directed Quartermaster Harman to evacuate all Army stores from Winchester.[16]

Scenes played out around Winchester mirrored events in many Southern cities. The town was abruptly sealed off; movement in and out was thereafter allowed only by military permit. Families secured passes and hurried away in pitiful refugee caravans. The bankers fled; inflation spiraled; rumors abounded. Near the courthouse square, carpenters worked on a symbolic project. Winchester's Union Hotel, which with a burst of early wartime enthusiasm had shortened its name to "Ion," restored the "Un."[17]

In the camps of the Valley Army there was, fortunately, a

different mood. The steady Federal approach brought home to these rebels the immense strength their foe had gathered while they had been squabbling among themselves, and this realization snapped the malaise of the Romney winter. Most rebels suddenly found themselves eager to meet the enemy. Loring's former troops were even willing to follow Jackson. Ceaseless Confederate reverses satisfied Private John Green that no one should allow himself the luxury of a furlough, much less the pleasure of leaving the army.[18] Private Dick Waldrop caught the same spirit: "I begin to feel as if it would be almost a disgrace for me to go home when my time expired, unless the tide of success should change and we win some important victories."[19]

A grim resolve began to supplant the vanished illusion of war as heroic romance. Private Hugh White of the Headquarters Guard put aside his hopes of attending divinity school and wrote his parents that he had decided to re-enlist: "I need not say how very important it is for the preservation of our army that as many of us as possible should stand firm in our places. . . . In doing this, *every one must sacrifice a great deal*."[20] This blunt affirmation of purpose was echoed throughout the Army's camps. The enemy was doing what furloughs and re-enlistments drives could not—reviving the Valley Army's morale. "I was never," concluded John Green, "in a better mood to fight. . . ."[21]

Green's general shared this fighting mood. Old Jack reacted to Banks's seizure of Harper's Ferry by ordering Ashby to scout the town and determine the chance of capturing the Federals there.[22] Jackson assembled the Army at Winchester and alerted all units to stand ready to move at all times.[23] Ashby contracted his cavalry in a tough screen north of Winchester.

Jackson's hope was that Banks might expose a detachment upon which he could pounce; such a reverse surely would keep Banks fully concentrated in the Shenandoah as Johnston desired. When General Hill withdrew his garrison from Leesburg as part of Johnston's withdrawal from Centreville, Jackson requested that Hill join him to give the Valley Army some striking power: "I greatly need such an officer, one who can be sent off as occasion may offer against an exposed detachment of the enemy for the purpose of capturing it. . . . The very idea of reinforcements coming to Winchester would, I think, be a damper on the enemy, in addition to the fine effect that would be produced on our own troops, who are already in fine spirits." He added a game conclusion: "If we cannot be successful in defeating the enemy should he advance, a kind Providence may enable us to inflict a terrible wound and effect a safe retreat in the event of having to fall back."[24]

From an officer whose force was so badly outnumbered this letter may have seemed fantastic to Johnston, who did not reply. Hill joined the main Confederate army south of the Rappahannock River near Culpeper, and the Valley Army was more isolated than ever before. It was sixty miles from Winchester to the nearest of Johnston's forces and ninety miles to the remnant of the Army of the Northwest under Brigadier General Edward Johnson. Yet Jackson refused to publish an appeal for all Valley men to join the Army lest the enemy learn its weakness. Stonewall did, however, explain something of his intentions to his friend Alexander Boteler: "My plan is to put on as bold a front as possible and use every means in my power to prevent [Banks's] advance whilst our reorganization is going on. . . . What I desire is to hold the country as far as practicable until we are in a condition to advance, and then with God's blessing, let us [make] thorough work of it."[25]

Events quickly pressed the Valley Army to throw out its bold front. On March 7 Banks rattled southward into Ashby's pickets. A furious skirmish ensued.[26] Jackson double-timed his infantrymen out to form a brave but pitifully thin line of battle two miles north of Winchester.[27] Throughout the afternoon a bitter wind brought them the sound of Ashby's fight, which finally faded as he drove the enemy off the field. The infantry brigades remained in line until night, then slept in place.[28]

The next three days were anxious ones around Winchester. Rebels deepened trenches, sandbagged their redoubts and cleared lanes of fire.[29] Major John Harman crated the last of the Army's stores. His responsibilities required him to maintain contact with the Army's supply base at Staunton, where his brother, Colonel Asher Harman, commanded, and as Banks closed on Winchester, John Harman jotted short bulletins to his brother. Often written with pencil and on small scraps of paper, these uninhibited personal notes caught the anxiety of a white-knuckled Valley Army:

March 7: I have just had an order from Gen'l Jackson to send his wagon to headquarters; this looks like we are about to be off. . . . What is to become of us God only knows.

March 8 [Here Harman referred to the alarm of the 7th]: At last the crisis is upon us. Everything is packed and ready for a move. Jackson will certainly make a stand if he can do it without the risk being too great.

March 9, 12:30 P.M.: . . . still here. I do not know how long we shall be here. It is a terrible state of uneasiness to be in, I can assure you.

March 10, 10 A.M.: I was to see the Gen'l this morning, and he talks as though he meant to fight. . . . There is no government property here that I know of, and all the wagons are loaded and horses harnessed and ready to move.[30]

The enemy continued to press. Federals along the District's western fringe were moving. General Shields's division, destined to become a part of Banks's command, had inched from Paw Paw to the vicinity of Bath by March 6. On the eleventh Shields occupied Martinsburg and established liaison with Banks.[31] The enemy fronts from west and north had finally joined by advancing against Winchester, much as Jackson had augured.

Jackson also had predicted that a juncture of these fronts would be a Southern calamity, but now something would not let him retire before the almost 40,000 Federals he confronted. The Yankees advanced on Winchester again shortly after noon on March 11, and Jackson deployed to meet them.[32] He was outnumbered roughly ten to one.

Stationed on a fortified hill called Fort Alabama, Captain Morrison's Headquarters Guard company watched the armies squaring-off. His men saw the enemy coming southward, first cavalry and skirmishers, then massive columns of infantry. They picked out Ashby thundering into action—he was easy to spot on his tall white horse—and watched as he shattered the head of the enemy column. More Federals darted forward, and a Southern brigade advanced against them in a ragged line. When the evening sun lit bayonets on the plain below, battle had not been joined, but cannon fire erupted from the east and indicated that Banks was dangerously near the Confederate right flank.[33]

Old Jack gave instructions for the Army to join its wagons, which he had ordered parked just south of Winchester, cook rations, and wait. As usual, orders concealed the next move. Captain Morrison led his company back to Headquarters, where Jackson inquired what he had observed from Fort Alabama that afternoon. He then told Morrison to billet his men for the night in a house across the street. The captain soon noted a gathering of star-collared officers at Headquarters. He supposed they were assembling to receive orders for the next day.[34]

The meeting of March 11 was more extraordinary than Morrison could have guessed. Jackson had summoned his brigade and regimental officers to a council of war, the first he had ever held. And it met to consider a course so startling that even Jackson felt the need for approval; he proposed nothing less than a predawn surprise attack. Let the Army finish supper, rest a few hours, then slip back through Winchester to attack Banks before daylight. It would encounter, he argued, Federals unnerved by the past few days of skirmishing, the first combat most of them had seen. Jackson thought that early morning darkness, surprise, and Confederate élan would combine to stampede the enemy.[35]

A bewildered silence met Jackson's proposal. Garnett, as senior subordinate, probably cracked this hush with a question which astonished Stonewall. Did the General not realize the Army was far south of Winchester? As ordered, it had marched until it found its wagons, which were some five or six miles south of town. Winchester was already abandoned.

There had been a mistake. The trains had somehow been ushered farther than Jackson intended when he started them south that afternoon.[36] An eight mile march was now needed to bring the infantry within striking range; someone ventured to suggest the attack could not be arranged in the time available. A vigorous debate followed. Jackson still hoped to strike. The Army could do without rest! Let it begin its march at once! His subordinates united against the idea. Their view was that troops who had done a day's work already could not trudge another eight miles during the night and rout ten times their strength at dawn. At length, Jackson conceded. He ordered the Army to continue southward in the morning and told Captain Morrison to evacuate the Headquarters Guard. The Shenandoah Valley Campaign of 1862 would begin with a Confederate retreat.

Accompanied by Dr. McGuire, Jackson joined the retreat about midnight of March 11. The pair rode silently a short distance, then halted to peer back at the city. McGuire took a last look toward his home below, then found himself staring at Jackson. The General was gripped by a rage born of frustrated ambition. On the large war maps in Richmond this withdrawal would be charted as a minor incident, another small column plodding south. For Jackson it was much more: an opportunity missed. Suddenly he blared: "That is the last council of war I will ever hold."[37]

Given the enemy's enormous numerical superiority, Jackson perhaps should have been thanking his council for holding him back from a disaster—a disaster which Jackson as Valley District commander would hardly have survived. But Jackson did not view it that way. He had held his last council of war.

Dejected, Jackson settled deeper into the saddle, turned his horse and trailed the Valley Army into a springtime of little hope.

6

KERNSTOWN

*I do not recollect of ever having
heard such a roar of musketry.*

—T. J. Jackson

By dawn of March 12 the only Confederate left in Winchester was
Turner Ashby, who sat at the southern end of Loudoun Street. As
always, he looked like a cavalryman. His seat was perfect: rein
and forearm made a straight line from bit to elbow; weight was
deep in the saddle. A black plume jutted out of his brown felt hat
and stabbed the sky behind him. Around his waist was a sash and
a handsome leather belt for pistol and saber.[1] He now commanded the Valley Army's rear guard.

Ashby waited until the enemy appeared, then turned and trotted
slowly out of town. Rumor had it that before Ashby reached
Winchester's outskirts, two Union riders suddenly blocked the
road ahead of him. Ashby charged, dropped one Federal with a
shot through the heart, jerked the other out of his saddle, and
carried him by the throat to the nearest rebel outpost.[2]

Much exaggerated, the story was nonetheless credited by some
Valley cavalrymen, a fact which highlighted a peculiarity of those
troopers: they were coming to believe their leader and themselves
capable of such feats. To an extent this was understandable, for
the Yankee cavalry against whom they had fought so far had
proven inept. Operations against them were a lark. "We thought
no more of riding through the enemy's bivouacs than of riding
around our fathers' farms," scoffed one rebel who was nineteen

when the war ended.³ Boys who had played knight-errant in the antebellum Valley tournaments had seen their fantasies come true, and Ashby's latest stunt seemed to them a fitting prelude to a springtime of gallantry.

This attitude frightened Jackson. To be sure, Southern cavalry had picketed the Valley frontier well enough during the winter,⁴ and there was no concrete evidence it would not continue to perform well. When Ashby was promoted to full colonel in early March, Jackson passed the news along by a friendly note,⁵ but he also began badgering Ashby to tighten his discipline. With the enemy now within easy striking distance, the Valley Army could ill afford a mounted arm entranced with notions of dashing adventure. Its vedettes had to be in place and alert, needs which posed a grim question for Jackson as early as the evacuation of Winchester: could the cavalry operate effectively with him in the field?

The bitter answer to that question would not come for two months. The Federals pursued the retreating Valley Army but at a distance, and Ashby's rear guard had only an occasional skirmish for amusement. This feeble Northern showing bespoke the military temperament of Major General Nathaniel P. Banks. An ardent abolitionist, one-time member of Congress, and influential member of the Republican party, Banks owed his command of Union troops in the Valley to political rather than military skill. Of the former he had much. During only his second term as a congressman, Banks had won the longest struggle on record for the speakership of the United States House of Representatives; when South Carolina seceded, he was retiring from the governor's mansion of Massachusetts. Political clout had brought him Lincoln's nomination to a major generalship, for which he was otherwise totally unqualified. Banks did not even look like a general. He was slight and much too short. His walrus mustache, which was absurdly big for him anyway, refused to be groomed properly; rather than curling down at the ends, the whole thing drooped straight down and concealed his mouth. To his credit, Banks had worked up from the poverty of a New England mill town, knowing hardships as harrowing as any soldier's, but he was no general.

Banks's timidity permitted the Valley Army an unhurried retreat from Winchester. It was at Woodstock on March 15; on

March 20 it was only twelve miles farther south at Mount Jackson, where it halted. A wagon train heaped with every item of conceivable military value from Winchester moved with the Army up the Valley Pike.[6] Paralleling the Army, Manassas Gap locomotives shuttled all rolling stock left in the District to the railhead at Mount Jackson. To insure that none of this equipment reached the enemy now holding Manassas Junction, Jackson detailed his Headquarters Guard to burn several bridges, including the Manassas Gap's 450-foot trestle at Front Royal. Lieutenant Sandie Pendleton, of Jackson's staff, saw his friends from Washington College marching off and joined this expedition. He recorded:

> The burning bridges presented one of the grandest spectacles I ever beheld. One bridge of considerable length was covered and drew like a funnel. A strong wind was blowing, and as soon as the fire was kindled at the east end of the bridge, it swept through and over it, catching the dry planks like tinder [and] made a mass of fire. It burned for some fifteen minutes, when the whole gave a crash and down went the brilliant, blazing structure, a splash and a column of steam and smoke rose up from the water below. . . .

Pendleton added a sober reflection: ". . . we were left in the darkness on the edge of a yawning gulf, to contemplate the destruction we had wrought."[7] More and more, the Army was coming to realize what war meant.

All of Virginia was learning this lesson. In response to a Confederate War Department requisition, the Old Dominion had called up 40,000 militia from her recent canvass of the state's male population, and 12,000 of them were slated for the Valley.[8] Jackson had no illusion about 12,000 men actually reporting for duty; he would have to work to get a fraction of that total. He was authorized to go get them when, on March 12, Governor Letcher issued an executive order empowering Confederate commanders in Virginia to rally every militiaman within the boundaries of their districts.[9]

Jackson mobilized the entire Valley militia at once. The response was good and included a bonus in the person of Jedediah Hotchkiss, the Shenandoah schoolmaster who was also an accomplished map maker. Hotchkiss had taught himself the art of topography during holidays and free study hours before the war, and he was without peer in the subject. Robert E. Lee had employed him in the Alleghenies during the fall of 1861, until typhoid forced Hotchkiss to return home. Oddly enough, Hotchkiss' initial application for commission had never been acted upon, which meant that he was still a civilian and would remain so throughout the Valley Campaign. Nevertheless, Hotchkiss, now recovered from his bout with typhoid, resolved to tender his services to Jackson and joined the militia units heading for the Valley Army.

Hotchkiss' observations at this time are revealing. At Staunton on Monday morning, March 17, he found three militia regiments from the upper Valley. Since many militiamen had volunteered already, the regiments were exceedingly thin; when Company A of one militia regiment was ordered into line, a solitary figure formed up. Nevertheless, those present at Staunton were ready to do their duty, and others joined them on the march north to Mount Jackson, filtering in by twos or threes. Hotchkiss noted that morale was high. Even the flotsam of the Valley Army's retreat—wagons of military stores and refugee carriages piled high with furniture and wailing children—did not depress the militia, and they covered a respectable sixteen miles in one day. Stonewall's induction officers at Mount Jackson matched this swift pace. The militiamen were given a recruiting lecture and advised to volunteer and secure the benefit of choosing the regiment with which they would serve. Many did so. The remainder were organized into a special battalion and put to drill.[10]

Hotchkiss talked his way past the Liberty Hall Volunteers standing guard at Jackson's door and secured an interview. The General looked tired, but he pumped Hotchkiss thoroughly about the militia and conditions in the upper Valley. Hotchkiss' detailed answers obviously impressed Jackson. Stonewall shortly appointed him to his staff and gave him his first job—all with three sentences: "I want you to make me a map of the Valley from Harper's Ferry to Lexington, showing all the points of defense and offense between those points. Mr. Pendleton will give you orders for whatever outfit you want. Good morning, Sir."[11] With those terse orders, the ablest topographer of the war went to work for the Valley Army; his maps were to contribute greatly to the speed and precision of its movements. Hotchkiss also began a diary which, supplemented by elaborate postwar research, became the most valuable source of information about the Valley Campaign.

As Hotchkiss began his new assignment, Jackson turned to a task which had been occupying a good deal of his time recently. Johnston wished the Valley Army to keep Banks too busy to support McClellan, and to this end Jackson was giving himself a thorough lesson in Shenandoah geography. Unfolding his maps, Stonewall traced the rebel retreat up the Valley Pike through Strasburg and Woodstock to Mount Jackson. South of this point, the Pike led through Rude's Hill, New Market, Harrisonburg, and Staunton, where the Virginia Central Railroad tied the Valley with Richmond. With the destruction of the Manassas Gap bridge at Front Royal, the Virginia Central was the only rail link open to the Army. And since this latter line lacked a spur to Mount Jackson from Staunton, the Army's supplies were piling up there. Staunton thus became Jackson's main warehouse, and its defense became a major factor in his maneuvers.

Nature dictated a second strategic problem. East of Strasburg a huge interlocking system of ridges called Massanutten Mountain (or simply the Massanutten) rose precipitously and surged up the Valley for fifty miles. For this distance the Shenandoah corridor was actually two corridors, the Luray Valley between Massanutten Mountain and the Blue Ridge and the Shenandoah Valley between the Massanutten and Alleghenies. This mountain divider was the salient geographic feature of Jackson's district, and he could never leave it out of his plans. It was always there to trouble him, a tangled green wall with but one way across: between New Market, in the Shenandoah, and the village of Luray, in the Luray Valley, was Massanutten Gap, the only pass in the rugged mountain for its entire fifty miles. The difficulties posed by this barrier were endless. Jackson could not simultaneously retreat up both the corridors it formed. Had he retired into the Luray Valley from Winchester, he would have surrendered the richer Shenandoah, exposed Staunton, abandoned the Valley Pike to the enemy and confined his forces to the muddy trails around Luray. On the other hand, retreat along the Pike left the Luray region unguarded and endangered Jackson's communications with Johnston. A Federal force east of the Massanutten could easily deny Jackson the

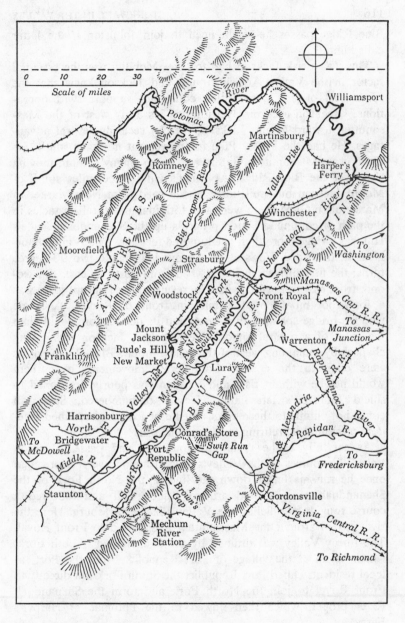

3. The Valley

Blue Ridge passes he might need to join Johnston if the latter called him.[12]

This was a risk Jackson had to take. Mobility was the essential factor in the Valley Army's future, and Jackson knew that the roads east of the Massanutten could not support swift operations.[13] Jackson accordingly withdrew his army west of the Massanutten toward Mount Jackson, thereby securing several advantages. He had the Valley Pike for movement north or south. He could cross Massanutten Gap to pursue an enemy column moving east over the Blue Ridge. At Rude's Hill (three miles south of Mount Jackson but well north of the road from New Market to Massanutten Gap) there were also formidable natural obstacles in the path of continued Union progress up the Shenandoah. Rude's Hill was a ridge more than one hundred feet above the Valley floor. Near it, the North Fork of the Shenandoah made two 90-degree turns; the first turn wrenched its bed from north to east, the second, from east to north again. The result of these abrupt jerks was a forty-foot moat about a mile in front of Rude's. A single wooden bridge spanned this moat, and its destruction would slam the gates of a natural citadel. Nevertheless, Jackson was taking chances by remaining west of the Massanutten: Blue Ridge passes were open to the enemy, Confederate movements over them would not be without risk, and Jackson was poorly positioned to shield Johnston's left flank. Heavily outnumbered, Stonewall could not eliminate these risks, but he at least had retained freedom of motion by retiring to Mount Jackson.

As carefully as he reviewed mountains and passes, Jackson traced the courses of the Valley's several major rivers. More than once he ran his finger down the line of the North Fork of the Shenandoah as it twisted around Rude's Hill and followed a course roughly paralleling the Valley Pike to Strasburg. Here the river curled around the Massanutten and flowed to Front Royal. The Luray Valley was drained by the Shenandoah's South Fork, which began at the village of Port Republic. From the Port, as local residents called Port Republic, the South Fork ran directly to Front Royal to join the North Fork and form the Shenandoah River proper, which then flowed to the Potomac at Harper's Ferry.

Valley rivers would be swollen with spring rains during the

coming months, giving their infrequent bridges special importance. Jackson's Headquarters Guard already had burned the Manassas Gap trestle over the South Fork at Front Royal. They also had burned the South Fork highway bridge in order to retard Federal movement into the Luray Valley. A second highway bridge over the North Fork at Front Royal was useless without its counterpart over the South Fork and was left intact. Jackson's own ability to enter the Luray Valley from Rude's Hill depended on possession of at least one of three bridges crossing the South Fork near Luray, and he doubtless told Ashby to watch them. Two other bridges, one over the South Fork near Conrad's Store and another over the North River (a tributary of the South Fork) at Port Republic, carried routes exiting the Valley to the east via Swift Run Gap and Brown's Gap, respectively. On the North Fork there was only one bridge, the structure near Rude's Hill.

The complexities raised by this skein of passes, streams, and bridges were compounded by unknown enemy intentions and uncertain Southern reactions. The Valley Army's situation would change not only with each movement Banks made but with those of McClellan and Johnston as well. Shifts by the main armies far beyond the Blue Ridge could make deadends of passes across it, could sacrifice the Army's remaining rail line, or even open roads leading into its deep rear. And Jackson could not neglect the second front he faced directly to the west. Shields had joined Banks from the Alleghenies, and thousands of additional Federals there were in range to do the same. To summarize, every troop movement in Virginia meant that Jackson had to rethink his position as he searched for some way to keep two enemy fronts separated and at the same time to answer Johnston's urgent need to keep Banks in the Valley. It is little wonder that Hotchkiss thought Jackson seemed weary.

II

Strategic reflection gave way to action on March 21. A sweating courier from Ashby informed Jackson that the feeble enemy pursuit, which had inched as far as Strasburg, had turned back to Winchester and that the cavalry chief was crowding the Union

rear with a few companies and Chew's battery.[14] Mindful of his
mission to shadow Banks, Jackson followed Ashby immediately.
Stonewall's haste was such that he did not pause to ready the new
militia battalion for action. There was time to alert only the experienced brigades: cook rations and prepare for march. The Army
raced twenty-five miles to the vicinity of Strasburg the next day. It
was the hardest march in months and cluttered the road with
hundreds of stragglers. As the Army slumped around its campfires, a new message arrived from Ashby.

Ashby had neared Winchester during the afternoon to find it
seemingly devoid of Federals. Only a handful of Federals were
visible from the heights overlooking the city. The cavalry had
spurred onward, flushing out one Union regiment and some artillery. A skirmish flared until sunset, when Ashby drew off and
dispatched a note reporting that the enemy force appeared to be
weak. His scouts had slipped into town and been told that Banks's
principal strength had been moving eastward toward the Blue
Ridge since noon. Four regiments remained as rearguard, and
they were supposedly under orders to withdraw the next day.
Ashby believed he could take Winchester at daybreak with a regiment of supporting infantry.[15]

This intelligence was confirmed by other sources,[16] and Jackson
lost no time. He pushed four companies of the Stonewall Brigade
under Captain John Nadenbousch forward to help Ashby and
pressured the rest of his army along on March 23. Here was the
exposed detachment for which he had waited; its destruction
might well keep Banks in the Valley.

Meanwhile, Ashby stepped up his pressure. He threw several
mounted companies which had joined him during the night against
the enemy around Kernstown, a hamlet two miles south of Winchester. The advanced companies of the Stonewall Brigade
reached Ashby between 9 and 10 A.M., and he fed them into a
seesaw skirmish. Captain Nadenbousch narrated: "We continued
to advance firing, when the enemy retired or fled rapidly, but were
soon heavily reenforced. Seeing this, I at once ordered forward
the reserve [which] . . . moved forward and reinforced our line,
which kept up a brisk fire, doing great execution. Colonel Ashby,
seeing heavy columns of the enemy [ahead], ordered us to fall

back, which order was obeyed, and the command fell back to the [Valley Pike]."[17]

This early retreat had a critical effect on the battle to follow by clearing the rebels from high ground north of Kernstown. It also prompted Ashby's party to bang away all the harder. Their one-sided fight continued until about 2:30 P.M., by which time the Federals had deployed several regiments and were forcing them steadily away from the high ground. Such was the situation when Confederate infantry began to fill the Pike within sight of Kernstown and Jackson arrived to survey the front.

Stonewall initially intended to avoid battle that afternoon and issued bivouac orders accordingly. It was a Sunday, and he had no wish to break the Lord's peace. Straggling had thinned his ranks severely; no more than 3,000 winded infantry were available, and Ashby counted less than 300 cavalry.[18] At the front, however, Jackson was forced to change his plans. He saw that from the ground won by the enemy during the morning, particularly from a knob called Pritchard's Hill where a battery was strafing Ashby, the Yankees could observe his troops spread along the Pike. Rebel delay thus offered the Federals an opportunity to entrench, to retreat, or to call for succor. With the enemy already counting his battle flags, Jackson was compelled to improvise a battle he did not want.[19]

The terrain before Jackson was typical of the Shenandoah: pastures surrounded by stone walls, well-tended apple orchards, and rolling wheatfields. Cow trails meandering in every direction provided access to any point on the field. Jackson noted that the column opposite Ashby, which he considered the principal enemy force, was in the wheatfields to the right (east) of the Pike. To advance directly against it risked crossing open terrain exposed to Union guns on Pritchard's Hill. Better ground was on the left. Parallel and two miles west of the Pike was a low ridge crested with oak, chestnut, and cedar. Mounting it presented no problem, and once there, rebels could pivot around the Federal right to wedge between them and Winchester. Jackson resolved to make that end run; he did not have time or manpower for anything more elaborate.

A spate of couriers dashed off with instructions for the Army.

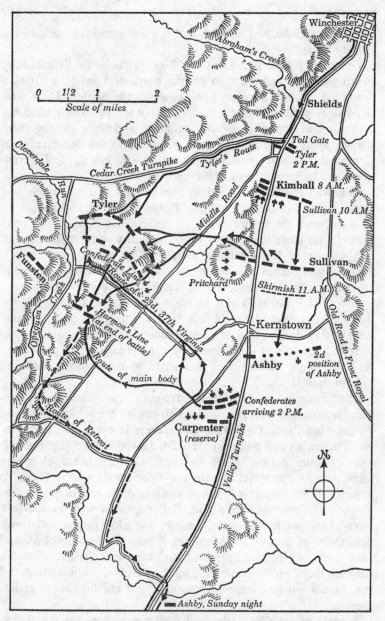

4. BATTLE OF KERNSTOWN, MARCH 23, 1862.
Redrawing of map prepared under the direction of Jedediah Hotchkiss for William Allan's *History of the Campaign of General T. J. (Stonewall) Jackson in the Shenandoah Valley.*

Ashby was ordered to divide his cavalry: Major Funsten would take half to the left to cover Jackson's flanking movement; Ashby would occupy the Federals east of the Pike with the remainder. Burks's brigade formed behind Ashby as a general reserve. Fulkerson's brigade was to seize the vital ridge and spearhead the sweep around the Union right; Garnett was to support it with the Stonewall Brigade minus its largest regiment (William Harman's 5th Virginia), which formed with Burks's reserve. The artillery would concentrate near Burks, then shift to the ridge as needed.[20] Hurrying west, Jackson passed Joe Carpenter's gunners as they fired one of their "alleged cannons" and sent a shell arcing gracefully into an old barn stuffed with Federal sharpshooters. "Good, good," cried Old Jack, clapping his hands with excitement.[21]

Shortly after 3:30 P.M. Fulkerson started toward the vital ridge. Federal artillery from Pritchard's Hill instantly lobbed shells around them, and the Southerners knew they would have a battle. Faces stiffened and breath grew shorter. Gamblers flung aside well-worn decks and fumbled for neglected Bibles. Double-timing along with the Rockbridge Artillery was a broad-shouldered nineteen-year-old, Ed Moore, who had joined the battery the previous Monday. He came from Washington College, where his father had tried to shelter him while his older brothers fought. Young Moore had tolerated this haven for as long as he could, found he was paying no attention to his professors, and won permission to enlist. He had been delighted with his first six days; the camaraderie of the battery was wonderful. Now he saw another side of army life. The concussion from an enemy shell battered Moore to his knees: "We began to feel that we were 'going in,' and a most weakening effect it had on the stomach."[22]

Stomachs calm or trembling, the rebels were quickly "in," and things began to go wrong. Fulkerson fanned out over the ridge and discovered the enemy as a storm of musketry broke upon his ranks. Jackson muddled the advance with contradictory orders to Garnett, one order directing him—or so at least Garnett thought— to aid Fulkerson with only one regiment, the second requiring him to throw his entire force into the battle. Garnett initially pushed ahead with the 33d Virginia. He soon received Jackson's second order and summoned his rear regiments to join him on the ridge. Jackson, unfortunately, had already found them sitting quietly where Garnett left them. Unable to locate Garnett, Stonewall personally led these three rear regiments toward the front.

Confusion quickly multiplied. Orders were reaching Garnett's regimental commanders sometimes through Garnett, sometimes from Jackson personally, and sometimes through the latter's aides.[23] As Garnett overtook Fulkerson, he learned that his rear regiments still were not up with the 33d. Then an aide informed him that Jackson was maneuvering those rear regiments. Though second in command of the Army, Garnett knew nothing of Jackson's intentions and feared some change of plan. He therefore cautioned Fulkerson that he was pulling the 33d to the rear. At the same time, Jackson was losing sight of two of the three regiments he was bringing forward; furious, he plodded ahead with only the 27th Virginia.[24] Some officer, it may have been Garnett or Lieutenant Colonel Andrew Jackson Grigsby of the 27th, came upon the Irish Battalion (which Jackson had dispatched from Burks to support Carpenter's battery) and gave it confusing orders. The battalion broke into two groups attempting to execute these orders and lost track of the guns they were to support.[25]

It was easily 4:15 or 4:30 P.M.[26] before the rebels untangled and the battle began in earnest. The Rockbridge Artillery arrived on the ridge beneath a fierce cannon fire that disabled one of its pieces. Jackson motioned the battery to the right of the Confederate line to answer Union guns on Pritchard's Hill. As the battery lurched off, a wide-eyed Ed Moore watched a shell slice through the two rear horses of his team, tear driver Bill Byrd's leg off, and maim another man.[27] Moore thought it was a ghastly introduction to war. While the queasy nineteen-year-old struggled to hitch two fresh horses, Captain McLaughlin wheeled the rest of the Rockbridge Artillery into position and opened fire. Carpenter's and Waters' batteries joined him.

Left of the guns, the 27th Virginia collided with a large force of Federals and withdrew to better ground. There it withstood two charges before the 21st Virginia came up on its right.[28] Private John Worsham was in the 21st's vanguard and counted five enemy flags tossing above a long line of battle: ". . . we opened fire at once and they scattered. In a few minutes I saw only two flags and soon after only one, which marched on our right to a pile of rocks on which it was planted. . . . A part of our regiment moved to a fence on the right, and facing the enemy in the field, fired at them. Some of [my] company were kneeling down, firing from behind the fence, some were standing straight up; soon all were standing and taking deadly aim as they fired."[29]

Left of the 21st, rebels were also meeting determined resistance. Nearing the edge of a clearing, Fulkerson's 37th Virginia spotted a Federal regiment on the other side. Both units sprang for a stone wall in the middle of the field. The 37th won that race and poured a point-blank volley into the enemy. The Federals fled, but another regiment stormed from the woods to the north.[30] Garnett had collected his 2d, 4th, and 33d Virginia but had failed to advance beyond Fulkerson, so that the rebel front now consisted of the artillery and the 21st Virginia on the right, Garnett's regiments in the center, and Fulkerson's brigade on the left. Between the right wing and the Stonewall Brigade the ground was open to enemy fire. Rather than expose his men there, Garnett squeezed them together in some cedars farther to the left, until they became somewhat intermingled.[31] For the present this did not matter, since the troops needed little direction. Kneeling behind trees, walls, or fences, Garnett's men found abundant targets. John Casler saw Yankee formations so thick "a bullet could hardly miss them if aimed low enough."[32]

The raging, swelling howl warned Jackson something was wrong. Strong bodies of Federals were still opposite Ashby, who was brilliantly feinting against them, yet the rebel flanking column was stalled, unable to make progress as Union battalions swarmed out of the woods to the north. Jackson sent Sandie Pendleton to reconnoiter. The lieutenant found a high knoll and quickly estimated Union numbers must exceed 10,000—the Confederates had fallen into a trap. "Say nothing about it," came Stonewall's reply, "we are in for it."[33] Victory was impossible; Jackson had to worry about saving the Valley Army. The only chance was to hold out until dark, perhaps an hour away,[34] then retreat under cover of night. Stonewall ordered Garnett to bring up the 5th Virginia and summoned Burks to get the balance of his brigade into action. The reserve regiments numbered 1,000 rifles.

On the firing line the Confederates were indeed "in for it." Ammunition began to run low. The Rockbridge Artillery endured a storm of shells and flying rocks as enemy gunners peppered a nearby stone wall.[35] The 2d Virginia's color bearer went down; Lieutenant J. B. Davis clutched the flag and was wounded; Private R. H. Lee grabbed it and was struck; and four more bearers fell from the 2d before the day ended.[36] Colonel John Echols of the 27th was hit. Colonel Jesse Burks, his uniform riddled, had a horse blasted from under him.[37] Along the worm fence that sheltered John Worsham and his buddies of the 21st Virginia, men were now recklessly straddling the rails to take better aim.[38] Some enemy banners were hit twenty and even forty times.[39] The Rockbridge Artillery was attacked by two Union regiments. As the Yanks vaulted a fence no more than two hundred yards off, McLaughlin's gunners dragged four pieces around and minced them with canister.[40]

The Federals were repulsed, but they came on again, lapping closer like the incoming tide. Southern ammunition was almost exhausted. Rebels borrowed from wounded comrades or frisked the dead for cartridges, yet their fire continued to slacken.[41] Desperate minutes passed.

The pressure mounted against Garnett. His men shot away their last rounds; Northern cavalry slipped around Major Funsten and snapped at the left flank, and Garnett faced the ultimate choice of a commander: whether to abandon a battle that seemed lost, though he had no orders to do so and had little comprehension of the over-all situation, or to stand and die awaiting instructions or help. Jackson had gone back to hurry up the reserves and could not be reached; nor were the reserves in sight. About 6 P.M., Garnett made his lonely decision and, without orders, pulled the Stonewall Brigade to the rear. "Had I not done so," he asserted, "we would have run imminent risk of being routed by superiority of numbers, which would have resulted probably in the loss of part of our artillery and also endangered our transportation."[42] Perhaps Garnett did save the guns and the trains, but at the price of uncovering Fulkerson on the left and forcing the entire line to withdraw. The retreat quickly became a rout.

By now the Army's reserves were nearing the fight. Colonel Harman reported at the head of his 5th Virginia and asked Jackson for orders. "Reinforce the infantry engaged," barked the General, who thought his front was still holding.[43] Without a clear idea of what to do, Harman marched for the sound of the guns

until he met the retiring Army. Then he received instructions from
Garnett to occupy a wooded hillock where he might protect the
retreat. Jackson soon appeared and was enraged to find the Army
flowing back around him. He collared a drummer boy and made
him beat the rally.[44] "Go back and give them the bayonet," he
shouted to men who complained that they had no ammunition.[45]
He cornered Garnett and rasped: "Why have you not rallied your
men? Halt and rally."[46]

Garnett screamed himself hoarse, but to no purpose. It was impossible to halt the intermingled regiments amid the noise and
gathering twilight. The Liberty Hall Volunteers of the 5th Virginia
streamed off the ridge with Lieutenant John Lyle sure at least a
thousand Yankees were using him for target practice.[47] Union
cavalry poured onto the field from the left and scooped up Captain Morrison, Lyle, and Jim Langhorne of the Headquarters
Guard and several hundred others from all regiments. Each gun
spitting a last shell, the Rockbridge Artillery rumbled to the rear.
Clem Fishburne's No. 3 gun did not get far before a wheel horse
was hit. In a dying panic it dragged the team and gun across a
stump, flipping the caisson over. Within seconds a Union regiment
was all around it and shooting down the gunners.[48] A gun from
Waters' battery overturned as one of its horses was killed. Sergeant Charles Arnell strained to upright the wreck until Federals
were but fifty yards away, then cut the traces and whipped the rest
of the team to safety.[49]

Garnett, meanwhile, galloped to the position held by Harman's
5th Virginia. Finding Harman, he told him that the day was lost
and that the 5th must gain time for the retreating infantry and
artillery.[50] The most anxious moments of the afternoon followed.
Harman was squarely athwart the enemy's path, and blue regiments were massing around him. He deployed hastily, hoping the
enemy might pause a few seconds until help arrived from Burks.
Federal regiments glowered at Harman across a clearing to the
north; his left was crowded with Northern cavalry; his right was
threatened by Union infantry—but the enemy allowed six or
seven minutes to pass. One of Burks's panting regiments finally
aligned on Harman's right, and the tide surged against these
rebels. Six, seven, and sometimes eight Union battle flags billowed
before the rebel line. The Southern regiments fought, fell back,

were raked in a cross fire, reformed and fought again. They sacrificed 20 per cent of their strength in as many minutes, but they bought the needed time. The enemy halted as night fell, and Harman slipped behind Ashby's skirmishers.[51]

The cavalry chief had also fought magnificently against heavy odds that afternoon. He had so harried the enemy on his front that they could not advance up the Pike to turn the Confederate right, and now he skillfully screened the Army's flight. Last from the field, Ashby and Chew blasted away until Harman's survivors completed their escape. Private George Neese of the horse battery rammed in a parting round and concluded: "Mother, Home, Heaven are all sweet words, but the grandest sentence I ever heard from mortal lips was uttered this evening by Captain Chew when he said, 'Boys, the battle is over.' "[52]

III

The Valley Army staggered back up the Pike marveling at the day's events. "It was a harder fight than Manassas," thought Sandie Pendleton[53]; ". . . the most desperate time I ever was in . . ," wrote George Harlow[54]; ". . . the most terrific battle yet . . ," exclaimed Jim Edmondson.[55] The two hours of incessant musketry known as the Battle of Kernstown had cost the Confederates 455 dead and wounded and 263 captured, total losses of one quarter of those actively engaged.[56] (On a per cent scale, the losses rivaled Southern casualties at Gettysburg.) Two guns were left on the field. Bull Paxton admitted to his wife: "We have had a severe fight today and were pretty badly whipped."[57]

Wandering through the darkness, one of Ashby's cavalrymen paused by a small fire and found himself warming hands next to Old Jack. The boy mustered his courage to speak: "The Yankees don't seem willing to quit Winchester, General."

"Winchester is a very pleasant place to stay in, sir," came the curt answer.

The trooper continued: "It was reported that they were retreating, but I guess they are retreating after us."

Jackson replied only: "I think I may say I am satisfied, sir."[58]

That satisfaction, amid the wreckage of a badly trounced army, might have been augury, except that it reflected a common-sense grasp of what had happened that day. Despite the unexpected enemy strength at Winchester, Jackson knew Union troops had been leaving the Valley. He had struck a very hard blow against the remaining Federals, and although his own force was battered, he believed the enemy had suffered more.[59] This battle could not be ignored, and it was logical to assume it would delay and perhaps prevent additional enemy departures from the Shenandoah. This was exactly what Jackson had been ordered to do, and here lay the cause for his satisfaction.

History would show Old Jack's estimate of the situation was essentially correct. Banks had been redeploying as called for by McClellan's Peninsula plan. One division of 11,000 men (Major General John Sedgwick's, which was on loan to Banks only for the advance on Winchester[60]) had already rejoined McClellan, and other units were taking up positions along the Manassas Gap Railroad east of the Blue Ridge. Another division, Brigadier General Alpheus S. Williams', had left Winchester for Manassas Junction on March 22, and Banks had departed for Washington about noon on the day of the battle.

The last Federal unit at Winchester was Shields's division of 10,000. Ashby had overlooked it on March 22 because Shields had kept most of it well hidden and had shrewdly uncovered only a token force to meet the rebel cavalry. Shields, a doughty Irish immigrant from County Tyrone, was everything Banks was not. He had learned the business of a general well at the head of an infantry brigade during the Mexican War. Shields's troops were Midwestern farmboys who knew how to bide their time and how to complement an able general with tenacious fighting. Northern losses at Kernstown were 568 killed and wounded,[61] less than Jackson imagined. Shields, however, knew the Valley Army was sixty miles from Johnston and did not believe it would have ventured a battle without large reinforcements. Further, he had been impressed by the Valley Army's fighting spirit. He estimated the Confederates had thrown 11,000 men at him and called them the "flower of the Southern army."[62] Fearing a new attack in the morning, Shields sent couriers after Williams' division with orders to turn around and march all night to reach Winchester by dawn of March 24.[63] Banks returned immediately.

McClellan wired approval of Williams' recall, for his Peninsula Campaign was supposed to be prefaced by pacification of the Shenandoah: ". . . push Jackson hard and drive him well beyond Strasburg, pursuing at least as far as Woodstock, and, if possible, with cavalry to Mount Jackson."[64] Unfortunately Banks could not push Jackson as hard or as fast as McClellan needed, compelling McClellan to vastly expand his plans for the Shenandoah. On April 1 McClellan informed his Valley deputy: "The change in affairs in the valley of the Shenandoah has rendered necessary a corresponding departure—temporarily at least—from the plan we some days since agreed upon [Banks's redeployment to Manassas]. . . . The most important thing at present is to throw Jackson well back, and then to assume such a position as to enable you to prevent his return. As soon as the railway communications are reestablished it will be probably important and advisable to move on Staunton, but this would require secure communications and a force of from 25,000 to 30,000 for active operations. It should also be nearly coincident with my own move on Richmond; at all events, not so long before it as to enable the rebels to concentrate on you and then return on me."[65]

McClellan had originally contemplated stationing only a few regiments along and north of the Manassas Gap Railroad. That territory was to serve as a buffer zone between Confederate partisans and vital Union communications along the Potomac. But now the "flower of the Southern army" was in the middle of that zone and McClellan was directing Banks to press one hundred miles to Staunton with 25,000 men. Kernstown thus lured the Union to undertake an extended Shenandoah campaign; it transformed a buffer zone into an active, and unexpected, sector of operations. McCellan did not want and could not afford such a sector, because it entailed a two-pronged invasion of Virginia. Neither McClellan on the Peninsula nor Banks in the Valley could readily support the other, and the rebels, as McClellan was already noting warily, now had the opportunity to mass against either Union prong.

But a more immediate problem for McClellan was that of how to garrison Washington. He had a promise to keep to Mr. Lincoln that the city would be entirely secure when he left it, and Kernstown derailed the orderly flow of troops from the Shenandoah upon which he depended to keep his pledge. Some of what was about to be revealed would have come regardless of Kernstown, because McClellan had started to decrease the forces detailed for Washington almost as soon as his corps commanders settled on the number, but the failure to get Banks's divisions to Manassas drove McClellan from any pretense of compliance with the dispositions that his corps commanders had voted as necessary for the city's defense. On April 1 he gave Secretary of War Stanton a list indicating that 73,456 men were deployed in a long arc covering the capital. That figure was comfortably above the number approved by the corps commanders; unfortunately, the location of these men bore no relation to what was agreed upon—at least, to what Lincoln thought was agreed upon—in March. McClellan tallied 10,000 men for the covering detachment at Manassas, a detachment which was supposed to comprise 25,000. And it was evident from the list that virtually none of the men McClellan placed at Manassas on paper were actually there. Part of the force was to come from troops McClellan suggested the government bring down from Pennsylvania! The garrison in Washington, which was to be 30,000 men, counted less than 20,000. McClellan added detachments which were in fact spread over all of northern Virginia, including Banks's command, to reach his assuring total, but he could not camouflage the weakness of the units actually present around the capital.[66]

McClellan could not end these numerical machinations. To supply a token force at Manassas, he ordered 4,000 men from the Washington garrison to that point on April 1. The next day the commander of the capital's defenses complained to Secretary Stanton that McClellan also had called on him to ready several of his best regiments for the Peninsula.[67] Without these units there would remain perhaps 13,000 or 14,000 men to hold the thirty miles of fortifications that ringed Washington. Stanton investigated and stumbled onto some incredible facts. There was not a single field battery in the city fit for service; the city's heavy artillery was manned by ill-trained infantry—the gunners had been shipped to the Peninsula; few cavalrymen in the District of Columbia had horses.[68] McClellan, it appeared, had used the requirement to garrison Washington as an opportunity to dump the sweepings of his army, untrained or half-equipped regiments he could not trust in the field. Stanton buttonholed the first generals he found and posed one question: Was Washington entirely secure? Their answer came back promptly: No.[69]

Lincoln's response to the information Stanton fed him shackled Union operations during the coming months. The President began to seek some means to establish the conditions under which the Peninsula Campaign was supposed to have begun—that is, 55,000 men stationed in and around Washington. Contrary to what Jackson's most enthusiastic admirers might assert, there is no evidence that Lincoln was concerned about the Valley Army at this time or, indeed, that he saw any immediate threat to Washington from any quarter. Lincoln simply was aware that his capital was not "entirely secure." The President wished to correct this, and he found the means in General Irvin McDowell's 30,000-man corps.

Bad luck seemed to plague Irvin McDowell. He had been compelled by politicians to lead the Union army to Manassas and fight a battle he knew it was not ready to fight in July 1861. In 1862 McClellan had scheduled him to embark for the Peninsula last. McDowell was still waiting around Washington to board his transports two weeks after Kernstown, and Lincoln decided he would not go at all. The President severed him from McClellan's command for garrison duty around Manassas. McClellan went to his grave believing McDowell conspired to arrange this, which was not true but which poisoned relations between the men now commanding the two largest concentrations of Union troops in Virginia.

Concerning McDowell's detachment, McClellan protested frantically, but the President would not relent: "I do not forget," he wrote McClellan, "that I was satisfied with your arrangement to leave Banks at Manassas, but when that arrangement was broken up and nothing was substituted for it, of course I was not satisfied. I was constrained to substitute something for it myself." Lincoln added a pointed inquiry: "Do you really think I should permit the line from Richmond via Manassas Junction to this city to be entirely open, except what resistance could be presented by less than 20,000 unorganized troops?"[70]

Next, Lincoln virtually stripped McClellan of all command over Federal forces in northern Virginia and the Valley, and, by not appointing a successor, the President kept the job for himself. Lincoln narrowed McClellan's authority to the Army of the Potomac and its drive toward Richmond. McDowell and Banks, whose corps heretofore had acted directly under McClellan, were made independent of the Young Napoleon. Lincoln created an autonomous military department extending from Washington east to the Blue Ridge and south toward Richmond for McDowell. His immediate task was to garrison Manassas Junction, from whence he would eventually advance south to Fredericksburg. The Shenandoah was designated a separate department for Banks. His mission was to beat back Jackson.[71]

On March 11 Lincoln had carved another independent department in Virginia. This one superseded the Department of Western Virginia in the Alleghenies and was known as the Mountain Department. Major General John C. Frémont, the famous "Pathfinder" who led America's 1848 expansion through the Rocky Mountains to California, was given command here,[72] largely because he had sold Lincoln the idea of a three hundred-mile push through the Alleghenies to an important Confederate rail junction at Knoxville, Tennessee. (Frémont would quickly abandon his idea of trudging through the mountains in favor of an advance southward along the Shenandoah corridor, so that the Valley Army's second front, which had been relatively quiet since Shields had joined Banks, was about to come alive once more.) Frémont wanted reinforcements for his Knoxville adventure, and Lincoln provided them by detaching Brigadier General Louis Blenker's division from McClellan; this transfer cost the Army of the Potomac another 10,000 men.[73]

No longer authorized to command his former subordinates McDowell, Banks, and Frémont, McClellan had reason to be concerned when he landed on the Peninsula in early April, and Kernstown was the source of his woes. That tiny battle had two immense results: it lured the Union to open and sustain a new sector of operations, and (an unexpected bonus for the South) it disarranged Washington's defense, setting the stage for Lincoln's crippling remedy. McClellan had hoped to clear the lower Shenandoah, get Banks to Manassas, and strike on the Peninsula with a united Army of the Potomac. But as of April 4 his Peninsula Campaign masterplan was abandoned. It had been replaced with four separate Federal armies operating in four tight little

compartments toward four different objectives. All four would be
co-ordinated, if at all, by Lincoln and Stanton, men completely
without military experience.

Jackson, of course, could know nothing of the contortions into
which the Union high command would twist itself as he stood by a
campfire on the night of March 23 and batted away the questions
of an annoying cavalryman. He never claimed that McDowell's
delay around Washington was a result of Kernstown. Jackson
after all was attempting to keep Banks in the Valley, the battle's
first result, not to cause detachments from McClellan's army, the
second result. Though generals are sometimes credited with power
to divine such things, they often do not understand how their
efforts interact with other influences to produce enemy reactions.
It is thus proper to credit Stonewall with no more than he had
done—which was, nonetheless, a great deal: he moved swiftly and
alertly to seize what appeared to be an excellent opportunity. And
though a tactical defeat, the Battle of Kernstown was among the
most productive battles the South ever waged.

On another count, Kernstown left Jackson as bitter and frustrated as it did his West Point classmate McClellan. Jackson
brooded for a week over Garnett's unauthorized withdrawal from
the front, then opened his door and beckoned Sandie Pendleton
into his office. The young aide knew something was wrong when
he spotted the scowling General. Wrote Pendleton: ". . . Genl.
Jackson directed me to go and arrest [Garnett] and relieve him
from command for 'neglect of duty'. . . ."[74] That was the first
Stonewall had said of it, and the news tore through the Valley
Army like an exploding hand grenade.

Garnett, who did not even know the charges against him at the
time,[75] was escorted to the rear under arrest. Jackson then filed
court-martial papers which cited seven specifications of Garnett's
supposed neglect of duty: (1) that Garnett initially advanced
after Fulkerson with only one regiment and then withdrew it, leaving Fulkerson unsupported; (2) that Garnett separated himself
from his brigade so that messengers from Jackson were unable to
deliver orders to him; (3) that Garnett was not with his leading
regiment as it entered battle; (4) that he did not have a regiment
in supporting distance of his leading regiment as it entered battle;

(5) that he allowed his regiments to become intermingled during the fight; (6) that "Garnett gave the order to fall back, when he should have encouraged his command to hold its position"; and (7) that as Harman's 5th Virginia entered the fight, Garnett ordered it to retreat.[76]

The gravamen of Jackson's complaint lay in the sixth specification, Garnett's unauthorized retreat. Stonewall did not care for independent action by his officers anyway, but a retreat without orders was intolerable. Stonewall was livid about that, and anger caused him to make some questionable charges. There was, for example, no regulation that required Garnett to escort his first regiment into battle. The first and fourth specifications probably reflected Jackson's own failure to tell Garnett what his mission was,[77] while the last item was directly refuted by Colonel Harman. In a report submitted before Jackson removed Garnett from command, Harman stated that he was ordered by Garnett to hold a position, not to retreat.[78]

Whether Garnett was correct to retreat without orders cannot be answered today. The reserves Jackson marshaled did successfully retard the enemy after the front collapsed; if Garnett had waited for them, the Confederates might well have held on till night and retired under its cover with significantly lower losses. Garnett knew help was on the way, because the order to bring up the 5th Virginia went through him. On the other hand, Garnett's brigade was out of ammunition when he pulled it to the rear. His regimental commanders unanimously asserted that he thereby saved not only the Stonewall Brigade but the entire Army, that if he had waited any longer the entire rebel line would have been overrun. The only criticism of Garnett from the rank and file who bore the weight of the enemy onslaught was that he did not retire soon enough.[79] These considerations escaped Stonewall. Jackson thought Garnett had pampered the Stonewall Brigade during the past months, and now he saw Garnett as the cause of the Army's rout. When Richmond suggested reinstating Garnett almost a month later, Jackson angrily replied: "I regard General Garnett as so incompetent a Brigade commander that, instead of building up a Brigade, a good one, if turned over to him, would actually deteriorate under the command."[80] This sort of invective was unusual for Jackson and implied that thwarted ambition fueled his rage.

Jackson's first battle as an independent commander had ended with his army flowing back around him, and that must never happen again.

Garnett was fundamentally a good soldier and a brave man. No question of his personal courage was ever raised. He was not as stern a disciplinarian as Jackson, but the Stonewall Brigade had fought well under him. Still, he did retreat on his own initiative. A military hierarchy must react severely to such initiative, especially when it is not clearly beneficial: such is the nature of any system dependent upon obedience. Garnett, a West Pointer, certainly knew he risked the wrath of that system when he gave his unauthorized order to retire.

The affair quickly became the sorriest in the history of the Valley Army. The Stonewall Brigade reacted to Garnett's arrest bitterly. For weeks Jackson was greeted by an icy silence whenever he encountered his old regiments.[81] Garnett fumed until a court-martial could be assembled in August, and only Jackson and Pendleton testified before renewed campaigning suspended it. The matter finally fizzled out, and Garnett returned to active duty. He died twenty-five yards from Union cannons leading a brigade in Pickett's Charge at Gettysburg. A few weeks earlier he had been a pallbearer at Jackson's funeral.[82]

The Valley Army would see other days as desperate as Kernstown, but no one would think of retreat; this was the one positive legacy of Garnett's removal. By it, Jackson made explicit what he demanded on the battlefield. He assigned positions to be held regardless of the danger and regardless of the price. To pull back when the situation seems hopeless is a natural instinct; Jackson demanded that his officers suppress it.

With the same earnest spirit, Jackson did all he could against the immediate consequences of defeat on the night of Kernstown. He summoned the recently organized militia battalion forward from Mount Jackson. Dr. McGuire was told to take whatever army wagons he required to evacuate the wounded. A few hours later the surgeon reported that he had not been able to locate sufficient transportation and some wounded men might have to be abandoned. The General's answer was that McGuire should impress civilian carriages.

"That requires time," McGuire warned.

"Make yourself easy about that," Jackson said. "This army stays here until the last wounded man is removed. Before I will leave them to the enemy, I will lose many more men."[83] The Valley Army would learn to do its duty under every circumstance.

RETREAT, REORGANIZATION, AND A QUESTION

*I have cleaned my gun and am ready
to take another pull at the Yanks
when opportunity occurs.*

—DICK WALDROP

By dawn of March 24, after all Confederate wounded were on their way to the rear, the Valley Army started southward from Kernstown. The deep boom of artillery rolled out behind it as Ashby and Chew dueled the advancing enemy.[1] At Newtown there was a lively scuffle. Then the Yankees paused, and Ashby's troopers carelessly lowered their guard. Jackson funneled his infantry across Cedar Creek, two miles north of Strasburg, and allowed them to break ranks for dinner, the first food most had eaten in twenty-four hours.

Ed Moore and his messmates of the Rockbridge Artillery were wolfing down a huge pot of beans when a Federal shell suddenly tore into their hillside. Moore gulped another bite. Then came another Federal shell, shrieking wildly as if hunting for the rebels. The enemy had swept Ashby from high ground north of Cedar Creek and gained an artillery advantage. Moore's section was ordered to meet the attack, and Moore, his stomach weakening again, shoved his beans at his brother.[2] In the melee that followed, Union gunners picked over the rebels, killing 4 and wounding others.[3]

This preventable affair must have renewed Jackson's doubts about the cavalry's ability to operate effectively with him in the field. Covering the rear was its duty, and it failed. The lapse was not due to excessive casualties at Kernstown, since only 8 riders had been killed or wounded there.[4] Nor was the cavalry's conduct at the battle entirely satisfactory. Jackson could not attach any blame to Ashby for his erroneous information on Federal strength[5] (Stonewall's other sources had been fooled by Shields also), but there had been confusion among the troopers led by Major Funsten on the left,[6] confusion which enabled Union cavalry to snap up many prisoners. And, with at least 600 men under his command,[7] Ashby had fielded less than 300 on March 23. When Jackson pressed this point, Ashby admitted the absence of many men: he had not expected an engagement until the next day and had ordered his companies to assemble accordingly. He also cited the poor physical condition of his men and horses because of insufficient food and rest during the preceding week.[8]

That the cavalry was short of many things could not be denied; a few days before Kernstown, one trooper had carried the spirit of knightly adventure to its illogical extreme by charging the enemy bareback armed with a club. Ashby was roused to inquire about weapons for his unarmed boys after this episode, though he did not press his requests.[9] Perhaps his role as combat leader left him no time to grapple with such details. More probably Ashby did not comprehend enough of military bureaucracy to know he must pursue his requisitions tirelessly. Whatever the cause, Ashby's regiment was not getting any better, and Jackson felt it necessary to ask other commanders if they could spare him some cavalry.[10]

Looking beyond the escalating problems with his cavalry, Jackson discovered solid support for gratification over the strategic outcome of Kernstown. The enemy was deploying strong forces against him. In his report of Kernstown to Johnston, which with less than full candor did not describe the ragged Southern retreat, Jackson stressed this concentration: "Though Winchester was not recovered, yet the more important object for the present, that of calling back troops that were leaving the valley, and thus preventing a junction of Banks' command with other forces, was accomplished. . . ."[11] Jackson also noted with special pride that the Confederate Congress voted a resolution of thanks to the Valley Army for its "gallant and meritorious service in the successful engagement with a greatly superior force of enemy, near Kernstown. . . ."[12] The Valley Army was running an uncommonly good sideshow.

On March 26 the Federal pursuit column retired a few miles, and Jackson leapt after it.[13] He was told by informers fresh from across the lines that the enemy was under the impression his army was retreating to Staunton preparatory to joining Johnston. "I will try and correct this error . . ," Jackson assured the latter.[14] Of course, Old Jack knew he could only correct it for the present by bluster, because the ravaged Valley Army could not risk another stand-up battle for a full month. It was in fact inevitably due for a long retreat. Its hope was that bluster would win time for a slow retreat during which to mobilize the Shenandoah.

Ashby rendered valuable help in the quest for time by developing a highly effective scheme to hinder Banks. Ashby stationed Chew's horse battery on a commanding hilltop to challenge the Federals whenever they advanced. The cavalry waited nearby to pounce on any enemy mounted detachment, which cowed the Federals into deploying their cumbersome infantry. When that slow process was nearing completion, Chew galloped off to another hill—and there were hundreds of hillocks in the Valley—for a repetition. Not until April 1 did Banks lurch beyond Woodstock. Ashby jumped him at once and played with the Union vanguard all day. This skirmish eventually ended at Stony Creek, where Chew furiously shelled the Yanks, Ashby's riders merrily burned a bridge over the creek, and the Federals came on too slowly to save it.[15]

The day before, Jed Hotchkiss had surveyed Stony Creek as part of the map-making project Jackson had assigned him and found it to be an excellent position from which to delay Banks.[16] The stream was deep and wide, and one quarter mile to the south were wooded hills offering rebel snipers good concealment. It was a comfortable seven miles north of Mount Jackson and ten miles north of Rude's Hill. Jackson concurred with Hotchkiss. He delegated the defense of this line to Ashby and sent an infantry brigade to assist. The balance of the Army was planted on the crest of Rude's Hill, so that the Confederates were formidably positioned. Ashby was well placed along Stony Creek to keep the enemy out of Mount Jackson for some days. Should the Federals push into Mount Jackson, Stonewall hoped to slow them again by destroying the bridge over the moatlike North Fork of the Shenandoah. And between that river and the Southern lines atop Rude's the ground lay as flat as a Midwestern prairie, completely exposed to rebel artillery. Banks ground to a halt in front of these lines and gave Jackson more precious time.

Jackson had a use for every hour Banks allowed him: his militia needed time for drill; his skeleton regiments needed time to rest and refit; his quartermaster required time to concentrate the Army's stores at Staunton, out of the enemy's path.

Among the most important equipment hurried south now was a giant Baltimore & Ohio locomotive, the 199. With other B & O rolling stock, some of it captured in Jackson's great haul at Harper's Ferry, the 199 had found its way to Mount Jackson. Stonewall resolved to get this valuable engine to Staunton, and the only way was up the Valley Pike. Squads of scavenger machinists went to work. They hoisted the locomotive with jacks, stripped everything removable except the huge rear driver wheels, swung it around, and lowered it onto the Pike. The strongest teams in the Valley were hitched to the engine by means of an ingenious rigging of front wheels and a chain with harnesses of forty horses. These stood more than one hundred feet ahead of the locomotive in ten rows of four animals abreast. A teamster mounted every fourth horse, and the chief engineer gave the signal to start.

The 199 screeched a few hundred yards along the Valley Pike to the brink of its first obstacle, a sharp descent just south of Mount Jackson. With whatever brakes it had left squealing and white hot to the touch, the iron behemoth slid down that slope and came to rest upright and headed in the proper direction. By the time the lathered horses had dragged it a quarter mile farther, fully onto the Shenandoah's North Fork bridge, that structure threatened to collapse and save Jackson the trouble of burning it. But his engineers threw together some pulleys and settled the 199 once again on the Valley Pike. Here it cracked the macadam surface and listed into the dirt beneath, to be reclaimed by the indefatigable engineers with jacks and timbers. Next came the struggle up the 30-degree incline of Rude's Hill, where hundreds of soldiers and civilians alike were impressed to man dragropes.

After many long hours the 199 gained the summit of Rude's Hill, having come a total distance of two miles; ahead lay forty more miles of rolling hills. The crew was greeted along each of those miles by open-mouthed children, frantic dogs, and old men who came to the roadside and told them that a locomotive could not be dragged cross country. The gainsayers seemed vindicated at the last moment, when the 199 broke loose and overturned only two blocks from its destination in Staunton. It lay mired in spongy earth like some prehistoric monster caught in a tar pit, but it was to be saved in a matter of days.[17]

Wiser after their first effort, rebels began to move other rolling stock south from Mount Jackson, and the equivalent of several short trains was eventually hauled up the Pike. Rebels even developed a certain flare for this mode of travel, and old men along the route stopped telling them it could not be done. Soon no one marveled at it. Sandie Pendleton noted casually in a letter one day: "As I looked out of the window just now, I saw a railroad car traveling up the turnpike, showing what war can do."[18]

The Army's April rebuilding also brought an overhaul of its brigade commanders. General Johnston ironically picked this juncture to return William Taliaferro, the politically influential colonel who had complained so bitterly about the occupation of Romney, to the Valley with the fresh stars of a brigadier general on his collar and orders to reassume the small 3d Brigade, which Fulkerson was handling well. It was now Jackson's turn to protest, which he did to both Johnston and Richmond, but it did no good.[19] Taliaferro's government friends insisted that he rejoin his former command. Fortunately, Taliaferro had returned with a better attitude, and he would prove himself leading the Army in battle. Jackson also requested a replacement for Colonel Burks, who had left the 2d Brigade on extended sick leave, but was unable to get action on his request and so placed the brigade under its senior colonel, John Campbell of the 48th Virginia.[20]

To replace Garnett in the Stonewall Brigade, Johnston dispatched Brigadier General Charles S. Winder. A West Pointer, Winder had earned a captaincy in the prewar Union army at the early age of twenty-six, had fought Indians in Washington territory, and had become known as something of a martinet. The regiment he headed before reporting to the Valley, the 6th South Carolina, was deservedly considered among the Confederacy's best. Tall and broad shouldered, with a high forehead and a frizzled chin beard, Winder was as good an officer as Jackson could have wished. He especially shared Stonewall's mania for discipline, and he was more than a match for the icy welcome awaiting him from the Stonewall Brigade.

Winder found his men in a foul mood as he assumed command on April 2. Garnett's abrupt arrest had come the day before and feelings were raw. Jackson had heightened the tension by reducing the Army's wagon trains; all tents and much other personal baggage had been ordered to the rear. Winder caught the resentment as he inspected the 33d Virginia. John Casler and some comrades began hooting: "More baggage, more baggage."[21] Later, Winder was openly hissed. He ignored the malcontents and found their colonel. Should such incidents continue, Winder told him, he would be held responsible.[22] The disturbances ceased. Winder went on to demand absolute enforcement of every regulation, even to the point of classifying those who overstayed furloughs as deserters.[23]

Similar reforms were occurring throughout the Army. The troops muttered about new and harsher regulations, but their grumblings were no longer the squawks of green recuits. The troops had begun to growl like veterans, a good sign. Observant Bull Paxton wrote of his regiment: "The soldiers . . . seem to exhibit the appearance of contentment and happiness. A mode of life which once seemed so strange and unnatural, habit has made familiar to us, and if peace ever comes many of them will be disqualified for a life of industry."[24] Captain John Graybill obtained a discharge from the service on April 23 and was writing within five days: "I have found the world more monotonous than I supposed. However, I am in fine spirits and hope to soon take the field again."[25] Shortly he did so, joining the cavalry.

Life with Ashby was increasingly attractive these days. The cavalry chieftain had learned that he could sneak cannons and skirmishers through the woods south of his Stony Creek line and pitch a few shells into the Federals on the other bank. These ambushes became a daily affair, the Yankees coming to expect them as they did their breakfast.[26] Old Jack rotated one brigade with artillery support to the front every three days to back these operations. The entire Army thus got training in close-range picket work and, more dramatically, had a chance to watch

Ashby. John Worsham's company of the 21st Virginia was easing into the forward sentry posts one sunny afternoon when the chieftain cantered by and instructed them not to fire unless Federals actually advanced. Accompanied only by a courier, he rode out to reconnoiter and drew hostile fire. His messenger's horse was shot dead. Ashby sat calmly under the hot fire and told the boy to loosen the girth and carry his saddle to the rear. Ashby remained motionless under enemy fire until the task was finished. Then he turned his clean-limbed horse and walked leisurely back to the Southern lines.[27]

Ashby was later to explain that he had a purpose in such displays of nerve. He told one of Jackson's staff that only stray bullets worried him, because they tended to hit those for whom they were not intended. He was not afraid of shots aimed directly at him, since Northern riflemen invariably missed their mark. Hence he felt safest sitting quietly in the open.[28]

Ashby's style of brash heroics was exactly suited to impeding Union progress up the Valley, but even Ashby could not contain Banks forever, and Jackson continued the strategic planning begun prior to Kernstown. He summarized the Valley sector for Major General James Longstreet (who temporarily commanded Johnston's army when the latter was called to confer with President Davis in early April) as follows: Banks's army was spread along the Valley Pike from Winchester to Stony Creek, where both sides held strong positions.[29] With his present force Jackson could not hope to do more than draw Banks farther on, but given reinforcements—Jackson requested an impossible 17,000 men from Longstreet—Banks might be turned and his rear struck. If only he had the manpower, Jackson wrote, "I could so threaten the enemy's rear as to induce him to fall back and thus enable me to attack him whilst retreating. . . . But, if the number asked for is not available, any that you send will, under Providence, have my best efforts expended upon it, and no stone shall be left unturned to give us success." To this crisp summary of his intentions Jackson added a significant thought: "If Banks is defeated it may greatly retard McClellan's movements."[30]

The movements to which Jackson referred were the evolutions of McDowell's forces around Manassas. Confederates regarded these forces as the vanguard of a Union overland offense until the first days of April. The scope of the Northern build-up on the Peninsula did not impress itself upon Richmond until then, after which Johnston received an urgent summons to review the situation with President Davis. Sequestered in the Valley, Stonewall heard nothing of these developments until Johnston returned from his conference and, about April 8, informed Jackson the decision had been made to concentrate his own army on the Peninsula opposite McClellan. Hastening to begin this redeployment, Johnston did not even consider that Jackson's expectations about Banks's defeat might apply as fully to Union forces on the Peninsula as to a Union army marching south from Washington. Instead, Johnston severely narrowed his thinking about the Shenandoah and gave Jackson new instructions reflecting that contraction. Johnston intended to leave behind him only General Ewell's division when he marched toward Richmond; Ewell was to cover the line of the Rapidan River near Orange. The Valley Army must continue slowing Banks in order to shield Staunton and the Virginia Central Railroad, one of the capital's major supply lines. Should Banks press onward vigorously, Jackson was to retire to Swift Run Gap (in the Blue Ridge opposite Harrisonburg). There he was empowered to call Ewell to his aid and give battle in such a way, it was hoped, as to keep the Virginia Central open and, as Johnston had desired from the first, to prevent Union forces from leaving the Valley.[31]

Several days later Johnston was gone, and Jackson was more isolated and exposed than ever. Stonewall penned his first note to Ewell on April 10 to inform him the Valley was quiet but that he planned to fall back if the enemy launched a determined drive.[32] Jackson and Ewell began corresponding over the complexities of Shenandoah geography two days later. They also pooled their intelligence on a new Union force, Blenker's division, which appeared to be en route to Banks from the Manassas area.[33]

These letters were interrupted by a burst of Federal activity. A Union mounted detachment boldly forded the upper reaches of Stony Creek on April 16. Near Columbia Furnace they snared virtually all of a sleeping rebel cavalry company. Ashby's troopers had not bothered to post pickets and were completely surprised; 50 men, their horses, baggage, and equipment were lost.[34] Afraid this sudden Northern initiative signaled the arrival of Blenker's 10,000 men, Jackson pulled his advanced infantry and artillery back to the main line at Rude's Hill and alerted Ashby to give up Stony Creek if pressed. Major John Harman prepared the railroad property still at Mount Jackson for destruction, and Ashby was ordered to attend to this if he retired.[35]

Before dawn on April 17 massed battalions of Federal infantry and artillery stormed Ashby's line, and the troopers fled for Rude's Hill, stopping only to chuck some torches into the railroad yard at Mount Jackson. Union cavalry was close behind them and entered the yard in time to save several engines.[36]

The North Fork of the Shenandoah was the last barrier between Banks and Rude's Hill, and it would not be a barrier unless the bridge over it was demolished. Ashby had entrusted this mission to Captain John Winfield, who paced nervously among twelve of his men at the bridge's southern end while Chew's guns and the last gray cavalry clattered over it. Blue cavalry was close behind them. Winfield's detail hastily tore up some flooring and stirred their torches into a pile of kindling. Grabbing rifles and carbines, they formed a line across the mouth of the bridge.

"Hold your fire," Winfield shouted as the enemy rolled toward them.

At the last second: "Boys, pick your man like a squirrel in a tree, and FIRE!"[37]

Enemy dead piled up on the far edge of the span. A few moments later the Federals were beaten off a second time, but they rushed in again, riding straight through Winfield's squad.

Union cavalry swarmed across the bridge, stamped out the flames and pounced on Ashby's troopers. Desperate hand-to-hand fighting followed. George Neese's crew of Chew's battery unlimbered half a mile away but dared not fire as the opposing forces were completely tangled.[38] Ashby was charged by four Yanks; one of their bullets hit his horse in the lungs and threw it into a death panic. The chieftain was almost taken, when a dismounted rebel ran out of the swirling dust and smoke to drop one assailant; Captain G. W. Koontz and Private Harry Hatcher each picked off another; the fourth ran.[39]

More Union squadrons dashed across the smoldering bridge, and the rebels were flung back upon Rude's. Captain Winfield swore the Federals were no more than a saber's length behind him as he fled. Neese heard the metalic rattle of their scabbards above the sound of his fleeing gun.[40] Ashby fell behind them all; to those watching from the main Confederate line he appeared to be leading the Union attack. No other horseman could have escaped on a dying mount, but Ashby made it. He was the last man to get within range of the Southern guns on Rude's, which blunted the Union onslaught. Dappled with sweat and blood, the magnificent charger carried Ashby by the roaring cannons and dropped. The cavalryman gave it a quick end, then sent for a huge black beast that few others could even mount. By nightfall souvenir hunters plucked the dead steed's mane bare. "Thus," sighed one rebel, "the most splendid horseman I ever saw lost the most beautiful war-horse I ever saw."[41]

It was a sad encounter for Jackson too. He watched his cavalry scatter for the first time, and he witnessed the loss of a vital crossing. A long-range Federal battery was pounding Rude's Hill within a few hours.[42] If this unusual enemy aggressiveness signaled that Blenker's division had swollen Banks's army to something over 30,000 men, the Valley Army was now outnumbered six or seven to one. Even the advantage of better ground could not compensate for this. Jackson reviewed Johnston's instructions about calling Ewell's division to reinforce him in the Blue Ridge if Union pressure grew unbearable and decided the time for that had come. At 2:50 P.M. on April 17 Jackson directed Ewell to head for Swift Run Gap, to which the Valley Army was already retiring.[43]

Banks did not pursue, allowing Jackson more time. Stonewall rode ahead into Harrisonburg to superintend a division of the Army's trains. All superfluous baggage was routed to Staunton. The remaining wagons rolled eastward under a heavy rainstorm.[44] The thin column of infantry followed, moving around the southern tip of the Massanutten Mountain range. By the evening of April 19, the Army was building its campfires in Swift Run Gap near the village of Conrad's Store, twenty miles east of Harrisonburg.

The new position actually exceeded Rude's Hill in natural strength. The Confederate camp lay between two spurs of the Blue Ridge on the east bank of the South Fork. The mountain spurs were pathless and gave the Army secure flanks, so that

Banks had only one approach to this camp—straight over the
river and into rebel guns. Jackson did not anticipate that Banks
could steel himself to make such an attack.[45] He also thought he
would check Banks's drive toward Staunton from this base, since
the cautious Yankee probably would not move south beyond
Harrisonburg and thus expose his flanks and rear to the rebels at
Swift Run Gap. A month-long retreat of almost one hundred miles
had taken the Valley Army to a haven where, for a little while, it
would be safe.

II

If the strength of the new position could be relied upon, early
warning from the cavalry should Banks approach could not. The
fiascos at Cedar Creek and Columbia Furnace attested that the
Valley cavalry was becoming less effective by the day. Chaos in
Ashby's command had become so well known that Richmond lectured Jackson that the cavalry would not only be without sufficient
officers but would also be in violation of recent conscription laws
if it was not properly organized.[46]

On April 19, for the first time, Jackson dispatched one of his
staff officers to supervise the cavalry on an important mission. To
keep Banks out of the Luray Valley, Jackson ordered Hotchkiss
to raze the three bridges over the South Fork of the Shenandoah
near Luray. This was not the sort of thing a map maker normally
would handle, but Jackson trusted Hotchkiss. He told him he
could employ all Southern cavalry in the Luray Valley for the
raid; however, Hotchkiss would have to find them first, since
Jackson had no idea where they were.

Hotchkiss eventually located the companies of Captains Sheetz
and Macon Jordan in an old foundry, where Jordan and most of
his boys were guzzling applejack. With more than the usual
hoopla, the riders assembled on Hotchkiss' orders and wove off
toward the first target, a red, covered bridge. There a detail separated to prepare the span for burning, while the rest of the column
moved farther downstream. Hotchkiss sensed trouble near the second bridge, concealed his men and explained the need for a careful scout. Some troopers loped off and soon returned with assur-

ances the enemy was nowhere around. Hotchkiss sent Sheetz to burn the bridge and told Jordan to sober up his company.

Unfortunately, there was no time to sober up; the scouts had overlooked a Federal task force of infantry, cavalry, and artillery with orders to save the bridges Hotchkiss was to destroy. Federal dragoons surprised Sheetz on the span and hurled him back upon the main body. Hotchkiss had only enough warning to tell Jordan to get his company into line and ride out to spot the enemy. Instead of forming his men, the besotted Jordan trotted after Hotchkiss. Federals swept up the road, and Hotchkiss was caught in a panic: ". . . our men broke at once except some 3 or 4, and a perfect stampede of them took place; the enemy pursu[ed] for 3 miles; every attempt to rally was unavailing, some men actually throwing away their guns, many their coats, blankets. . . . I never saw a more disgraceful affair—all owing no doubt to the state of intoxication of some of the men, and to the want of discipline." Some drunks were so terrified they scampered over the Blue Ridge and did not rejoin the Army for days. Almost alone, Hotchkiss managed to outrun the Federals and to burn the red bridge as he retraced his steps to Swift Run Gap. He complained to his wife that evening: "When Ashby's men are with him they behave gallantly, but when they are away they lack the inspiration of his presence, and being undisciplined, they often fail to do any good."[47]

The map maker's report of this episode to Jackson was as blunt as his letter home, and it was more than Jackson could tolerate. On April 24 he moved to correct the cavalry's indiscipline with the following order:

> The General Commanding hereby orders Companies (A–K) of Ashby's cavalry to report to Brigadier-General Taliaferro, and to be attached to his command; the other companies of the same command will report to Brigadier-General Winder, to be attached to his command. Colonel Turner Ashby will command the advance-guard of the Army of the Valley when on an advance, and the rear-guard when in retreat, applying to Generals Taliaferro and Winder for troops whenever they may be needed.[48]

In effect, Ashby was stripped of his command. Winder and Taliaferro would see to its supply and training, and Ashby was left with nothing more to do than borrow his men when the situation permitted.

Jackson's decision was as unexpected as the snowstorm which hit the Valley that same day[49]; Stonewall's decision also revealed again his own inability to work skillfully with his subordinates. Better cavalry discipline might have been achieved by explaining to Ashby that it would conserve the lives of his men and prevent stains upon the reputation of his command. There is no evidence Jackson attempted this approach. Jackson at least could have offered some explanation for his action, but he was never a diplomat.

The blunt order reassigning his troopers was delivered to Ashby without elaboration. The enraged cavalryman stormed into his headquarters, kicked some shavings onto the fire, and slumped before it in a black mood. Hotchkiss found him in this mood and listened patiently as Ashby spun an irrational fantasy about Stonewall mistreating him by ordering that the cavalry be drilled. "He seemed to think," recorded Hotchkiss later, "that although he had so many companies he could easily manage them all himself and that it was [unnecessary] to have them drilled."[50] Ashby grew bitter, ranting that his command was organized under special permission from the War Department in Richmond and that Jackson could not legally interfere. Ashby's regimental surgeon tramped in from the snow to hear Ashby pouting that if he were of equal rank with Jackson, he would challenge him to a duel.[51] That, of course, was not possible, but Ashby did strike a blow: he sent General Winder his resignation to be forwarded to Jackson. With it went the resignation of Major Funsten.

This news traveled fast. Quartermaster Harman revealed his sympathies as he informed his brother at Staunton: "A great calamity has befallen us; there is a rupture between Ashby and Jackson. . . . Ashby will not submit, and we are in great danger from our cracked-brained Genl."[52] When he received Ashby's resignation, Winder galloped to see the paladin immediately and helped him talk out his frustrations. Then he persuaded the chieftain to let him intercede with Jackson. Throughout the night, Winder rode through the snow between Ashby and Jackson, finally arranging a conference on the morning of the twenty-fifth at the latter's headquarters.

Men of two different worlds confronted one another at that meeting. Ashby was a courageous loner. His was a world where freeholders assembled when danger threatened, drove off the enemy, and trotted home to till their fields—just as Ashby had done when rowdy railroad workers threatened his home during the 1850s. Jackson, a West Pointer, was imbued with the rigid traditions of the professional army in which soldiers did exactly what they were told. Ashby was a cavalier at heart. He rejoiced over acts of personal courage and admired them in his enemy. Never was his whole concept of a leader better expressed than when he advised his surgeon that a commander "should go to the front and take risks in order to keep his men up to the mark."[53] Jackson was more pragmatic. He once heard a rebel officer regret that his men had shot down a gallant Federal officer doing just what Ashby prescribed. Jackson instantly rebuked that officer: "Shoot them all. I do not want [the enemy] to be brave."[54] Jackson's unremitting discipline made his infantry as Spartan as any in the Confederacy; Ashby's system stunted his cavalry at a tournament mentality.

Ashby's was a dying tradition, but this day it prevailed. The meeting ended as the cavalier stomped from Headquarters and announced to some of his riders that he was quitting Stonewall to organize a new command totally separate from the Valley Army. Those present volunteered in a trice, and Jackson was helpless. Every Valley trooper would want to follow Ashby, and if denied they would be too demoralized to do any good. Disorganized cavalry was better than none at all. The impasse was settled, Major Harman chuckled, "by Gen'l. Jackson backing square down."[55] The cavalry was detailed back to Ashby. Jackson thus saved face, since the cavalry technically continued under his direction. Ashby in reality resumed unfettered command. As he had no concern with paper organization anyway, his dignity was assuaged, and he withdrew his resignation (as did Major Funsten).

New problems arose for Jackson as the Army reorganized itself under the provisos of recent Southern draft laws. The inevitable disorder in such a reshuffling was compounded by conflicting laws from the Confederate and Virginia state governments. The South was attempting a general conscription, the first such attempt in American history, and it was a confusing process. During February, Virginia had thoroughly canvassed its population for all males eligible for the militia; on March 10, Virginia had drafted 40,000 of these militia, who were destined to fill "volunteer" units. The result of these moves was to bring the militia into the volunteer army. Volunteers had the option either to re-enlist or to wait out their terms, at which time they were mustered out of the army and rostered with the militia. But since militiamen were being siphoned off to fill depleted volunteer units, a mustering out was followed by a mustering back in, frequently back into the same company and for the duration of the war.[56] The earlier plan of the Confederate Congress, the Furlough and Bounty Act, also applied to Virginians. It granted re-enlistees furloughs, bounties, and the right to change their branch of service. Many of those who stayed with the Valley Army through Kernstown did so seeking some loophole in the Virginia law or waiting to switch their branch. At virtually the last moment, April 21, the Confederate Congress dashed these hopes by enacting national conscription of all males without the transfer privilege but with the right to elect company and regimental officers.[57]

This rolling barrage of legislation hit everyone, even Jackson's Headquarters Guard. It had already taken such heavy casualties that it needed a large infusion of militia draftees. Thirty-three conscripts joined one day, with more slated to arrive the next. The original volunteers learned that the new men, who would have a majority by morning, planned a block vote for their own candidate in the company election. The volunteers howled to their regimental commander, Colonel Charles Ronald, and got swift relief. Ronald scheduled the election that night, and after he managed to have all sentries released from Headquarters duty, the volunteers fielded a majority of two.[58] Those two swung the election for company captain to quiet, devout Hugh White. White, whose ambition was to attend divinity school, accepted the job with serious qualms. He found many things about army life "irksome."[59] He had no military education and assumed his duties with only the preparation of a quick mind and a willingness to learn. Not all units chose even this well; some proven officers were defeated and a few utterly unfit men elevated to their places. Jackson sent officers who failed to gain re-election home, and the ever watchful Hotchkiss recorded "quite a stampede."[60]

Across the Valley Army's camp, the Rockbridge Artillery had difficulties of another variety. Its superb reputation lured recruits until its rosters bulged with 240 men, far too many for the 6 guns left after Kernstown, so it was decided to convert the unit into an artillery battalion of three batteries. Two new companies were organized, captians were elected, and everything was arranged— then the additional cannons failed to arrive and the project died. A second set of elections had to be conducted, and Lieutenant William Poague won the captaincy. He had to pare the battery down to 150 men; those not selected were allowed to transfer or detailed to guard prisoners.[61]

The effects of the reorganization period were extremely debilitating in Ashby's cavalry, because the scramble to join it continued regardless of the ban on transfers contained in Confederate draft laws. On April 21, for example, almost an entire company was organized of transferees from the Stonewall Brigade's 2d Virginia.[62] The new unit was one of more than twenty companies in Ashby's regiment. The exact number of companies cannot be determined today, but estimates ranged all the way from twenty-one to twenty-six companies.[63] Whatever the total, it was more than twice authorized regimental size and more than Ashby could discipline, train, equip, and lead in battle. Yet Ashby did not realize or would not admit that his command had grown beyond his ability to control it.

Somehow, the rank and file of the Valley Army maintained a characteristic sense of humor during this reorganization. In Chew's battery George Neese found himself elected to the post of chief gunner. Neese considered this a good joke: "I know very little about gunnery, in fact, nothing except that a gun in good health never shoots backward." He resolved to learn, but did not expect much success mastering the technical principles of gunnery: ". . . I can plainly see that if I ever acquire any efficient knowledge of practical gunnery it will have to be gathered on the battlefield, a rather dangerous place to be experimenting with fireworks. . . . If any Yanks should happen to get hurt by my first attempt at gunnery, it will be their fault, not mine."[64]

There was humor, and there was hope. The Army's enthusiasm was growing. Rather than being broken by defeat at Kernstown, morale was actually bolstered, since the men believed they had fended off 15,000 to 20,000 Yankees that day and were not reluctant to congratulate themselves about it.[65] As word of Kernstown spread up the Valley, hundreds of furloughed men voluntarily cut short their leaves and returned to ranks. Offers of help arrived from as far south as Lexington, where Superintendent Francis H. Smith of the Virginia Military Institute tendered the service of the Corps of Cadets.[66] Another reinforcement, the 10th Virginia, came from Johnston's army. Recruited from the Valley, the 10th had served through the winter with Johnston and agitated constantly to be returned to the defense of its home. It finally won a transfer and on April 21 marched into Swift Run Gap to become part of Taliaferro's brigade. The newcomers were immediately assailed with dire yarns about life under Stonewall. The 10th would soon get enough of it, John Casler taunted; Old Jack would make them earn their bread.[67]

Though the cavalry was inefficient and some infantry were bitter about conscription, the Army's over-all condition was better than might have been anticipated a month earlier. It had three capable brigade commanders in Winder, Taliaferro, and Campbell. It numbered more than 8,500 infantry by the end of April,[68] and Ashby counted perhaps 1,000 sabers. The trains were lightened and mobility enhanced by discarding much cumbersome baggage. The troops had been toughened at Kernstown and during the retreat. Most important, the Shenandoah's citizen soldiers were ready for a real fight. The militia which Jackson had distrusted since the beginning of the war finally was integrated into regular units. The foolishness of elections and luring volunteers to reenlist with bountiful furloughs was past. Everyone was in "for the duration."

Several notable additions to Jackson's staff completed the reorganization. With strong recommendations from his friend Sandie Pendleton, Henry Douglas, formerly an infantry lieutenant with the 2d Virginia, joined as a special aide. A "wide awake, smart young man"[69] was Hotchkiss' evaluation of the youth who had practiced law before his twenty-first birthday and who later wrote an invaluable memoir of his service under Jackson. Stonewall called Lieutenant Colonel Stapleton Crutchfield to become his chief of artillery; during the coming weeks Crutchfield would coordinate the Army's batteries in a dozen skirmishes and battles.

Once a student under Jackson at V.M.I., Crutchfield subsequently served on the faculty with him for six years, and his abilities were so considerable that Stonewall even overlooked the fact that he liked to sleep late.[70]

The post of assistant adjutant general had been vacant since Colonel Preston's departure in January. Equivalent to the modern position of chief of staff, his job exacted tedious yet vital attention to detail; not until late April did Jackson satisfy himself on a candidate, the Reverend Robert L. Dabney. A distinguished Presbyterian clergyman—he had taught ecclesiastical history at Union Theological Seminary in Richmond—Dabney had no military experience and traveled to Swift Run Gap to dissuade Stonewall. Nonsense, said Jackson: "Rest today and study the Articles of War and begin tomorrow."[71] Dabney walked out of Valley Army Headquarters a major.

The preacher's appointment sparked a round of quipping among the irreverent of the Army. Among them was the new colonel of the 27th Virginia, Andrew Jackson Grigsby, who joked: "I concluded that Old Jack must be a fatalist sure enough when he put an Ironside Presbyterian parson as his chief of staff. But, I have bright hopes of headquarters, seeing they are no longer omniscient."[72] Dabney ignored the jokes and dug into the Articles of War. A man of boundless intelligence, he proved himself quickly, even to Grigsby.

With Dabney's appointment Jackson essentially had filled his staff, one of the best assembled during the war on either side. Jackson's aides, like any staff, struggled with the paperwork that encumbered Headquarters, but they had other duties as well. Battlefield orders which were too important for the carefree messengers provided by Ashby were carried by Jackson's aides. They were often found at the front helping to steady the line. Sometimes they even led major portions of the fighting; Crutchfield, for example, often supervised the Army's batteries with little direction from Jackson.[73] Not surprisingly, many staffers graduated to field command. Lacking a trained cadre of junior officers who could be trusted with combat missions away from the Army (bridge burnings and the like), Jackson was also compelled to delegate these tasks to his staff. (This was becoming particularly true where Ashby's cavalry was involved.) Much more than paper monitors,

Jackson's carefully picked staff members were extensions of the General on and off the battlefield, and their zeal helped immeasurably to lead the freshly reorganized Army through the tests that awaited.

III

"My plan is to put on as bold a front as possible and to use every means in my power to prevent [Banks's] advance whilst our reorganization is going on. . . . What I desire is to hold the country as far as practicable until we are in a condition to advance, and then, with God's blessing, let us [make] thorough work of it."[74] Thus had Jackson outlined his plan to Alexander Boteler before leaving Winchester, and much had been done to fulfill the preliminaries. Yet as surely as the plan fostered hope, it also posed a serious question: What next? The Valley Army was as ready to advance as could be hoped, but much of the Shenandoah had been given up to the enemy.[75] The Army's presence in the Valley amounted to a narrow bridgehead across the South Fork near Conrad's Store, and rumors persisted that this toehold would be relinquished if the Army was called to reinforce Johnston, which seemed increasingly probable. Would the Shenandoah be abandoned?

Even had Old Jack been disposed to answer such a question, he could not have done so now, for he himself was stymied. The retreat into the southern Shenandoah prompted thoughts of cooperation with General Johnson's remnant of the Army of the Northwest located west of Staunton. Johnson, however, had arrived at Valley Army Headquarters on the evening of April 19 with a discouraging report.[76] Frémont's vanguard, under Brigadier General R. H. Milroy, was pressing toward Staunton (from whence Frémont intended to begin his march up the Valley toward Knoxville, Tennessee). Frémont's command was scattered and concentrating slowly; still, Johnson had only 2,500 men and had begun a retreat which would settle him only six miles west of Staunton.[77]

That retreat placed Johnson between enemy fronts to the north (Banks) and west (Frémont). While Banks probably would not advance as far south as Staunton and thus expose his lines of communication to Jackson at Swift Run Gap, he had other options. Banks could thrust far enough south to threaten Johnson's rear so that he would have to retire, and Staunton would fall to Frémont. Banks could unite with Frémont via the Harrisonburg and the Warm Springs Turnpike and present a combined force of almost 45,000 men. Jackson feared this move most, for the Valley Army could do little to protect either Johnson or Staunton against such a host. It was also entirely possible that Frémont could defeat Johnson and capture Staunton regardless of Banks or Jackson. There seemed no remedy against these permutations, and the Southern generals parted without a plan.

Jackson received more bad news on April 21: Federals were massing on the Rappahannock River opposite Fredericksburg. Five thousand of McDowell's men were already poised there, and the bulk of his command was ten miles north. Because Fredericksburg was less than sixty miles directly north of Richmond, the Confederate high command anticipated McDowell would shortly open a second front against the capital. A stopgap force assembled to resist McDowell under Brigadier General Charles Field had already burned the Rappanhannock bridges and retired some distance south of the river.[78]

Profoundly disturbing, the letter that jolted Stonewall with this information bore the signature of Robert E. Lee, and in this there was encouragement. Lee requires no introduction today, although he was largely unknown beyond the borders of Virginia during the spring of 1862. The war so far had been a succession of thankless tasks for Lee: a hectic mobilization of Virginia, a hopeless campaign in the Alleghenies and a fight against impossible odds along the coast of Georgia and the Carolinas. He recently had left the Atlantic seaboard for Richmond and another lackluster assignment, Commanding General of Confederate Armies. Impressive in title only, the post confined him to a desk bereft of clearly defined authority.[79] The job at best made Lee an adviser to the President and at worst his military handmaiden, although, under a nebulous grant of authority from Davis, Lee was allowed some freedom to supervise the smaller Confederate armies.

It was not exciting duty, and Lee did not relish it. Yet he sought to do his best, and perhaps to his own surprise he performed one of his most valuable services to the Confederacy during the spring of 1862 by setting a goal for Jackson. Since beginning his new duties, Lee had watched a gradual dispersion of Confederate forces across central Virginia and the Valley. While Johnston retained over-all command of this area, he was so ensnarled on the Peninsula that he had not communicated with Jackson since early April and had written only once to Ewell.[80] With great skill, and little actual authority, Lee moved to fill this vacuum. In his letter briefing Jackson on the Union concentration opposite Fredericksburg, he advanced a basic strategy to guide Southern operations. The threat to Richmond from Fredericksburg must be eliminated.[81] The South could not stand an enemy onslaught from the Rappahannock; it would almost certainly bring the destruction of Johnston's army. Lee suggested that Jackson, with the assistance of Ewell's division, might be able to reduce the pressure from Fredericksburg[82] by routing Banks. Lee reasoned, no doubt, that Banks's defeat would expose the strategic flank of Federal forces near Fredericksburg, thereby discouraging a Union attempt to cross the Rappahannock.

Jackson replied on April 23, explaining to Lee that he did not think he could be much help. Banks was at New Market, where he posed a threat to Staunton's rail link with Richmond; Jackson in turn posed a threat to a direct move on Staunton by Banks, but Stonewall could not do much more than threaten without Ewell. Jackson's intention remained an attack on some exposed portion of Banks's army or, voicing a possibility that increasingly fascinated him, a maneuver into the Federal rear. Unfortunately, Banks presented no opportunity for a sudden blow, and Jackson offered Lee nothing better than hope that the enemy would make a careless move soon. With a twinge of guilt, he added that this offensive plan violated the spirit of Johnston's orders of early April.[83] Later that day Jackson received further word of General Field's predicament near Fredericksburg. Seeing no possibility of action in the Valley, Jackson wrote Lee again to suggest that Ewell's division might be used to best advantage by sending it to Field.[84] Jackson already had halted Ewell's march to Swift Run Gap and told him to await further instructions.[85]

These messages were unusually negative for the truculent Jackson. Lee was unable to disguise a note of disappointment in his next dispatch, dated April 25: "I have hoped in the present divided condition of the enemy's forces that a successful blow may be dealt them by a rapid combination of our troops before they [the enemy] can be strengthened themselves either in their position or by reinforcements." Lee left the chances for success of such a move in the Valley to Jackson's estimate. He also pointed out that Southern intelligence indicated the North had weakened its forces twenty-five miles northwest of Fredericksburg at Warrenton; Jackson and Ewell might lunge at this point. If this was not feasible, Ewell could join Field, for whom Lee was prying 8,000 men from other sectors, and deliver a surprise attack at Fredericksburg. Lee did not insist that Jackson choose any of these alternatives—the distance between them was too great for such control—and emphasized that he only made suggestions as to how McDowell might be neutralized. But he tailored his conclusion specially for Jackson: "The blow, wherever struck, must, to be successful, be sudden and heavy. The troops used must be efficient and light."[86]

Jackson mulled over this letter at length, for it subtly yet significantly expanded his mission. Johnston's instructions of early April were defensive: protect lines of supply from the Shenandoah to Richmond, retard Banks, but give battle in the Blue Ridge where the chance of a severe defeat was lessened. Without precise authority to do so,[87] Lee had authorized Jackson to strike, and to strike beyond the Valley if necessary,[88] two things Johnston never explicitly sanctioned. Jackson was no longer to struggle merely to hamper enemy progress up the Valley; he was to attack at a place of his own choosing as an integral part of Richmond's defense. What Lee authorized might achieve all Johnston desired, but it would be more dangerous than awaiting an attack atop the Blue Ridge and could put Jackson beyond the point where Johnston could reinforce him or he Johnston. It might also catapult the Valley Army from a sideshow to main attraction.

Stonewall hurried back to his maps. He first noted the most recent changes. Banks had inched his way into Harrisonburg on April 26; in response, Jackson had directed Ewell to resume his march to the Blue Ridge.[89] Marking these shifts, Jackson recapitulated the over-all situation: two campaigns were currently underway in Virginia. One belonged to McClellan, who had established himself on the Peninsula and ground forward fifteen miles to Yorktown, site of the Revolutionary War siege. There he had been bluffed by a theatrical little rebel garrison which put on a facade of great strength and had laid siege to the city. The delay enabled Johnston to arrive at Yorktown, and the main armies faced each other in trenches fifty miles southeast of Richmond. McClellan's tortoiselike advance did not surprise Jackson; he remembered him from West Point and told his staff: "McClellan lacks nerve."[90] This was perhaps true, but McClellan did have 100,000 men and dozens of heavy guns, force enough to dictate the pace at which his campaign would proceed. Johnston had about 55,000 men and was seeking to stay out of McClellan's grasp; Johnston was already anticipating another strategic retreat nearer the capital. McDowell's forces were rapidly assembling at Fredericksburg, preparing, Jackson supposed, to join McClellan by an overland descent upon Richmond from the north. McDowell's numbers would soon exceed 30,000; Field had less than 12,000, even after the reinforcements provided by Lee joined him.

The second campaign in the Old Dominion was that of the Valley Army, and unlike the first, it was at a rough equilibrium. Banks could not go on to Staunton with the rebels at Swift Run Gap; the rebels were too weak to drive Banks out of the Shenandoah. But the first side to maneuver wisely might upset this balance in its favor. Banks had 22,000 men at Harrisonburg, and what he intended was unknown. Jackson was relieved to note, however, that Blenker's division (which had been ordered to join Frémont) had passed through the Valley and had not joined Banks as Jackson had feared when the rebels retreated from Rude's Hill. Finally, Milroy's 2,000- or 3,000-man vanguard of Frémont's forces (about 20,000 total when joined by Blenker), was pressing Edward Johnson back toward Staunton and threatening to upset the tenuous Valley balance.

Old Jack's calculations convinced him there were at least 160,000 Federals operating across Virginia; perhaps half that number of Confederates opposed them. Such odds could only be redressed by maneuver, and Jackson and Ewell led the only movable Southern columns. Johnston, Field, and Edward Johnson were each nailed in place by powerful Union forces. The war had unfolded so that, at this particular movement, only Jackson, with Ewell, was free to move. The Valley Campaign that Jackson had

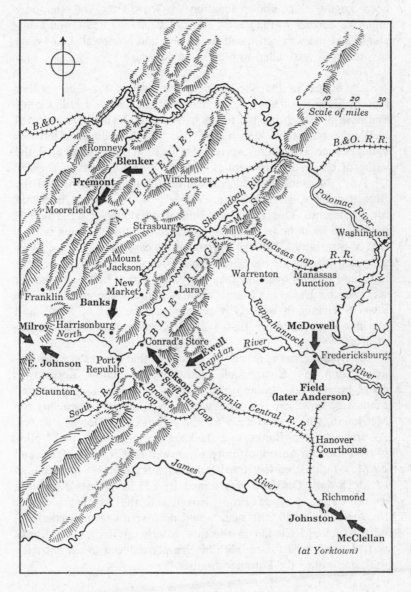

5. GENERAL SITUATION, APRIL 30, 1862.

been waging since the evacuation of Winchester was the only offensive means available to stop McClellan's Peninsula Campaign. But the war continued to spread, and Stonewall had to act before Ewell was called to plug some new gash.[91]

Swift action in the Shenandoah was needed for still another reason. Since the Valley Army had evacuated Rude's Hill, Banks had been boasting that the rebels had fled the Valley. He reported to War Secretary Stanton on April 19: "I believe Jackson left this valley yesterday."[92] On April 22: "Jackson has abandoned the valley of Virginia permanently, *en route* for Gordonsville. . . ."[93] On April 24, Banks placed Jackson near Stanardsville, east of the Blue Ridge.[94] On April 30 he claimed: ". . . Jackson is bound for Richmond. This is a fact, I have no doubt. . . . There is nothing to be done in this valley this side of fortifications on this side of Strasburg."[95] Banks overstated his case slightly, since Jackson was clinging to his Shenandoah toehold at Swift Run Gap, but there was no question that the Valley Army had been pushed well south. Union rail and canal communications across the lower Shenandoah were fully restored by the end of April, and all that was asked of Banks after Kernstown seemed accomplished.

Abraham Lincoln therefore reasoned that Banks's redeployment from the Shenandoah, contemplated before Kernstown, could be revived. Rather than leading to garrison duty around Manassas, however, this shift was to provide reinforcements for McClellan, who wailed daily for the return of McDowell's forces. Assurances from Banks that Jackson had departed the Valley offered Lincoln an opportunity to answer McClellan's pleas, and on May 1 the President transferred Shields's division from Banks to McDowell. Once he was joined by Shields (Shields's march would be by way of Front Royal and the Manassas Gap), McDowell, with 40,000 men, would push south from Fredericksburg to join McClellan in the final attack on Richmond. Banks was to retire to Strasburg with his gravely reduced force, entrench well, and police the Potomac frontier.[96]

Lincoln's new strategy was exactly what Lee anticipated from Fredericksburg in his letter of April 25, and it was the reason he kept prodding Jackson to strike somewhere in central Virginia or the Valley. Stonewall's blow would, it was hoped, dislocate whatever the enemy planned from Fredericksburg by stripping McDowell's flank and making it dangerous for him to cross the Rappahannock, and that, ultimately, would relax much of the pressure on the Confederate capital. The Valley was rapidly changing from sideshow to center stage. Shields had to disentangle himself from the Shenandoah and join McDowell for the crucial march to Richmond; Jackson had to prevent just such a contingency.

As he sought to prevent McDowell's advance, Jackson began planning from a fresh perspective. During his retreat up the Valley, Stonewall's orientation had necessarily been north-south and confined to the corridor between the Massanutten Mountain and the Alleghenies. He had looked sideways only with fitful glances toward Johnston's flank. Now, freed of the obligation to dangle before Banks to keep him off Johnston's flank and coiled at the important road junction of Swift Run Gap, Jackson could spin his maps around and consider the Shenandoah from its east-west axis. He could think in terms of four directions, and the mountains and rivers that had narrowed his periphery now became avenues rather than obstacles. The strategic options at Swift Run Gap were almost endless. Jackson could slip out the back door of the Gap and maneuver northward along the eastern shoulders of the Blue Ridge to attack the Warrenton area. He might attempt to storm west through Massanutten Gap and isolate Banks at Harrisonburg. Further reflection made Jackson hesitant about this scheme, since Banks could conduct a delaying action in Massanutten Gap that might enable him to get his main force to New Market in time to repel the rebel attack. More interesting was a dash down the Luray Valley toward Front Royal and the deep Federal rear around Winchester; such a raid would certainly clear Banks out of the upper Valley. Jackson outlined all of these courses to Lee on April 29.[97]

And there were still other possibilities. His broad hands gripping his knees, his back becoming rigid, Stonewall stared ahead fixedly as he pondered an answer to the insistent question: What next?

INTO THE MOUNTAINS

Our movement, or rather Jackson's,
had entirely bewildered us.

—ED MOORE

In the early hours of April 30 Private Joe Kaufman of the 10th Virginia was roused by a fife and drum corps pounding through the camps of the Valley Army at Swift Run Gap. Kaufman was marching westward by 4 A.M., and with mounting excitement he guessed the Army was going after Banks. The rebels pressed forward, deployed, and made much noise before Union positions outside Harrisonburg. The veins in Kaufman's neck were throbbing in anticipation of his first battle, but the next orders directed the Army back toward camp. Oddly enough, it did not go there either. The column turned from the road to Swift Run Gap and headed south.

What next? The only answer was a cloudburst, through which the bewildered troops shuffled along the east bank of the Shenandoah's South Fork to a bivouac five miles south of Swift Run Gap. Kaufman drew one half pound of bacon, his only ration for the day, ate, and went to sleep beneath a spiteful rain which would outlast the night.[1]

By morning the road had disintegrated into a wilderness of mud. Kaufman sank to his knees with each step as the march continued southward. Wagons and guns settled to their axles in mud.[2] Shoving and sliding by his cannon, Clem Fishburne recalled the drive on Romney and swore the morass had no bottom.[3] George

Neese had to use fence rails twice to pry a horse out of the slush.[4] John Apperson abandoned the road and took his chances in the quicksand-dotted forest alongside it; whole regiments lost cohesion around him as the Army wallowed into the night.[5] "The men became perfectly reckless, and plunged into mudholes and ponds of water with a yell or a laugh," wrote Hugh White.[6] Only the cursing heaped on Jackson tied together the troops.[7]

Next morning the sun was out. Hotchkiss took the entire 42nd Virginia ahead to repair the road, "the worst," he groaned, "I ever saw in the Valley of Virginia."[8] Other staff members joined Old Jack as he lugged rocks to shore up chuckholes.[9] By force of habit and with much profanity, the column continued its advance along the Shenandoah's South Fork to reach Port Republic by nightfall. (As they encamped, some rebels noted menacing bluffs on the far side of the river, but few would have guessed that six weeks hence they would defend those bluffs from Federals trekking up this very road from Conrad's Store.) The rebels had covered fifteen miles in two and a half days, a stern initiation to the Valley Army for newcomers like Joe Kaufman. His diary entry for the day read: "I begin to think Old Jack is a hard master from the way he is putting us thru. . . . My feet have given out but still I have to travel on. Oh, how I wish peace would be declared!"[10]

The suspense in ranks was equally painful. There was absolutely no hint where the Army was going, though the troops grumbled about likely destinations in low, almost sullen tones.[11] One thing was clear: the Army was drawing away from Banks. On May 3 it toiled eastward up into Brown's Gap of the Blue Ridge —out of the Valley. The Shenandoah was abandoned. There was little enthusiasm when the eastward march was resumed the next day. The road wound southward along the Blue Ridge to the Virginia Central Railroad at Mechum River Station. During the march several comely girls taunted the troops for deserting the Valley, and that stung worse than the last three days on the road.

All the rolling stock in this part of the state had been assembled at Mechum River Station to meet the Army, but the result was disappointing, five or six short trains at most. As each regiment reached the station, Jackson sorted out the sick and barefoot and packed them into the splintered baggage cars[12]; some men were pressed together as tightly as they could stand.[13] Most were too

dejected to wonder why the locomotives were on the uphill end of
the trains, or why two special engines, leviathans boasting six
great rear driver wheels for negotiating the Blue Ridge, were raising steam.

With a jolt that mashed everyone together, the lead train suddenly lurched uphill, slipped back as its driver wheels lost trac-
tion, then gathered steam and strained westward—back toward
the Shenandoah. Rebels along the track stood gawking, amazed
that Old Jack was heading back to the Valley he had abandoned
only yesterday. Surely he was crazy!

The destination proved to be Staunton, whose population was
as amazed as the Army. The town had felt itself within Union
grasp since April 17, when news came of the Confederate retreat
from Rude's Hill. Two days later a false alarm about Yankees "at
the gates" emptied Staunton's hospitals and banks; patients and
money were hurried off to Charlottesville. The Staunton *Spectator*
followed. General Johnson pulled back to within six miles of Staunton and began to evacuate his stores from the town. Then came
whispers that the Valley Army had disappeared from Swift Run
Gap. Whispers grew into rumors that the Army had left the
Shenandoah for good, touching off a new wave of refugees. May 4
began with a report that 10,000 Federals were descending on
Johnson, and the remaining citizens prepared for the worst. Instead, about noon and without as much as a rumor preceding it,
the Valley Army chugged into town from the east. Jackson's
muddy, barefoot boys entered Staunton as conquering heroes.
Tension dissolved into a county-fair atmosphere.[14]

Jackson arrived on horseback before dark and was worried at
the carnival mood his troops had created. He immediately sealed
off the town to prevent word of this celebration reaching the
enemy. Country people who came in to greet friends and relatives
with the Army were not permitted to return home. Strong picket
detachments were posted on roads leading to Harrisonburg, and
rumors flared that Banks would be attacked. Jackson detailed
some riders to sweep west toward Johnson's forces and arrest all
persons heading that way.[15] New rumors claimed Frémont was the
target.

A battle was obviously near, because Jackson was marshaling
every man within his District, a sure sign of a fight. The Army's

infantry and artillery concentrated around Staunton during the next two days. Ten of Ashby's companies reported for duty. Jackson previously had accepted Superintendent Smith's offer to field the Virginia Military Institute Corps of Cadets,[16] and the cadets paraded smartly into Staunton. In solid ranks and natty gray uniforms, the 200 youths sparked much admiration, especially among the girls.[17]

The concern with appearance even touched Jackson. Perhaps because he was again around the cadets he had taught to be neat, he checked his own grooming. He got a haircut and retired the United States Army uniform he had worn until then. In its place he donned the coat and trousers of a Confederate major general,[18] and, correctly attired, he reviewed the Corps of Cadets in a formal parade. The ladies made a splendid outing of the review, and the spirit of romantic adventure flickered once again in the Shenandoah.[19]

Yet romance never replaced hard work in the Valley Army, as was evidenced by its final victory in the month-old struggle to salvage the B & O locomotive 199. That giant had resisted all manner of attempts to extract it from the bog into which it had overturned within sight of Staunton's rail yard; yet by working literally day and night, persistent Southern engineers at length dragged it free, and rebel infantry detraining from Mechum River Station saw the 199 being reassembled on the tracks of the Virginia Central. Federal informers trapped inside Staunton by the Southern cavalry net ought to have made note of this victory, for it revealed something of importance: these rebels did not give up easily.[20]

Jackson had prodded efforts on the 199, but most of his attention while at Staunton was devoted to other matters. He learned that Brigadier General Edward Johnson's vestige of the Army of the Northwest included six battle-hardened regiments—25th, 31st, 44th, 52d, and 58th Virginia and 12th Georgia—and three batteries: Lusk's, Raine's, and Rice's. Johnson had organized his infantry into two brigades of three regiments each and had done a creditable job holding them together against superior numbers during a long, isolated winter. A West Pointer twice breveted for gallantry during the Mexican War, Johnson was a fighter, and he was well liked by his men. At Jackson's orders, Hotchkiss established liaison with Johnson, borrowed some of his men, and reconnoitered the vanguard of Frémont's forces under General Milroy.[21]

Frémont's vanguard had been the Army's target since leaving Swift Run Gap, but the problem was how to get at it. A rough equilibrium had existed in the Shenandoah during late April, and the Valley Army's shift to Staunton had not greatly changed that balance. The rebels needed some strategic opening to gain the initiative, and with timing so perfect it appeared foreordained, the Yankees provided that opening. Banks withdrew to New Market from Harrisonburg[22] (preparatory to dispatching Shields to Fredericksburg), a move which eased pressure on Staunton from the north. Hotchkiss returned to Valley Army Headquarters late on May 6 with additional good news. Milroy had recoiled to the west, and Johnson was already on his trail. The Army unexpectedly had been given the breathing room it needed, and it did not hesitate. Jackson joined Johnson's pursuit of Milroy with all of his brigades early on May 7.[23] Jackson was so intent on shrouding the goal of this march that he slipped away from his staff that morning and departed Staunton by the road south to Lexington. Only later did he detour by a side path to the road which led west from Staunton and upon which the Army was marching. Even members of the staff were so ignorant of the General's intentions that, when they mounted to follow him, they knew merely that Jackson had departed for Lexington and accordingly rode south.[24]

When the errant staffers overtook the Army, it was in the foothills of the Alleghenies. Tiered ridges loomed above it. The column leaned into the ascent, and the rebels began to climb.

For those of the Valley Army who once had styled themselves "Loring men" during the march on Romney, this route was familiar: most of them had sweated over these slopes on their first marches of the war. One of the V.M.I. cadets now marching with the Valley Army, B. A. Colonna, had been with the 21st Virginia briefly when it left Staunton during the summer of 1861. Catching sight of the 21st today, Colonna had to reflect on the changes eleven months had introduced. In June 1861 each company of the regiment was allotted four Conestogas to haul trunks and tents. Many companies had hired additional vehicles for still more personal baggage. Almost all men had started with hundred-pound packs full of "necessities"—items that gradually were thrown away as the owner realized what it meant to march like a pack mule. One rebel wrote of those early days:

> After we had trudged along some five miles in a sweltering sun, I tried to give my six-shooter away, but could not find any one to accept it, and over in the bushes I threw it. I then unbuckled my Damascus blade, made an offer of that, but was likewise refused, and it was thrown into the bushes. I then tried to give away a blanket, but no one would accept, so away it went. I thought, probably, the war would end before the winter. By the time we reached the summit of the mountain nearly all the men in the regiment had disposed of their extra appendages by leaving them in the bushes.[25]

Colonna had witnessed all of this eleven months earlier, but now everything he saw had a lean, strictly utilitarian look. There were no tents and no trunks. The entire 21st possessed only a handful of wagons. The soldiers carried no more than a musket, a light haversack, and one blanket. Colonna laughed: "I doubt whether the whole of Jackson's army had as much impedimenta as the 21st had on leaving Staunton in 1861."[26]

Southern uniforms, or the lack of them, also amused the neat Colonna. The Army had grown shabby as a year of war tattered the bright attire of the previous spring. Comfort rather than looks was now the single criteria for apparel. Civilian clothes abounded. Stiff boots had given way to brogues with wide, thick bottoms and flat heels. The towering busbies and shakos that adorned the ranks —and blew off in a strong wind—during the early days had been replaced with homemade slouch caps. Dick Waldrop of the 21st Virginia ambled along in a pair of pants at least six sizes too big and with legs the size of salt sacks; he loved them, for they allowed plenty of stretching room.[27]

Stragglers had grown wise with their ways too. A standard joke had it that an accomplished straggler could feign more misery, spin more tales of woe, and find more to eat than ten ordinary soldiers. Colonna recollected many stragglers along the way "looking unhappy."[28] Many others ranged far beyond the roadside. Ed Moore and Clem Fishburne of the Rockbridge Artillery, for example, schemed to make a sidetrip to visit some young lady friends when the Army left Staunton. Fishburne backed out at the last moment, and Moore went on alone. The attractive girls regaled him with food and drink, and he did not rejoin the Army until the close of its next battle.[29]

Those in ranks on a given day resorted to gibes and banter to lessen their fatigue. Caparisoned officers were a sure target, and the happy ridicule one regiment could dump upon the unwary lieutenant who sported a feathered cap or a braided coat would fill a tome. The same sort of greeting was directed at members of different branches. Filing around a cannon stuck in the mud, infantry and cavalry alike would rack their brains for catcalls to worry the gun crew.[30] But the infantry's special target was the cavalry, or, as the foot soldiers called them, the "Buttermilk Rangers." Infantrymen had a secret envy of those who escaped walking and exacted a merciless verbal revenge. A mounted company was greeted with hoots and howls: "Where's your buttermilk jug? . . . Jump down and carry that crow bag . . . Mister, let me pop a cap on your little gun." Sometimes the marchers would cry with mock alarm: "Jim, stop. Don't cut that roll from the back of the gentleman's saddle." If the rider fell for the prank and twisted around, he was jeered all the more.

One day a lone trooper was to retaliate mightily for such harassment. Meeting a foot column, he endured the usual gibes in silence until someone mocked the courage of all horsemen with the supreme insult: "Ten thousand dollars for a dead cavalry-man."

The trooper reined up and retorted: "I tell you what, if this war lasts much longer, damned if I don't give ten thousand dollars for a live infantryman." The thought struck home, and the trooper departed in peace.[31]

When circumstances made it worthwhile, there could be combined operations. An old cannoneer recalled one stratagem: "Artillerymen, who had tender consciences (and no muskets), seldom if ever shot stray pigs, but they did sometimes, as an act of friendship, wholly disinterested, point out to the infantry a pig which seemed to need shooting, and by way of dividing the danger and responsibility of the act, accept privately a choice part of the deceased."[32]

If a messmate was dipping too deeply into the company pot, his companions would sneak the extra food from his haversack and substitute rocks.[33] And if a boy wandered away from his regiment during the night and asked directions of a strange unit, everyone within hearing would answer, each differently. Roaring with laughter, they would chant: "Does your mother know you are out?"[34]

Such was the Valley Army as it clambered into the Alleghenies. The troops had changed the military to conform to their own notions as fully as they had been molded by it. These rebels were not professionals, often were boyish, but they would prove themselves fierce fighters.

II

The pursuit of Milroy took the rebels into Highland County, rough country where there was great opportunity for, and danger of, ambush. Johnson ambushed a regiment of the Federal rearguard on May 7, killed a few, and herded the rest westward. He also bagged a prisoner who boasted that Milroy had 6,000 men and was about to receive 6,000 more. Later that day Union artillery appeared out of nowhere to shell Jackson's brigades and forced them to retire a short distance.[35] That shift widened to a five hours' march the gap between Johnson and Jackson. The enemy now certainly knew the former had been reinforced; Jackson hoped, however, that Milroy might yet be ignorant that the entire Valley Army was present.

Jackson was stirring before 5 A.M. the next day,[36] riding ahead with Hotchkiss to catch Johnson. They began to pass Johnson's rear units that afternoon on the slopes of Bull Pasture Mountain near the village of McDowell, where Milroy was reportedly encamped. Leaving the main road, Hotchkiss ushered Stonewall up a narrow, boulder-clogged gorge tufted with dead and stunted brush. The gorge grew steeper, parted around a stand of young pines and leveled into a large spur of Bull Pasture Mountain called Sitlington's Hill where Johnson was arraying his advanced regiments. The officers exchanged salutes and rode out to discuss the terrain.[37]

The rebels were confronted with two ridges running roughly parallel. Sitlington's Hill, where Jackson, Johnson, and Hotchkiss

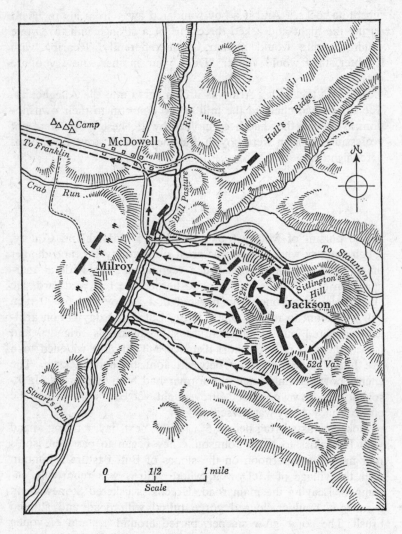

6. Action at McDowell, May 8, 1862.
Redrawing of map prepared under the direction of Jedediah Hotchkiss
for William Allan's *History of the Campaign of General T. J. (Stonewall) Jackson in the Shenandoah Valley.*

were standing, formed part of the long eastern side of this parallel. About a mile away (and west of the Bull Pasture River) was a place called McDowell, a tiny mountain crossroads. The enemy camps lay around McDowell and along the western rim of the parallel ridge. The rebels held higher ground and might have decimated Milroy's camps with their guns, except that the sole approach to the rebel heights, the gorge through which Jackson and Hotchkiss had just come, seemed impassable to artillery. Storming the Federal lines was equally impracticable. The enemy rested on the west bank of the rain swollen Bull Pasture River. The bridge across that stream bore the Staunton–Parkersburg Pike, which snaked down Bull Pasture Mountain and joined the bridge just in front of Northern artillery.[38]

Jackson fanned his scouts to search for some path by which to attack and sent Hotchkiss to devise a means to bring artillery to Sitlington's Hill. In the meantime, Jackson's three brigades were some miles to the rear, so an immediate attack was out of the question. Old Jack left Johnson to defend the front and joined his staff at the base of Bull Pasture Mountain.

Johnson was troubled by one aspect of his position. The summit of Sitlington's Hill was a rough curve with the convexity towards the enemy. The ends of the curve rose into shaley spines and offered good defensive ground, but not so the middle, which was vulnerable from several sides. Johnson deployed his aggressive 12th Georgia in this middle sector. To its left went the 52d and 58th Virginia. To the right went the 44th Virginia. Somewhat to the 44th's right rear was the defile leading down from Sitlington's Hill, the only route open to the Southerners. As they arrived, the 25th and 31st Virginia were placed in reserve near that defile. On the slopes of Sitlington's Hill beyond the front lines, snipers from both armies were already at work.[39]

About 4:30 P.M. the skirmish fire swelled.[40] Federal gunners backed their gun carriages into V-shaped holes to gain elevation and began hammering the Confederate crest.[41] Rebel pickets on the right scampered in shouting the enemy was behind them, and blue regiments smashed against the 44th Virginia. Johnson quickly had to empty his reserve. He sent the 25th Virginia to bolster the 44th and ordered the 31st to a wooded hillock on the far right commanding the gorge, while he anxiously counted new

Northern regiments threading across the Bull Pasture bridge.
Evidently the enemy was reinforced. Perhaps it was the 6,000
men his prisoner had boasted of yesterday. The approaching
Union column seemed too thin for that number, but its weight was
soon banging against Johnson's right and making the fight "very
terrific." Johnson appealed to the nearest of Jackson's brigades,
Taliaferro's, for help.[42]

Repulsed at first, the Federals probed around the extreme Confederate right. After less than an hour of heavy combat the Virginians on the right expended their ammunition and surrendered a
portion of the crest, and the 31st Virginia was in danger of losing
its vital hillock near the gorge.[43] Such was the situation when General Taliaferro's infantry began to appear. No longer the bickering
subordinate he had been at Romney in January, Taliaferro hurled
his men at the enemy. His 23d Virginia joined the 25th in a
mulish defense. A few companies of Fulkerson's 37th Virginia
arrived ahead of the rest and moved to reinforce the 31st.[44]

With night approaching, the enemy massed against the Confederate center. Rebels here stood on lower ground than those on the
flanks, and evening shadows were stretching out so as to veil the
enemy on the slopes below the center. Silhouetted against the
lighter sky, the 12th Georgia made an excellent target and took
severe losses without being able to reply effectively. Orders were
given to evacuate this exposed ground, but the Georgians
screamed they would not run from the enemy. Several times their
colonel dragged one end of the regiment back only to see it rush
out again as he went to withdraw the other wing. Boys from the
44th Virginia also refused to occupy a reserve post and joined the
firing line with other units.[45] The flow was in two directions, however. Rebels on the left were making an awkward attempt at volley fire, a rotating drill whereby one rank stepped out to fire, then
retired a few paces and lay on the ground to reload while the next
rank delivered its volley. The brigade commander, Colonel W. C.
Scott, watched with rising anger as the volleys grew more ragged,
the pauses to reload longer, and the distance some men retired
greater. As the firing increased against the center, some of Scott's
men fell back even farther and burrowed into the ground for shelter. Scott tried to rouse them with appeals to pride, and when that
failed he began to ride over them, forcing the shirkers into line.[46]

7. "Following Stonewall." A wartime sketch by Confederate artist William L. Sheppard depicting the march on Romney. (Courtesy of the Museum of the Confederacy)

8. *below:* A highly romanticized depiction of Ashby's exit from Winchester on March 12, 1862. The scene is typical of the myths that grew up around Ashby. (From *Wearing the Gray,* by John Esten Cooke, New York, 1868)

9. *opposite, above:* Captain R. P. Chew, commander of Ashby's mounted battery. (U. S. Signal Corps Photo No. 111-BA-1251, Brady Collection, in the National Archives. Courtesy of the National Archives)

10. *opposite, below:* Typical Valley Army cavalry men. (Courtesy of the Library of Congress)

11. Recruiting at Woodstock when the war was still a romantic adventure. (Courtesy of the Virginia State Library)

Both sides were now losing cohesion. Several battalions of straying Federals wandered up a dark draw to within fifty yards of Scott's line and shattered it with a surprise volley. The rebels fled, as did the Yanks, who were startled by their own fire.[47] Colonel Samuel Gibbons of the 10th Virginia was killed and his regiment frittered away in stopgap counterattacks. General Johnson crumpled down with his ankle torn apart; Taliaferro took charge and skillfully deployed to hold all night if necessary.[48]

Johnson was carried from the field; his wound was serious and would keep him out of action for months. Jackson met his ambulance halfway down the mountain. Concerned about protocol, Stonewall had sat out the battle, because, having delegated Johnson to hold the front, he felt the presence of a higher ranking officer would interfere. Pausing to reassure the writhing Johnson, Jackson quickly took hold. He ordered Hotchkiss to tell Taliaferro to hang on until he could bring Winder's 1st Brigade up from the rear. Campbell's 2d Brigade was already on its way up the clogged gorge to the battle. Unable to make headway on horseback through the jammed crowd of Campbell's infantry, Hotchkiss stumbled up on foot to find chaos. Hundreds of men were roving about shouting for comrades or looking for their units. Those still on the line were mingled together like a swarm of bees.[49]

Despite the confusion, Taliaferro was able to hurl Campbell's regiments to the right and blunt a final enemy attempt to turn that flank. About 9 P.M. the musketry sputtered to a conclusion. Fires immediately blazed around McDowell as General Milroy burned his camps and retreated northward toward his depots at the village of Franklin.[50] In the springtime of Southern defeat, the Valley Army had won a battle.

Jackson detailed the V.M.I. cadets and the Stonewall Brigade to collect dead and wounded. It was gruesome duty. The wounded had to be manhandled down the gorge on crude stretchers made of rifles and blankets; bounced and sometimes dropped, their shrieks were hideous.[51] Confederate casualties were 75 killed and 428 wounded, with fully a third of that total coming from the 12th Georgia.[52] The rebels had possessed both superior strength (Milroy numbered only 3,000 men, even after reinforcements reached him, and committed only 2,200 to the fight, while Jackson eventually engaged 6,000 troops) and the advantage of high ground, and yet their losses were double those of the enemy. That ratio spoke well of Union courage.

Compared to later engagements of this war, the fight at McDowell was an affair of gnats; by 1864 it would not have been rated as more than a skirmish. It was primarily a stand-up soldier's fight and significant mainly as notice to the enemy that the recently reorganized Confederates were still in the war—yet it was unquestionably a victory. The Federals were gone by morning. Jackson verified their flight and gave Richmond a one-sentence report: "God blessed our arms with victory at McDowell yesterday."[53]

III

The Valley Army spent May 9 regrouping around McDowell; it continued the pursuit of Milroy on the tenth. Jackson wished to shove Milroy as far from Staunton as possible and hoped, in the process, for an opening to cleave into Banks's rear from the Alleghenies. He instructed Ewell (now at Jackson's old camps in Swift Run Gap) to converge upon Banks with him if the Yankee retired because of this thrust.[54]

Jackson next countered a possible march by Banks to reinforce Frémont. The town of Franklin in the Alleghenies and the New Market area in the Shenandoah were linked by roads running through three gaps: the North River, the Dry River, and Brock's. Banks might use any of these roads to move toward Franklin, to which Frémont was reported en route with large forces. Stonewall could not allow such a junction. He took Hotchkiss aside from the marching columns, away from all listeners, and gave him a new assignment. Shaking his long index finger like a schoolmaster, Jackson told Hotchkiss he wanted the gap roads blockaded by dawn of the next morning. "Take a squad of couriers . . ." Jackson continued, "and send me back a messenger every hour telling me where you are and what you have done."[55]

Hotchkiss dug his spurs in and galloped off on a fifty-mile circuit through McDowell, back to the Valley, and into the Alleghenies from the east. Oppressed by a sense of urgency, he reviewed his task as he rode: first, corral some reliable cavalry—Stonewall already had suggested certain men, but Hotchkiss rejected them because their commander was a drunkard; second, find some tools—the cavalry of course would not have any; third, pinpoint the probable bottlenecks and plug them by daylight. It was the kind of hard duty the Army was learning to expect and to master. Hotchkiss had commandeered Captain Frank Sterrett's company and was trotting into the North River Gap before dawn. The rebels moved dangerously far up that defile, requisitioned axes and crowbars from the trappers who lived thereabouts, and set to work. They burned every bridge along the way. They felled trees and rolled great boulders of limestone across the road. Daylight found the work progressing well, and Hotchkiss moved on by way of Emanuel Church and Ottobine Church to Dry River Gap and completed his task, while a separate detachment did similar work in Brock's Gap. Every sixty minutes Hotchkiss dispatched a rider to Stonewall with news of his progress.[56]

Hotchkiss' couriers overtook the Army as it plowed through tangled country where the only sign of life was an occasional cabin festooned with hunters' trophies: antlers, bearskins, and turkey wings. One day's head start allowed the enemy to hang just out of rebel reach behind a smoke screen they laid down by setting fire to the forests.[57] Often unable to see to either side, the Confederates crept onward through smoke and gusts of fire, growing more weary and disgruntled every hour. Their misery was heightened as the supply train fell behind and rations grew scarce.[58]

Trying to supply an army the destination of which he never knew, attempting to prod a wagon train along a road that was no better than a buffalo trail, Quartermaster Harman found his own version of Hell in the Alleghenies. Advance planning was impossible. Several times he ventured to ask the objective, which finally brought him a stern rebuke from Stonewall. That was none of Harman's concern, snapped the General, who handled the inquiry with characteristic want of tact. Instead of doing anything for Harman, the General crabbed that he was not working hard enough. Crusty, profane Harman "thanked him for his candor and told him I would resign."[59] At that Stonewall admitted much of

the fault had been his own; he subsequently became "quite
friendly," and Harman joined Ashby as one of the few men ever
to back Jackson "square down."[60]

Outside Franklin, thirty miles north of McDowell, Milroy cam-
ouflaged his lines with acres of burning hardwoods and made a
stand. Jackson sparred with him on Sunday, May 11.[61] The rebels
endured a sweltering night and formed on Monday morning looking for a fight. As usual, they guessed wrong. Orders for the day
specified morning worship[62]: Old Jack was making up for the
religious services which military necessity required him to cancel
the previous day. Major Dabney donned his robes to preach in a
wide sward that rose gently to a wall of pines. His theme was the
war as God's punishment for sin, a message punctuated by the roll
of Northern artillery and the billowing pine smoke that surrounded the Army.[63]

Jackson attended this worship, and observers did not think he
stirred an inch during Dabney's entire sermon. Devout as he was,
however, his attention occasionally roamed from his friend's
words to the sound of Northern guns. Frémont's arrival at
Franklin with the bulk of his army was imminent, if not already
accomplished, which discouraged Jackson from seeking another
battle in the mountains. Beyond this, there was the situation in the
Valley to preoccupy him. Banks was obviously preparing some
major new maneuver from New Market, a possibility which
greatly worried General Lee at Richmond. Writing to Jackson on
May 8, Lee had surmised that Banks's withdrawal from Harrisonburg to New Market betrayed his intention to reinforce General
McDowell at Fredericksburg. Lee accordingly thought Ewell
should move from Swift Run Gap to strike Banks on the march to
Fredericksburg.[64] This message gnawed at Stonewall, because he
did not want to lose Ewell and because he did not believe Banks
would abandon the Valley. And even if Banks were to leave the
Shenandoah, to hurl Ewell upon him alone was to foolishly scatter
the Southern forces Lee himself had wisely sought to unify. Yet
Banks clearly was about to do something, and with Frémont at
Franklin, Jackson's hope to do Banks serious damage by carving
into his rear from the Alleghenies vanished. It was evident Stonewall must try something else to stop Banks; everything he could
now expect from the drive into the Alleghenies had been achieved.

Jackson had begun this drive with more than his normal secrecy. The demonstration before Harrisonburg on April 30 was not an invitation to battle but a ploy to mask the march of Ewell's division, which occupied the camps at Swift Run Gap while Federal scouts were thrown back from there. Jackson then attempted to slip away so quietly that Banks would not notice the substitution. In case he was spotted on the march to Port Republic, he gave the appearance of abandoning the Shenandoah by crossing the Blue Ridge to Mechum Station. When he reached Staunton he circled the city with pickets and allowed no one to leave, lest news spread that the Valley Army was there. Aware his own movements were the talk of talkative civilians, Jackson had left Staunton on May 7 by a road he did not intend to follow.

Ingenious as these deceptions were, they were not initially successful. Banks detected Ewell's arrival and the direction of Stonewall's march by May 2[65] and informed Frémont that Milroy was the probable target.[66] Banks lost contact with the Valley Army shortly thereafter, however, and would not rediscover its exact whereabouts for three weeks. Milroy's intelligence provided additional warning; he knew of Jackson's arrival at Staunton by May 7.[67] He had time to call for aid and reach the comparative safety of McDowell, where reinforcements joined him on the morning of the battle.

The purpose of the Valley Army's Allegheny drive was similar to that of the Romney expedition. On May 1, as on January 1, the junction of two Federal fronts was a possibility Jackson had to prevent. Now, as four months earlier, his initial concern was to batter the Union fronts apart, so he went after Frémont. The latter's advance was crowded back into Franklin and the gaps between that city and the Harrisonburg–New Market area were blocked. Banks and Frémont thus could not unite any place south of New Market, and a meeting north of New Market would demand several extra days. Jackson thereby gained priceless time and space, while also relieving the pressure on Staunton. Further, he had Lee's permission to augment the Valley Army with Johnson's command.[68] (The question of whether Lee's permission was sufficient to authorize this union highlighted an increasingly dangerous uncertainty in the Confederate high command. But with Johnson wounded there was no one with sufficient experience to take over his little force, and with Frémont fifty miles from Staunton, there was little need for it in the Alleghenies. The practicalities of the situation dictated that these rebels join the Valley Army, and Jackson knew there were some permissions better left unquestioned.) His men had wondered: What next? Old Jack's answer had been to keep the enemy divided and to clear the Southern flank in the mountains.

Jackson now turned to the principal object of his operations: Banks—and by his defeat, the immobilization of McDowell's hosts at Fredericksburg and those of McClellan on the Peninsula as well. Jackson received additional word from Ewell concerning Banks's activities no later than May 13.[69] Banks was indeed preparing to march, and Ewell calculated it would be to Fredericksburg. Jackson still suspected Banks would aim for a junction with Frémont, probably around Winchester, yet Stonewall knew he could not predict the enemy's movements. He realized only that it was time to return to the Valley. He started back to the McDowell crossroads after Dabney gave a benediction on May 12, and his correspondence with Ewell took up a relentless theme: "What news have you from Banks?"[70]

That same day, even as Jackson began his march, Banks divided his command, part of it leaving New Market for Strasburg with him, while Shields's division traversed the Massanutten Gap and pivoted northward in the direction of Manassas Gap and the road to Fredericksburg. A hundred miles to the east, General McDowell had crossed the Rappahannock, occupied Fredericksburg, and begun to rebuild the bridges there.[71]

Jackson's return to the Shenandoah exhausted his already weary men. Food remained scarce; stragglers abounded.[72] Private Jim Hall of the 31st Virginia wore through his shoes. There were no extra pairs, but in the Valley Army having no shoes was not an excuse to stop. Hall had to keep marching; one day he limped eighteen miles barefoot.[73] The V.M.I. cadets were knotting their shoes together with twine.[74] A rainstorm destined to last five days had broken on May 12. The torrents meant wet clothes and blankets, mildewed food, useless firewood, swollen creeks to ford, and dirty springs from which to drink—all that and the endless, bottomless mud.[75] The Liberty Hall Volunteers exploded with profane disgust when their company wagon lost a wheel and their mess gear clattered into the muck.[76]

Jackson chose this improbable time to impose a further strain with new march regulations. Henceforth, each regiment would halt every hour, stack arms, and rest exactly ten minutes; at no other time could men leave ranks. Exactly one hour was allotted for lunch. Only tools, mess equipment, and officers' baggage were to be carried in the wagons. Roll would be called immediately before leaving and immediately after reaching every camp. The regulations filled a page of tightly spaced fine print, of which one section read: "During marches men will be required not only to keep in ranks, but the proper distances must be preserved, as far as practicable, thus converting a march, as it should be, into an important drill, that of habituating the men to keep in ranks. . . ." Jackson's emphasis lay with that last phrase about keeping the men in ranks. Straggling must end. Appropriately, this order was headed: "Headquarters, Valley District, *Camp on the Road.*"[77]

Regulations, fatigue, rain, hunger, and bitterness over the draft proved too great a torment for fragments of the 27th Virginia, and, near McDowell village, they rebelled. Their original twelve-month enlistments had expired, and they flung down their arms and proclaimed themselves free men. Colonel Grigsby appealed to Jackson for guidance.

When Grigsby's appeal arrived at Headquarters, Major Dabney was on hand and saw Jackson erupt. "What is this but mutiny?" he roared. "Why does Colonel Grigsby refer to me to know what to do with a mutiny. He should shoot them where they stand."

Dabney wrote quickly as the General dictated ruthless instructions: Grigsby was to parade the mutineers before their regiment at once, briefly explain the nature of their misconduct, and offer an opportunity to resume duty. All those refusing would be shot within the minute. Faced with immediate execution, the rebellious troops moped off to camp and caused no further difficulties.[78]

More than anything else, this abortive rebellion reflected the physical exhaustion of these men. Only with fatigue overcoming reason could they have fancied Jackson might yield to them, and the failure of their attempt was total. The incident did not even break the Army's pace. It struggled to the western edge of the Shenandoah by May 15. Jim Hall hobbled another fifteen miles barefoot that day.[79] Joe Kaufman summarized the day in his diary: "I feel very much worsted. It has begun to rain again. Very hungry."[80]

Ironically, the only men still eager to continue the drive, the V.M.I. cadets, left the Army on May 15. The Board of Visitors of their college had decreed that they must return to studies. Jackson wished to retain them for coming battles and was as disappointed as the cadets. They headed for Lexington with long faces but not without an order from Jackson commending them for "the promptitude and efficiency with which they have assisted in the recent expedition."[81]

Friday, May 16, was officially proclaimed by President Davis as a day of fasting and prayer throughout the Confederacy. The Valley Army remained in camp in observance of this proclamation. Divine services were held, which Hospital Orderly John Apperson believed was a fine idea; prayer had been ignored recently by many, although he thought the Army had already been fasting for quite enough time.[82] The rain continued, and the troops had neither shelter from it nor protection from the spongy ground. Captain H. W. Wingfield of the 58th Virginia wrote in his diary that the camp was "so rainy and disagreeable . . . we are but little rested."[83] It occurred to Ted Barclay of the Headquarters Guard that he turned eighteen today. He could not have imagined a year earlier that he would spend this birthday hunched beneath a downpour wearing a uniform he had not been able to wash for three weeks.[84]

Ashby's cavalry, meanwhile, continued to romp about the Shenandoah. Jackson detailed some troopers to drive captured cattle out of the Alleghenies. They did so, then turned the herd into a field and left it to scatter.[85] Ashby was sick during early May and unable to accompany the Army to McDowell or give any leadership to the riders left in the Valley.[86] During these days, Bill Wilson, a nineteen-year-old transferee to the cavalry, recorded much jolly fun in his diary as many gallants took up racing to amuse themselves.[87] One company had not had a roll call in weeks, and a payroll did not exist, but no one seemed to care.[88]

Mutiny in the Stonewall Brigade, a frazzled Army, an unreliable cavalry—Jackson had these problems as he prayed on May 16, and, as he would discover within forty-eight hours, he had still others.

DICK EWELL'S DILEMMA

*Gen. Jackson has stayed much longer
than I anticipated.*

—Richard S. Ewell

A fortnight prior to the Confederate day of fasting and prayer, on April 30, Major General Richard S. Ewell's division had entered the Shenandoah. Eager to meet the famous Stonewall, Ewell's boys paraded through Swift Run Gap four abreast with every band blaring *Listen to the Mocking Bird*.[1] Their introduction to Stonewall was to find him gone without a trace.

The neighborhood did, however, boast many attractive girls whose acquaintance Ewell's boys could make. Twenty-three-year-old Captain John Nesbit headed a company of mountaineers from a Georgia regiment. Sharing a common bond with the Blue Ridge people, the Georgians were quickly at ease—". . . it was so homelike," recollected Nesbit.[2] His mountain men found their way to many pretty girls, and any they missed were looked after by an Alabama regiment. To insure high times at their nightly dances, the rebels also learned the whereabouts of neighborhood stills, and the war passed as painlessly as they could desire.[3]

If these newcomers to the Shenandoah were much like Jackson's boys, their commander, Richard Ewell, likewise shared traits with Stonewall. He was highly exacting. Ewell was particularly enraged to receive a "don't know" for an answer, and his couriers dreaded him more than the Yankees when they "didn't know." He would not accept information relayed from "reliable sources";

what his scouts had not themselves seen, Ewell did not want to hear.[4] Ewell, like Jackson, could also be eccentric to the point of comedy. His camps chuckled over the fact that Ewell, an excellent cook, restricted himself to a concoction called frumenty (hulled wheat boiled in milk with sugar, raisins, and egg yolk) in deference to a possibly imaginary ulcer. He habitually tilted his bald, bomb-shaped head to one side to talk, and when he spoke it was with an explosion of soldier's profanity—all uttered with a noticeable lisp.

Ewell's had been a life dedicated to the profession of arms. Acceptance at West Point had been a boyhood dream, which Ewell fulfilled when he entered the Academy in 1836. As a cadet he displayed solid academic skills and excellence in equitation; he was, in fact, the only rider in the Valley whose horsemanship rivaled Ashby's. Ewell graduated in 1840, relished combat during the Mexican War and spent the next decade and a half as a cavalry captain chasing Indians across the western frontier. Ewell was good at that and liked to boast that he had learned everything about leading 50 cavalrymen and had forgotten everything else. "In this he did himself injustice . . . ," objected one of Ewell's admirers, who noted that Ewell displayed a fine tactical eye on the battlefield and maneuvered units as large as a division with ease.

Resigning from the U. S. Army to join the South at the start of the war, Ewell won rapid promotion in the Confederacy. He was commissioned a lieutenant colonel of cavalry in April 1861 and had a brigadier general's stars and an infantry brigade by June. He became a major general by January 1862 and found himself charged with a full infantry division. That frightened him a little, for a year earlier he had been a cavalry captain. He lay awake some nights at Swift Run Gap wondering what to do with this division, and occasionally he demanded of his officers: "What do you suppose President Davis made me a major general for?"[5]

Ewell's division, like its general, had not had an opportunity to prove itself during a frustratingly inactive winter with Johnston's army at Centreville. Few of its regiments had seen action, but its mettle was sound. Brigadier General Isaac Trimble, an 1822 graduate of West Point who had served well in the U. S. Army and as a Baltimore railroad executive, headed one of Ewell's brigades. At sixty years of age Trimble was a fragment of ancient history to his young soldiers, but he knew something about modern war. In April of 1861, while others were prattling about the romance of war, the white-thatched Trimble had commandeered a train and roared north from Baltimore burning bridges to delay Federal troops in transit to Washington. Nor did age soften Trimble's discipline; during the division's recent reorganization, when an officer Trimble deemed to be competent and brave was voted out, he compelled a new election and made it clear who was to win.[6] His command was a representative collection of deep South units: the 15th Alabama, 16th Mississippi, 21st Georgia, and 21st North Carolina.

Brigadier General Arnold Elzey, a Marylander, headed another of Ewell's brigades. Elzey, a West Pointer, had served with distinction in almost every battle of the Mexican War and had led the decisive Southern counterattack at the First Battle of Manassas. His command, though fielding only two instead of the normal four regiments, was among the South's best. The 13th Virginia received its excellent initial training from an officer the war would make immortal, A. P. Hill. The 13th was currently under Colonel James Walker, who, as a V.M.I. cadet, had won immortality at the Institute by challenging then Professor Jackson to a duel. Elzey's other regiment was the 1st Maryland of Colonel Bradley Johnson. A Princeton graduate, lawyer, and former Maryland state's attorney, Johnson was something of an orator, a skill he would make use of in the Valley. His troops were earnest men who cared enough about the Confederacy to filter south to its armies, although at its arrival at Swift Run Gap the regiment was wracked by morale problems. Some of the Marylanders had decided the Confederate Conscription Act did not apply to their state, and that therefore the ban against transferring branches of the service likewise did not apply to them. The Confederate Government thought otherwise, and much bitterness resulted when the Marylanders' petition for a transfer to the cavalry was rejected.[7]

Completing the infantry was Brigadier General Richard Taylor's Louisiana Brigade, consisting of the 6th, 7th, 8th, and 9th Louisiana and an attached infantry battalion. The 6th Louisiana was essentially an oversized gang of raucous dock workers from the New Orleans waterfront—"hardy fellows, turbulent in camp and requiring a strong hand . . ." was Taylor's estimate of them.

The 7th, on the other hand, was the sort of polished military machine Jackson sought to make of the Valley Army, and it was considered capable of stopping a herd of elephants. The 8th was a regiment of French-speaking Acadians, most of whom had never strayed more than ten miles from their bayou homes before the war. Gallic pride prompted them to field a fine regimental band, and they were likely to finish even the weariest day with a concert. The 9th came from the privileged world of north Louisiana, where large plantations sprawled along the Mississippi. Wealthy planters and their sons made up this regiment.[8] But most amazing of all was Major Roberdeau Chatham Wheat's infantry battalion of so-called "Louisiana Tigers." Cutthroats and hooligans from the back alleys of Mississippi River towns, the Tigers left even their fellow rebels shaking. They were fierce in battle: at Manassas some had thrown away their rifles and charged with knives. They fleeced the dead of both armies under an absurd banner with the words "as gentle as" inscribed beneath a lamb, and only the experienced hand of Major Wheat kept them in tolerable order. Six feet four inches tall and two hundred forty pounds, Wheat had learned to savor combat during the Mexican War, and afterward emerged as a notable soldier of fortune in Cuba, Nicaragua, and Mexico and with Garibaldi in Italy.[9]

General Taylor was also a man who commanded respect. When two of Wheat's men broke into the brigade guardhouse to free some imprisoned Tigers, Taylor had the intruders court-martialed and executed within hours. Even the Tigers were a little tamer after that.[10] A Yale graduate, Taylor had an impressive educational background, having also studied at Harvard and Edinburgh, Scotland. He was the son of former President Zachary Taylor and brother-in-law of Jefferson Davis, and he worked as hard as his connections were good. His brigade's particularly impressive march discipline, for instance, was the product of his strenuous effort. As Johnston withdrew from the Centreville–Manassas area during March, Taylor was disgusted by the rampant straggling, a symptom of indiscipline which infected his own command. He began to root it out at once. He taught his men to bathe their feet at the end of each day, showed them how to heal sores, and gave advice on picking boots. The brigade's standard uniform was modified to include two pairs of boots per man. By riding at the

rear of his command to encourage those who fell behind (sometimes he gave them short lifts as well), Taylor set an example
which his officers copied. The men responded with their best
efforts and soon regarded straggling as a disgrace.[11] Excepting the
tenuous discipline among the Tigers, Taylor's was a model brigade.

Attached to Ewell's splendid division were the 2d and 6th Virginia Cavalry Regiments under Colonel Thomas Munford and
Lieutenant Colonel Thomas Flournoy, respectively, officers who
had schooled their riders well. Two artillery units, Captain A. R.
Courtney's (Richmond) battery and Captain John B. Brockenbrough's Baltimore Light Artillery, were also with the division.[12]
All units were ready for hard fighting. Still, as days and then
weeks passed at Swift Run Gap, the division began to doubt that
it would ever see action under Stonewall.

Ewell shared these doubts, for Jackson had assigned him a passive mission. Stonewall, on the evening of April 30, had returned
to Swift Run Gap from his demonstration outside Harrisonburg to
give Ewell a hurried briefing.[13] He explained that he hoped to
reach Staunton and link up with Johnson. Ewell was to remain in
the Gap where he could block Banks's advance on Staunton. At the
same time, he was to prevent Banks from detaching any portion of
his army out of the Shenandoah, but Ewell could not leave it himself. Jackson emphasized above all that Ewell must not leave the
Valley until he, Jackson, could return from the Alleghenies. Perhaps by design, Ewell's chief of staff, Captain Campbell Brown,
found a copy of the court-martial charges against Garnett in
Stonewall's old headquarters that night.[14]

So Ewell settled down to watch and wait, a wait interrupted by
frequent reminders from Jackson to stay put.[15] Stonewall regarded
co-operation with Ewell as so important that he relaxed his precious silence enough to keep Ewell tolerably up to date on his
movements. He corresponded from Brown's Gap on May 3,[16] and
again the next day, reiterating that he was pressing on to Johnson's aid.[17] Jackson wrote shortly after his arrival in Staunton,[18]
twice on May 6,[19] and again when the Valley Army marched
out of Staunton.[20] At 5:10 A.M. on May 8 Jackson confided his
exact location and Milroy's estimated strength to Ewell.[21] On

May 10 Ewell received Jackson's note that he hoped to cleave into Banks's rear from the west and that Ewell should press Banks if he fell back as a consequence.[22] Of everyone in the Confederacy, Ewell alone received some news about Jackson's Allegheny drive.

But though Ewell knew where Jackson was, he could not understand why he was there. Ewell did not grasp the full complexities of operations in the Shenandoah, and to him it appeared that Jackson was loping farther away on a comparatively insignificant mission—especially when Jackson described the capture of some wagons in one of his dispatches. Wagons, Ewell groused, "General Lee at Richmond will have little use for wagons if all [the Federals] close in around him . . ."[23]

The frequent messages showing Jackson always higher in the Alleghenies made Ewell nervous, a nervousness aggravated by new orders from without the Valley and new enemy moves within it. General Lee wanted action somewhere in central Virginia or the Valley. He was funneling every man he could find to that region, his last hope as McClellan ground toward the Confederate capital and McDowell's threat from Fredericksburg grew. Lee drained other fronts to free a brigade of North Carolinians under Brigadier General L. O'Bryan Branch and ordered it to Gordonsville, twenty-five miles southeast of Swift Run Gap. He scraped together a few more regiments and dispatched them to join Branch. This column was designed to cut the Manassas Gap Railroad, and Lee, on May 5, suggested that Ewell lead the raid at his first opportunity.[24]

Lee's concern remained a shift by Banks to Fredericksburg. He advised Ewell of this possibility on May 6 and again on May 8. He counseled in the message of the sixth that there was no necessity for his (Ewell's) presence at Swift Run Gap if Banks left Harrisonburg, which Banks did that day.[25] Lee on the eighth suggested that Ewell redeploy his division to Gordonsville to intercept Banks if he moved toward Fredericksburg, as appeared increasingly probable.[26]

Lee informed Jackson of his communications with Ewell, and these were the messages which had troubled Stonewall as he listened to Major Dabney's sermon outside Franklin. If they vexed Jackson, they evoked a long string of Ewell's curses. Lee's suggestion of a raid on the Manassas Gap Railroad and the maneuver to Gordonsville both clashed directly with Jackson's desire to have him remain in the Shenandoah. Since Lee had not issued a specific order, the choice between his arrangements and Jackson's was dumped in Ewell's lap. His decision was to stay at Swift Run Gap.

Fresh intelligence soon made Ewell regret this decision. On May 11 he garnered something definite about enemy activity at New Market: Shields was ready to march for Fredericksburg, and the balance of the Federals under Banks was cooking rations for a move to an unknown point. Ewell offered this information to Jackson on May 12.[27] Ewell desperately wanted to attack Shields when he separated from Banks, but he was manacled to Swift Run Gap by Jackson's orders. The best he could do was free Colonel Munford with elements of his 2d Virginia Cavalry to harass Shields. Frustrated by this inadequate measure, Ewell began to recall the stories he had heard of Jackson's insanity. He complained to Munford: ". . . I could crush Shields before night if I could move from here. This man Jackson is certainly a crazy fool, an idiot. . . . Mark my words, if this old fool keeps this thing up, and Shields joins McDowell, we will go up at Richmond."[28]

Colonel Walker of the 13th Virginia arrived at Ewell's headquarters and heard more of the same. "Colonel Walker," Ewell bellowed, "did it ever occur to you that General Jackson is crazy?"

This was a tempting question for Walker. A confrontation with Professor Jackson had cost him his V.M.I. cadetship within months of graduation, and he had shouted some ugly words about Jackson at the time. When Walker mentioned something about this incident, Ewell demanded the whole story. It seemed that while Jackson was butchering a lecture one day, Cadet Walker, who ranked at the head of his class, began to discourse on some more interesting topic. Jackson called for quiet, but the chatter persisted, evidently from Walker's corner. Jackson then resorted to stern punishment, and Walker presented a disrespectful written objection to Jackson's charges. A court-martial followed in which there was much bitter testimony about whether Walker had actually done all the talking. The trial concluded after sixty-two pages of statements with an expelled Walker demanding satisfaction from Jackson on the field of honor. Superintendent Smith was

concerned enough to urge Walker's father to get the livid youth
home before "serious difficulty" erupted. Fortunately this was
done; there was no duel, and Walker went on to enter the University of Virginia Law School.[29] Now, ten years later, Walker's
division commander was inviting him to pitch into his former professor. It was tempting, but Walker replied with a lawyerlike restraint: "I don't know, General. We used to call him 'Fool Tom'
Jackson at the Virginia Military Institute, but I do not suppose he
is really crazy."

That was not the answer Ewell wanted. "I tell you," he ranted,
"he is as crazy as a March hare."[30]

May 14 brought Stonewall's reply to Ewell's information that
Banks and Shields would soon separate, and the reply fortified
Ewell's doubt of Jackson's sanity. Old Jack took only cursory note
that even a portion of Banks's command might head for Fredericksburg. He suspected instead that Banks and Frémont would
seek to unite around Winchester. If Banks did retreat down the
Valley toward Winchester, Jackson wrote, Ewell should pursue
him so vigorously the enemy would fear an immediate attack
should any force be disengaged from the Valley.[31]

Banks was retreating from New Market by now, but additional
orders checked Ewell before he could start after Banks. These orders were from General Johnston, his first in a month. Johnston's
army was drawing nearer Richmond, and as it did, Johnston, like
Lee, begin to think of the forces spread across central Virginia
and the Valley. He was unhappy to discover, however, that Lee
already had begun to maneuver these detachments. On May 10
Johnston dictated a testy complaint to Lee, griping that the government had denied him the information he needed to direct these
forces, forces which were still under his command.[32] It was Johnston's way of telling Lee hands off, and he strengthened it on May
13 with letters to both Jackson and Ewell. The communiqúe to
Jackson has not survived, but the letter to Ewell makes it clear
that Johnston was bluntly reasserting authority over the Valley: "I
have written to Major General Jackson to return to the Valley
near you, and, if your united force is strong enough, to attack
General Banks. Should the latter cross the Blue Ridge to join
General McDowell at Fredericksburg, General Jackson and yourself should move eastward rapidly to join either the army near

Fredericksburg or this one. I must be kept informed of your movements and progress, that your instructions may be modified as circumstances change."[33] Apparently neither Johnston nor Lee had any idea what the other was demanding from the Shenandoah forces, and Johnston's newly expressed intention to modify his orders for that region as circumstances changed made it almost certain that his orders would conflict with Lee's at some point.

The call to action Ewell read in Johnston's letter (received on May 14 or 15) was echoed by the next communications from Jackson. Stonewall reported he had nearly re-entered the Shenandoah and asked the location of the Federal army there and what strength Ewell could mass against it. If Banks was crossing the Blue Ridge, Jackson wanted Ewell to send his cavalry to delay the Federals until the Valley Army could catch up.[34]

Jackson finally hinted a willingness to consider that Union forces could be en route to the east, but the circumstances had changed by this time—Banks and Shields had parted. The former was digging massive earthworks at Strasburg. Rebel cavalry spied Shields marching toward Front Royal on May 13 and again on May 14.[35] Johnston and Jackson both spoke of attacking Banks's army, but Ewell alone comprehended this army was in two separate columns. Given this situation, Ewell judged that Johnston's orders compelled him to track Shields. That course, however, meant abandoning Jackson, and Ewell was not a man to forsake a comrade, even a crazy one. Ewell reviewed his dilemma in a sorrowful letter to his niece:

> I have spent two weeks of the most unhappy I ever remember. I was ordered here to support General Jackson, pressed by Banks. But he [Jackson], immediately upon my arrival, started on a long chase after a body of the enemy far above Staunton. I have been keeping one eye on Banks, one on Jackson, all the time jogged up from Richmond, until I am sick and worn down. Jackson wants me to watch Banks. At Richmond, they want me everywhere and call me off, when, at the same time, I am compelled to remain until that enthusiastic fanatic comes to some conclusion. Now I ought to be en route to Gordonsville, at this place, and going to Jackson, all at the same time. That is, there is reason for all these movements and which one is taken makes it bad for the others. The fact is there seems no head here at all, though there is room for one or two. I

have a bad headache, what with the bother and folly of things. I
never suffered as much with dyspepsia in my life. As an Irishman
would say, "I'm kilt entirely."[36]

Ewell grew frantic for action as he stressed to Jackson: "On
your course may depend the fate of Richmond."[37]

"If Bank goes down the Valley, I wish you to follow him"[38]—
those words of Jackson's lay somewhere in the welter of dispatches scattered atop Ewell's desk (no less than twenty-four
messages by May 16, not counting those written by Ewell). Ewell
recalled Jackson's words on May 16 and pondered them. Following Banks down the Valley would fulfill at least the portion of
Johnston's instructions concerning an attack on Banks. It promised action and a release from this war by courier. The flow of
words might continue for days while Banks burrowed at Strasburg
and Shields marched, and a harassed South needed victory, not
words. With a dispatch ringing of the Valley Army's style, Ewell
decided to go after Banks and summoned the column under General Branch at Gordonsville (which was still poised to strike the
Manassas Gap Railroad) to march on Luray: "You cannot bring
tents," he cautioned Branch. "No mess chests, trunks, etc. . . .
We can get along without anything but food and ammunition."[39]
Ashby had recovered sufficiently to resume his command and
promised to add the weight of his cavalry.[40]

The next day, Saturday, May 17, Ewell's offensive plans were
again mired in the war by courier. Ashby had informed Jackson
that neither Banks nor Shields had left the Valley. However, the
cavalry chief had relayed an erroneous report of Union reinforcements streaming westward from Winchester to Frémont. In a
dispatch Ewell received on the morning of May 17 Jackson therefore advised that Ashby could not unite with his advance. Instead,
Ashby was to completely cloak the Valley Army's march as it
moved directly to Harrisonburg and thence down the Valley. "[I]t
may be," wrote Jackson, "that a Kind Providence will enable us to
unite and strike a successful blow."[41]

Ewell finally knew that Jackson wanted to attack in the Valley
and was coming on fast to get into position. But it seemed too late
for Ewell to join that effort. He now had a report from Colonel
Munford that Shields had crossed the Blue Ridge and was striking

east with 6,000 or 7,000 men and 36 guns.[42] The railroad bridge Jackson had burned at Front Royal in March was fully repaired by May 17, and 1,000 of Banks's men deployed around Front Royal to secure it.[43] The enemy was clearly shifting formidable strength eastward, and Johnston's orders of May 13 apparently required at least Ewell's division to conform to that shift.

Was there no alternative? Ewell dictated a letter to Lee, knowing Lee would forward it to Johnston, in hope of getting a satisfactory response from one of them. Ewell summarized his own orders for Branch to proceed toward Luray and he noted Shields's eastward route of march. Then he posed the essential question in view of Shields's departure from the Valley: What now was his—and Jackson's—mission?[44] Ewell hurried this letter off by courier and waited anxiously for the next post. It brought no definite orders from anyone, and, after rethinking the situation once more, Ewell decided he could not delay moving eastward after Shields any longer. He started preparations for this shift during the afternoon of May 17, conveying word of its necessity to Jackson.[45]

Still later that day, Ewell was handed another bulletin from Jackson. This message had been penned before receipt of Ewell's most recent message and again evidenced Jackson's strategic blindspot regarding Shields. Presuming no Union forces had left the Shenandoah, Jackson directed Ewell to have his division at New Market by May 21. But at least acknowledging the possibility Banks might cross the Blue Ridge, Jackson wrote that if this happened, Ewell must trail the Yankees until he, Jackson, arrived. "But," concluded Jackson, "this cannot be determined upon until we know what the enemy is doing."[46]

Ewell must have endured an attack of his dyspepsia as he studied this dispatch. He knew what the enemy was doing; he could not understand this "enthusiastic fanatic" Jackson. Was that fanatic determined not to accept the division of Banks's army? What would Jackson say when he realized that division? Would he ever realize it? What should be done in the meantime? Should Ewell desert the Shenandoah to follow Shields on the eve of the Valley Army's drive against Banks? Cussing wildly, Ewell's answer was personal action. He would ride at once to face Jackson and settle the matter.

DOWN THE VALLEY

*God grant that we may be enabled
to make a good lick.*

—JOHN HARMAN

On the evening of Saturday, May 17, as Ewell resolved on personal action, the Valley Army re-entered the Shenandoah from the Alleghenies. After those stark, scorched mountains, the budding Valley was paradise. It was the first day in five without rain; long rays of sunlight gradually broadened and fell upon clear lakes and pools. Cherry and peach orchards were in magnificent bloom; fields were lush with clover— ". . . how our weary horses did revel in it," laughed Ed Moore.[1] Camp was made that evening on the road from McDowell village to Harrisonburg at Mount Solon, about twelve miles southwest of Harrisonburg. Prosperous, white-fenced farms surrounded the Army, and famished rebels spread across the countryside.

Ed Moore borrowed a horse to forage cavalry style, finding abundant reward in a comfortable Dutch household. The family felt pity for the hungry Moore and sent him back to the Army with a ham wedged in the saddle with him, a bucket of butter dangling from one arm and a box of pies from the other. His horse promptly took a bad fall, but Moore's instincts were true. He dropped the reins and balanced his treasures; when his mount recovered its feet, not a morsel had slipped an inch.[2]

General Ewell had seen many foragers such as Moore when, after daylight on May 18 he reached the camp at Mount Solon after a long night's ride. What he discovered prompted afresh the thought that Jackson was crazy. Every hour counted now, yet the Valley Army would not march today. It was Sunday, and Jackson did not wish to breach the Lord's peace with warlike activities. Thousands of troops were napping or cooking or washing their clothes[3]; worship services were slated for later in the day. Perhaps the hardest thing Ewell ever did was not to bolt for his division and whisk it away from this "crazy fool" Jackson, but he had come this far, so he kept coming.

Ewell found his way to Stonewall, and the two generals retired to an old mill.[4] Both men knew as they began their discussion that the Confederate war picture was darker now than during March. In April the Battle of Shiloh had been lost in Tennessee, with 10,000 Southern casualties. Strategic Island No. 10 in the Mississippi River had fallen to Union Major General John Pope the day after Shiloh. New Orleans had surrendered by the end of April. Most of Tennessee was under Federal sway by then, and a 100,000-man Federal army was edging toward the Tennessee–Mississippi line. McClellan, meanwhile, was again on the move toward Richmond. Johnston had withdrawn from his Yorktown lines on May 4. The great Confederate naval base at Norfolk, Virginia, was abandoned on May 9, leaving the Southern ironclad *Virginia* without a port and forcing the crew to scuttle it on May 11. The whole tragic prospect was eased only by the Valley Army's success at McDowell, and amid so many disasters it did not seem to count for much. When the little victory was announced in Richmond, McClellan was thirty miles away with 100,000 men, and the city's sidewalk strategists gathered to denounce the Valley Army's offensive as too rash.[5]

Urgently, then, Jackson and Ewell scanned their maps. The situation was as follows: The night before, Jackson finally had accepted the reality of Shields's march for Fredericksburg. Banks was known to be at Strasburg. Frémont's command was hunkered down between Staunton and Winchester at Franklin and did not threaten the rebels immediately; the Union front west of the Valley was briefly neutralized. The Confederate column under General Branch was marching from Gordonsville to Luray in accord with Ewell's orders; Ewell's own division was at the southern end of the Luray Valley.

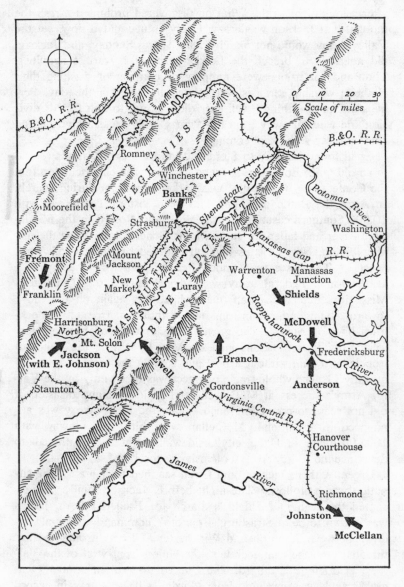

7. General situation, May 18, 1862.

Jackson and Ewell suddenly sat bolt upright. The enemy had committed a classic blunder: the Federals in central Virginia were dispersed in four parts (the detachments of Frémont, Banks, Shields, and McDowell) over a wide arc—just at the moment when the forces of Jackson, Johnson, Ewell, and Branch, a total of 20,000 men, were within three days' march of each other by interior lines within the arc of the Union troops. The possibilities were dazzling. But to exploit this blunder a Southern concentration must be effected and a blow delivered before Shields spearheaded a drive from Fredericksburg and sealed the fate of Richmond.

Robert E. Lee also knew the future of Richmond would be determined during the next week, and he had hinted as much in a letter (dated May 16) which Jackson opened not long before Ewell's arrival. Lee had written under pressure; on May 15 Federal gunboats had bombarded Confederate positions only seven miles outside Richmond. The enemy had been driven off, but might return. Lee gave Jackson this news and advised him again of the importance of stopping what remained of Banks's army in the Valley from moving to Fredericksburg, or possibly to the Peninsula. Then came the crux of his message, Lee's final call for action: "A successful blow struck at [Banks] would delay, if it does not prevent, his moving. . . . Whatever movement you make against Banks do it speedily and if successful, drive him back toward the Potomac, and create the impression, as far as practicable, that you design threatening that line." These were electric words, yet Johnston's recent tirade about interference from Richmond constrained Lee to add a dousing qualifier: "But you will not, in any demonstration you may make [upon Banks], lose sight of the fact that it may become necessary for you to come to the support of General Johnston, and hold yourself in readiness to do so if required."[6]

Jackson handed this letter to Ewell, who read the portion concerning Banks with pleasure. Routing Banks in the Valley might bring the recall of Shields and would certainly check additional detachments from the Shenandoah. Banks was the nearest target Jackson and Ewell could hit and thereby hinder Union movements from Fredericksburg. With Shields gone and Frémont at a halt, Banks was isolated. Now was the time to smash him!

There was a rare opportunity in the Valley, but there was also a problem: Johnston's letter of May 13, which ordered Jackson and Ewell to conform to Union movements east of the Valley. Did this order permit an attack on Banks, or should the rebels be hastening after Shields? Ewell goggled at Jackson through his pop eyes as he offered that question, and Stonewall did not know what to answer. The previous evening, when Stonewall comprehended that Shields was beyond the Blue Ridge, he posed the question of his and Ewell's assignment to Johnston via telegraph. Jackson explained that he planned to unite with Ewell, mash Banks, and knife into the Alleghenies near Strasburg to menace Frémont's rear so as to prevent a renewed effort against Staunton by the Pathfinder. But if Johnston wanted him to move east, he would of course do so. Stonewall had requested specific instructions via telegraph.[7] Since none had come, it was obvious Johnston was undecided or had replied by a mounted courier.

To understand where he stood at this juncture, Old Jack broke down the conflicting orders under which he had campaigned for the past month into their components. Reduced to essentials, they ran something like this:

1. In mid-April Johnston had directed him to protect the Valley while retreating to Swift Run Gap, which Jackson had done.

2. In late April Lee had urged him to strike so as to hinder Union movements from Fredericksburg (thus ultimately relieving pressure on Richmond). Jackson had completed the groundwork for this strike.

3. On May 13, unaware of the division of Banks's army, Johnston had ordered Jackson to pursue "Banks"[8] if the latter crossed the Blue Ridge, which half of "Banks" had done.

4. On May 16, aware of the division of Banks's army but apparently without knowledge of Johnston's desires, Lee had urged Jackson again to smash Banks in the Valley.

5. Conclusion: Jackson was beset with instructions none of which exactly fitted the situation as it existed.

The generals drummed their fingers until Ewell exploded. His division was in the Valley, he exclaimed, and he would follow

Jackson's orders, not Johnston's. If Jackson would give the word, he would lunge down the Valley after Banks, not east after Shields.[8] Lee would certainly approve such a thrust; but as Lee had stressed, his authority over the Valley was at best complementary to that of Johnston, and nothing Jackson and Ewell did for him must impair their ability to respond to Johnston's orders. They would not have such ability if they engaged Banks in the lower Valley. Both men sitting among the floor bags in an ancient Shenandoah mill understood Ewell's proposal strained the scant discretion permitted by Johnston to the absolute limit.

Stonewall said nothing for a moment, then ambition overthrew restraint, and he agreed. History would judge more harshly than Johnston if the opportunity before them was allowed to pass. Jackson formally requested Ewell to prepare a statement of his dilemma and drew up the following solution:

> Headquarters Valley District
> Mount Solon
> May 18, 1862

> Major Gen. R. S. Ewell,
> Commanding Third Division
> Army of the Peninsula:

> General:

> Your letter of this date, in which you state that you have received letters from Generals Lee, Johnston and myself requiring somewhat different movements, and desiring my views respecting your position, has been received. In reply I would state that as you are in the Valley District you constitute part of my command. Should you receive orders different from those sent from these headquarters, please advise me of the same at as early a period as practicable.

> You will please move your command so as to encamp between New Market and Mount Jackson on next Wednesday night, unless you receive orders from a superior officer and that of a date subsequent to the 16th instant.

> I am, General, your obedient servant,

> T. J. Jackson
> Major General[9]

Action at last! Ewell, who avowed an enthusiastic atheism, was thankful enough to attend the Valley Army's morning worship with Jackson. Then they parted, Ewell fairly bouncing onto his horse and thundering off to ready his division.

Stonewall also accelerated, for time was now his principal opponent. Shields would billet at Fredericksburg within the coming week, so the Valley Army must strike quickly. Discipline on the march must be tightened further: the Army was ordered to move automatically at 5 A.M. each morning.[10]

That same day, as Jackson and Ewell conferred, Shields was thirty miles from Fredericksburg.[11]

The Confederate sprint began on May 19. Jackson's column shot across the North River at the village of Bridgewater. Wagons had been placed side by side across the stream with planks laid between the wagons, forming a crude span, but one that served.[12] Couriers spurred ahead of the Army with important orders. Ashby was again directed to gather his riders, sweep Federal scouts back to Strasburg, and nail Union attention to that point.[13] Ewell was again summoned to march for New Market. Evidently some sort of secret code, the message was actually a signal for Ewell to continue toward Luray with the bulk of his division. Only Taylor's Louisiana Brigade was to join Jackson near New Market.[14]

Southern columns were converging on a wide front. On May 20 Branch was near Madison on his way to Luray. Ewell was in the Luray Valley. Jackson reached Harrisonburg and ordered his troops to store their knapsacks. This was Old Jack's cue for hard fighting. "We knew there was some game at hand then," wrote John Casler, "for when General Jackson ordered knapsacks to be left behind he meant business."[15]

From Harrisonburg Jackson's column pushed northward over familiar ground. The march gathered speed along the Valley Pike, and once more the rebels were in sight of Massanutten Mountain. That tangled mass loomed to their right, halving the Valley, impenetrable save for the New Market–Luray Gap. By supper time on May 20 the column had covered almost fifteen miles from Harrisonburg and bivouacked a little south of New Market within sight of the Gap.

Taylor's Louisiana Brigade was not far behind Jackson. His

Louisianians had tramped steadily around the Massanutten all morning on May 20, then pounded north along the Valley Pike. Their entire march was textbook perfect: every soldier was in ranks; every officer was at his post; there was not a single straggler. Late that afternoon the brigade's pelican-bedecked banners rose into view of Jackson's camp, where road-weary men were pulling off their shoes. Troops who have marched twenty miles and more in a day do not take to their feet without cause, but the Louisiana Brigade brought veterans of Kernstown and McDowell to the roadside in awe.[16]

General Taylor's narrative of this moment was exquisite: "Neat in fresh clothing of gray with white gaiters, bands playing at the head of their regiments . . . stepping jauntily as on parade, in open column with arms at 'right shoulder shift,' rays of the declining sun flaming on polished bayonets, the brigade moved down the broad, smooth pike and wheeled onto its camping ground."[17] At the command "Order arms!" hundreds of rifles butted the ground in unison. "Front! Right dress!" and fifty companies aligned without a wobble. These were men for whom there would be much work in the coming days. Probably anticipating a commendation for the excellent discipline of his command, Taylor sought out Jackson, whom he located perched on a fence sucking a lemon.

Jackson received, quizzed, and dismissed Taylor with four sentences, for he was less inclined to talk than ever.[18] Ewell, whose division was still east of the Massanutten in the Luray Valley, had received a new order from Johnston that day. It was dated May 17—it was thus written *before* either Jackson's telegram or Ewell's letter of the seventeenth, asking what was desired of them, could have reached Johnston—and, with hardly more words than had just passed between Jackson and Taylor, it abandoned everything the Valley Army had striven for since the evacuation of Winchester. Johnston's order was born of his fundamental strategic preference for massing strength by giving up territory and fighting only when there was nowhere else to retreat and no other friendly forces to muster. Johnston explained: "My general idea is to gather [at Richmond] all the troops who do not keep away from McClellan greatly superior forces."[19] Johnston at last understood that Shields was east of the Blue Ridge and that Banks was fortifying Strasburg, and he doubted the Valley Army could now make an important diversion in Richmond's benefit. Hence, the Valley would be weakened to strengthen his own army. Orders recalling Branch's column to the capital had reached Branch on May 20, and Branch was now hurrying toward Richmond via Hanover Courthouse[20]; Johnston's newest orders also required Ewell to march for Richmond. Jackson and Ewell were given permission to attack Shields if an opportunity arose, but in all events Ewell must start east at once. Only Jackson would remain to confront Banks. Ewell had received the dispatch early on May 20, halted, and relayed it to Jackson.

It was a moment of intense drama in the Shenandoah. Union forces here were estimated to number 15,000.[21] Without Ewell and Branch the Valley Army could accomplish little against Banks and must revert to a sideshow. Yet the Army had its orders. It was Jackson's duty to comply. He could not appreciate the over-all situation as viewed from Richmond nor know how an order which appeared wrong to him might be part of a larger plan. Nor was it a subordinate's right to such knowledge—that was the premise of Stonewall's own impenetrable silence.

Jackson groped within himself for the will to release Ewell, but it was not there. Within himself Jackson clutched ambition, not obedience. There remained one hope, Lee. Lee had nurtured the Shenandoah offense; perhaps he could save it. Perhaps he could do no more than stretch his tenuous authority into another qualified permission to keep going, but given only that much, the Army would strike. Three or four days were all it needed. To his swiftest courier, Jackson entrusted this plea to be telegraphed from Staunton:

Camp Near New Market, Va.
May 20, 1862.

General R. E. Lee:

I am of the opinion that an attempt should be made to defeat
Banks, but under instructions just received from General Johnston,
I do not feel at liberty to make an attack. Please answer by
telegraph at once.

T. J. Jackson
Major General.

Having taken one step toward insubordination, Jackson went all the way. He returned Johnston's message to Ewell with the endorsement: "Suspend the execution of the order for returning to the east until I receive an answer to my telegram."[22]

Had General Loring halted his Army of the Northwest during the march against Romney and surreptitiously petitioned Johnston that some other move be made, his conduct would not have been more insubordinate than Jackson's. Jackson had just directly countermanded the express orders of a superior officer, a graver offense than those for which Jackson had demanded Loring's court-martial. If Johnston had developed some plan to relieve Richmond by the sudden arrival of Ewell's division, Jackson might have ruined everything. It would profit the Confederacy nothing to crush Banks if it lost Richmond in the bargain, and this was the risk Jackson had assumed. It was little wonder General Taylor found him disinclined to conversation.

What Lee did with Jackson's appeal remains a mystery, yet it cannot be doubted that he acted upon it. His first thought must have been to persuade President Davis to simply override Johnston's orders. It is unlikely Lee attempted that, however, because it was the sort of thing Johnston would have protested to his grave, and Johnston is not known to have made any such protest.

It is much more probable that Lee learned that Jackson's problem had been solved two days earlier. Subsequent to his order of May 17 Johnston had received Ewell's letter of that date—the letter addressed to Lee—asking for clarification of his orders now that Shields was east of the Blue Ridge. Lee had forwarded this request to Johnston's Headquarters, where it arrived about 2 P.M., May 18. Johnston instantly understood the crisis in the Shenandoah and replied immediately: "The whole question is whether or not General Jackson and yourself are too late to attack Banks. If so, the march eastward should be made. If not (supposing your strength sufficient) the attack."[23]

Later that same day, Johnston dictated another note to the Valley. This letter was in all likelihood prompted by receipt of Jackson's message from Mount Solon, and, knowing more certainly Ewell's location than Jackson's, Johnston replied by way of the former. Even more so than the first, this communiqué emphasized what the Valley Army must accomplish: ". . . the object you

have to accomplish is the prevention of the junction of Gen.
Banks' troops with those of Gen. McDowell."[24] Johnston concluded with an expression of his "full confidence" in his Valley
commanders and directed Ewell to forward this note on to Jackson. (Nothing in the messages of May 18 altered Johnston's instructions for the detachment under General Branch to return to
the Richmond area, and Branch continued his march toward
Hanover Courthouse, some fifteen miles directly north of Richmond.)

Following receipt of Jackson's plea of May 20 Lee must have
reviewed correspondence concerning the Shenandoah and discovered Johnston's letters of the eighteenth. (Since Ewell's May 17
letter had reached Johnston by way of Lee, it is obvious Lee was
aware of the crisis and reasonable to assume that he was most interested in Johnston's replies to the Valley.) Even a verbal report
about these two dispatches would have assured Lee that Johnston
had given the Valley Army the very task he had urged of it for
weeks. Lee would have also realized that if the dispatches traveled
at only a normal pace they would reach Ewell and Jackson no
later than midnight of May 20; and since Johnston had sent two
dispatches, at least one would almost surely reach its destination.
Any orders Lee could have sent in reply to Jackson's plea would
have merely supplemented the good news already in the Valley,
and it may be questioned that he felt any need to reply.[25]

The Valley Army had weathered another crisis; both Johnston
and Lee now agreed that Banks had to be kept from McDowell's
forces. Jackson allowed himself a moment of personal thanks
that the specter of insubordination had also vanished; his countermand of Johnston's May 17 order had become augury. Sometime
during the night of the twentieth he assured Ewell their campaign
to halt McDowell's march from Fredericksburg would continue,
then he visited the Louisiana Brigade. Some hours later, as General
Taylor was forming his Louisiana regiments in the half dawn,
Jackson returned with the morning's marching orders: North.[26]

The Army quickly reached the strategic crossroads at New
Market. The rebels strode down Congress Street to Cross Street,
where Jackson motioned to the right: East. The turn produced
some murmurs from the Louisiana men, but kindled little excitement among those familiar with Old Jack's ways: ". . . we were

getting used to Jackson's divergences from the straight road ahead," wrote one rebel.[27] The column swerved east toward Massanutten Gap.

The day grew sultry with summer heat. Thousands of shuffling feet kept a pall of dust above the troops. Dirt caked in their mouths; it coated their eyes and lips; it scraped at their necks, wrists, and ankles. Their shoes filled with dirt and pebbles. Talk ceased in the ranks, and nothing was heard save the drone of sweat flies.[28] The Army began the passage through Massanutten Gap.

Fifty minutes of each hour the Army climbed, aching for the ten minute pause allowed under Jackson's new road orders. Those who had started from Swift Run Gap with Old Jack on the last day of April had since plodded two hundred and thirty miles, most of the way through mud, mountains, and burning forests. They had had only four days of rest, and many were in a stupor: "We are very wearied by the march, in fact, virtually worn down. A night's rest appears to do us no good—just as sleepy and languid in the morning as when we sleep in the evening," panted Private Jim Hall.[29]

Seventy miles to the east, another column was toiling through dust and heat that day. It was Shields, drawing still nearer to Fredericksburg.

Late on May 21 the Valley Army wound down the Massanutten Mountain, crossed the Shenandoah's South Fork and bivouacked near Luray. Taylor, who had ridden beside Jackson all day, shot him a puzzled look. After two days of strenuous marching, his Louisianians were at a rendezvous with Ewell's division barely twenty miles from where they left it. Ewell's main body had reached this rendezvous by a hike straight down the Luray Valley. Taylor was baffled. The Army was obviously not going to Strasburg. It could not possibly catch Shields. To keep from concluding that Jackson was insane, Taylor decided he must be an unconscious poet, who "as an ardent lover of nature desired to give strangers an opportunity to admire the beauties of his Valley. It seemed hard times to be wandering like sentimental travelers about the country, instead of gaining 'kudos' on the Peninsula."[30]

Jackson, of course, offered no response to Taylor's stare. He gave his reins a shake and rode to oversee the final merging of Edward Johnson's and Ewell's forces into the Valley Army. Three of Johnson's regiments (12th Georgia and 25th and 31st Virginia) were added to Elzey's brigade of Ewell's division. Johnson's other brigade, Scott's (44th, 52d, and 58th Virginia), was also assigned to Ewell, as were all three of Johnson's batteries. By reshuffling two units already with Ewell, Richmond had recently created a special force called the Maryland Line. The government intended for political reasons to collect all Maryland units in this command; for the present, the 1st Maryland—formerly of Elzey's brigade— and Brockenbrough's Baltimore Light Artillery formed its nucleus under newly arrived Brigadier General George Steuart. Steuart was a West Pointer from Maryland who had seen much action while a cavalry captain in the prewar United States Army, and Jackson noted Steuart's background as he decided the Maryland Line would continue under Ewell. Ewell's division thus grew to a full complement of four brigades and the attached Maryland Line. Jackson's three brigades—commanded by Winder, Campbell, and Taliaferro—comprised the Army's other division and remained under his personal control. The long-envisioned concentration of Confederate forces from central Virginia and the Valley was a reality. With Ashby's cavalry and the 2d and 6th Virginia Cav. of Ewell, the Army numbered perhaps 17,000 men and 50 guns, and everything it would accomplish must be achieved with this force and no more.[31]

The march continued on May 22, as the rebels headed down the Luray Valley over a miserable road. They trudged for hours through ankle-deep ruts, and their exhaustion grew more acute. ". . . [A]lmost tired to death," Jim Hall scribbled in his diary.[32] Indeed, many themes of the Valley Campaign rose toward a climax this day. Ashby rejoined the Army with the bulk of his command, having left four companies south of Strasburg to prolong the demonstrations against Banks[33] and one company near Franklin to observe Frémont.[34] Ashby had finessed his mission opposite Strasburg well, but Jackson still feared his riders were incapable of sustained operations. A problem from the Confederate reorganization during the spring surfaced in the 1st Maryland, where the initial enlistments of some men who had desired transfer to the cavalry expired. The bitter would-be cavalrymen now demanded discharges. Colonel Bradley Johnson refused, and half the regiment swore to fight no longer. Johnson thereupon disarmed the mutineers and placed them under guard in the custody of the steadfast half.[35] Old Jack, meanwhile, continued to mold his infantry. He announced a new rule that before battle two men should be detailed from each company to succor the wounded; only those men, identified by a red badge around their hats, were authorized to leave ranks during the fight. To implement this rule, roll would be called immediately after every engagement.[36] Jackson was determined to tighten discipline, and his youths continued to ignore him. Joe Kaufman saw his house from the column that day and dropped out to spend a refreshing afternoon at home.[37] These motifs and others—the compartmentalization of the Federal high command, Shields's redeployment to Fredericksburg, Lee's warnings of danger from that point, and Jackson's ceaseless considerations on the question "What next?"—had primed the Shenandoah for the events to follow the march of May 22.

The Army bivouacked that night within ten miles of Front Royal.[38] Tension gripped the scene; during the afternoon the men had been ordered to clean their weapons.[39] That meant battle the next day. The rebels talked gravely of the prospect while they oiled their muskets, then ate their meager rations, and took fitful rest. Silence enfolded the Valley Army, a silence broken only by the crickets and a rustle from the ambulances of the 4th Virginia, where Hospital Orderly Apperson was readying bandages for the morrow.[40]

II

A scant twenty miles from the Valley Army's camps in the Luray Valley were those of Banks at Strasburg. Unlike the rebels, Union soldiers were well contented and amply fed. They had heard rumors that afternoon that the rebels might be approaching, but they took little heed.[41] More interesting was the current gossip about Banks, who was now transporting himself in a carriage. Northern troops strolled the brightly lit streets of town during off-duty hours and mobbed the sutlers' wagons, where they could buy oysters, lobsters, and the finest cheeses and meats. A traveling minstrel show had come to town, and laughter roared from a canvas theater.[42]

Only Banks did not join that laughter, for his command was scattered and much reduced from the 22,000 men it had boasted after Kernstown. Shields had taken a full division of 10,000 men to Fredericksburg, not the 6,000 or 7,000 suspected by Confederates. Banks was also required to keep small detachments along the Manassas Gap Railroad from Strasburg to Manassas. The largest such detachment was roughly 1,000 men of the 1st (Union) Maryland Infantry at Front Royal; most of the other detachments were east of the Blue Ridge and beyond supporting range. Banks's effective strength around Strasburg was less than 7,000: 4,500 infantry, 1,800 cavalry and 16 guns.[43] Though his forces were strongly entrenched, Banks recognized that fortifications could not protect him from a determined assault, and he worried that Ashby's demonstrations south of Strasburg for the past week might prelude such an assault. His sadly out-of-date intelligence located Jackson eight miles west of Harrisonburg and Ewell at Swift Run Gap, but he more accurately estimated these divisions to number 16,000 and believed he was their target.[44] On May 22 he begged reinforcements from Secretary Stanton, warning of "the persistent adherence of Jackson to the defense of the Valley and his well-known purpose to expel the Government troops from this country if in his power. This may be assumed as certain. There is probably no more fixed and determined purpose in the whole circle of the enemy's plans."[45] Had Banks been privy to the insubordination Jackson had just risked to keep the Shenandoah offense alive, he could not have written more shrewdly; Banks's only mistake was that he could not envision the Valley Army already less than ten miles from the Union outpost at Front Royal.

Stanton made no known reply to Banks's forecast, for he was occupied with other fronts that May 22. A telegram had reached Washington from General McDowell at Fredericksburg that day, and with seven words it sentenced the Confederacy to an early end: "Major General Shields' command has arrived here."[46] The descent on Richmond could commence. Everything was prepared:

wagons were heaped with five days' rations; beef cattle on the hoof were distributed to the brigades; four new bridges spanned the Rappahannock.[47] McDowell reported to McClellan that very day: "I have received the orders of the President to move with the army under my command and cooperate with yours in the reduction of Richmond. . . ."[48]

May 22, 1862, was a glorious day, twenty-four hours during which McClellan's partially reassembled Peninsula Campaign stood on the edge of success. There was even to be a triumphal parade to mark the upcoming victory. President Lincoln and several of his Cabinet members were journeying to Fredericksburg to issue McDowell final instructions.[49] Following the conference, they would be treated to a grand review of McDowell's army— four divisions totalling 40,000 men and more than 100 guns—before it marched south for the "reduction of Richmond."

In Richmond, President Jefferson Davis and his Cabinet shared no bright prospects. McClellan was inching steadily up the Peninsula from the east, and the city was awash with badly frightened people. The Confederate Congress had adjourned and evacuated Richmond with demoralizing haste. The Treasury Secretary kept steam up in a special train holding the South's gold reserves; the Secretary of War had discreetly begun to pack his records for "removal."[50] President Davis had bundled his family off to North Carolina and almost despaired that Johnston could reverse what he termed "the drooping cause of our country."[51] On May 14, with McClellan twenty-five miles away, the Cabinet debated where Johnston's army should rally if Richmond fell.

A prickly tension was mounting throughout Richmond, a tension fueled by the growing conviction that the government was losing control. "The enemy are at the gates. Who will take the lead and act, act, act?" demanded the *Daily Dispatch*.[52] A correspondent for the Memphis *Daily Appeal* wrote of "groups of excited men at every corner; dense crowds before the bulletin boards of the newspaper offices; long lines of army wagons rattling over the clamorous pavements; . . . couriers, covered with dust of the road, on broken down horses in feeble gallop towards the War Department."[53]

Portents of disaster multiplied: The Government took control of telegraph lines south and west of Richmond; foreigners literally besieged the passport office.[54] Every shop in town, even bookstores, was selling packing cases and trunks.[55] The Richmond & Danville Railroad dismantled its repair shops for shipment south; planks were being laid across the railroad bridge spanning the James River to speed any escape attempt by Johnston's army.[56]

On May 20, Davis promised publicly that the capital would be defended to the end. That same day McClellan crossed the Chickahominy River—twelve miles from Richmond. Coffee soared to $1.50 per pound; tea was selling at seven times the usual price. Some rents doubled. The price of boots rose to an unattainable $30 per pair.[57]

On May 22 McClellan extended his right wing northward as if to invite McDowell's march from Fredericksburg. McClellan occupied Cold Harbor—eight miles from Richmond.[58] On the twenty-fourth he held Mechanicsville—five miles from Richmond.[59] Union observation balloons floated into view above the city. "Every day the two armies are shelling each other . . ," wrote one government clerk in his diary.[60]

Johnston ordered the Confederates near Fredericksburg, now under Brigadier General Joseph R. Anderson, to join him before Richmond.[61] Anderson marched southward, but on May 27 forwarded ominous news: McDowell seemed to be pursuing him. McDowell's main body was already six miles below Fredericksburg. McDowell's advance guard was even farther south—less than forty miles from McClellan.[62]

THREE DAYS OF RUNNING BATTLE

All sorts of a mixed-up fight ensued.

—HENRY DOUGLAS

On Friday, May 23, the sun rose over the Shenandoah at 5 A.M. and found the Army of the Valley resuming its advance toward Front Royal. The day stoked up early. Southern ranks were shriveling from heat prostration before noon; sweating profusely, stomach and legs convulsed with cramps, men slumped to the ground vomiting. Hundreds of stragglers lagged behind, and Hospital Orderly Apperson watched whole squads of his 4th Virginia melt from ranks.[1] Many infantrymen lacked even the spirit to jeer Ashby's cavalry as it splashed over the South Fork of the Shenandoah on a new adventure.

Ashby's riders may have guessed they were the initial wave of a general attack. Their objective was to rupture communications between Banks at Strasburg and his detachment at Front Royal by striking Buckton Station, where a Federal outpost guarded a trestle midway between the towns. Riding almost to within sight of the enemy post by a sheltered path, Ashby dismounted and dodged forward to reconnoiter. Federal guidons warned him that he faced two companies of Indiana and Wisconsin infantrymen, farmboys who would not scatter like Yankee cavalry. Tents for perhaps 150 Federals stood in rows near a stout brick depot. That building was sandbagged and manned like a redoubt, and behind it lay the Passage Creek trestle, on both sides of which the enemy was also dug in.[2]

Ashby quickly rejoined his troopers, formed a rough line, and charged. The Yanks were surprised but rallied inside the depot to turn back the first rush. Ashby shouted for a second dash. Vaulting fences and ditches, the rebels roared in like Indians. The bluecoats had driven loopholes through the depot walls and kept up a steady fire on the circling Confederates. Captain Sheetz was killed; Captain Fletcher went down. Captain Winfield's horse was shot from under him. Winfield rolled free, gathered a squad, and hacked into the Union fort. After five minutes of room-by-room fighting he emerged with a Federal banner wound around his arm, signaling the post had fallen.

Federal survivors pulled into their revetments at the western end of the bridge. Ashby burned the depot, slashed telegraph wires, and massed his men to go again. "Forward boys," he thundered, "we'll get every mother's son of them."

Yelping rebels swarmed into a leaden hail. They recoiled, charged again, and more troopers fell. Ashby drew off, but not without a characteristic show of nerve. He halted to ponder still another charge, and the Federals began to bang away at him. Ashby ignored them until a bullet tore the ear off his black charger. Such was his horsemanship that a few soft words kept the animal quiet, and to a private who urged his retreat, he merely replied: ". . . that was only a stray ball, but you'd better see to yourself."[3] The paladin had not routed his enemy today, but he would never fear them. For now, however, he had done all he could and headed for Front Royal.

The fast-paced, almost dizzying action at Buckton was a portent of things to come. Colonel Flournoy, with his own 6th Virginia Cavalry and all of Munford's 2d Virginia not still east of the Blue Ridge, also struck the Manassas Gap Railroad west of Front Royal. All links between it and Strasburg were severed by noon, then Flournoy rode for Front Royal.[4] West of the Massanutten Mountain, Captains G. W. Myers and Edward MacDonald boldly flung the small mounted contingent there upon Banks. In a perfectly timed feint they occupied a hill outside Strasburg and entrenched at dusk. Darkness prevented Banks from knowing how weak the Confederates were and gave him the whole night to worry about them.[5]

While rebel cavalry isolated Front Royal, the infantry closed on it from the south. Jackson learned during the morning that the Union's 1st Maryland regiment garrisoned the place. Still unaware that half of his own 1st Maryland was disarmed and under guard in custody of the other half, Jackson ordered his Marylanders to the Army's van.

This summons found the Marylanders strung along the wayside on one of the Army's hourly rest breaks. Their mood was sullen: "silent, lifeless and without spirit," one of them recalled.[6] Colonel Johnson could feel their hostility as he scanned Jackson's order, and his waxed handle-bar mustache seemed to droop; these men were not capable of leading the Army into battle. Then, suddenly resolved on a desperate gamble, Johnson called them to attention and began reading Stonewall's order: "Colonel Johnson will move the First Maryland to the front with all dispatch. . . ." Johnson brandished the order at his sulking troops and threatened he would return it with an endorsement that the regiment was too demoralized to fight because some of them had been denied transfers to the cavalry. He was ashamed to be a Marylander, Johnson ranted. He worked himself into an orator's frenzy, ending his harangue by shouting: "Go home. . . . Boast of it when you meet your fathers and mothers, brothers, sisters and sweethearts. Tell them it was you who, when brought face to face with the enemy, proved yourselves . . . to be cowards."[7]

The ploy worked. Nineteen- and twenty-year-old soldiers may sulk for a principle, but they will not permit such a slur on their recently acquired manhood. Those under arrest clamored for their arms, and the Marylanders strutted to the van.

Four miles from Front Royal, Jackson once again unexpectedly "diverged from the straight road ahead." With his vanguard, he turned right onto Gooney Manor Road, which bore east, seemingly straight into the Blue Ridge. Within a half hour the Marylanders climbed five hundred feet and began to wonder whether, after all else, they must scale the Blue Ridge as well. But the road finally twisted northward to enter Front Royal via a well-sheltered back trail.[8] Old Jack was at his secretive best, even if he punished his soldiers as a consequence. Pines packed closely together along the new road slowed the air, so that the shade was more stifling than refreshing, and dog-tired rebels remembered the balance of this day through a haze.

About 2 P.M. a single Yankee was spotted dozing under a fence. The fellow glanced lazily at the first company of rebel skirmishers, looked harder as Confederate officers emerged from the woods, fired a wild shot, and ran. The attackers quickened their pace; Bradley Johnson's troops were jubilant when they realized they would face the "bogus" 1st Maryland.[9] Stonewall flung his vanguard across the southern approaches to Front Royal like a net; the Marylanders and Wheat's Tigers served as the center, with the remainder of Taylor's brigade supporting them on either flank.

The rebels pounded up the last rise before Front Royal to find the village dominated by the high ground on which they stood. The village lay about a mile off; two miles beyond it, the forks of the Shenandoah River met at right angles, the North Fork flowing from the northwest, the South Fork, from the southwest. Near the confluence, the rebuilt Manassas Gap Railroad viaduct spanned the South Fork. The enemy camp rested nearby and on the same side of the South Fork as the rebels; inside Federal lines was a flinty ridge, Richardson's Hill, where two Northern guns were planted. Though he could confidently expect to bag the enemy, Jackson was more intent on capturing the two highway bridges lying near the Union camp. One bridge (also recently rebuilt) spanned the South Fork a short distance upstream (southward) from the viaduct. The main highway, an essential thoroughfare, crossed the South Fork bridge, the peninsula between the two forks, and the North Fork's highway bridge and ran thence to Winchester.

Jackson swiftly grasped these features and opened his attack, one which he hoped would be an exercise in collecting prisoners. The Marylanders dashed ahead, blasting at some Federal snipers in a large hospital. "Can't you take that building?" General Steuart urged. Johnson's men answered with a yell as they crashed into the place.[10] They swept on and cleared the main highway into Front Royal (which the vanguard had left at Gooney Manor Road); Jackson dispatched a courier to bring his rear brigades straight down this road. Wheat's Tigers cleared the village and threw the enemy back upon Richardson's Hill before Northern artillery shelled their ragged line to a stop. Colonel Crutchfield, handling the Army's artillery for the first time, ordered up the closest of Ewell's batteries, only to discover its short-range guns could not reach the enemy. Unfamiliar with Ewell's pieces, he sent for every long-range gun in the division.[11]

Rebels listened for the scream of friendly shells and heard instead the piping scream of a locomotive churning through the middle of the battlefield. Was it a troop train, perhaps the first of many? Anxious moments passed, then a heavily laden Union supply train chugged into sight from the east. No matter what his previous service, the engineer had no experience to equal this stop. The battle was raging around him; civilians were in the streets of Front Royal rounding up stray Federal soldiers, and Wheat's Tigers were swarming toward him looking like the train robbers some of them were. The trainman slowed but could not reverse his direction, and a squad of Tigers ousted him from his cab and triumphantly began to toot the engine's whistle.[12]

Confederate artillery still had not appeared,[13] and Jackson goaded the Marylanders and Tigers on without it. The enemy fought for time and won more than an hour, then the game was up. As Taylor began skirting his 6th Louisiana Irishmen around the Federal right, Flournoy's cavalry began gathering like vultures across the South Fork of the Shenandoah. The Yanks set fire to their tents and ran for the highway bridges. Jackson began to count his prisoners, but he was disappointed. The Tigers could not resist rifling the Union camp, and the Federals were allowed to reach high ground north of the North Fork bridge, which they set afire behind them.[14]

Despite vastly superior numbers on the field the Valley Army was in trouble. The highway bridge across the South Fork was safe, but if its twin over the North Fork was lost the enemy might escape and a further advance would be slowed or stopped. This had to be prevented at all costs. Jackson gave Taylor a nod, and his entire brigade stormed toward the burning span. "[I]t was rather a near thing," Taylor recalled. "My horse and clothing were scorched, and many men burned their hands severely while throwing brands into the river."[15] A long section of floor collapsed in front of the rebels, but by bearing to the right in single file they gained the opposite bank, only to spy the enemy disappearing toward Winchester.

"Oh," moaned Jackson, who was among the first over the charred span, "what an opportunity for artillery. Oh, that my guns were here."

Jackson peered back across the rivers, impatiently hoping to see his batteries and brigades pouring through Front Royal on the main road cleared by the 1st Maryland. Perhaps in his eagerness and amid the heat of the day and the smouldering bridge he thought he saw them, for he shouted to his nearest aide: "Order up every rifled gun and every brigade of the Army."[16]

But if Jackson was seeing the bulk of his command it was a mirage. Ashby had supplied one of his least disciplined companies to serve as couriers for Headquarters today, and the message Jackson had sent earlier for the rear units to advance by the direct route into Front Royal was never delivered. The courier, a youth never near combat before, had panicked and fled. Jackson's latest order to press forward found the rear units making a fruitless detour along Gooney Manor Road.[17]

Old Jack was forced to improvise. Flournoy had alertly forded the North Fork with several companies when the enemy began to retire, and Stonewall ordered him to pursue. Three miles north of Front Royal on the road to Winchester, at Cedarville, the Federals were overtaken. Almost 1,000 strong, they deployed to make another stand.

Flournoy had no more than 250 riders, but they were to relish a moment of romantic glory. They came on across clean green fields, bugles blaring, four company guidons whipping in the breeze, sabers and pistols flashing. Some men rode with reins in their teeth and weapons in both hands. A point-blank fusillade dropped many of Flournoy's troopers, but the rest waded among the Federals hacking and shooting. The four-times stronger enemy broke before them.[18]

A short distance away, Jackson sat aglow. He had his prisoners at last. Never, he exclaimed, had he seen such a gallant charge[19]—high praise from the reticent Stonewall. The riders merrily rounded up hundreds of prisoners and escorted them to Front Royal. One of the two Union cannons was also taken at Cedarville. Two of Flournoy's privates discovered the other piece abandoned outside Winchester and spirited the trophy back to the Army.[20]

Other rebels had also done well. Captains Myers and Mac-Donald succeeded completely with their bluff opposite Strasburg: at dawn on May 24 Banks believed a full division was south of him on the Valley Pike.[21] Rail and telegraph communications between Strasburg and Front Royal had been slashed, and roughly 900 of the latter's garrison had been killed, wounded, or captured.[22] Strategically, Jackson had delivered a master stroke. Screening his approach behind the Massanutten, he had punched through the Union line guarding the Manassas Gap Railroad at its weakest point, and now he hung on Banks's flank between him and Fredericksburg—all at a cost of little more than 100 Southern casualties.

Late on the evening of the twenty-third the victorious commander rode weary and alone through the bivouac of the Louisiana Brigade near Cedarville. Jackson sat down at General Taylor's campfire almost without a word. Many hours elapsed, some of them beneath a brisk shower,[23] and Taylor deduced that the mute Jackson was at his prayers.[24] Doubtless so. Yet even prayer often yielded to speculation about the immediate future.

While seated by the campfire Jackson visualized a triangle, the base of which was the twelve-mile road between Front Royal and Strasburg. The Valley Pike ran northeast from Strasburg eighteen miles to the apex of the figure at Winchester. A second road ran northwest from Front Royal to Winchester and completed the triangle. The Valley Army's offense would probably unfold along or within this triangle depending on which of four courses Banks elected. First, if Banks misread the situation (that is, construed the Army's attack as merely a raid with limited objectives), he might remain at Strasburg while detaching a small column to reclaim Front Royal. Second, he might retreat westward into the Alleghenies to join Frémont, probably near the village of Wardensville, in West Virginia. Third, he could retreat to Winchester; this course would enable him to protect his capacious warehouses there and to stay between the Confederates and the Potomac. Fourth, he might try to outguess Jackson. Banks might assume the rebels would swoop directly from Front Royal to Winchester.

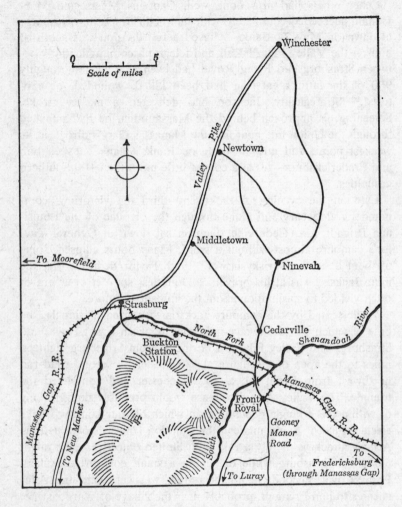

8. JACKSON'S STRATEGIC TRIANGLE, MAY 24, 1862.

Such a move would open the way for Banks's escape via Front Royal and Manassas Gap; he could simply bide his time until the Confederates were a good distance down the road to Winchester, then slip across their rear to the east.

Another set of givens plagued Jackson. He had estimated Northern strength at 21,000 or 22,000 in late April and thought Shields took only 6,000 of them to Fredericksburg. Not counting Shields, the casualties inflicted today, and necessary detachments, it was conceivable that Banks still had 10,000 to 15,000 men at Strasburg.[25] Stonewall thus erroneously calculated that Banks's strength was not much less than his own. Further, Jackson could also suppose, quite correctly, that Union troops were well rested, while the Valley Army was depleted by excessive straggling. Ewell's forces were relatively fresh, but their capabilities were unknown. Taylor's brigade and Bradley Johnson's 1st Maryland had fought well, although the sight of Major Wheat's Tigers pillaging the enemy camp disturbed Jackson, the difficulties Crutchfield experienced with Ewell's guns warned him that co-ordination with this division would not be flawless. Jackson therefore thought it prudent to keep the Army together on May 24, at least until he discovered something of Banks's intentions.

From the constraints of geography, enemy options, and relative strength, Jackson sought a plan. Two possibilities emerged. First, the Valley Army could seek Banks by crossing the base of the triangle to Strasburg. This would position the rebels to blunt a thrust on Front Royal or to pursue if Banks fled into the Alleghenies. Should Banks retire directly to Winchester, however, the Confederates probably could not catch him before he reached the high ground west of the city, ground which offered good defensive positions. Second, the Army could advance northwestward, directly from Front Royal to Winchester and doubtless could outfoot Banks there. Should the enemy bolt eastward from Strasburg, however, the rebels would have to countermarch from Winchester and possibly not be able to overtake the Federals before they gained Manassas Gap. As the critical goal of the Valley Army's offense was to prevent the union of Banks's and McDowell's forces, this second course appeared no better than the first.[26] Frustrated in his analysis, Jackson renewed his prayers.

II

At 6 A.M. on May 24 Trimble's brigade of Ewell's division was probing down the road from Front Royal to Winchester[27]; Ashby added the weight of his command to this probe.[28] The bulk of the Valley Army was not immediately behind Trimble, since, because of bridge repairs and a time-wasting detour along Gooney Manor Road the day before, most brigades had camped around Front Royal and spent their early daylight hours filing over both forks of the Shenandoah.[29] The Stonewall Brigade did not move until 8 A.M.[30]; one of Campbell's regiments had not marched by 9 A.M.,[31] and Taliaferro started even later.[32]

Jackson, whose inclination was probably to slice directly down the Front Royal–Winchester road with the entire Army, had not committed himself to such a plan.* He recognized that he must have more information, and with his infantry still milling around Front Royal he believed he had time to get it. He recalled General Steuart's career with the United States Cavalry and detached him from his Maryland Line to gather crucial information. Steuart was ordered to take Ewell's mounted regiments and intercept the Valley Pike nine miles south of Winchester at Newtown. If Banks was there, the cavalry must delay him; if he was not, the riders could relay that fact.[33] Scouts from Ashby's command also rode west to observe Strasburg.[34] The Army's ultimate course awaited the outcome of these reconnaissances; in the meantime, Trimble continued his march toward Winchester. Jackson joined him.

Banks, meanwhile, was preparing to take to the Valley Pike, or, as he explained later: ". . . to enter the lists with the enemy in a race for the possession of Winchester."[35] Portions of his wagon train were in retreat at 4:30 A.M. Still dreading an attack from the nonexistent division supposedly above Strasburg, he deployed his cavalry to parry that thrust. The infantry was readied with what

---

* See Appendix A for a fuller discussion of what is known and what can be deduced of Jackson's plans and marches on May 24.

Banks considered "incredible celerity," yet they were not heading down the Pike for Winchester until after 9 A.M.[36]

By 9 A.M. Jackson had pressed six or seven miles north of Front Royal on the Front Royal–Winchester road with Trimble's brigade, so that Union and Confederate vanguards were now traveling on opposite sides of Jackson's triangle. Trimble already stood closer to the apex and could have entered Winchester some hours ahead of the Federals—if only the advantage of an early start had not been neutralized by want of information. Banks presumably had 10,000 to 15,000 men somewhere along or within the triangle, and Jackson did not know where. He had hoped his cavalry would discover the enemy's direction of march, but since the Federals did not evacuate Strasburg until midmorning, Jackson could have had no positive news. If any word arrived from the scouts observing Strasburg, it was merely that Banks was preparing to move.

Move where? Jackson was harassed by a fear that Banks would scurry east through Manassas Gap. In doing so, Banks would follow the base of the triangle to Front Royal and destroy the North Fork highway bridge just north of there, rendering Jackson unable to recross and interdict the Federal movement. Only the 12th Georgia had been detailed to watch Union prisoners at Front Royal and would be helpless if Banks hurled his entire strength against it. Once past the Georgians, Banks would find the road eastward clear, the one thing which Lee and Johnston had at long last come to agree must be prevented. As he attempted to corner Banks, Jackson was compelled to remember that his operations were governed more by the strategic situation outside the Valley than by immediate tactical considerations within it. He had to think about the dire consequences of McDowell's 40,000 men at Fredericksburg being strengthened further by Banks and to understand that it was more important today to prevent additional enemy forces from leaving the Shenandoah than to destroy them. These factors in mind, at 8 A.M. or perhaps a little later, Stonewall dared go no farther northward; he halted Trimble three miles north of Cedarville (near the hamlet of Ninevah) to await news from the cavalry,[37] dismounted at a farmhouse, and asked for breakfast.[38]

This halt consumed the forenoon. The rear brigades of Ewell's division caught up with Trimble and also halted; Jackson's late-starting brigades pushed forward rapidly to bring the rear of the Army to Cedarville by 11:00, then they too halted. Thousands of men sprawled along the roadside swatting flies. Ewell joined Jackson in the farmhouse near the head of the column, and the two generals pondered the situation.

About 11 A.M., a panting, hatless courier interrupted this conference. The boy was from General Steuart, who had reached Newtown an hour earlier and found the Valley Pike crowded with Union trains.[39] Steuart had attacked and scattered the enemy wagons. This was the first definite information Stonewall had received, and it was hopeful news. It indicated Banks was running for Winchester and might be spread along the Pike where Southern guns could decimate him. Banks had missed his opportunity at Front Royal, and Jackson now dared to split the Valley Army. He ordered Ewell to stand fast around Ninevah with Trimble's, Elzey's, and Scott's brigades as a general reserve while he himself backtracked to Cedarville, from whence a trail ran west seven miles to the Pike at the village of Middletown. As a final check, he sent Hotchkiss ahead to feel for Northern pickets along this trail, and Hotchkiss uncovered a strong Union picket less than two miles west of Cedarville.[40]

That settled the matter. Jackson had all the hints he needed that Banks was running for Winchester. He bugled his men to their feet and marched for Middletown about noon.[41] Ashby and Chew took the lead, stiffened by the two long-range rifled guns of the Rockbridge Artillery under Captain Poague's personal direction. Wheat's Tigers escorted the guns and capered along hoping for another fight and more plunder.[42] They were trailed by the remainder of Taylor's command and Jackson's three brigades. All of these men were exhausted, and many were limping in obvious pain. Their road grew rough and muddy; the terrain was hilly and heavily forested; a light rain commenced, and two hours vanished despite cries for haste from Jackson and his staff.

Halfway to Middletown, Union riders dashed onto the road and entangled Ashby in a slow joust for time.[43] Behind him, the Confederates marched and stopped, marched and stopped, and another hour vanished. The drizzle ceased.

It was approximately 3:30 P.M. when the rebels burst onto high ground overlooking Middletown. Federal wagon trains, ambulances, and cavalry were jammed on the Valley Pike before them. Stone walls on either side of the road corseted the enemy into a thin line that stretched out of sight both to the north and south, an artillerist's dream. Chew and Poague wheeled their pieces into range while the Tigers opened up with rifle fire from behind a stone wall, and a lopsided fight ensued. The first Southern shells crushed some Union wagons and clogged the road. "At a half mile range," wrote George Neese, "we opened on the flying mixture with all of our guns, and as our shells plowed gap after gap through the serried column it caused consternation confounded, and vastly increased the speed of the mixed fugitive mass."[44]

The slaughter spilled onto the neighboring fields as fresh Northern cavalry squadrons blindly spurred forward to hew their way to Winchester. Staff Lieutenant Henry Douglas gathered a hundred Tigers behind a fence to stop them, and the Tigers did not waste their shots: the front rank of Union cavalrymen fell in a tangled pile. Other riders could not check their pace and plunged into the heap, until Douglas beheld a "shrieking, struggling mass of men and horses, crushed, wounded and dying."[45]

Thrashing horses, bleeding men, and smashed wagons covered the Pike.[46] General Taylor cantered up to see his Tigers "looting right merrily, diving in and out of the wagons with the activity of rabbits in a warren." (When the Tigers spotted their stern general this pillaging ceased, and they promptly snapped to attention, looking, wrote Taylor, "as solemn and virtuous as deacons at a funeral."[47]) Jackson was too busy to reprimand them as he quizzed local civilians. How many Union regiments had come this way? How many guns? At what hour? The answers told him little.

At this critical time, 4:00 P.M., Union artillery joined the fracas.[48] Jackson traced the shells southward to what looked like strong blue formations deploying south of Middletown. Other officers agreed. Stonewall immediately instructed Ewell to send him Elzey's and Scott's brigades and to hold Trimble's in place for further orders.[49] Banks appeared to be concentrated between Strasburg and Middletown where a decisive battle now loomed. Ashby, in charge of a task force consisting of his own cavalry, Chew's battery, Poague's rifled guns, and a few companies of the

7th Louisiana, was dispatched northward in pursuit of the enemy who had escaped the ambush along the Pike[50]; meanwhile the bulk of the Army lunged southwestward toward Strasburg.

Taylor's brigade led the way through Middletown amid wild cheers from liberated civilians. Flags were unfurled and the bands sounded off, each with a different tune. "Everything in Middletown turned out to greet us: men, women, girls, children, dogs, cats and chickens . . ," wrote Private Bob Barton of the Rockbridge Artillery.[51]

Progress was less rewarding outside the village. The Federals took a strong position west of the Pike, and Union artillery dueled skillfully with Taylor's brigade. When Taylor rode forward to reconnoiter, Northern gunners concentrated a heavy fire against him. One shell exploded directly beneath his horse. Taylor and an aide were showered with dirt, the edges of their saddle blankets were blown away, but neither men nor mounts were as much as nicked.[52] The enemy continued their stand long enough to force Taylor into a time-wasting deployment, then disappeared, running north for the Potomac via backroads.

Jackson finally deduced that these Federals had represented only Banks's rear guard; the main Federal body had obviously already cleared Middletown before the rebels struck—but two invaluable hours were spent to ascertain this.[53] Old Jack's men had tramped fifteen miles or more, several of them at a run during the skirmish around Middletown, but he would not pause now. The rebels about-faced, and some regiments exploded as they guessed their destination: Winchester!

Ewell was already on his way there. It was one of his many eccentricities that when battle neared he grew positively afraid someone else would get into it before him,[54] and he had been chafing all afternoon. Federal infantry had shoved Steuart's cavalry away from the Pike at Newtown, and the cavalryman had rejoined Ewell near Ninevah with news of heavy enemy columns to the west. Then came Jackson's message to detach Elzey and Scott for a confrontation above Middletown. Ewell predicted that Jackson had been lured the wrong way, and he saw an opportunity to beat his chief to the first shot. He accordingly resumed his advance north about 5 P.M. He had only Trimble's brigade, the Maryland Line, and the cavalry under Steuart, but he moved within two miles

THREE DAYS OF RUNNING BATTLE

of Winchester by dark, boldly drove in enemy pickets, and brushed with them through the night.[55]

Ewell's road toward Winchester had been clear; on the Pike, Jackson met the wreckage of Banks's army. Abandoned wagons littered the road for miles, some with teams still hitched.[56] Other vehicles were smashed or overturned, with contents scattered. Muskets and rain capes, ornate footlockers stuffed with gaudy uniforms, songbooks and sutlers' stores were thrown about in abundance—". . . a general wreck of military matter," wrote one eyewitness.[57]

This wreckage saved Banks. Stonewall himself was unable to resist a moment of plunder—without food since breakfast, he instinctively dug into one overturned wagon until he found a stale cracker for his supper[58]—and Ashby's boys, tempted by first choice of the spoils as they chased the enemy north from Middletown with the guns under Colonel Crutchfield, went wild. Many roped two or three horses and rode off to their homes.[59] One cavalryman hammered into a barrel, to strike whiskey; he dropped to his knees before the gushing brew and filled himself.[60] Another drunk piled sacks of booty behind his saddle, then in front of it, then across it. He spotted a beautiful saddle and tossed it over the bags. Arms full of wine flasks, he mounted in an effort to wobble off. Instead, horse and rider collapsed.[61]

With the rebel cavalry dwindling, the artillery contingent of Ashby's task force (which was five or six miles north of the main body of infantry under Jackson) became dangerously exposed. The guns outdistanced the few companies of supporting Louisiana infantry shortly after leaving Middletown, and by the time the gunners sighted Newtown, Ashby had only half a hundred men still covering the cannons. The artillerymen halted, and Colonel Crutchfield, who was with Poague's rifled guns, rode back towards the main body begging for help. He urged a few dozen men of the 7th Louisiana forward, but even Taylor's marchers could limp onward no faster. Only Ashby's ransacking cavalrymen, who were all around, could do any good. Crutchfield appealed to pride; he swore; he threatened. It was in vain: "Unable to force or persuade them to abandon this disgraceful employment and return to their duty, I returned to Newtown, and after consulting Colonel Ashby we concluded it would be imprudent to push the pursuit further

. . . especially as there were but 50 cavalry, under Major Funsten, remaining with us, the residue being eagerly engaged in plundering the captured trains."[62]

The enemy detected this halt. A Union battery swung around, and an artillery duel followed while Banks gained Winchester.[63] Ashby could have swept the field with two hundred men; as it was, he sat helpless and shamefaced for several hours, until Jackson reached Newtown with the head of the infantry column. What Jackson snarled about Ashby's troopers was, mercifully, not recorded. The enemy withdrew, and the General said to get going. Chew's battery was too spent to obey,[64] so Poague's rifled guns and Ashby's handful took the van. Just behind came Jackson and his staff, then Winder's brigade with Colonel John Neff's 33d Virginia in front. It was now night.

The Pike was lit for a mile north of Newtown by burning wagons. The frolic of Ashby's command has given the enemy time for this, Jackson thought bitterly[65]; once again, the cavalry had failed. Beyond the wagons the Army was engulfed by a night as dark as Jackson's rage, and the march slowed to a crawl.

"Moving at a snail's pace and halting," wrote gunner Bob Barton, "and then moving again and halting again, falling asleep at the halts and being suddenly wakened up when motion was resumed, we fairly staggered on, worn almost to exhaustion by the weariness of such a march."[66] Ed Moore left a similar narrative, commenting that of everything he endured during four years of war, this night was the worst.[67]

A volley roared from the dark. Ambush. Colonel Neff's infantry gave a thunderous reply, and then only the screams of the wounded lingered.

The Valley Army's advance probed onward slowly and cautiously[68]—into another ambush. The enemy was all around, in front, to the east and to the west of the Pike. "Charge them, charge them," Jackson ordered Ashby's cavalry.[69] The tense riders drew a volley and stampeded. Poague's gunners jumped under their caissons to avoid being trampled.[70] Men of the 33d Virginia were run down, and the regiment was left in such confusion it could not be rallied.[71] Winder attempted to bolster his front with the 2d and 5th Virginia, but they wandered into a swale as a blazing ammunition wagon began to explode.[72] Some men of the 2d and 5th

thought the explosions were artillery and fled toward an open
field. There they were mistaken for Federals and shot down by
their own comrades until Colonel Grigsby forced his 27th Virginia
straight down the Pike and drove back the enemy.[73]

Winder pushed two companies from the 5th Virginia, boys born
in Winchester, to the van.[74] Stalking the orchards of childhood,
these rebels kept up a slow battle against a tenacious Federal rear
guard. What was left of the deathly-tired Army wove after them like
drunks. Men swore they napped as they marched.[75] Ever watchful
John Apperson observed that many of his friends simply fell in
the road and slept, reducing his regiment's strength by three
quarters.[76] Only two men showed no weariness: Ashby, erect on
his ebony warhorse, and Old Jack, silent, expressionless.[77]

The General's thoughts were on the high ground around Winchester. He recalled the withering fire from the Union battery on
Pritchard's Hill during the Battle of Kernstown and wanted no
repetition.[78] When the Valley Army passed Pritchard's, Jackson
knew that Banks had only one other possible defensive position, a
series of hills running north–south along Winchester's western
limit. If Stonewall could secure these hills, Winchester would be
free.

Between 2 and 3 A.M.[79] Colonel Fulkerson of the 37th Virginia
stumbled out of the night with an urgent request. His men were
finished; half already had collapsed and more were lost with every
step. The Army must rest, he pleaded, or it would be nothing
more than a skirmish line by dawn. Jackson listened and knew
Fulkerson was right. In an unusual response, he explained:
"Colonel, I yield to no man in my sympathy for the gallant men
under my command, but I am obliged to sweat them tonight, that
I may save their blood tomorrow. The line of hills southwest of
Winchester must not be occupied by the enemy artillery. My own
must be there and in position by daylight. You shall, however,
have two hours rest."[80]

The Army slumped down; men simply dropped wherever they
stood.[81] A blurry-eyed Henry Douglas noticed Jackson and Ashby,
two silent sentinels, pacing at the head of the Army. This alone he
recalled. Douglas touched the ground, and sleep was instantly
upon him.[82]

III

Jackson stood sentry over the Army for two hours. Ashby disappeared during the vigil, and Old Jack continued his watch alone. Much of this time he spent regretting that another Sabbath had come which he must violate with battle, then he gave the word to move. A morning mist was gathering over the wheatfields and orchards surrounding Winchester.[83] Stonewall determined to use that cover and enjoined silence on his troops.[84] A mute shadow, the Army advanced.

The line of hills that Jackson feared took form west of Winchester and to the left (west) of the Pike. One hill was four hundred yards south of the main line and commanded the road. "You must occupy that hill," was Jackson's laconic order to Winder.[85] The Stonewall Brigade charged at once, meeting, curiously, no resistance.

Winder's troops clambered to the summit and grasped the situation with a glance. Banks had stationed some units east of the Pike, but his principal force studded the hills west of the road, where Jackson expected to find it. From the Pike, the Federal line ran roughly half a mile to the northwest along these hills, but near its end, the Union position curved forward somewhat, so that the Union right flank enfiladed (from the left) the hill just taken by Winder. Manning the Federal heights were 3,000 or 4,000 men and a dozen guns; shrouded by the mist, the enemy looked stronger.[86] Union artillery began to plaster the rebel hill with startling accuracy and drove the Stonewall Brigade back from its crest.[87]

Ewell, east of the Valley Pike where the morning mist thickened into a fog, heard but could not see this cannon fire. He nevertheless promptly opened his attack. During the night, Jackson had sent Ewell a map of the area and the simple orders: "Attack at daylight."[88] Ewell needed no urging other than gunfire to carry out Jackson's orders, and he closed on Winchester's southeast corner, with the entire 1st Maryland of Colonel Johnson ahead as skirmishers. Johnson groped through a dense fog until he lost contact with rebel units on all sides of him. Unable to see twenty

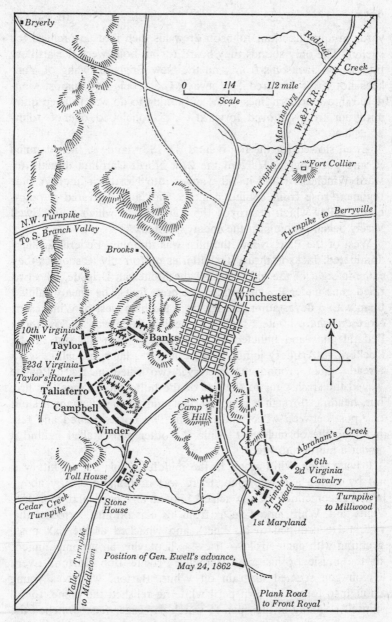

9. Battle of Winchester, May 25, 1862.
The original of this map, prepared by Jedediah Hotchkiss in 1863, accompanied Jackson's official report of the Valley Campaign.

yards in any direction, Johnson drew his men into an orchard for shelter. The only sounds they heard for an hour were the artillery thunder on Jackson's front and the New England twang of Yankees not three hundred feet away. The rebels had almost wandered into Northern lines. "The only thing to do was to keep quiet until our troops moved forward . . ," concluded one of Johnson's men.[89]

Ewell slowed for the fog behind the Marylanders, then damned it, and got moving. He sent the 21st North Carolina directly toward Winchester, and it did wander into Northern lines. A blue regiment rose from behind a stone wall and delivered a point-blank volley which destroyed the Tarheels, at which point Ewell wisely began probing for the enemy left flank.[90]

West of the Pike, where the mist was thinning, Federal artillery dominated. Jackson thrust his batteries up to reply as soon as they came in sight of the hill taken by the Stonewall Brigade. The two rifled guns under Poague gained the crest first. The enemy saluted them with a devastating barrage from the hills west of Winchester. Northern sharpshooters took post behind stone walls below those Federal guns and inflicted heavy damage: when the rest of the Rockbridge Artillery joined Poague minutes later, casualties were already piled around the battery's two rifled pieces.[91] Poague waved the fresh guns to the left of the hilltop to answer this fire, but, heading through a gate, the first gun carriage caught a stout oak post between wheel and cannon. The horses reared and fell, jamming the obstacle fast, while the other guns stalled behind it under a murderous fire.

Private Alex Whitt stood in the middle of this hell. Whitt was not by nature a heroic man; there was nothing of Ashby about him, yet something heroic seized him at this particular moment. Veins taut, Whitt jerked an ax from his caisson and darted to the wreck. He dropped to his knees and whacked at the oak post, grunting with each stroke—". . . as if playing an accompaniment to the music of his axe," thought Private Bob Barton. Every Union gun seemed to train on Whitt. Barton, who was young enough to forget his own peril while he relished the scene, found himself standing in the open to watch as "eager faces watched the axe-man to see what would happen when the post should fall. Presently the last lick was struck and the post fell and the straining, struggling horses sprang forward with the gun, while the cool headed [Poague] called out above the din, 'Corporal Whitt from this hour.' "[92]

There were other Alex Whitts' in the Valley Army this day. Carpenter's battery, then Cutshaw's (formerly Waters') entered the melee. They aligned on Poague's right under a crossfire from Northern artillery to the front and left. Cutshaw was killed and all his officers were either killed or wounded. Carpenter lent the survivors a lieutenant and ordered a mass fire on a Union battery to the north. After much punishment the Federal guns retired.[93]

The four crews Poague ordered to the left found the position untenable and rejoined him near the Rockbridge Artillery's rifled pieces.[94] Here Private Lanty Blackford watched the driver of his No. 5 gun stagger off with his arm in shreds. Then Private Washington Steuart's face was smashed by a Minié ball. Bob Barton heard a scream and saw John Gregory carried away. He spun and saw friends drag Bob McKim from the field. A wheel of Barton's gun was hit, showering him with splinters. Undaunted, he ran for a new wheel.[95] Not far distant a second gun of the Rockbridge Artillery lay crippled and useless.[96]

Poague brought his serviceable pieces to bear on the stone walls that protected enemy sharpshooters and blasted them away, but he could not match the superior range and position of the Union guns. On the reverse slopes of the artillery hilltop, Winder's men lay nose down as shells burst around them and bluebottle flies swarmed over bloody patches of ground. Even the combative Colonel Grigsby could do nothing more than stand and swear at Banks for a shrapnel hole in his sleeve. Colonel Campbell was severely wounded as he extended Winder's position to the left (west) with his brigade; Jackson bolstered Campbell's left with Taliaferro's brigade, but still the line was pinned down by heavy artillery fire.[97]

The Army was stalled. Winder ordered the rebel artillerymen to cover and found Jackson. The enemy right flank must be turned, he shouted. Jackson concurred. "I shall send you up Taylor," he promised and personally spurred to give the orders.[98] As he might have expected, he located the Louisiana Brigade coming forward alertly and in good order toward the sound of battle. Jackson found Taylor, pointed out the hill which anchored the right flank of the Federal line, and said four words: "You must carry it."[99]

Taylor gazed over Jackson's long index finger to his objective. A small stream known as Abraham's Creek ran northwesterly from the Pike just behind Winder toward the enemy position and might afford some shelter during an approach to it. A march of at most a mile up that stream should bring his men to the foot of the hill on which rested the right flank of the Union line; from there the ascent would not be steep. Only two fence rows would slow the climb. The real test would come beyond the fences, for there the slope was completely exposed to Federal infantry and artillery.

The Louisiana Brigade began to slosh up the creek bed; alongside it trotted Jackson. Richard Taylor was ecstatic. The peacock in him was delighted that after two days his command had become the Army's workhorse. He was about to take his brigade into combat as a unit for the first time, and it would be to carry the decisive point in plain view of both armies—and especially under the eyes of the tight-lipped Jackson, who was observing everything with his piercing stare. Taylor imagined the battle slackened as both sides craned to catch sight of his neat lines. They must be perfect! Federal artillery began to drop shells around the brigade and some Louisianians ducked.

"What the hell are you dodging for?" Taylor rasped. "If there is any more of it, you will be halted under this fire for an hour."

The troops looked as if they had swallowed ramrods, but Jackson stared reproachfully. There was no excuse for such language on a Sunday. He put his hand on Taylor's shoulder: "I am afraid you are a wicked fellow," he said and turned back toward Winder's position at the center of the field.[100]

Taylor was too excited to smile. He reached the base of the Federal hill and adjusted the dress and cover of his lines. He cautioned Major Wheat on his left flank to be ready for enemy cavalry. Then to the front. His lone saber flashed, and as it did, a breeze tore away the last tatters of the morning fog. Five pelican-bedecked battle flags began to flap.[101] "Attention, forward march."

Three thousand men stepped off on the left foot. With a strict cadence, ninety paces per minute, a forest of burnished steel paraded up the hill. Taylor twisted occasionally to check the alignment. It did not falter, though enemy shells chopped and chewed his ranks. Men stepped up to close the gashes. They skirted trees and reformed, vaulted fences and reformed, preserving a perfect formation. Private John Worsham of the 21st Virginia crawled from his place in the field where Campbell's brigade lay to get a better view: "That charge of Taylor's was the grandest I saw during the war; . . . every man was in his proper place. There was all the pomp and circumstance of war about it that was always lacking in our charges. . . ."[102]

Northern cavalry advanced from the left. Wheat's Tigers fanned out to meet them; with one volley they crushed the attack. Directly ahead of them, the rebels could now see Union gunners frantically limbering their pieces. Taylor rose in his stirrups and bellowed a command that John Worsham heard a mile away: "Forward, double quick, charge!"[103]

The Louisianians surged across the brow of the Federal position. East of the Pike, Ewell was also after the Yanks. General Trimble found Banks's left flank, and at his suggestion Ewell circled it with Trimble's Alabama and Mississippi regiments.[104] Rebels were springing forward everywhere with explosive cheers. Even Jackson, silent, wooden-faced Old Jack, sensed the climax and waved his cap around his head like a child, shouting: "Let's hollar. Order forward the whole Army to the Potomac."[105] The Union line crumbled.

Trimble from the east, Winder from the south, and Taylor from the west careened toward Winchester in pursuit of the enemy. There would later be heated argument over which Confederate unit entered town first, but all agreed that the wildest scenes of the day took place in Winchester. Half the town was engulfed by smoke from blazing Union warehouses. Citizens were everywhere, beating out the flames, laughing, shrieking, crying. They fairly dragged the rebels aside and smothered them with affection. Wrote John Worsham: "On passing through Winchester, the citizens met us with cheers and were perfectly wild with delight. . . . The bullets were flying through the streets, but it made no difference to those people; it seemed that joy had overcome fear. Such a scene I never witnessed."[106]

Captain Jim Edmondson elbowed through town at the head of his company and wrote: "I never saw such a demonstration as was made by the citizens—the ladies especially as we passed through—every window was crowded and every door was filled with them and all enthusiastically hurrahing for our generals and soldiers. I have never seen such an exhibition before."[107]

Federals were barricading some intersections in a bid for time. Some were arrayed around the courthouse square, but they scattered as the 5th Virginia's Winchester boys sprinted down side streets and charged the square. Citizens vied with soldiers to mop up other pockets. They sniped with handguns hidden since March; those without weapons threw kitchen knives and pots and even buckets of boiling water down on the Yanks. Southern batteries somehow lashed through the mad streets and opened up whenever the civilians could be driven out of the way.[108] Banks's army spilled out of Winchester in hopeless rout.

The Southern victory needed only to be crowned with a grand sweep of cavalry. This was the moment for Ashby to storm after the enemy like a firedrake. Ashby! Jackson suddenly realized he had not seen Ashby since before daybreak.[109] The Union mob streaming northward for the Potomac was the perfect target for him, and none of his riders were at hand. Nor was Steuart present. "Never was there such a chance for cavalry," wailed Stonewall. "Oh, that my cavalry was in place."[110]

Jackson spurred on, determined to do the cavalry's work. He forced his gunners to lash their jaded teams forward; when those animals could pull no farther, he ordered the gunners to unhitch them and charge like cavalry. Hundreds of Yankees were taken, but the impulsive pursuit could not be sustained.[111] Panic hastened the Union flight, but even victory could not overcome the rebels' exhaustion. The pathetic battery horses staggered along the Martinsburg road a few miles and quit. Pallid infantrymen sank around them. "The physical man was so weakened it was impossible to go farther," declared one Virginian.[112] These men had marched a hundred miles during the past week and had been fighting for the past thirty hours with hardly a pause. They could do no more.

Three miles north of town, Jackson ordered Sandie Pendleton to find the cavalry regiments under General Steuart and get them into action. After scouring the field, Pendleton located Steuart three miles east of Winchester. He had sat there all morning. His men were resting quietly along the roadside as their mounts grazed in a clover field.

Pendleton spat out Jackson's orders: "Ride." Steuart refused. He considered himself under Ewell's direct command and, in by-the-book military fashion, said he had been awaiting and must continue to await orders from his immediate superior. Pendleton rode to find Ewell, whose amazement over Steuart's conduct evoked his blackest oaths. The cavalry started in a short time,[113] but still two hours too late.[114]

During the afternoon Ashby joined Steuart with a handful of troopers. He later explained his mysterious absence with the simple report that he had circled the right end of Ewell's line to cut off an enemy detachment.[115] By so doing, contrary to Jackson's orders,[116] Ashby had squandered one of the finest cavalry opportunities of the war, and it was a blunder which could not be remedied. Ashby and Steuart finally combined at least 800 sabers, but they were too late for decisive action. Banks had been handed the time he needed to regroup. He pulled some artillery into line outside Martinsburg, and the rebels backed away. The Federals were safely across the Potomac by sundown.

Nevertheless, the Valley Army's triumph had been splendid; ". . . the rout was more complete than that at Manassas," boasted Hugh White.[117] Total Confederate casualties during the three-day fight from Front Royal to Winchester were only 400 killed and wounded.[118] Banks had been driven from the Shenandoah with the loss of 3,500 men, half his force, of whom 3,000 were prisoners.[119] More than 9,000 small arms, 2 cannons, warehouses of urgently needed medicine ("more medical stores than you ever heard of," gloated Quartermaster John Harman[120]), droves of cattle and sheep, tons of food, and other stores were taken. Swearing merrily, Harman calculated the booty's worth at something like a half million dollars.[121] It had been a glorious Sabbath in the Valley.

That same day, Sunday, May 25, McDowell had four bridges across the Rappahannock at Fredericksburg, and McClellan bombarded Confederate lines in the suburbs of Richmond.[122]

THREE DAYS OF RUNNING BATTLE:
THE AFTERMATH

*A certain plan I had much at heart had been
adopted and was on the eve of execution when
I received orders changing it.*

—IRVIN MCDOWELL

Jackson the soldier obeyed necessity and fought Banks on a Sunday; Jackson the Christian would not profane the Sabbath by writing a letter. His initial report of the fight from Front Royal to Winchester was dated Monday, May 26.[1] Johnston received that report the next day and replied eagerly: "If you can threaten Baltimore and Washington, do so. It may produce an important diversion. . . . Your movements depend, of course, upon the enemy's strength remaining in your neighborhood. Upon that depends the practicability of your advancing to the Potomac and even crossing it."[2]

Johnston wrote more in desperation than hope; that same day, May 27, McClellan hurled a reinforced division against Branch's brigade at Hanover Courthouse, fifteen miles due north of Richmond. Branch had been called back by Johnston from his march to join the Valley Army just three days before Jackson attacked at Front Royal, and frustration at missing events in the Shenandoah perhaps led him to make a stand at Hanover. The result was predictable; outnumbered Confederates were driven south with heavy losses. On their heels came couriers with General Anderson's report that McDowell seemed to be marching south in pursuit of Anderson's forces retiring toward Richmond. McDowell's advance guard was already less than twenty-five miles from Hanover.[3]

The Union verged on decisive action the next day. McClellan's forces around Hanover burned and looted without opposition. Morning reports confirmed McDowell's southward advance; "there can be no doubt" of McDowell's approach, Johnston wrote to Lee.[4]

Just as certainly, Richmond verged on chaos that May 28. The morning papers carried an appeal from Mayor Joseph Mayo declaring, "The hour of battle and decision is upon us," and urging the citizens to meet with him at City Hall. Hundreds came and heard Mayo suggest what once had been unthinkable: if Confederate authority collapsed, the city might be exposed to devastating riots and pillage. Mayo's solution was the immediate formation of a home guard to protect citizens and their property, and it was greeted with wild applause. As if to underscore Richmond's plight, transport trains started to disgorge the casualties from Branch's rout at Hanover the previous day. Carloads of dead and wounded and tales of "terrific slaughter" from demoralized deserters only increased the prevailing dread.[5]

Johnston, meanwhile, was pondering a last-chance battle to keep the Confederate Government in Richmond. On Johnston's map of the Peninsula was a ragged plus sign depicting McClellan's current position. The vertical arm of that cross was McClellan's front, which ran generally north–south. The horizontal line was labeled Chickahominy River, which flowed eastward past Richmond on the north before curling southward to the James. McClellan was compelled to straddle the Chickahominy so that his right (northern) wing could link up with McDowell. Johnston had been weighing an assault on this exposed flank for several days, but news of McDowell's approach prodded him to action. He now *had to* throw part of his army north of the Chickahominy and crush McClellan's right wing before McDowell arrived to swell the Union host to 150,000 men.

It was after 1 P.M. on May 28 before Johnston finished sketchy orders for a dawn attack on McClellan's right.[6] The seventeen hours that remained were not sufficient to arrange it properly, and those familiar with the over-all situation betrayed their pessimism regarding Johnston's chances. The Richmond City Council began enrolling the home guard of old men and boys proposed only that morning. The Army Provost Marshal made ready to burn enormous stockpiles of tobacco leaf. Under cover of dark, the Secretary of War began carting the archives he had packed several weeks earlier to the railway station.[7] A violent thunderstorm broke over Richmond.

Confederate division commanders gathered at Johnston's headquarters outside Richmond during that storm for a briefing by Major General Gustavus W. Smith, who would lead the attack on May 29. It had showered heavily during the past month and the Chickahominy was swollen beyond its banks, Smith began. Worse, Federal outposts held the Chickahominy bridges which the rebels must use, so that the main attack could not even be launched until those structures were captured. That task was assigned to the only Confederate unit north of the Chickahominy, Major General A. P. Hill's division, and it was not a good choice. Hill's division had been formed the day before and included one brigade, Branch's, which had been weakened by its drubbing at Hanover Courthouse; yet there was no time to get more experienced troops into position to take the bridges. Assuming the spans were won, other divisions must funnel over them and across quagmires to assault enemy lines bristling with heavy artillery. There was no chance to achieve surprise.

Several officers interrupted Smith to argue against this slugging match. The obvious alternative was to outflank McClellan by circling to the north around his right, but there was no time for maneuver. Smith was of the opinion that a head-on assault could not be avoided: ". . . it would be a bloody business, called for, however, by the necessity for prompt action if we expected to beat McClellan before he was joined by McDowell."[8]

Smith summarized: Hill's untested, two-day-old division must capture several Chickahominy bridges so the main columns could cross that treacherous river to attack a carefully entrenched foe. And there were but forty-eight hours in which to win a decisive victory. The Confederates would be fighting east of the Fredericksburg–Richmond road, so that if success was not achieved within two days McDowell could slash into their rear.

Johnston thought to himself about problems Smith had not considered. While Smith thrust at the Union right, Johnston had to retain some divisions south of the Chickahominy to keep McClellan from storming Richmond. Fourteen years later Johnston said of the prospect for communication between his separated wings: "I supposed that the bridges and fords of the little river would furnish means of sufficient communication between the two parts of the Confederate army."[9] Here lay the ultimate admission of tactical despair. About to gamble for his capital, Johnston could only "suppose" the halves of his army would fight in concert.

Yet, if Johnston dared, this last-chance battle might be avoided. A courier had brought him word before the conference that McDowell had about-faced and was returning to the Rappahannock. The Southern cavalry shadowing McDowell did not know why but they were certain about his new direction of march.[10] The question was whether to credit the report. Johnston's opinion of cavalry was notoriously low, though this intelligence came from a young brigadier general named J. E. B. Stuart, and Johnston thought well indeed of "Jeb." But had Jeb actually seen the withdrawal? Could he vouch that McDowell had given up a winning hand? If Johnston held off his attack on the authority of this report and it proved false . . .

Johnston drifted back to the reality of a room crowded with long-faced generals, one of whom, Major General James Longstreet, was arguing vigorously for immediate action.[11] Johnston hesitated, listened for a moment to the storm swirling outside, then announced his most fateful decision of the war. He canceled the attack on McClellan's right.

May 29 dawned quietly, without rain, and morning reports confirmed McDowell's retreat. Richmond listened in vain for cannon fire, then slowly began to realize it would not need a home guard to preserve order. Confederate authority would not collapse here. President Davis skimmed his office work and galloped out to observe the battle; as usual, Johnston had not shared his altered plans with the Chief Executive. Davis found whole divisions parked along the roadside in confusion: "I found Smith's division halted, and the men dispersed in the woods. Looking for some one from whom I could get information, I finally saw General Hood, and asked him the meaning of what I saw. He told me he did not know anything more than that they had been halted."[12]

Recall orders had not reached some units until the early hours of May 29, even as they were wading toward their attack positions.[13]

Robert E. Lee rode directly to Johnston's headquarters that morning,[14] and only then did Lee learn of McDowell's countermarch on May 28. Perhaps only then did he read Jackson's dispatch from Winchester announcing: "During the last three days God has blessed our arms with brilliant success."[15] The Valley Army (of which Lee had heard nothing after May 20) had carved its way to Winchester, and now McDowell had abandoned his descent on Richmond. Doubtless Lee joined those who linked McDowell's countermarch with "brilliant success" in the Shenandoah. At the last hour of the last day, the Valley Army had won through.

In Washington, the sense of impending victory, so strong on May 22, had weakened since 11 P.M. of May 23, when first word of the fight at Front Royal arrived. In this report Banks estimated rebel strength at 5,000.[16] By midnight he relayed hearsay estimates of rebel strength as 20,000.[17] He soon reported that Ewell held Front Royal with 6,000 to 10,000 men and Jackson was south of Strasburg with his command.[18] Banks's warnings were magnified by Brigadier General John Geary, who patrolled the Manassas Gap Railroad east of the Blue Ridge. Geary howled that Jackson was passing north of him and moving eastward in the general direction of Centreville with an army of 20,000; Geary reported additional thousands south of the railroad near Warrenton.[19] Luck favored the South with Geary's dispatch, for the Federals had just lost contact with General Anderson's Confederate force,[20] which was retreating from Fredericksburg to Richmond. Now here were thousands of rebels supposedly swarming into the Warrenton area northwest of Fredericksburg. Had Anderson joined Jackson for a general offensive? Lincoln and Secretary of War Stanton did not know.

For the first time in his presidency Lincoln was truly the Commander-in-Chief. The Valley Army had struck in a region where three of Lincoln's independent departments—those of Frémont, Banks, and McDowell—abutted, and any Northern reaction there must affect McClellan as well. None of the generals involved could act decisively in the over-all situation, since each commanded only his own department. Lincoln stepped into this breach.

The Commander-in-Chief discerned two contrary options. He could forget all else and concentrate McDowell around Washington to assure its safety. Yet this did not seem justified on the evening of May 24. Secretary Stanton sent four regiments to Banks from Washington and Baltimore on the twenty-fourth,[21] and there was every reason to suppose Banks would survive. Nor did a passive stance satisfy Lincoln, who, like Jackson, had been studying his map of Virginia. If Jackson was hurtling down the Valley or even east from the Blue Ridge, there could hardly be significant Confederate strength in the rebel rear around, say, Harrisonburg. With that thought Lincoln clutched a plan. At the same hour Jackson was piercing Banks's rear guard outside Middletown, at 4 P.M., May 24, Lincoln ordered Frémont to abandon his Knoxville project and move from Franklin toward Harrisonburg: "The exposed condition of General Banks makes his immediate relief a point of paramount importance. You are therefore directed by the President to move against Jackson at Harrisonburg and operate against the enemy in such way as to relieve Banks."[22]

Within the hour Lincoln also instructed McDowell to forego his movement on Richmond (scheduled to begin on May 26) and lead two of his four divisions, a total of 20,000 men, to the Shenandoah. McDowell's objective was to capture the Valley Army, orders which McDowell called a "crushing blow."[23] At that moment, 5 P.M., May 24, the Valley Army won its Valley Campaign.

Because Lincoln soon did fear that the Valley Army might approach Washington and because he unloaded that anxiety on McClellan, the traditional view of his crucial May 24 orders has been that they were motivated by this fear. There is no hard evidence to support this view. As of 5 P.M. Lincoln knew only that Jackson might be advancing east from the Blue Ridge[24] or down the Valley toward Winchester,[25] and Banks wired at 8 P.M. that the entire alarm was a mistake and that he would reoccupy Strasburg immediately.[26] Lincoln took no action on May 24 to bolster Washington's garrison; instead, troops were sent from Washington to the Valley. His orders to Frémont and McDowell show concern for Banks, not for Washington. Even Secretary Stanton, who considered a rebel drive against the capital likely and who knew the city's garrison was not strong, routed Union troop trains directly from Baltimore to Banks all day.[27] McDowell went to the Shenandoah to bag the Valley Army, an offensive rather than a defensive strike.[28] Perhaps the President wished to give sluggish McClellan a demonstration of what decisive action could accomplish, but whatever his thoughts, he gave no hint that fear of the Valley Army controlled him when he issued his May 24 orders and changed the course of the war.

Only as reports of a collapse at Winchester were added to other bad news on May 25 did Lincoln and Stanton begin to worry about the Valley Army approaching Washington. Banks sought to minimize the extent of his rout, but he also relayed intelligence that the rebels, with reinforcements expected, would invade Maryland via Harper's Ferry and Williamsport.[29] Sporadic pro-Southern rioting flared in Baltimore.[30] The disappearance of General Anderson's rebel force from Fredericksburg remained unsolved. General Geary not only reiterated that Jackson was moving eastward from the lower Valley but also relayed a rumor that as many as 10,000 rebel cavalry were pressing northward from Warrenton.[31]

Coupled to the disappearance of Anderson's command from Fredericksburg, Geary's dispatches were especially grim. Stanton imagined the enemy capable of anything and read these dispatches as proof that Anderson had eluded McDowell. He pestered the latter for assurances Anderson was not heading toward the Valley.[32] McDowell's well-reasoned response could not alleviate the Secretary's fears, which were aggravated by escalating alarms from Geary. On May 26 Geary again reported that Jackson was pouring east over the Blue Ridge to surround him.[33] "[I]n consideration of the hopeless circumstances surrounding us," Geary wrote, he fled with his entire force to Manassas.[34] Stanton spread the panic: Bristoe Station, forty miles east of the Blue Ridge, was abandoned on his orders.[35] At the van of McDowell's column moving to the Valley, Shields neared Manassas Junction on May 26 ready to fight his way through it.[36] Absurd as hindsight makes it, there was a genuine fear on the part of some high Union officials on May 25 and 26 that the rebels were nearing Manassas in force.

Two or three hundred half-armed Southern cavalry were responsible for this farce. Ewell, it will be recalled, had sent Colonel Munford with a detachment of his 2d Virginia Cavalry east of the Blue Ridge to track Shields in mid-May. Munford had ended his vigil when Shields passed Warrenton. By this time Munford's companies were swollen with unarmed recruits, and he was sent to secure arms in Richmond. Many of his riders returned to the Valley, but some had remained to observe Geary and his command.[37] It was this motley handful that Geary multiplied into the rebel hordes that haunted Stanton. The only other known Confederate force east of the Blue Ridge during this period was one company of Ashby's command,[38] and it merely burned Manassas Gap bridges deserted by Geary.[39] These cavalrymen thus did as much as anyone in the Valley Army to throw a scare into the Federal Government.

Southern riders, however, were only the first of Stanton's worries. The Secretary also was dogged by the knowledge that Washington's garrison probably could not withstand even a cavalry army. When McDowell was held at Manassas after Kernstown the capital was entirely secure, and Stanton did little thereafter to tone up the flaccid garrison McClellan had provided. So little was done that when, on April 19, Stanton gave surprise orders requiring the garrison to assume the city was under attack and actually deploy to resist, it took four hours to assemble 4,100 men at several Potomac bridges, and many of them lacked ammunition.[40] He confided to Banks on May 9: "The probabilities at present point to a possible [rebel] attempt upon Washington. . . . Washington is the only object now worth a desperate throw."[41] Yet there is no record of Stanton prowling Washington's defenses to insure their adequacy. Of course, a Secretary of War normally does not attend to such matters, but since he and Lincoln had virtually become the Union high command in Virginia the job properly devolved on him. Stanton had ignored the job, while at the same time allowing McDowell to dip into Washington's garrison before his scheduled descent on Richmond. Four regiments from the capital were on the Rappahannock by early May.[42] On May 11 four of the best regiments remaining in the city were siphoned to Catlett's Station as replacements for a brigade which strengthened McDowell.[43] Another regiment left Washington for Fredericksburg as late as May 22.[44]

It is one of the war's unnoted ironies that Stanton, so indignant over McClellan's chicanery in March, himself let Washington be stripped of defenders, yet Union records amply document the fact that the city was no better defended after Winchester than after Kernstown, and Stanton cannot evade culpability in this. He had personally supervised the deployment of McDowell's forces. McDowell noted some of the major shifts in the Washington garrison in dispatches to Stanton.[45] McDowell submitted frequent reports tallying the strength of his army and its subordinate command, Brigadier General James Wadsworth's Military District of Washington.[46] These reports openly charted a steady drain on the forces around Washington. The report of Saturday, May 24, which Stanton must have combed eagerly, was especially revealing of Washington's exposed situation. Wadsworth's effective aggregate strength was given as 18,779 men, and 3,300 of them were forty miles away at Catlett's Station; Wadsworth even doubted those 3,300 were still under his command. Stanton flashed special orders returning those men to Wadsworth,[47] but telegrams did not move them any closer, and there were other skeletons lurking among the neat rows of numbers. With a lawyer's passion for detail, Stanton noted that one of the regiments supposedly at Washington had marched for Fredericksburg on May 22; of the less than 15,000 "effectives" in the city, 2,000 were unequipped[48]; there was a total of only 300 cavalry fit for service.[49] Even the news, if Stanton heard it, that there were units available but not tallied in McDowell's report soured: those units proved to be several squadrons of cavalry so disorganized that even McClellan, who never felt he had enough men, had ejected them from the Peninsula.[50] Had Stanton been willing to empty Washington's military stockades and hospitals, he might have placed a man every ten feet around the capital on May 25.

Stanton did not stop to classify the fears which were battering him to the fringe of hysteria. Whereas the day before he had weakened Washington to bolster Banks, the afternoon of May 25 saw him drag one of McDowell's brigades back to Manassas and another into Washington.[51] Stanton wired the governors of thirteen states that Jackson was advancing full force on Washington and begged them to rush their militia to its rescue.[52] He seized operating control of every railroad in the North to speed the rescuers[53] and thereby immeasurably fueled his own crisis mentality.

After the war, zealous admirers of Jackson would claim the entire Union shared Stanton's fears for Washington; they would write of a panic-stricken North pouring men into the capital,[54] but this was not true. What panic there may have been was confined to a handful of public officials and journalists. Some governors did issue alarming mobilization orders in response to Stanton's plea for militia. Ohio's Governor David Tod relayed the "astounding intelligence that the seat of our beloved Government is threatened with invasion."[55] Governor John Andrew of Massachusetts announced that a "wily and barbarious horde" was menacing Washington as he ordered his militia to assemble on Boston Common.[56] The Boston *Daily Advertiser* thereafter reported a "ferment" in Boston,[57] probably attributable more to the assembling militia than fears for Washington. The New York *Herald* headlined that 500,000 men responded to the governors' calls,[58] a report often cited by Jackson's admirers, though it was totally inaccurate.

The North was not stampeded by the Valley Army's drive. The stock market recorded no unusual activity from May 24 to 30. The New York *Times* immediately advised that stuffing Washington with militia would only produce undue excitement on the home front and assured its readers on May 27 that the Valley Army was already retreating.[59] One looks in vain for any large-scale evidence that the Union feared for Washington's safety during May 1862. One finds, rather, complacent comments such as that in a Philadelphia *Inquirer* editorial: "Strategic combinations, well made, have doubtless been in a slight degree disconcerted by the hurried retreat of General Banks. . . . But it is very improbable that any permanent damage has been done."[60]

Nor is there any evidence of panic in the streets of Washington itself. The *Sunday Morning Chronicle* of May 25 reported simply that Banks had retired safely to Winchester, where he had been heavily reinforced. The *Chronicle*'s front-page story concerned Benjamin Franklin's ledger kept while Postmaster General.[61] The *National Intelligencer* denounced rumors of a Southern advance on the city as absurd and devoted its principal attention on May 27 to an analysis of United States relations with Mexico.[62]

One reporter, who had witnessed the frenzy in Washington following the defeat at Manassas a year earlier, compared it to the current mood of the capital: "The alarm of the night of [May] 25th by no means was as general as it was [after Manassas]. We are all surprised, vexed; some of us are a little glad, though, that the enemy is doing something besides everlastingly running away. We don't apprehend any great catastrophe."[63]

But Abraham Lincoln did apprehend a catastrophe, at least during the afternoon and evening of May 25. Rumor stacked on rumor in the White House, and the President recalled glumly that this was the agony he had dreaded since McClellan first broached his Peninsula scheme. McClellan had assured him it would never happen, but he also had promised to leave 55,000 men around Washington. Fear and frustration marked every word as Lincoln wrote McClellan that day: ". . . Jackson's movement is a general and concerted one, such as could not be if he was acting upon the purpose of a very desperate defense of Richmond. I think the time is near when you must either attack Richmond or give up the job and come to the defense of Washington."[64] Later, perhaps after a briefing by Stanton, the President wrote McClellan again to tell him the city was "stripped bare," adding: "If McDowell's force was now beyond our reach, we should be utterly helpless. Apprehensions of something like this, and no unwillingness to sustain you, has always been my reason for withholding McDowell's force from you."[65]

That last sentence has been cited as the strongest support for the traditional view that Lincoln diverted McDowell from Richmond for fear of the Valley Army.[66] As we have seen, however, this diversion had already taken place for offensive purposes when Lincoln penned those words. But while Lincoln's concern had not been the cause of McDowell's new orders, it did make them irrevocable. By May 25 Lincoln's concern was such that he was deaf when McDowell argued that he should go to Richmond as planned. More than anyone else, McDowell perceived the gravity of the error Lincoln was making. He lectured the President: ". . . by a glance at the map it will be seen that the line of retreat of the enemy's forces up the valley is shorter than mine to go against him. It will take a week or ten days for the force to get to the valley by the route which will give it food and forage, and by that time the enemy will have retired. I shall gain nothing for you

12. *left:* General Robert E. Lee.
(Courtesy of the Library of Congress)

13. *below:* General Joseph E. Johnston.
(Courtesy of the Library of Congress)

Classmates at West Point, Johnston and Lee
found themselves issuing conflicting orders
to the Valley Army in May 1862.

14. *below:* The Battle of Kernstown. This contemporary engraving by Alfred R. Waud evidently depicts the final moments of the battle, as Waud carefully included fleeing rebels and the setting sun. (From April 12, 1862, issue of *Harper's Weekly,* reproduced courtesy of the Virginia State Library)

15. *opposite, above:* Ashby's charge at Middletown. (Courtesy of the Virginia State Library)

16. *opposite, below:* Federal scouts approaching Strasburg, June 1, 1862. In this wartime sketch by Union artist Edwin Forbes, the last Confederate trains can be seen (center, left) pulling through Strasburg to escape the Union pincer operation set in motion by President Lincoln seven days earlier. (Courtesy of the Virginia State Library)

17. *above:* Brigadier General Edward Johnson.   18. *above:* Brigadier General Isaac R. Trimble.
19. *below:* Brigadier General Charles S. Winder.   20. *below:* Brigadier General Richard B. Garnett.

The brigade was the basic combat unit of the Valley Army, and on successive fields these brigadiers held center stage of the Valley Campaign. (All four photographs on this page courtesy of the Library of Congress) there, and shall lose much for you here [at Fredericksburg]. It throws us all back, and from Richmond north we shall have all our large masses paralyzed, and shall have to repeat what we have just accomplished."[67] He complained to General Wadsworth: "If the enemy can succeed so readily in disconcerting all our plans by alarming us first at one point, then at another, he will paralyze a large force with a very small one."[68]

McDowell had read the minds of Lee and Jackson, but Lincoln did not appreciate his vision. The President's orders stood. General Shields left Fredericksburg for the Valley on May 25, and Major General E. O. C. Ord's division followed the next day. At Stanton's direction, most of Ord's command moved first by water to Alexandria, thence to the Valley, in order to afford Washington some additional temporary security.[69]

(To counteract the melodrama which has confused the Valley Campaign, it must be stressed here once more that Washington had not been an actual or feinted target for Jackson and that fear of Jackson did not dictate Lincoln's crucial redeployments of McDowell either in April or May. The rebels had wintered in 1861–62 within a few miles of Washington, had watched its fortifications grow, and could not have believed Jackson's small force capable of bothering it. The Lee–Jackson correspondence of this period does not contain the word "Washington," and there is only one possible allusion to it, Lee's letter of May 16 in which he suggested Jackson threaten the "Potomac line" after Banks was routed. Johnston, writing on May 27, was the only Confederate to mention a demonstration toward the city, and this came as an afterthought to the victory at Winchester. The Valley Campaign, then, had developed as follows: Lincoln, admittedly concerned for the safety of Washington, demanded that McClellan garrison it strongly before he sailed to the Peninsula in March, but McClellan failed to provide an adequate garrison. Lincoln discovered this failure after Banks was detained in the Shenandoah by the Battle of Kernstown on March 23 and, to establish the agreed preconditions of the spring campaign and not from any fear of the Valley Army, he detached McDowell from McClellan's army; McDowell eventually moved south to Fredericksburg. Lee urged Jackson to interfere with McDowell's operations from Fredericksburg by a strike in the Valley which would have repercussions in eastern

Virginia; Jackson launched his drive with this goal in mind, and Lincoln, for offensive reasons, ordered McDowell to move to the Valley on May 24. On May 25 and 26 Lincoln and Stanton did briefly believe Washington was threatened, a belief that was a Confederate bonus and that served principally to render McDowell's rerouting irrevocable. Finally, Stanton ordered Ord's division of McDowell's force to move to the Valley by water via Alexandria, thereby delaying Ord's column. The time lost by this detour was paid for in the Shenandoah and made more certain the Valley Army's escape from Lincoln's counterthrust.)

There is, finally, an ironic footnote in the chronicle of the Union's response to the Valley Army's drive; this footnote concerns the reprieve of May 28 which appeared so miraculous to the Confederates at Richmond. As Shields's and Ord's divisions left Fredericksburg for the Shenandoah, McDowell sent his remaining forces south of the Rappahannock to conceal their departure.[70] It was this sham—and McDowell's march south from Fredericksburg was never more than that—which scared Johnston to the brink of a last-chance battle on May 28. Had McDowell actually been en route for Richmond—indeed, had his sham only continued a little longer—Johnston would have sacrificed his army before McClellan's guns on May 29. But as it was, the nightmarish jolt McDowell gave Johnston was all the help McClellan was to receive from him. McDowell soon called another of his divisions to the Shenandoah, and the second front against Richmond dissolved.

II

"[Jackson] will paralyze a large force with a very small one"— that was McDowell's warning as his divisions lumbered off on a mission he knew to be a blunder, and it was high praise and fitting reward for the Valley Army. The redeployment of McDowell's divisions climaxed a disruption of Union strategy so complete that the campaign which produced it has become a classic of the soldier's art. The student of large-scale military operations is richly rewarded by a study of the Valley Campaign from Kernstown to Winchester, for it offers both examples of the successful application of almost every principle of war as well as object lessons highlighting the consequences of disregarding these principles. Particularly in the realm of strategy, the art of maneuvering an army across a large area against an opposing army, the Campaign illustrates certain lessons with a clarity rarely matched in military history.

First, the Valley Campaign illustrates that an offensive does not leap full grown from the mind of its planner. It begins, rather, with a series of suggestions, of alternatives typified by the Lee–Jackson correspondence prior to May 1, and it develops in an atmosphere of vaguely understood enemy intentions, strength, and location. By the end of April Frémont's advance had driven Edward Johnson back on Staunton, Banks had mustered a powerful column at Harrisonburg, and a dual threat to Richmond was worsening from Fredericksburg and the Peninsula. Stonewall had no solution to this imbroglio as he left Swift Run Gap on April 30; it cannot be asserted that he definitely planned more than to drive Frémont away from Banks.[71] Jackson thought he saw a path into Banks's rear after the victory at McDowell on May 8 and plunged toward Franklin hoping to seize it. This proved impossible, so Jackson retraced his steps to the Shenandoah determined to try something else. On this march, from May 12 until May 17, he clung to the mistaken notion that no part of Banks's column would leave the Valley, and the intelligence he received did not clarify his picture of the situation. Ewell (correctly) sent word that portions of Banks's force were moving east, while Ashby (erroneously) reported they were moving west. Such contradictory reports are the rule in war rather than the exception. Jackson's constant demand was properly for more information.

As late as May 17 Jackson did not know how he might best exploit a possible victory over Banks. He informed Johnston that the Valley Army might "try" to move into the Alleghenies from the Strasburg area after dealing with Banks, thereby threatening Frémont from the rear and compelling him to retreat farther from Staunton.[72] Lee's suggestion that a demonstration along the Potomac would be valuable may have turned Jackson's thoughts to this goal, and Johnston's suggestion that he might cross the Potomac ended any idea of re-entering the mountains. Finally, the halt just north of Cedarville on May 24 clearly reveals Jackson was unsure how to corner Banks as late as 11 A.M. that morning. At no time was the Valley Campaign ever a fixed itinerary in Jackson's mind.

The tentative nature of military planning has as a consequence a second lesson, a lesson chiseled into the story of this Campaign: the greatest possible independence must be awarded to a commander struggling to execute his inevitably provisional strategy. It was to protect this independence that Jackson so loudly protested Loring's withdrawal from Romney in January. The correspondence between Lee and Jackson reads like a textbook on this point. From his desk in Richmond, Lee sought to co-ordinate Confederate operations; he did not dictate them, and Lee was careful to emphasize that his own thoughts on how McDowell's threat might be countered were speculations and not orders. Lee replied to Jackson's various proposals: "I cannot pretend at this distance to direct operations depending on circumstances unknown to me and requiring the exercise of discretion and judgment as to time and execution."[73] Here Lee highlights a valuable truth: subordinate commanders exist because discretion and judgment in the enemy's presence are essential. If an officer is not capable of the necessary decisions, no outside direction can substitute; if he is capable, none is needed. Lee set the basic goal of this Campaign; Jackson planned and executed it, and Lee was well rewarded for trusting Jackson to his own resources.

Third, a crucial principle of war—concentration of maximum force at the point of decision—is vividly illustrated in both its negative and positive applications through this Campaign. The principle itself, like all axioms of war, is readily comprehensible. Clausewitz expressed it thusly: ". . . to concentrate our power as much as possible against that section where the chief blows are to be delivered and to incur disadvantages elsewhere, so that our chances of success may increase at the decisive point. This will compensate for all other disadvantages."[74]

Starting in obedience to this principle, the Union spring offensive ended in tragic violation of it. McClellan set out to capture the enemy capital by an end run with his entire army; for all his faults as a commander, he at least planned to keep the Army of the Potomac together. Unfortunately for McClellan, the Battle of Kernstown made it impossible for him to keep his army together and simultaneously guard Washington in the manner Lincoln desired. McClellan chose instead to inflate Washington's garrison with nonexistent or worthless troops. Discovery of that duplicity led directly to the severing of both Banks and McDowell from McClellan's control. The detachment of McDowell from the Army of the Potomac was especially unfortunate. His 30,000 men at Fredericksburg were too powerful merely to guard the approaches of Washington yet too distant from McClellan or Banks to actively support either.

After Kernstown, Lincoln increasingly became supreme commander of the Union armies across Virginia, a role in which he ignored the need for concentration again with the dispatch of Blenker's division (10,000 men) from McClellan to Frémont for operations against Knoxville. This was a gross blunder. Frémont had 19,000 men without Blenker,[75] an adequate force to defend his Mountain Department. McClellan was launching a possibly climactic struggle for the enemy capital, and every available Union soldier belonged with him. The conquest of Richmond would have outweighed anything Frémont might have won in the Alleghenies. Frémont should have been kept on the defensive with only sufficient strength to prevent Confederates opposite him from reinforcing Richmond. A Southern attack in the Alleghenies might even have been encouraged, for rebels pushing west there could not be at Richmond. Instead, Frémont advanced without concentrating his forces and thereby provided Jackson a superb strategic opening: Milroy was dangerously far from the bulk of Frémont's command when the Valley Army started after him.

By ordering McDowell to Richmond in May, Lincoln attempted to reunify his armies. It would have been best for McDowell to go by sea, since an overland march risked his destruction before reaching McClellan. Lincoln, however, would not uncover Washington, but he did brace McDowell with an additional 10,000 men. Unfortunately, Lincoln drew these reinforcements from the sensitive Valley. Banks was left with less than 10,000 men to garrison a large area and a long rail line, and his inadequate force was as a result thinly spread. (It should also be noted that, during May, Lincoln was preparing to give up Frémont's advance on Knoxville and direct him toward Richmond by way of Salem, Virginia.[76] This course was preferable to the original plan for

Frémont, but it still kept Frémont isolated and out of range for co-operation with other Federal armies.)

Shields's transfer was arranged after Banks claimed Jackson had fled the Valley, but the Battle of McDowell signaled that Jackson had not. Immediately after Jackson left his front, Frémont reported that the rebels were returning to the Valley.[77] Even before this, Banks, reversing earlier claims, wired that Jackson and Ewell were both in the upper Valley,[78] and similar warnings came from at least one other source.[79] Washington seems simply to have ignored these signals in favor of reports more compatible with its notion of where the Valley Army should be. As he moved eastward, Shields assured the War Department that rebels in the Valley were not there to fight but to delay his own division and then retreat to Richmond via Charlottesville.[80] Washington adopted Shields's view, and late May found Union armies badly positioned: Frémont had too many men where they were not needed; Banks had too few where they were; Shields was on his way to Fredericksburg from whence, with McDowell, he faced a potentially dangerous march of one isolated army toward Richmond. Finally, responding to the Valley Army's offense, Lincoln further scattered his forces. Some of McDowell's brigades moved toward Washington; some of his divisions went to the Shenandoah, and the remainder feinted an advance on Richmond.

While Washington squandered its strength, Richmond sought ever greater concentration of its resources. Lee worked energetically to bring units from as far south as Georgia to the Peninsula and increased Johnston's army by many thousands. Lee's letter to Jackson of April 25 catches so clearly the essence of the principle of concentration of force that it deserves repetition. Lee wrote: "I have hoped in the present divided condition of the enemy's forces that a successful blow may be dealt them by a rapid combination of our troops before they [the enemy] can be strengthened themselves either in their position or by reenforcements."[81] A worthy companion to Lee's letter came from Jackson, who had explained his need for Loring's command and the subsequent march on Romney by writing Johnston on Christmas Eve 1861: ". . . our true policy is to attack the enemy in his present position before he receives additional re-enforcements, and especially never to permit a junction of their forces at or near Martinsburg."[82]

It is with such vision that campaigns are won. Jackson's goal after leaving Swift Run Gap at the end of April was to unite with Edward Johnson; during the same march he gathered up the small V.M.I. Corps of Cadets. The cadets may have been young, but they had muskets and knew how to use them, and Jackson did not overlook a reinforcement of 200 any more than he did one of 2,000. Stonewall's next strategic move was to join Ewell for the attack at Front Royal. He fought this battle with virtually the entire Valley Army, posting only a handful of cavalry south of Strasburg. The road to Staunton was thus temporarily opened for Frémont, a risk Jackson took to insure preponderance of numbers on the battlefield.

An integral aspect of Southern concentration of force was an effort to prevent the enemy from achieving the same thing. This desire possessed Jackson from the day he assumed command in the Valley and saw he must contend with two enemy fronts. The quest to keep those fronts apart led him to Bath and to McDowell. The persistence with which he pursued this matter was evidenced after the Battle of McDowell on May 8 when he had Hotchkiss block passes between Franklin and the Harrisonburg–New Market area. It was Jackson's desire never to leave enemy columns an open road by which to unite.

The concentration of Southern forces in the Valley, though ultimately successful, was not easily achieved, which points to a fourth lesson of the Campaign: in war it is usually difficult to continue toward a chosen objective, even as basic an objective as concentration. During the spring of 1862 Lee desired to combine Southern detachments in central Virginia and the Valley for a major diversion to stop McDowell at Fredericksburg. This was certainly the Confederacy's best hope. But even Lee lost sight of this goal when, on May 8, he urged Ewell to attack Banks if he ventured to Fredericksburg. Such a blow would have been struck without Jackson's and Johnson's commands, and it is questionable whether anything approaching the results of the descent on Winchester could have come from such an attack.

Johnston, too, wished Jackson and Ewell to unite against Banks. Yet, under the pressure of McClellan's approach and Shields's departure from the Valley, Johnston temporarily relinquished hope of a Valley attack. In his letter of May 17 he stated that Jackson and Ewell might join to attack Shields, but then Ewell must reinforce Richmond while Jackson watched Banks, orders which would have dispersed the Confederates at the very moment they had an opportunity to crush Banks. Fortunately Johnston was wise enough to return freedom of action to the Valley Army after he saw Ewell's letter to Lee of May 17 and rethought the strategic situation.

Jackson's response to Johnston's orders of May 17 was another example of the strain involved in holding to the objective. Johnston's instructions to send Ewell east were clear and peremptory. Jackson, however, suspended Ewell's movement when he appealed to Lee, a virtual renunciation of the exacting obedience by which Stonewall had always lived. His hand must have trembled as he wrote Lee, but Jackson resolved to exhaust every possibility before he abandoned a course he believed to be correct. For the military historian, failure to maintain the objective is among the easiest mistakes to detect. For the soldier, it is among the most difficult blunders to avoid.

Constant planning, freedom to carry through the product of this planning, concentration of force, and maintenance of the objective —these were elements, among many, of victory in the Shenandoah. And there is nothing particularly difficult to understand about these elements; they are simply the result of earnest effort. The Valley Campaign has been termed a brilliant strategic conception, and so it was, but brilliance sprang from much hard work. Constantly rechecking his information, Jackson at length found a sensitive point which he struck with his whole strength. That done, he had fulfilled his mission as a commander, and even had McDowell not been diverted from Richmond, Stonewall could have done no more. "Duty is ours," Jackson once declared, "consequences are God's."

III

Tactics is the art of maneuvering units on a battlefield. It is fully as demanding as the realm of strategy, and in the tactical realm, Valley Army leadership from Kernstown to Winchester was often disappointing.

At Kernstown, on March 23, confusion snarled the Confederate advance and gave the enemy time to meet it with ample reserves, and this confusion was largely attributable to Jackson. Garnett's court-martial after Kernstown was suspended before the accused could testify, but in a preliminary document Garnett wrote that at the beginning of the battle Jackson gave him only a vague instruction to support Fulkerson and that he (Garnett) entered the battle supposing the Confederates were to attack Northern artillery on Pritchard's Hill.[83] Stonewall admitted under questioning at the trial before it was suspended that he never revealed his plan to Garnett.[84] Jackson thus sent Garnett, who was second in command of the Army and at the head of its largest brigade, into battle without specifying what he was to accomplish. Garnett also claimed that Jackson initially directed him to support Fulkerson with only one regiment.[85] Jackson denied giving such an order, but the fact that Garnett, a brave man under fire, believed he had received it underscored the turmoil in which the Confederates operated that day. At Kernstown, Stonewall's secretive ways backfired.

The Battle of McDowell on May 8 was fought largely under General Edward Johnson, whose record was not distinguished. Confederates standing on the defense there suffered significantly heavier losses than their attackers, and by the close of the engagement Southern regiments were intermingled worse than at Kernstown. Nor had Jackson kept his rear units concentrated that day, with the result that the Valley Army was committed to the battle piecemeal.

The operations from May 23 to 25 saw improvements in Jackson's handling of the Army. He made excellent use of his cavalry on May 23: Ashby's and Flournoy's raids along the Manassas Gap Railroad denied the Federals at Front Royal any help from Strasburg. On May 24 Jackson demonstrated a fine understanding of the interplay between strategy and tactics. When the information he needed on Banks's location failed to arrive, Jackson halted north of Cedarville to await it. By this halt he conformed his tactics to the over-all situation. The Army's offense would have lost its goal had Banks slipped east through Front Royal. On the other hand, if Jackson could be certain the Union army would not escape eastward, he could look for later opportunities to crush it. The hours lost around Cedarville, if unfortunate

from a tactical point of view, were nevertheless wise strategy and
made more probable the Army's ultimate success. That Stonewall
did not reach Middletown until midafternoon reflected no lapse of
leadership, as some have thought,[86] but rather a careful analysis.

Arriving at Middletown, Jackson was again uncertain about
Banks's location. It was afternoon and perhaps logical to think
that the main body of Union troops was already north of this
point. But enemy formations were visible to the south in seemingly heavy force, and Jackson turned to meet them. To have
chanced leaving any large portion of the Union army south of
Middletown was to seriously endanger the Valley Army's own
supply trains and to renew the possibility of a Federal breakout
through Front Royal. These were risks Jackson could not take.

At Front Royal and Winchester, Jackson displayed skills that,
because of his rapid rise from brigade to army commander, he
had not had time to master when he marched on Romney. When
he discovered that the Union 1st Maryland regiment occupied
Front Royal, he shrewdly threw his own Marylanders against
them; he witnessed the excellent combat discipline of Taylor's
Louisianians and assigned them the decisive task at Winchester.
Jackson clearly had given some thought to matching units to missions. He also co-ordinated movements better than he had during
the Romney offense and Kernstown, although this remained a
weak point. He explained to Winder and to Taylor exactly, if
briefly, what he wanted them to do at Winchester. During the
early hours of May 25 Jackson sent Ewell simple but adequate orders to arrange a simultaneous dawn strike. Finally, Jackson was
now careful to be where he was needed. He was among the first
Confederates to cross the burning North Fork highway bridge at
Front Royal on May 23; at one point he was actually in the way
of Flournoy's cavalry as it chased the enemy to Cedarville[87]; he
was with Trimble's brigade as it advanced toward Winchester on
May 24, and he stayed with the van for the duration of the drive,
almost singlehandedly dragging his weary men onward. In this respect, he was not at all the same officer who had allowed Loring
to dawdle for hours outside Bath on January 4.

Against Stonewall's achievements as a battle captain were balanced some extraordinary lapses. He thrashed the Federals at
Front Royal on May 23 only to end moaning that his artillery was

not present to help prevent their escape. He was forced to improvise a pursuit and to demand superhuman heroics of Flournoy's
squadrons. Southern artillery did fearful destruction along the
Valley Pike the next day, but the cavalry was scattered and could
not exploit this destruction. Worse still, none of the at least 800
cavalry in the area moved promptly to exploit the victory that was
won at Winchester on May 25, and Jackson was again left to
moan and improvise.

Responsibility for these disjointed blunders rests ultimately
with Jackson as commander of the army which made them.
Others, however, had also blundered. Colonel Crutchfield, Jackson's chief of artillery, for instance, had not sufficiently famil-
iarized himself with Ewell's artillery prior to the engagement at
Front Royal. He had no idea where Ewell's long-range guns could
be found,[88] which seems inexcusable for a man in his position.
The time lost locating these pieces helped permit the enemy's initial escape and necessitated the second fight at Cedarville.

An effective pursuit was eventually made after the action at
Front Royal, but none was carried through after the action at
Middletown on May 24; Ashby's command disintegrated following that skirmish. Two explanations have been offered for the dismal showing of Ashby's cavalry on May 24, but neither is completely satisfactory. In 1867 Captain Chew explained the
disappearance of Ashby's troopers by noting that as Federals fled
in every direction, rebels naturally became scattered in pursuit,
and Ashby, who stayed on the Valley Pike, had no chance to reassemble his men.[89] Doubtless Chew is correct to an extent. The fact
remains, however, that large numbers of cavalrymen near the Pike
refused to cease looting and join Crutchfield when ordered to do
so.

Captain James Avirett, Ashby's regimental chaplain, offered the
second explanation. He insisted that Ashby's command did not
disappear at all on May 24. Rather, he claimed that Ashby had
only a few companies available that day because most of the Valley cavalry was already spread around the Shenandoah on missions assigned by Jackson: ten companies, or nearly half Ashby's
force, stationed in the Alleghenies to observe Frémont; four companies deployed south of Strasburg; one company deployed east
of Front Royal; two companies guarding prisoners; at least one

company sent to scout Strasburg from the east; and some men detailed to act as couriers for Headquarters.[90] Like Chew, Avirett is correct to an extent. Ashby's cavalry was partially dispersed on the twenty-fourth, but the complete fragmentation Avirett described is doubtful. Captain Harry Gilmor wrote after the war that his company alone, not the ten asserted by Avirett, was left to observe Frémont.[91] Gilmor was corroborated by Trooper Bill Wilson, who noted in his diary for May 22: "That portion of Ashby's cavalry which has been camped for the last three or four weeks at Mt. Crawford, Lacey Springs and this place [New Market] together *with ten companies just returned from accompanying Jackson on his expedition to McDowell* [italics supplied by author] received marching orders [which directed them to cross the Massanutten Mountain with Ashby]."[92] It is true that one or two companies were detached from Ashby's immediate control to act as scouts and couriers for Headquarters, while four companies were deployed above Strasburg.[93] But even deducting all of the detachments cited by Avirett which were not specifically refuted by Gilmor and Wilson accounts for only eight companies of a command which Avirett numbered at twenty-six companies.

It was also true, as Chew noted, that Ashby dispatched Major Funsten with several companies to strike the Valley Pike north of Middletown and broaden the front of the Confederate attack on May 24.[94] Funsten, however, rejoined Ashby on the Pike during the afternoon.[95] From the time of Funsten's return there seems no reason other than poor discipline that at least three or four hundred riders (the equivalent of only eight or ten companies at normal strength)[96] were not with Ashby.

As it was, Ashby finished the day with 50 men, after a debacle Jackson had foreseen and was powerless to avert. Jackson had exceeded his authority when he assigned the cavalry to Winder and Taliaferro for drill at Swift Run Gap, and this merely produced Ashby's resignation. Since the cavalry chieftain had continued to ignore Jackson's insistence on better order, the cavalry's behavior on May 24 was inevitable. It was Ashby's harvest for months of neglected training and discipline.

What Stonewall desired from Ashby at the Battle of Winchester is not known, though whatever it was, it was not done. Jackson complained in his report: "Upon my inquiring of Ashby why he was not where I desired him at the close of the engagement, he stated that he had moved to the enemy's left, for the purpose of cutting off a portion of his force."[97] A circuit around the Federal left would account for the duration of Ashby's absence, but it remains an unsatisfactory explanation, since this quarter of the field was so foggy Ashby could not have seen the enemy he supposedly intended to bag. Further, Ashby must have known the bulk of Southern cavalry (under Steuart) was already arrayed opposite the enemy left east of the Pike, so that riding eastward would merely strip all mounted protection from the Valley Army's other wing. Jackson apparently had given him orders to be at a specific place by the close of the action, and the reason why Ashby failed to be there remains unclear. The uncertainty, however, frees Jackson from all but nominal responsibility for this Ashby failure.

Not insuring the presence of other units to take Ashby's place on May 25 was a mistake on Jackson's part. He had seen Flournoy in action at Cedarville, and Steuart had gained valuable information around Newtown. The squadrons under Steuart were obviously excellent, yet there is no record of Jackson giving Steuart battle instructions prior to Winchester. Jackson sent Ewell instructions during the early hours of May 25; he might easily have added a few words to place Steuart where he wanted him at dawn. Jackson gave Ashby orders for the day; why did he not give Steuart any? It was even more inexcusable that Jackson did not summon Steuart immediately after Taylor's charge decided the battle. At this juncture he knew Ashby was not present, but Jackson waited until he was three miles north of Winchester before sending Pendleton to find Steuart.

Perhaps Jackson assumed Steuart would not need orders when the situation clearly demanded attack, but if this was the case, Stonewall had overlooked a badly confused chain of command. Steuart presumed when he rejoined Ewell after his reconnaissance to Newtown on May 24 that he was once again under the former's control. According to his chief of staff, Ewell was under the impression Jackson would retain control over all cavalry.[98] What Stonewall intended is not known; evidently he failed to explain precisely who commanded whom. As Steuart was left with the idea he was under Ewell, it was, technically, correct for him to sit

out the battle waiting for properly transmitted orders from the latter.

In sum, Jackson failed to reap all that his strategy made possible because of a major tactical flaw, an inability to wield his army
as a single weapon. He had made strides toward overcoming this
problem, but it remained serious. If the faults of other officers had
aggravated it, they could not erase it. Perhaps the speed of his
marches had been so great and the exhaustion of men (and of
himself) so acute that mistakes were unavoidable. Perhaps. But in
his stern way, Jackson must have prayed that there be no more
disjointed blunders.

IV

Consequences, lessons, evaluations: these were not the concern
of the men who triumphed in the Shenandoah. Victory was a
more personal thing for them. It meant a visit home or the bliss of
a real bed. As the Army regrouped from the pursuit of Banks on
May 25, Jackson camped it several miles from Winchester and issued his usual directive prohibiting unauthorized soldiers in the
city,[99] an order which received as little attention now as it had during the winter. Johnny Williams invited Ed Moore to spend a
night at his house, which they found crowded with privates and
officers alike.[100] Randy McKim of the 1st Maryland savored three
days around Winchester reveling in civilized life and "the enjoy-
ment of the ladies' society in particular."[101]

And there was food—courtesy of the Union army. Before
Stonewall could secure the enormous abundance of captured
stores, his men had picked through them, liberating oranges,
lemons, figs, dates, oysters, lobsters, sardines, pickles, coffee,
sugar, cheese, hams, and meat.[102]

And there was drink—crates of the finest brandies and wines.
Two Marylanders captured a dozen bottles of champagne and resolved to place them beyond risk of recapture, so they quaffed
every bottle. The next day their regiment marched, causing one of
the Marylanders to admit in later years: "I have not forgotten the
terrors of that day's march, particularly in the early hours until
some friends gave me a bottle of Rhine wine. It healed my sor-

rows . . . and enabled me to make the march with comparative comfort. Many years have since rolled by; many varied experiences have I undergone, but never since have I attempted to put away six bottles of champagne in one sitting."[103]

The boys slept, bathed, ate, drank, and sought out the girls. They riddled Federal breastplates (which were advertised as protection against all harm) at target-practice sessions.[104] They began to replace their meager wardrobes from a warehouse of Federal uniforms, until it almost seemed that Banks's army had returned.

New regulations boomed from Headquarters as the Army revived. All men found wearing Union garb, Jackson directed, should be arrested and confined until they could be identified as Confederates.[105] Daily drills resumed. To aid Major Harman, who was evacuating prodigious amounts of booty, Jackson summoned every wagon in the Shenandoah, civilian and military, to Winchester.[106]

No chorus of squawks greeted these orders, for the troops had come to understand the purpose behind the ceaseless activity of their stern commander. On May 26 Jackson praised their triumphs in a General Order and added: "The explanation of the severe exertions to which the Commanding General called the army, which were endured by them [sic] with such cheerful confidence, is now given, in the victory of yesterday."[107] Old Jack won by trading sweat for blood. This his men understood: ". . . our loss was small," concluded John Casler about the fight from Front Royal to Winchester, "it being a kind of a one sided fight all the time. General Jackson 'got the drop' on them in the start, and kept it."[108]

Part III

13

UP THE VALLEY

*This trip has broken me down
completely and at one time.*

—JAMES EDMONDSON

On May 28 the Valley Army, which could not have known that it had already achieved everything desired of it, left Winchester and moved toward the Potomac to begin the demonstrations Johnston hoped would bring important relief to Richmond. Colonel Munford had returned from Richmond and his mission to secure arms for his 2d Virginia Cavalry. He now led his entire regiment on a raid to burn B & O bridges around Martinsburg.[1] Winder's Stonewall Brigade marched toward Harper's Ferry and collided en route with 1,500 Yankees from the town's garrison. The enemy was routed in twenty minutes and pursued to within sight of Bolivar Heights, which barred the southern approaches to Harper's Ferry.[2] Jackson joined Winder with the rest of the Valley Army by midnight.[3]

The Army thus was massed twenty miles northeast of Winchester—and rumors of impending disaster were beginning to circulate. Before Jackson left Winchester, an elderly civilian had collapsed at his door gasping that McDowell was marching for the Shenandoah. Shields led McDowell's advance and was making a forced march toward Front Royal, he stammered. The old gentleman swore he had seen Shields's division on the road and that he had galloped for twelve hours to bring this news. Jackson had listened attentively to his story, perhaps hoping it was correct, but he did not act upon that hope; civilian reports were notoriously inaccurate.[4]

This civilian report, however, proved to be painfully accurate. The counteroffensive Lincoln had launched to capture the Valley Army was building up steam, and the rebels would contend with this counterthrust throughout the waning weeks of their Valley Campaign. Lincoln's admirably flexible strategy had been plotted on the afternoon of May 24 when Lincoln knew little more than that rebels were chasing Banks along the Valley Pike. The President deployed Frémont's army in the southwest as an anvil against which McDowell's divisions could hammer as opportunity offered. Frémont was ordered to plug the Confederate escape route from the lower Valley by capturing Harrisonburg. McDowell would then strike the Valley Army wherever it was cornered.

Unfortunately for Lincoln, Frémont altered this plan by disregarding his instructions to enter the Valley around Harrisonburg; instead, he was moving through the Alleghenies to Moorefield before turning east to enter the Valley at Strasburg. One of Frémont's reasons for this shift was the obstruction of the passes between Franklin and the Harrisonburg–New Market area by Hotchkiss after the Battle of McDowell. Justified or not, Frémont's decision eliminated the flexibility from Lincoln's strategy. His march to Strasburg would inevitably lead him into the Valley at approximately the same time and at a point approximately opposite McDowell's entrance. Frémont thus converted Lincoln's flexible strike into a difficult pincer movement—but with Jackson obligingly sitting outside Harper's Ferry and disregarding reports of his peril, this pincer began to look better every day.

To summarize: late May found Federal pincers converging on the Valley Army's rear. Frémont was approaching Strasburg from the west; McDowell's two divisions, with Shields in the van, were nearing Front Royal from the east. The balance in the Shenandoah Valley suddenly shifted heavily in favor of the Union.*

---

* For an account of this extraordinary phase of the Valley Campaign from the Northern viewpoint, see Appendix B.

On May 29 Stonewall brandished his main force before Union entrenchments on Bolivar Heights. He threatened Harper's Ferry from the east by sending Colonel J. W. Allen's 2d Virginia Infantry to seize Loudoun Heights, on the Shenandoah River's right bank. Since Federals had cleared the Shenandoah of all boats, Allen employed the simple expedient of having each man hold the tail of a horse while a cavalryman swam it across the river. Southern artillery opened up during the afternoon.[5]

The following day dawned with a heaviness in the air. The rising sun was hazy and clouded by dark rain clouds stacking up swiftly in the east. Southern guns opened up again, while infantry poked energetically for weak points along the enemy front.[6] As Jackson watched this demonstration, Generals Winder and Elzey joined him. Winder mentioned that the Harper's Ferry garrison apparently had been heavily reinforced, which set Jackson on edge. Then Elzey, a man renowned for his courage, remarked that some long-range Union guns were implanted across the Potomac. "General Elzey, are you afraid of heavy guns?" snapped Jackson, who turned to receive a troubling dispatch and then spurred to the rear.[7] Elzey flushed, though he said nothing. Stonewall had been too tactless to realize he had just humiliated one general in the presence of another.

Fatigue and worry sharpened Jackson's want of tact on the thirtieth, for he had been receiving grim dispatches all morning. Scouts east of the Blue Ridge confirmed that Shields was moving on Front Royal and reported (erroneously) a second column pressing toward Winchester under McDowell. Other intelligence sources claimed Banks was heavily reinforced and ready to recross the Potomac below Martinsburg.[8] Frémont had been pinpointed coming north from Franklin on the road that could carry him to Strasburg.[9] If the enemy struck vigorously, every Confederate in the lower Shenandoah might be a prisoner within forty-eight hours.

Jackson said nothing about these newly discovered developments because he was too tired for even his normal few words. He ordered the Army to march back toward Winchester, then curled under a large tree for a short nap.† When he awoke, Alexander R. Boteler, the Valley's representative in the Confederate Congress and a newly appointed special aide on Jackson's staff, was drawing him on a pad. The General reached for the sketch, examined it, and mused as if very far away: "My hardest tasks at West Point were the drawing lessons, and I never could do anything in that line to satisfy myself, or indeed, anybody else."

Jackson studied the clouds and saw that they would break soon. Suddenly returning to the present, he pulled himself into an upright position and told Boteler: "I want you to go to Richmond for me. I must have reinforcements. You can explain to them what the situation is here. Get as many men as can be spared, and I'd like you, if you please, to go as soon as you can."

Boteler asked for details of the situation he must explain. This was usually a forbidden question, but Boteler, a friend who had helped talk Jackson out of his resignation in February and to whom Jackson had revealed his intentions the previous March, had the General's confidence. Jackson shared as much as he knew. Shields and Frémont were probably planning to link up around Strasburg, he said. Banks's resurrected army and the Harper's Ferry garrison would probably pursue as the Confederates withdrew toward Winchester. Stonewall was confident he could puncture this circle and was equally confident of regaining the initiative if reinforced. Ambition fired, he intimated plans for a great new drive: "If my command can be gotten up to 40,000 men, a movement may be made beyond the Potomac which will soon raise the siege of Richmond and transfer this campaign from the banks of the Potomac to those of the Susquehanna."

Boteler realized the Susquehanna flowed through central Pennsylvania and stared at Jackson askance. The General made no response; he merely continued giving instructions to Boteler. The aide was to proceed to Charles Town, a few miles south of Harper's Ferry, where he would find a train waiting which would take him to Winchester. Boteler was to continue from Winchester

---

† This nap, extremely unusual for Jackson during a time of crises, foreshadows the curiously passive role he was to play a month later during the Seven Days fighting around Richmond, a campaign that saw him fail as totally as he had succeeded in the Valley. See *infra*, note 57; Chapter 14, notes 5–10, 88; and Appendix C.

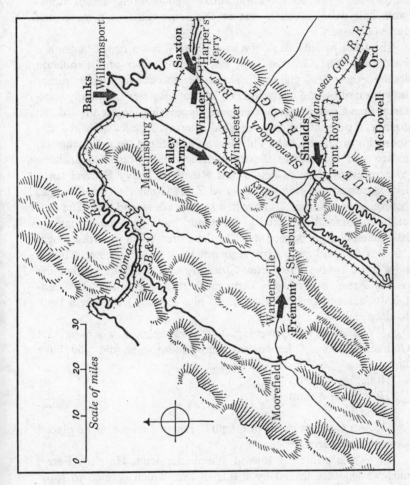

10. Situation in the Lower Valley, May 31, 1862.

by road and rail to Staunton and Richmond, where he was to relay word of the Valley Army's plight. Boteler departed immediately, but, as he was uncoupling all cars except one from the train in Charles Town, Jackson and Sandie Pendleton appeared. Stonewall, still weary, took a seat in the coach without a word and dozed off again.[10]

The train hissed out of the tiny Charles Town depot beneath a hard rain. The General slept on, while Boteler and Pendleton focused their field glasses to search for the enemy, whom rumor now located behind every mile of horizon. Boteler eventually spotted a lone Confederate horseman whipping his mount toward the train as if pursued by half the Yankee army. Boteler nudged Jackson, who ordered a halt. The rider, a messenger from Winchester, closed and handed up the most disheartening dispatch Jackson ever received: Shields held Front Royal! A heavy Federal force had surprised the garrison, Colonel Z. T. Conner's 12th Georgia, before noon that day. Conner had lost his nerve and fled. The second in command had tried to surrender, but a gray-haired captain had taken charge, burned most of the stores taken in Front Royal on May 23, and pulled the regiment back to Winchester. Shields now stood twelve miles from Strasburg and the Valley Pike; the Valley Army was roughly forty miles from that point. Woodenfaced, Jackson tore the dispatch to bits (a habit) and went back to sleep.[11]

At Winchester that evening, Old Jack erupted when he met Conner. "Colonel," he barked, "how many men did you have killed?"

"None."

"How many wounded?"

"None, sir."

"Do you call that much of a fight?" ranted Jackson as he placed Conner under arrest.[12]

The rebels retreating toward Winchester from Harper's Ferry, meanwhile, were lashed by sheets of rain which seemed to foretoken worse days ahead. These men intuitively understood they were "in for it." Jim Hall realized something was very wrong when his regiment suddenly began a forced march that carried it almost to Winchester by the evening of May 30.[13] When cannon fire roared from the rear, thousands of heads jerked around anxiously. It was the Confederate rear guard under General Winder attacking Bolivar Heights to screen the retreat. Before he took the train at Charles Town, Jackson had ordered this assault and pledged to hold Winchester open for Winder—if possible.

Before dawn on May 31 Jackson no longer thought it possible to remain at Winchester. He roused Hotchkiss at 3 A.M. to explain the situation as he grasped it. Federals were closing on every side; the Valley Army probably would have to fight at least one Union column that day and must pass through Winchester from its bivouacs north of town as speedily as possible. Jackson wanted Hotchkiss to return to Harper's Ferry and guide Winder back to the Army, if necessary by pioneering a trail for him through the Alleghenies.[14]

At this point Jackson was operating in a true fog of war, a host of conflicting misconceptions of enemy activity. The actual Federal situation at daylight on May 31 was as follows: Shields's entire division was coiled around Front Royal; Shields hesitated to spring, however, because his support, Ord's division, was a day's march behind him. (This gap was the result of Stanton's having detoured Ord through Alexandria several days earlier.) There was no column under McDowell closing on Winchester, although the skittish General Geary was probing the Blue Ridge twenty miles east of Winchester with a regiment and giving the appearance of such a descent. Frémont's 15,000 men were cooking breakfast approximately twenty miles west of Strasburg, and Frémont had announced his intention to occupy that town by 5 P.M. this day.[15] Banks had one cavalry regiment south of the Potomac.[16] This spearhead posed no threat to Jackson but was sufficient, when magnified by excited scouts, to cause him needless concern. Banks informed Lincoln on May 31 that the 6,000 men he now commanded were not ready for active service.[17] Brigadier General Rufus Saxton, in charge of 7,000 men hastily packed inside Harper's Ferry, also wired Washington that his command was too worn down to join the pursuit.[18] Weariest of all, the Valley Army had trudged twenty-five miles the preceding day and was camped some miles north of Winchester on the Valley Pike.

Though the balance hung in Union favor, it was not certain the Federals could exploit their advantage. Lincoln and Stanton continued to direct the Northern divisions, a task for which they were neither adequately situated nor trained. Further, Shields and Frémont each were more blinded by the fog of war than Jackson. Each correctly believed the Valley Army outnumbered his own force, and neither knew where the rebels were. Frémont already had flung out a wave of spies. Some penetrated as far as Strasburg only to be captured; the rest scurried back without useful information, and Frémont plodded forward very cautiously.[19] Shields was grappling with the same dilemma faced by the Valley Army on May 24: he had not located the enemy and could not act intelligently until he did. If Shields moved to Strasburg with his entire command, the rebels might slip behind him through Front Royal before Ord's division arrived there. If Shields remained at Front Royal, Frémont might have to face Jackson alone, and if Shields split his division between Strasburg and Front Royal, either fraction would be heavily outnumbered if it encountered Jackson. Shields had not mastered this dilemma when Ashby, in his most valuable service of the war, attacked Union outposts north of Front Royal with Chew's battery and most of his reassembled cavalry. Shields pushed out a brigade to meet this noisy challenge, and Ashby retired stubbornly to draw the Federals northward toward Winchester. With Ashby's threat hovering over him, Shields grew more reluctant to dash for Strasburg.[20]

While Northern generals faltered between options, Jackson acted on the only course open to him. Stonewall knew little of enemy intentions, but three things were evident: one, Shields held Front Royal; two, both Shields and Frémont were dangerously near Strasburg; and three, the Pike through Strasburg was the only road on which the Valley Army could escape with the stores captured from Banks at Winchester. These certainties made Old Jack's decision simple: he had to reach Strasburg before the enemy.

At dawn of May 31 the bedraggled, overloaded Valley Army began its trek to Strasburg. The day, mercifully, was clear and warm.[21] First came the trains, a jumble of captured U. S. Army wagons, civilian berlins and surreys, buckboards and drays and Conestogas. Stonewall had impressed everything on wheels to evacuate his booty, and now Major Harman had to conjure up one of his transportation miracles for the Army. Harman's column

was a traffic jam he estimated to be eight miles in length.[22] Hotchkiss claimed the trains stretched eight miles "when well closed
up."[23] Eight miles would have swallowed thousands of vehicles,
and it is little wonder Harman could only count them by the
mile.

Federal prisoners, on the other hand, were accounted for to a
man. There were 2,300 of them, and they crowded the rear of
Harman's caravan. "We have no place to put them, and they are
in the way. I wish now they had been paroled," groused the
quartermaster.[24] Only the 21st Virginia was available for guard
duty, and the Federals repeatedly threatened to get out of control.
One of the surrounded rebel guards, John Worsham, almost felt
himself a captive: "One of the Yankee prisoners marched at my
side, talking about what he was going to do with me when they
were retaken, and how he would take care of my gun."[25]

Trailing the prisoners was Valley Army Headquarters. In Henry
Douglas' classic but most unromantic description, Headquarters
was simply Jackson, "the worst-dressed, worst mounted, most
faded and dingy-looking general [anyone ever saw], with a staff
not much for looks or equipment."[26] But what it lacked in ac-
couterments Headquarters supplied with energy. Harman was
ably shepherding the trains; Hotchkiss was guiding Winder's rearguard. Colonel Crutchfield was forming a flying wedge of artillery
to cover the flanks. Henry Douglas, Sandie Pendleton, and others
bound the Army together as they shuttled Jackson's terse dispatches at a breakneck pace—the General kept them too busy to
worry, Douglas would gratefully recall.[27]

Jackson betrayed anxiety only by an occasional twist in his saddle to glance back at the infantry regiments behind him. Sustained
by the knowledge that their General swapped sweat for blood,
those regiments kept coming. First came Taliaferro's and Campbell's brigades, the latter now under its third commander since
April, Colonel John M. Patton of the 21st Virginia. Ewell came
next, pouting that his division had been shunted toward the rear
where it might miss five minutes of the next fight. His men were
beyond such thoughts; the division included many of the Army's
best diarists, but the strain of this march silenced them. Jim Hall
recorded only four words about May 31: ". . . marched way
above Middletown."[28] The gloss was even stripped from Taylor's

brigade. His Louisianians wove along trailing their muskets in the mud; their once-polished bayonets were tarnished. The white leggings that had made Taylor so proud only eleven days earlier hung limp around the ankles. Regimental bands were mute; the pace lagged; the fresh uniforms of gray were in tatters.

Then came the stragglers. Thousands of them sprawled across the rear of Ewell's division and onto surrounding fields in a crescent-shaped horde. Many of these stragglers found unexpected aid from Flournoy's and Munford's cavalrymen. Wrote Munford: "Hundreds of our best infantry fell by the wayside, but [overcoming their instinctive feud with the infantry, the riders] would help them, often taking them up behind them on their horses, or carrying their rifles or allowing them to hold on and be supported by the stirrups as they limped forward."[29] Much of the Army's real fighting power was strewn helpless in its wake.

Noon of May 31 found the Army spread along the Pike for fifteen miles. On each of those miles a few squadrons of Federal cavalry could have revenged the slaughter at Middletown on May 24. Rumors of such an ambush constantly rocked the rebel column. Frémont, then Shields, then Frémont again supposedly held Strasburg.[30] The thought of that village weighed on every mind. Who awaited there?

The answer was delivered by silence. Not one Federal crossed the Army's path. At dusk of May 31 the main column collapsed on the banks of Cedar Creek, only two miles north of Strasburg, and Taliaferro's brigade pushed even closer.

Farther north, Winder's task force remained on the Pike. Hotchkiss—of all people!—had gotten lost after Jackson dispatched him to guide Winder,[31] and the ensuing delay critically exposed the rear guard. Daybreak of May 31 saw Winder's group camped outside Harper's Ferry and divided by the Shenandoah River. Several hours were consumed as troopers ferried the 2d Virginia over the river from Loudoun Heights. As before, each infantryman paddled across clinging to the tail of a horse. Then Winder started a marathon with his remarkable little detachment. This detachment included the doughty 1st Maryland, still full of fight and still riddled with dissension. Within days it would break the best of Frémont's army, and within weeks it would disband because of continued protest over Confederate conscription laws.

The battered Rockbridge Artillery was present, as were all five of the regiments that Jackson, a year ago, had believed "promising."

Winder reached Winchester after a day-long march without pausing to eat; for the 2d Virginia it was the second day without rations. Men were fainting in ranks, but Jackson had left instructions to reach Strasburg by 7 A.M. the next morning, June 1. Winder accordingly bugled his dazed troops to their feet, but many could not, or did not, respond. John Casler decided he had had enough and fell out to find a meal; Casler was joined by at least 500 others.[32] Winder pushed the remnant southward across the battlefields of Winchester and Kernstown, and on, and on. About 10 P.M., as the rebels draggled past the charred Union wagons below Newtown, Winder realized they could not reach Strasburg by dawn. The shell of his brigade that remained with him was outnumbered by its stragglers. Better to lose his force in battle, Winder mused, than to string it along the Pike for enemy cavalry to collect. Pointing his men into an orchard, he let them sleep. Every soldier left in ranks had pounded out more than thirty miles, those of the 2d Virginia more than thirty-five miles, in approximately fourteen hours.[33]

Eighteen hours had elapsed between the dispatch of Hotchkiss to Winder and the latter's halt, and those hours had evened the balance in the Shenandoah. The enemy was near in heavy force, and the Confederate rear guard was badly isolated, but the bulk of the Valley Army was closer to Strasburg than either Frémont or Shields. The first side to move in the morning would tilt the balance in its favor, and Jackson was an early riser. Indeed, the wagon trains were given no rest at all; Stonewall ordered Major Harman to hustle them ahead throughout the night. Scouts had located Frémont less than five miles west of the Pike, and Jackson told Ewell to meet the Pathfinder at early dawn.

Dick Ewell greeted that challenge with much happy profanity. His division was moving against Frémont by 5 A.M. on June 1. He found the Pathfinder's vanguard, an apology for an infantry screen, and rolled it up without effort. Taylor sideslipped Frémont's right and accelerated the Union flight: ". . . it was nothing but a 'walk over.' Sheep would have made as much resistance as we met. Men decamped without firing, or threw down their arms and surrendered, and it was so easy that I began to think of traps."[34] But the Federals sprang no traps. Frémont had been hammered some miles west of the Pike by 10 A.M. Shields's heavy infantry brigades unaccountably made no appearance whatever. An unsupported pack of Federal cavalry which ventured west from Front Royal was neutralized with a couple of cannon shells, and the last Southern wagons creaked safely up the Valley Pike toward New Market.[35]

Winder resumed his march south at sunrise the same day. His troops were absolutely silent as they listened gloomily to the sound of Ewell's guns. "The men exchanged glances," wrote Marylander Randy McKim, "but no one spoke a word, though the same thought was in every mind, 'We are cut off now—it is all up with us.'"[36] The day was not yet warm when rumors seared through ranks: Shields was awaiting them at Middletown. The rumor flared again when the village came in view. The Confederates formed little more than a skirmish line as Winder deployed to struggle onward.[37] One of his aides, Lieutenant McHenry Howard, was all the mounted strength Winder fielded. Howard bolted to the front and spotted a band of horsemen watching him intently. Howard galloped out, perhaps hoping for nothing more than to draw enemy fire, but he found Ashby.

"Is that General Winder coming up?" Ashby shouted.

Howard whooped yes, and Ashby relaxed. Winder arrived, and the cavalry chieftain pumped his hand; he had not forgotten Winder's friendship during his resignation crises at Swift Run Gap. "General," Ashby beamed, "I never was so relieved in my life. I thought that you would be cut off and had made up my mind to join you and advise you to make your escape over the mountains to Gordonsville."[38]

Ashby's canny smile assured Winder this would not be necessary. The road ahead was clear. Winder reached Cedar Creek and halted while his stragglers rejoined. Colonel Johnson of the 1st Maryland estimated that at least a thousand men caught up during the halt,[39] and hundreds more lagged behind them.[40] Ashby dispatched riders to warn these men to strike southwestward through the Alleghenies until they could return to the Army. Then Winder burned the Cedar Creek bridge and marched. He reached Strasburg by noon and allowed his magnificent troops to sleep.[41]

When those men reopened their eyes, the day had drawn to a

gray dusk and the Army's retreat had resumed. Like veterans, and despite all they had endured, Winder's rebels formed ranks and shuffled off. Behind them, Union pincers from east and west slammed shut, twelve hours too late.

II

Forty-eight hours of hard marching and light skirmishing had carried the Valley Army through a ring of 50,000 enemy troops. As the rebels cleared Strasburg, their faith in their General and in themselves soared beyond limits. They gazed at Old Jack with awe, assuming that he thrust to the Potomac anticipating the enemy counterthrust and that the escape was a brilliantly calculated maneuver.[42] Actually, Jackson had done no more than push his retreat along the most logical route and to the threshold of physical exhaustion. Brilliance had sprung once again from hard work.

Indeed, the escape somehow seemed too easy. Frémont had sparred feebly with Ewell; Shields had held Front Royal since noon of May 30 but none of his men had neared Strasburg until late on June 1. This almost disinterested Union effort might signal that a trap would come from another direction, probably from beyond Massanutten Mountain. Jackson gazed at that tangled barrier and recalled how well it had screened the Army's advance down the Shenandoah in May; it could cover a Federal thrust southward as well. Even while Confederates congratulated themselves around Strasburg, Shields could be driving into the Luray Valley to bottle up the rebels via Luray and Massanutten Gap.[43] The South Fork bridges near Luray which Hotchkiss could not destroy in April with Ashby's drunken cavalrymen offered Shields easy passage from Luray to New Market, where he would bestraddle the Army's single escape route. That must not happen! A detachment from Ashby's command spurred at once to burn these bridges[44]; Colonel Crutchfield followed to check their work.[45] There could be no drunken follies this time.

There were none. Crutchfield confirmed destruction of all structures, but this offered no real safety. If Shields was in the Luray Valley, the Massanutten would screen him for days, and it was possible that this resourceful enemy could find a passable ford across the South Fork and reach New Market. The Valley Army once again had two enemy fronts with which to contend, a northern (Frémont) and an eastern (Shields), and Jackson commenced a protracted retreat to avoid being wedged between them. Jackson was worried enough to march throughout the night of June 1, though his troops were pallid from fatigue. He would not, however, lessen their burden by abandoning one of his booty-topped wagons—that was not Stonewall's way. Every wagon must make the retreat. The guards must account for every prisoner, the drovers, for every steer. The Army began one of the most difficult operations imaginable: "I am inclined to think we are going to be hard up," was Major Harman's prediction.[46]

That forecast quickly proved true. Ashby and Flournoy deployed their cavalry regiments to guard the rear. Soon after dark, Yankee riders clattered up the Pike shouting they were "Ashby's cavalry." One of Ashby's companies was on patrol, and the Federals were allowed to approach. They were almost inside Southern ranks when they charged and scattered the Confederates. Munford's 2d Virginia Cavalry was scattered by fleeing riders. Munford's horsemen in turn stampeded and overran the Louisiana Brigade, which loosed volleys into the riders. The mélee threatened to overwhelm the Army until General Taylor gathered the dockhands of his 6th Louisiana and took over the rear. Throughout a night of intermittent hail and stinging rain, Taylor held the snapping Union cavalry at bay.[47]

Dawn of June 2 brought a second fiasco. Rebel cavalry came up to relieve Taylor, but General Steuart bungled this simple maneuver and lost control of his troopers. The Confederate cavalry was again herded back into its infantry as the enemy exploited this blunder. Several of Munford's men were wounded by nervous rebel sharpshooters, and only a daredevil stand by Ashby stopped the rear guard from dissolving. He inspired 50 straggling infantrymen to form a line in the enemy path. At virtually the last instant he bellowed to fire, and a pointblank volley ended the Federal pursuit for the day. At Ewell's request, Jackson permanently assigned Munford's and Flournoy's regiments to Ashby. Steuart rejoined Ewell's division, where he headed one of the brigades (Colonel Scott's) of Edward Johnson's former command.[48]

For the men behind the cavalry screen, these days and nights blurred into a ceaseless ordeal. Rain poured down in a crackling stream. The wagon trains were far ahead and there was no food; men survived on whatever they could beg along the wayside. Officers lost their commands; units were intermingled; straggling reached epidemic proportions.[49]

"The road was shoe-mouth deep in mud," wrote one Alabamian. "My feet were blistered all over, on top as well as on the bottom. I never was so tired and sleepy."[50] One weary scavenger had the luck to find a hot meal but fell unconscious before he could eat it.[51] Cavalry Captain John Winfield was so weak his troopers had to lift him into his saddle.[52] The rebels lost count of the miles and grumbled they would rather fight than bear such punishment.[53]

The retreat from Harper's Ferry demanded the courage of a battle, and it was far more costly. The Army lost 400 men fighting its way north from Front Royal to Winchester; it lost thousands of stragglers on the retreat, and the Army's effective strength could hardly have been above 12,000. Captain Jim Edmondson of the 27th Virginia recalled: "I never saw a Brigade so completely broken down and unfitted for service as our Brigade. . . . I am satisfied that the Brigade has lost at least 1,000 men broken down, left on the way and captured. . . ." Edmondson was pained to admit that his own reliable company had lost at least 100 men from these causes. His entire regiment (which had numbered 418 one month ago) had shriveled to 150.[54] The toll was especially severe among officers. Some regiments were led by majors, and one, the 42d Virginia, by a captain.[55] Even men like Major Harman were nearing the end of endurance: "If I get through this safely," he despaired, "Gen'l Jackson must either relieve me or reduce the train. I will not be worked so any longer. . . ."[56]

Jackson was as weary as Harman.‡ He had been tired as early as May 30, when he had napped before enemy lines outside Harper's Ferry, but he continued to push himself now. He was everywhere, steadying the rear guard, helping Harman untangle the wagon trains, directing his staff, but he was expending his last

_____

‡ The crippling effect and causes of Jackson's weariness are discussed in Appendix C.

reserves of strength. Night after night, Hotchkiss noted that the General had but little rest.[57]

By June 3 the flagging rebels crossed the Shenandoah's North Fork below New Market to the familiar ground of Rude's Hill. The bridge they used was also familiar; it was this structure which Ashby's riders had failed to destroy in April. This time the destruction of the bridge had been arranged with much care. The roofing was stuffed with dry, split wood. Scattered through piles of kindling on the floor were two dozen artillery shells and several kegs of gunpowder. After the last straggler limped over it, the bridge was completely destroyed.[58]

The rebels hoped for a brief rest here, but it did not come. New rains deluged the Army that evening. The hollow in which the Headquarters tent was pitched became a creek bed; Hotchkiss noted that Jackson "was almost afloat . . . from the heavy rainfall."[59] Frémont's engineers somehow got a pontoon bridge across the North Fork, and his cavalry advanced at daybreak. They did not get far, however, before the stream began to swell from the night's downpour and snapped the Union bridge.[60]

Jackson squelched his desire to lunge at the enemy cavalry isolated on his side of the river and turned to a more desperate problem. Ashby's scouts had located Shields moving south through the Luray Valley, indicating Jackson's fear of being bottled up from behind was justified. When Shields discovered that the bridges over the South Fork leading from Luray to New Market were burned, he might attempt to gain the Confederate rear via the bridge at Conrad's Store, so Southern cavalry burned it as well. The enemy fronts would remain divided for a few more days, days in which the arduous retreat must continue.

The problem was where to retreat. Jackson's engineers reported they could not bridge the North River, which separated the Army from Staunton. The stream was higher than it had been for twenty years, and only the wounded were ferried across it on rafts.[61] Jackson already had sent his prisoners over the Blue Ridge at Waynesboro; if the Army followed, it would be safe, but at the price of abandoning the Shenandoah. Stonewall detected a better haven twelve miles southeast of Harrisonburg, at Port Republic. An important bridge crossed the North River there, and Shields was likely to strike for it when he found the span at Conrad's Store destroyed. If the Confederates could occupy Port Republic first, they could keep Shields from Frémont and spring at whichever enemy column approached first. Further, a road from that village would permit the Army's escape, if necessary, eastward through the Blue Ridge at Brown's Gap.

The march for Port Republic began. On June 5, already the seventh day of the race from Harper's Ferry, the rebels tramped through Harrisonburg and out a muddy road to the southeast. Harman's trains were quickly mired down. Fifty men from each brigade were detailed to help, but progress was slow.[62] Ashby reported that Frémont was again advancing. That night the Valley Army floundered to a halt in a dangerous position, stuck in the mud halfway between Harrisonburg and Port Republic. It would need time to complete its escape.

III

No one understood the Army's peril better than Turner Ashby. His scouts warned him that Frémont's unusually aggressive cavalry was Brigadier General George D. Bayard's brigade, hardy regiments which Shields had lent to Frémont. He also knew that one of Bayard's regiments was led by a veteran English soldier of fortune, Sir Percy Wyndham. The Valley Army's adventurous Major Wheat had fought beside Wyndham with Garibaldi in Italy and knew him to be a skillful soldier, which made more ominous his boast to capture Ashby. Some who knew the rebel chieftain believed he was delighted with Wyndham's spirit, for it promised a more resourceful enemy to conquer.[63]

All who knew Ashby were certain he was pleased with his promotion to brigadier general on May 23. The promotion was at Richmond's initiative; Jackson had opposed it and apparently did not even congratulate Ashby. Nevertheless, at Ewell's insistence (and because Ashby now ranked the other cavalry commanders), Old Jack had added Munford's and Flournoy's regiments to Ashby's command. On June 6 Ashby assembled at least 1,000 sabers to defend the Army's mud-bound wagon trains.

There was little activity that morning. Flournoy's 6th Virginia Cavalry fended off light attacks during the afternoon. Ashby kept his own regiment and Munford's in reserve until suppertime, then allowed the troopers to turn their mounts out to graze. The skirmishing promptly grew fiercer. Thinking they would retire, Major Funsten ordered Ashby's old companies into ranks. At that moment, with Ashby's companies facing away from the enemy and Munford's men dismounted, the Federals stormed up the road.

"Follow me," Ashby shouted.[64] Never taught how to maneuver, Ashby's boys about-faced in wild disorder, but they followed their general in a mad rush for the enemy. These Yanks had never faced an Ashby charge, and its fury startled, then shattered them. A headless mass of Union men and horses boiled back toward Harrisonburg. A few Yanks attempted to rally and were trampled; the Union banner was scooped up from the mud, as was the Englishman Sir Percy Wyndham. Reminding the braggart of his pledge to snare Ashby, crowing rebels led Sir Percy away, the maddest prisoner anyone ever saw. One Southerner wrote of the mercenary: ". . . he would have stopped right there in the road and engaged in fisticuffs if he could have found a partner."[65]

This was cavalry action as Ashby loved it, quick and fierce. As some 60 prisoners were herded off, he spied more Union cavalry approaching. Another challenge! Ashby borrowed two infantry regiments, the 58th Virginia and 1st Maryland, from Ewell and drew up a hasty plan. Munford would dangle the cavalry athwart the Harrisonburg road and lure the Federals onward until they presented their naked flank to the infantry, which Ashby would conceal in woods on the right of the road. Ashby was aglow with the joy of the hunt, and an admiring rebel was heard to say: "Look at Ashby. See how happy he is."[66]

The fun was short-lived. The Pennsylvania Bucktails, a crack battalion of Federal sharpshooters, had already infiltrated the wooded position Ashby hoped to secure. Carelessly advancing without a vanguard, the rebel infantry under Ashby stumbled into an ambush. The 58th Virginia bolted with the first volley, and only Ashby could have rallied it. He seemed that evening to be the very embodiment of a hero, and he was everywhere, weaving his sleek mount between the tangled hardwoods, shouting, steadying, leading. Suddenly his horse crumpled. He rolled free, bounced up, and ran at the enemy. The 58th followed.

Colonel Johnson swung his 1st Maryland upon the Union flank

under a galling fire. Private Sindal was hit in the mouth, Perry, in the lungs, Tarr, in the head. Color Sergeant Doyle spun around clutching his stomach; Corporal Taylor caught the banner and was cut open. The flag changed hands twice again in another thirty yards, but the advance did not falter. The rebels hurled the Bucktails into a clearing and picked off dozens of them.

By then Munford had joined the fight and was driving the Federal attackers back toward Harrisonburg. In fifteen more minutes Frémont's best cavalry and infantry were butchered and his pursuit blunted. It had been a good day for Ashby—and his last. As the hot firefight ended, rebels looked for Ashby to be on the enemy's tail, but he was not. Now they remembered that his horse had fallen. They returned to that spot and found him close by, lying dead with his face toward a fence which had sheltered the Union line.[67]

Ashby's death, like his life, has been obscured by romance. Henry Douglas portrayed Ashby's end with the classic military stereotype, the mortally wounded commander expiring in the arms of a grieving lieutenant.[68] Even the exacting Hotchkiss could not pierce the romantic veil. His diary notes that Ashby had been mistaken for a Yankee and killed by his own men as he finished scouting the Federal line.[69] Perhaps the most reliable account came from Major William Goldsborough of the 1st Maryland:

> Ashby was everywhere, encouraging and animating his men, until at last his horse was struck by a bullet and went down. Springing to his feet, and waving his sword over his head, he rushed forward, calling to his men to follow. He had not taken half a dozen steps, when he fell, pierced through the body by a musket-ball, and died almost instantly. No dying words issued from his lips, and the last command he was heard to give was, "Forward, my brave men!"[70]

Troopers escorted the body to the rear in disbelief. Ashby was the first general of heroic reputation to fall in Virginia, and his youngsters had never imagined that heroes really die in war. Word spread through the Army of its loss, and all activity ceased. "There is a gloom throughout the whole camp," wrote Trooper Bill Wilson, "an awful stillness that can be almost heard."[71] The corpse was carried to Port Republic. Wrapped with a Confederate flag, it remained during the night. Cavalrymen came to mourn over it, honoring Ashby in death as they had followed him in life, singly or in little bands. Many sobbing openly, they thought their sad thoughts and rode off as they saw fit.[72]

Jackson was interrogating Sir Percy when the news reached him. He dismissed Wyndham at once, and gloom enveloped Headquarters. Jackson went to his room and locked the door. The staff heard him pacing a long, long time,[73] perhaps examining his own relations with the slain leader. Surely he prayed earnestly for his soul. When the time came to report officially this phase of the Campaign to Richmond, Jackson bestowed an extraordinary tribute on Ashby: ". . . as a partisan officer I never knew his superior; his daring was proverbial; his powers of endurance almost incredible, his tone of character heroic; and his sagacity almost intuitive in divining the purposes and movements of the enemy."[74] Never again did the taciturn Jackson award such praise, and Ashby had earned it. He had rendered much valuable service, particularly with the feint before Strasburg from May 20 to 22 and by his fight with Shields on May 31.

Yet, only a month before Ashby's death, Jackson had confided to Alexander Boteler that Ashby had "such bad discipline and attaches so little importance to drill that I would regard it as a calamity to see him promoted [to general]."[75] Ashby had earned this opinion too. Rarely since mid-April had Jackson given Ashby's cavalry an important mission without detailing one of his own staff members to supervise. Hotchkiss was detailed to burn the bridges on the Shenandoah's South Fork in April. Hotchkiss, not Ashby's scouts, had reconnoitered Milroy's position before the Army had entered the Alleghenies. When Jackson wanted the Allegheny passes between Franklin and the Harrisonburg–New Market area blocked, he had again assigned Hotchkiss the task. Ashby was entrusted with an independent mission in the Buckton Station attack on May 23; Jackson, however, had guarded against failure there by committing a larger force under Flournoy to the same work of cutting rail and telegraph communications some miles nearer Front Royal. The next day Jackson had flung a mounted column to Newtown. He had not sent Ashby, whose riders knew every byway in the Valley, but Steuart, who previously had commanded no more than a single company of U. S. Cavalry and whose men were strangers to the region. Colonel

Crutchfield had checked the work of Ashby's bridge-burning parties during the retreat from Harper's Ferry. Even the prime achievements that can be claimed for Ashby—that Jackson was usually well informed of Union movements, while the enemy remained ignorant of his—resulted as much from Stonewall's own deceptive ways and from the poor quality of Northern cavalry as from Ashby's efforts.

Ashby was not exclusively at fault for the weaknesses which sometimes made his squadrons worthless. Stonewall had made incessant demands on him for information and security; since the beginning of the Campaign, Ashby's troopers had been kept on patrol and the picket line, work which kept them off the drill field. The vast expanse of the Shenandoah could only be patrolled by numerous small parties, and this too prevented close supervision by Ashby. Many of those who disgraced him had only enlisted during March and April, immediately before the Valley Army's explosive May drive, and Ashby had had little opportunity to fashion soldiers of them. Further, each Southern cavalryman was required to furnish his own horse. No central reserve of remounts existed (as it did in the Union army), and when a horse was lost there was nothing for the owner to do save leave to find another. Much of the Valley cavalry's rampant absenteeism arose in this way.[76]

It was also true, as Ashby's defenders pointed out, that Jackson's control over his infantry was sometimes tenuous. Infantrymen were as willing as Ashby's troopers to loot or slip home. Jackson never made professionals of his infantry. But—and here lay the essential difference—starting with volunteers who thought much like Ashby's, Jackson drilled those boys until most would stay in ranks at critical times if physically able. On May 24 Jackson brought a much larger percentage of infantry to Winchester than did Ashby of cavalry, and the infantry were as exhausted as the cavalry. Any doubt about whose methods made the better soldier, Jackson's or Ashby's, was resolved along the Valley Pike between Middletown and Winchester.

There were many competent men in Ashby's cavalry, but he never mobilized their abilities; he never made a real attempt to organize his command. A few hours per month could have been spared for drill. Smaller, more compact regiments could have been formed to provide additional officers. Ashby never grasped the importance of such things. He admitted as much when, during his stand off with Jackson at Swift Run Gap, he protested to Hotchkiss "that Jackson was treating him very badly in desiring to divide his command into two regiments and requiring him to drill them. He seemed to think that although he had so many companies he could easily manage them all himself and that it was unnecessary to have them drilled."[77] The lost opportunities of May 24 and 25 did not alter Ashby's view. On the day of his promotion to general he asserted that though his discipline was ragged, it did not worry him. His men followed when he led, and that alone was important.[78]

Ashby relied upon sheer courage to answer every challenge. He always fought with incredible boldness, staking his life each time on a conviction that the valor aroused in his men through his own fearlessness was ample substitute for discipline—and at the same time revealing that he, like his men, had succumbed to generations of Southern thinking that glorified cavalry action as glittering adventure. General Taylor sensed this delusion and complained: "Graceful, young cavaliers, with flowing locks, leaping cannons to saber countless foes makes a captivating picture . . . but ''tis not war.' Valor is necessary now as ever in war, but disciplined, subordinated valor, admitting the courage and energies of all be welded and directed to a common end."[79]

Such a union of energies never existed in Ashby's command, where every trooper was a general. One who rode with Ashby's regiment remembered: "It was more like a tribal band held together by the authority of a single chief. Increase of numbers rather diminished than increased its efficiency as a whole and made it more unmanageable."[80] Ironically, it was this very tribal band mentality which denied Ashby's troopers their dream of a glittering adventure. Flournoy's well-schooled companies at Cedarville on May 23, not Ashby's carefree squadrons, made the one truly romantic cavalry charge of the Campaign. Ashby's riders were offered their chance for a grand charge two days later, but the band was not together to strike Banks as he fled north from Winchester.

Still, Ashby's courage was magnificent; his bravery as a battle captain must be weighed against his failures as an administrator, and which was greater becomes a matter of opinion. Any summary of his career must stress that he was out of step with his times and therefore never able to achieve his full potential in them. "Riding his black stallion," remembered Henry Douglas, "he looked like a knight of the olden time . . ."[81]; and so he was. Ashby was a splendid paladin, and, as such, he was also an anachronism, a knight-errant at the dawn of modern, total war.

TRAP AND COUNTERTRAP

*The balls whistle by our heads
as fast and thick as ever
I saw hail fall in Georgia.*

—PVT. T. M. HIGHTOWER

Saturday, June 7, was a quiet day, the most peaceful time since the Valley Army had left Harper's Ferry. Beneath azure skies, Ashby's body was carried across the Blue Ridge for burial at Charlottesville. It was attended by a guard of honor from the company he had led to war as a captain fourteen months earlier. Captured Federals and their guards, many with uncovered heads, lined the road in respectful silence.[1] Colonel Munford became the new chief of cavalry.[2]

Ashby's dying fight had bought the time the Valley Army needed to complete its escape. The wagon trains had lurched beyond Frémont's grasp, and Jackson informed Richmond that there seemed little prospect for renewed action in the Valley.[3] Stonewall maneuvered throughout the seventh to tempt Frémont to attack, but the latter declined.[4] Nor was there any sign of Shields in the Luray Valley. The Confederates had escaped from almost certain encirclement on May 31 to get ahead of and between their pursuers; they were, apparently, safe.

Toward evening Jackson gave up the attempt to draw Frémont out, left Ewell to watch him, and moved his own division to Port Republic. The Port, as local residents called this cluster of a few dozen buildings, presented the most difficult terrain problem the Valley Army ever faced. The village lay on a peninsula formed by two streams, the North River which flowed from the northwest and the South River which flowed from the southwest; these streams merged into the South Fork of the Shenandoah. Stretching northeast from the confluence along the left (west) bank (see Map 11) of the South Fork was a line of bluffs which dominated all ground on the right (east) bank. The region's only bridge spanned the North River near the Port and bore a road which climbed the bluffs and led on to Harrisonburg; Jackson had just arrived by this road. Another highway led southwestward from the village to Staunton. Exit from the Port to the east was by a road crossing a ford (known as the lower ford) in the South River, on the eastern bank of which the road divided. One branch ran across several miles of wheatfields, thence through heavy forests to Swift Run Gap; the other branch led through the Blue Ridge at Brown's Gap. The Valley Army had utilized these two roads on its march from Swift Run Gap to join Edward Johnson in May. Shields was believed to be following the Army's previous route south from Swift Run Gap and could only approach the Port on the right bank of the South Fork, an approach which could be covered by Confederate artillery on the left bank bluffs. Finally, near the southern edge of the Port was a second ford (known as the upper ford) which was little used at the time.

To keep Shields from Frémont and to keep his own retreat route through Brown's Gap open, Jackson had to hold the bluffs, the North River bridge, and the fords in the South River. He accordingly stationed his division on the bluffs with adequate artillery support,[5] but then got careless. A single cavalry company was placed at the lower ford,[6] and only a dozen infantrymen under Captain S. C. Moore were assigned to watch the upper.[7] Jackson quartered his staff in Port Republic at the home of Dr. George Kemper, one half mile southwest of the North River bridge, without even bringing over the Liberty Hall Volunteers to protect Headquarters. Worse, he allowed Harman to park the entire wagon train on the Staunton road just south of Kemper's house. Some cavalry was brought over to guard the wagons but was placed too far south to be any help if the trains were struck from the north.[8] Shortly after midnight the first report on Shields for several days was received: the vanguard of his force had been

spotted a few miles northeast of Port Republic. Jackson sent two
companies from Ashby's regiment to investigate, then retired.[9]

These dispositions separated the Army by river from its wagon
trains and left those trains virtually unguarded. These were the
trains Stonewall had striven to protect all the way from Winchester, and his surprisingly careless exposure of them suggests
that the fatigue plaguing him since at least May 30 was clouding
his judgment.* Sandie Pendleton, jotting a short letter home that
very day, noted: "Gen. Jackson is completely broken down."[10]

The Sabbath (June 8) dawned quietly enough to seem unnatural. Headquarters slept late; it was approximately 8 A.M. as the
staff collected on Dr. Kemper's porch.[11] The only business was a
dispatch from the cavalry sent to locate Shields; they had encountered a Northern patrol and driven it several miles before sighting
a regiment of Union cavalry. That regiment was now advancing
toward the Port, though the dispatch did not tell how fast.[12] Jackson sent the bearer back for more information, then decided to
check for himself. He advised Ewell of the situation and ordered
him not to provoke Frémont until something definite was ascertained about Shields.[13] Following this bother, Stonewall hoped to
hear Major Dabney preach. He already had told Dabney that he
would keep the Sabbath holy if the enemy would leave him alone,
and the hawk-nosed cleric was lying on his cot outlining a sermon
for Winder's brigade.[14]

Jackson had not kept a Sabbath holy since May 18, and this
troubled him, but he would do no better today. While he was still
on Kemper's porch, a single courier came galloping toward Headquarters howling that Yankee cavalry was in sight of Port Republic. As if to punctuate that alarm, a Union shell exploded over
Port Republic. Jackson glanced down Main Street and saw all
the rebel cavalry south of the North River bridge riding away in
every direction. The Army's rear was defenseless.

The staff scattered in a trice. Hotchkiss rode to alert the wagon
trains. Jackson, Harman, Sandie Pendleton, and others spurred
across the North River bridge to the left bank under a spray of
Union pistol fire. Federal cavalry splashed up to Main Street from

---

* See Appendix C.

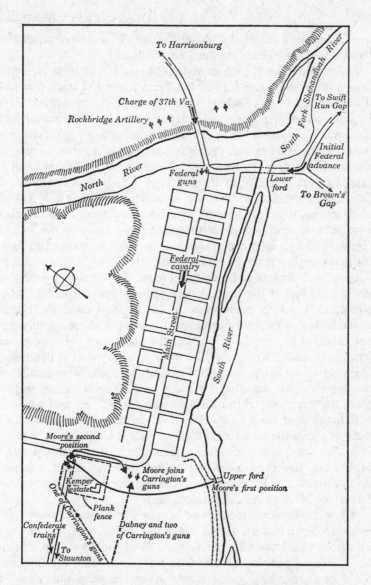

11. SKIRMISH IN PORT REPUBLIC, JUNE 8, 1862.
The above is reproduced from a tracing of an original in the Hotchkiss
Papers, Library of Congress. The original (prepared under the direction
of Jedediah Hotchkiss in 1896) reconstructed wartime Port Republic
with infinite care; unfortunately, the original is no longer reproducible.
Troop locations and movements have been added by the author and
are approximate.

the lower ford to capture Colonel Crutchfield and to discover the Army's wagons jammed on the Staunton road.[15]

The twelve infantry pickets under Captain Moore were lazing at their post on the upper ford of the South River (Moore's first position on Map 11) as Federal bullets began to spatter around Port Republic. The first shots startled them, and another round had them pulling on their boots and double-timing for the Kemper estate. Captain Moore was probably seeking orders, but Kemper's house was empty when he arrived. Moore spotted Federal cavalry entering Port Republic to the north; to the south were miles of Confederate wagons, ridiculously conspicuous with newly issued white canvas tops.[16] If Moore's eyes had been keen, he could also have seen Federal scouts alerting their main body to the wagon trains. In the greatest decision of his life, Moore resolved to fight for those wagons from the Kemper property.

On a knoll surrounded by a panel fence, Dr. Kemper's yard was like a little fort at the southwestern edge of Port Republic. Main Street ran generally southwestward to that fort from the North River bridge, turned 90 degrees to the west, and rose gently for one hundred fifty yards to intersect the Staunton road. The panel fence surrounded Kemper's yard in such a way that it paralleled Main Street for sixty yards to the Staunton road, then paralleled the latter toward Staunton for some yards. To attack the wagon train, the Yankees had to turn right with Main Street and advance uphill with their flank crowded against the fence; that would slow them and give the rebels time for two volleys of rifle fire. Accordingly, Moore placed his dozen men along the Staunton road behind Dr. Kemper's fence and waited (Moore's detail was just southwest of the intersection of the Staunton Road and Main Street; see Moore's second position, Map 11).

A few hundred yards south of Moore was Captain James Carrington's 6-gun battery. It had joined the Valley Army the day before from Charlottesville, but Colonel Crutchfield had found it to be so ill-equipped that he sent it to the wagon train for supplies. Some of Carrington's gunners were seventeen years old; none of them had fired a shot in anger. Fleeing Southern cavalry had shaken them already, and now they saw Union cavalry trotting along Main Street. Carrington's battery began to lose cohesion and slip away.[17]

Moore's men watched the enemy approach, licked suddenly dry lips, and wiped sweating palms on their pants. Breath came in short gasps through the nose. The enemy turned the corner below, unaware of the waiting Confederates. The distance was less than two hundred feet when 12 rebels rose and fired. The Yanks staggered, and Moore's men charged down Main Street toward them, loading and firing as they came. The Yanks ran.

Two, perhaps three, minutes were won, but the enemy was regrouping. Moore returned to the post from which he had just surprised Federal cavalry (Moore's second position on Map 11) and rejoiced to find one gun from Carrington's battery unlimbering behind the plank fence, a much-needed weapon as Federal cavalry was advancing again up Main Street, this time in battle formation. Federal skirmishers were already darting behind outbuildings and tree stumps to keep rebel heads down along the fence. There was no time for the rebel gunners to knock down the fence or even elevate their piece. Gunner L. W. Cox yelled to load canister, but there was none. He shouted for anything, and Private Julius Goodwin stuffed a bag of powder and a round shell into the gun. Cox rammed the shell home and jumped around to hook his lanyard to the primer. Fumbling seconds passed.

Through cracks in the fence, rebels saw the gleam of Union sabers and carbines in the morning sun. They could smell the mottled sweat on Federal horses, their nostrils flared and red.

The enemy broke into a charge. They were in half-pistol range. The rebel gun barked. The shot blew down the fence and sent splinters flying down the street like pinwheels. The shell was wide of the enemy and not a Federal was scratched, but they reined up in sheer amazement.

Major Dabney now roared into the fight. He had ridden south from the Kemper house after the first alarm, collided with Carrington's fleeing battery and talked Carrington into gathering two crews who thought they knew how to load. As Moore's party halted the enemy a second time, these two guns swept across Kemper's front yard with Dabney, a half-dressed Presbyterian preacher, waving them on. Their first shots blasted the Yankees into alleys along Main Street. Moore's men joined these guns and helped pen the enemy for valuable minutes. Theirs was a display of individual courage rarely equaled throughout the war.[18]

Jackson, meanwhile, rode to the Valley Army's camps for help. He did not know what force Shields had thrown against him, but he knew that only a handful of Federals could exploit his careless disposition of the Army. It would not take many to burn the North River bridge and trap him on the same side of the river with Frémont. Jackson dashed through Poague's Rockbridge Artillery shouting: "Have the guns hitched up, have the guns hitched up."[19] He hastened on to Winder's brigade and ordered it to the Port.[20] Couriers jabbed their mounts toward Taylor's camp with word to come at once.[21]

Returning to the bluffs above the Port, Stonewall saw a blue-clad gun crew unlimbering at the far end of the North River bridge. Jackson ordered the first of Poague's guns to arrive to shell the blue-clad men, but a chorus of voices protested that those men were Confederates. Poague yelled that he had visited Carrington during the night and knew his men wore blue uniforms.

Jackson rose in his stirrups to call the blue-clad gunners to the safe side of the stream: "Bring that gun up here." The men ignored him.

"Bring that gun up here, I say," Jackson repeated.† The gunners screwed their piece to its highest elevation and blasted the ground from his feet. Federals!

"Let 'em have it," raged Old Jack, who turned to hurry back to his infantry.[22] He found Fulkerson's 37th Virginia alertly heading for the sound of battle. "Charge right through, Colonel," he demanded, waving his cap around his head as he had done at the Battle of Winchester.[23]

Two Union guns were blazing away from the bridge, Poague's cannons were belching from the bluffs and Carrington's were firing from the vicinity of Kemper's home as Fulkerson charged. He had no time to deploy. His Virginians advanced in a long column. Northern artillery fired point blank as the rebels hurled onto the span. The front rank dropped; the bridge heaved and both sides collapsed, but the understructure was secure. When the

---

† Historical romance credits Jackson here with an attempt to trick the Federals into bringing their gun across the bridge by impersonating a Union officer. Jackson certainly was desperate at this point, but there is nevertheless no basis in reliable records for the story that he was trying to capture the gun by ruse. Rather, he simply thought it was a Confederate gun.

smoke cleared, Confederates held the Union guns, had swung them around, and were shooting down the Federals as they ran for the lower ford.[24] Colonel Crutchfield escaped his Federal guards in the confusion. The little band of heroes from Dr. Kemper's property danced down Main Street shouting that the wagon trains were safe, though badly startled. The teamsters had decamped smartly at the first alarm and were barreling up the Staunton road; one driver did not check his frantic pace until he neared Staunton, a distance of fifteen miles.[25]

Before Jackson could descend to inspect the captured guns a new alarm riveted him to his artillery along the bluffs. Federal infantry sallied up the road from Swift Run Gap. Confederate batteries greeted them. The Federals wavered, and rebels increased their fire until the enemy ran for shelter.[26] But, as if in echo, cannon fire swelled from the west: It was Frémont! Jackson knew Ewell confronted Frémont with only three brigades, but he was too concerned with the situation at Port Republic to spare reinforcements. Ewell must handle Frémont on his own.

The previous evening, when Jackson marched for Port Republic, Ewell had camped on a ridge line which commanded an open dale seven miles northwest of the Port and two miles southeast of a hamlet called Cross Keys. A creeklet threaded along the northern face of that ridge, and maple groves bordered it on the north and south. With Taylor's brigade called away to support Jackson against a grave threat, Ewell had fewer than 5,000 men and decided to hold tight on his ridge in a line of battle facing to the northwest. Trimble's brigade was placed on the right, Steuart's brigade, on the left. Five batteries barred the road to Port Republic in the center; behind the guns was Elzey's brigade.[27]

Frémont began an advance of sorts against these lines about 10:00 A.M. on June 8. The Pathfinder later boasted of the lusty blows he struck,[28] but the Confederates experienced the day as a poorly co-ordinated series of spiritless Union attacks. "They made no bayonet charge, nor did they commit any particular ravages with grape or canister, although they state otherwise," scoffed Ewell.[29] Frémont did not commit the men who had tested Edward Johnson at the Battle of McDowell; instead, he sent in Blenker's division, a horde of befuddled German emigrants who spoke little

English and understood less of the reasons for the war. The 15th Alabama alone held up the Union advance for fully an hour.[30] General Elzey opened up the Southern artillery with good effect; Northern guns answered wide of the mark.[31] It was noon before the fight quickened. Two Northern regiments wandered into the 44th Virginia—130 rebels. The 44th gave one sharp volley and chased the enemy from the field.[32] The 1st Maryland thrashed three consecutive attacks within an hour.[33]

Frémont aimed his main thrust against the rebel right, where Trimble's command was posted along a brushy fence facing an open wheatfield. A brigade of Blenker's Germans started across this field, and Trimble paced down the length of his line telling his men to stay low and hold their fire. The Federals swashed through the creeklet in solid ranks and tramped up the ridge. On they came, until Trimble gave the word and a murderous flash snapped the Union line. Two more volleys cleared the slope, and Trimble bolted forward a mile. His Georgians tried repeatedly to close, but the Federals were running too fast. Trimble was positive he could outflank the entire enemy line and asked Ewell for reinforcements.[34]

Ewell wisely did not permit Trimble to entice him. Though he had suffered few casualties, Ewell had had two brigade commanders, Elzey and Steuart, wounded by stray Union shells.[35] Scouts reported a Federal turning movement against the Confederate left,[36] which would explain the Pathfinder's anemic attacks thus far. Patton's (formerly Campbell's) and Taylor's brigades arrived from Jackson during the afternoon, and Ewell massed them protectively near his center. Later, after the enemy failed to attack against his left, Ewell advanced over feeble opposition, and by nightfall he held the ground from which Frémont initiated the encounter.

Historians have termed the desultory fighting on Ewell's front the "Battle of Cross Keys," although, like the fight at McDowell, it was essentially a rambling skirmish. It was significant primarily as proof of Ewell's development into a first-rate division commander. He had shown bold initiative on May 24 when he advanced to Winchester without awaiting Jackson's orders; he had resourcefully held off Frémont outside Strasburg; today he demonstrated he knew when to avoid combat. Perhaps his only fault was the common tendency to overrate the damage inflicted. Ewell gave Jackson a personal report that the fighting had ended well and that at least 2,000 enemy fell during the day.[37] (Frémont actually had suffered far less: 557 men killed or wounded and another 100 captured.[38]) Ewell also handed Jackson a copy of Frémont's order of battle taken from a captured staff officer. It was clear from this roster that Frémont had had six infantry brigades and several cavalry regiments engaged or available; he had outnumbered the rebels two to one. Ewell's losses were half those of the enemy, less than 300 men, and he now knew what President Davis "made me a major general for."

Only General Trimble was unsatisfied. He believed the Confederates had stopped short of routing Frémont and pestered Ewell when he returned to Headquarters to make a night attack. Ewell had the good judgment to refuse, lest the operation interfere with Jackson's intentions for the morrow, but he gave Trimble permission to see Stonewall. Jackson heard him briefly, then told him: "Consult General Ewell and be guided by him." Trimble tried again, and Ewell shook his head a second time. "You have done well enough for one day. . . ," he said.[39] For Jackson to have allowed a subordinate such discretion was his supreme, if unspoken, compliment.

Old Jack spent the twilight hours of June 8 pondering this extraordinary day. Shields's arrival was particularly disturbing, because his exact strength was unknown. The timing of Federal assaults near Port Republic also gave cause to suspect that Shields had established communication with Frémont. The latter had declined battle on June 7, but today he had attacked at roughly the same hour as Shields. Shields had remained passive during the afternoon, yet Jackson had to consider the possibility that enemy forces were acting in concert, in which case the Valley Army might be trapped between two enemy fronts. (In fact, Shields and Frémont had not established communication.) Jackson had been straining to avoid such a trap since November, but he abruptly decided to accept the risk. The enemy offered battle, and ambition goaded Jackson to accept: he would attack in the morning.

From Ewell's description of his own fight, Jackson could estimate Frémont's strength at between 12,000 and 15,000 men. Shields's command was probably smaller and closer to Port

Republic. Frémont's miserable attack invited a counterattack and promised an easy victory. Still, if it lost to Frémont, the Valley Army would have two rivers and Shields's unbroken force in its rear. If the Valley Army beat Frémont, the latter had the Valley Pike by which to escape a punishing pursuit. The alternative was to strike Shields. If the Army lost to him, its retreat from Port Republic into the safety of Brown's Gap was comparatively easy. If victorious, the Army could hope for an effective pursuit of Shields, who had only the poor road to Swift Run Gap for withdrawal. But one problem was inherent in any attack on Shields: Confederates could not abandon the left bank of the Shenandoah's South Fork, because this would allow Frémont to plant his guns there and decimate the Confederate attack. Thus the entire Army could not be concentrated against Shields; some Confederates would have to remain on the left bank of the South Fork.

With that thought, Jackson formed his plan. He suddenly saw the need to hold the left bank was an opportunity, not a problem, for it opened the way to a new round with Frémont. It would allow him to attack both enemy forces in a single day. Jackson decided to bluff Frémont with a light force, crush Shields, secure his own rear, and then turn on Frémont. Stonewall would meet trap with countertrap.[40]

The audacity—perhaps the word is rashness—of Jackson's plan can only be understood in relation to the terrain. The Valley Army lay north and west of Port Republic, Shields, north and east of it. Jackson now planned for the Army to cross south over the North River bridge, which was battered during the morning skirmish, and then cross east over the South River, which had no bridge. Both streams were high from recent heavy rains. Assuming Shields was beaten quickly, the rebels then faced a reverse march over the South and North rivers to fight Frémont, and Jackson planned to win both victories in a matter of hours. Military history before and since offers no parallel.

It is uncertain when Jackson made this decision, but it could hardly have been earlier than dark, or about 9 P.M., on June 8; it was only then that Ewell reached Headquarters with detailed information concerning Frémont.[41] Whenever the decision was made, there was little time left to prepare the dual victory. Taliaferro was directed to hold Port Republic and the heights above the village with his brigade. Trimble, who desired action against Frémont so badly, was chosen to bluff the Pathfinder with his brigade and the brigade under Colonel Patton. This left Jackson four brigades to strike Shields: the Stonewall Brigade and three brigades of Ewell's division. Ewell may have been told before he departed Headquarters to lead his brigades through Port Republic at daylight.[42]

The staff knew another battle was at hand when Major Harman emerged from the General's room grumbling that he must feed and resupply the Army before morning, then spirit his wagons off to Brown's Gap, an almost impossible feat. Sandie Pendleton whistled under his breath and mused: "Jackson is crazy again." Henry Douglas recalled his own surprise years afterwards: ". . . the General seemed to like traps and, at any rate, was not yet satisfied with the risks he had run and the blows he had inflicted. . . . We were getting used to this kind of aberration, but this did seem rather an extra piece of temerity."[43]

Time pressed. It was midnight (probably after the tiring visit of General Trimble) before Jackson rode to see about bridging the South River, an essential task if the four brigades for the attack on Shields were to cross it twice during the next ten hours.[44] Stonewall personally supervised his engineers as they stripped the sides off cargo wagons and dragged them into the stream. The wagons were placed end to end with boards from an adjacent sawmill laid from one to the next. The makeshift bridge looked secure in the faint moonlight, but dawn would show otherwise.

Jackson returned to Headquarters at Dr. Kemper's home before 2 A.M., when Colonel Patton arrived for special instructions on his mission opposite Frémont. "[M]ake a great show," Jackson said; deploy, skirmish, retire, and deploy again until he, Jackson, had finished with Shields. Patton asked how long that would be. "By the blessing of Providence," Stonewall replied earnestly, "I hope to be back by 10 o'clock."[45]

Shortly thereafter, the General threw himself onto his bed without even pausing to unbuckle his sword[46] and fell into a waking doze that was as near to sleep as his ambitions would allow. Only four hours remained before his hastily stitched-together attack must begin, and that was not enough time. Some batteries had been unable to locate the ordnance train and had no shells[47];

many supply wagons had been unable to find their regiments in the dark.[48] The trains had not cleared Port Republic as dawn neared, and a bottleneck in the village was building as the infantry moved toward battle.[49]

II

Time pressed. General Winder, still camped north of the North River and having no knowledge that a battle was planned, received orders at 3:45 A.M. of June 9 to have his brigade at Port Republic within an hour. He arrived by the appointed time and was told only to cross the South River. Calling up the 33d Virginia, which had been detached for picket duty, Winder stumbled onto the wagon bridge.[50] It proved unstable from the first,[51] and considerable time was lost on it.[52] Already off schedule, Old Jack led Winder's vanguard down the east bank of the South Fork. Poague's Rockbridge Artillery and Carpenter's batteries joined the advance.

Federal skirmishers were encountered a mile down the road. Jackson motioned to drive them off and surveyed the ground. He was facing to the northeast: ahead of him, between the South Fork on the left and the forested base of the Blue Ridge on the right, was a mile of level, dew-covered wheatfields. A spur jutted out from the Blue Ridge and commanded this plain; atop the spur was a coaling, a flat area where charcoal was produced. Cannon shells already searching for the gray line came from this post. Running northwesterly from the coaling to the river, directly ahead of the rebels, lay a worm fence. The main Union infantry line was behind it.

The hands of Stonewall's watch showed 7 A.M.,[53] and he knew the rebels must work swiftly if they were to meet Frémont by 10 A.M. He started the 2d and 4th Virginia and Carpenter's battery through the forested base of the Blue Ridge to take the coaling. Poague was ordered to answer the enemy artillery with his long-range pieces, while Winder deployed the rest of his brigade to advance across the wheatfields. The hasty Southern attack began.[54]

Union artillerists gauged the range to the rebel infantry, and

Northern fire swelled powerfully; 10, 12, perhaps 15 guns thundered from the coaling and from the enemy line to the north. Confederates ducked the first salvo and looked back for help—and saw that the road from Port Republic was empty. Where were the other rebel brigades? A short ride to Port Republic would have given the answer. The Confederates were snarled around the bridges there. Not even the Stonewall Brigade was completely through this jumble. Neff's 33d Virginia was stalled back there someplace, and his report of the battle contained a lucid account of havoc in the Southern rear. Approaching Port Republic, Neff asked one of Winder's aides where the brigade was. The aide, Neff wrote, "replied he was not sure whether it was on the Brown's Gap road or whether it would go down the river. . . . I pushed on, but before I got to the [North River] bridge I found the way blocked by wagons, ambulances, artillery, and infantry; it was with great difficulty and considerable loss of time that I at last got my regiment across the main bridge, and encountered almost every obstacle in crossing the temporary one across the [South River]. I was without any definite knowledge as to the whereabouts of the brigade, but took it for granted it was somewhere on the battle-field. . . ."[55]

Chaos erupted behind Neff as he wandered off to find his brigade. The board flooring of Jackson's makeshift bridge collapsed, leaving only enough planks for men to trickle across it in single file. Major Dabney, in charge at Port Republic, did not have the means to repair the bridge and could not convince the troops to wade the stream. Artillery, cavalry, and wagon trains continued to plow through the jammed infantry,[56] until the peninsula between the North and South Rivers was swamped by what Dabney termed "almost inextricable confusion."[57] Whatever battle orders Jackson had left with Dabney were lost in this confusion. General Taylor, obviously without instructions, squeezed over both rivers, then parked his brigade a few hundred yards downstream from the crossing and allowed his men to cook breakfast.[58]

A mile north of Taylor, Jackson looked to the Stonewall Brigade's flanking column for relief from Northern guns on the coaling. He was disappointed. Carpenter's battery quickly abandoned the attempt to flank the Union artillery and returned to fight with Poague in the wheatfields. The 2d and 4th Virginia

(which together numbered less than 500 men[59]) continued to
hack their way through dense stands of mountain laurel. The Virginians crept within one hundred yards of the coaling and counted
6 long-range guns. Three regiments of Union infantry supported
them. Too heavily outnumbered to attack and knowing what had
happened to Garnett for retreating, Colonel Allen of the 2d Virginia filtered some marksmen forward to pick off enemy gunners,
but two wild shots from overanxious rebels spoiled his plan. Federal gunners swung around, firing grapeshot, a shell packed with
clusters of iron balls, and riddled the Southerners.[60]

The Stonewall Brigade was neutralized. The 5th and 27th Virginia had been shelled to a halt in the wheatfields; Colonel Allen's
messenger soon informed Jackson that the 2d and 4th Virginia
were reeling back under the deadly Union grapeshot. The 33d
Virginia still had not found the battle. Colonel Neff was lost, utterly ignorant of the enemy position and forced to rely on rumors
to find his lines:

> I came up to an ambulance which the driver told me belonged to
> the Second Virginia Infantry, and from him I learned that the Sec-
> ond Regiment had gone up the same road upon which I was then
> moving. I continued to march in that direction, expecting to meet
> with General Winder or some of his aides. [In fact Neff was head-
> ing into the laurel thickets in the direction of the coaling.] . . . I
> had gone, as I supposed, half a mile farther, when I met several
> members of the Fourth Virginia, who told me the regiments were
> falling back, and their regiment was ordered back to support Car-
> penter's battery. I was now in the woods; there was sharp firing in
> front of me; I was totally ignorant of our position or that of the
> enemy, and scarcely knew what to do. I accordingly halted the regi-
> ment and rode forward to ascertain, if possible, something of the
> condition of affairs.[61]

The condition of affairs was grim. All chance of a dual victory
was gone, and Jackson realized that just defeating Shields would
not be easy. The entire Army would have to be concentrated
against him. Taliaferro was summoned to the front with his brigade. Stonewall ordered Trimble to ease away from Frémont,
burn the bridges at Port Republic, and join the battle. Unless

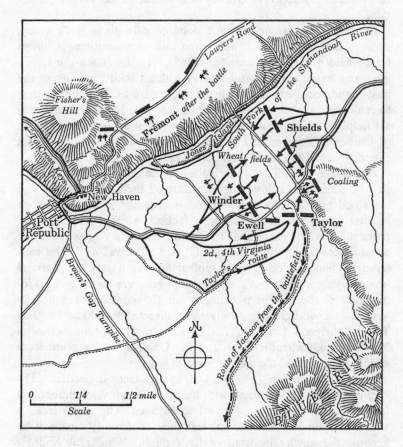

12. BATTLE OF PORT REPUBLIC, JUNE 9, 1862.
Redrawing of map prepared under the direction of Jedediah Hotch-
kiss for William Allan's *History of the Campaign of General T. J.
(Stonewall) Jackson in the Shenandoah Valley.*

Trimble was careful, and lucky, Frémont would follow and plant his artillery on the left-bank bluffs of the South Fork, heights from which Confederate artillery had shredded the enemy yesterday.

Confederate guns might have done equally good work today, except that many of them had no ammunition. Colonel Crutchfield scoured the rear for rifled pieces to match the Union guns and found battery after battery without shells, a result of the past night's congestion among the wagon trains. It required time to refill these limber chests, and until that was done Southern guns sat helpless while rebels below the coaling were butchered. Some of Carpenter's pieces had to be withdrawn after firing their last rounds,[62] and Crutchfield could only replace them piecemeal.[63]

About this time, Taylor's brigade double-timed toward the battle with some men still wiping breakfast off their faces. Taylor had not stood on formality and waited for orders; he had come when he first heard the battle explode. Jackson hurried Taylor's lead regiment, the 7th Louisiana, to bolster Winder's regiments in the wheatfields. "Delightful excitement," said Stonewall as Taylor cantered up and saluted. Taylor replied he was happy the General was enjoying himself but suggested that pleasure might turn to indigestion if the Northern cannons on the coaling were not silenced. Jackson agreed instantly[64] and directed Hotchkiss to guide Taylor's brigade (less the 7th Louisiana, which remained with Winder in the wheatfields around the Union left to a point from which Taylor could charge the Federal guns.[65]

Winder, meanwhile, made a courageous tactical decision. The enemy seemed to be present with heavy force, greater numbers, in fact, than the Valley Army now had engaged. The rebels faced a worse rout than at Kernstown, and they could only escape it by keeping the enemy ignorant of their plight. Winder accordingly aligned his 5th and 27th Virginia on the 7th Louisiana and attacked. Poague's and Carpenter's batteries rolled forward with him. He had little hope of driving the Federals from behind their worm fence, but he might, if willing to take the losses, check them long enough for Taylor to strike.

Winder took the losses. His men dodged through a devastating fire to a fence within two hundred yards of the enemy line and held fast. Yankees hidden along the riverbank caught the 5th Virginia in the flank. The 27th was torn by a "perfect shower of ball."[66] All along their fence, rebels fired and ducked and died. For thirty long minutes this unequal contest continued, then ammunition grew scarce. Disheartened Confederates began to slip away. Winder prayed for Taylor's attack. Nothing happened. Ten minutes passed, then ten more. Winder begged Jackson for reinforcements. Stonewall grudgingly ordered Colonel Walker, who was leading Elzey's brigade, to hurry his 31st Virginia to Winder, but it was too late. Winder decided to reserve the 31st in anticipation of what was to come.[67]

Winder's volleys weakened as man after man shot away his last cartridge. Courage gave way to strength, and the rebel front collapsed. A few companies rallied, only to wash away as advancing Yankees flowed over them. Winder spotted Lieutenant Davis of Poague's battery fleeing with his gun and implored him to make a stand. Davis tried, but his gunners began to drop. Federals were only a hundred yards away when the gun was loaded. Davis fell pulling the lanyard, but the piece was lost. Winder thrust the 31st Virginia forward and saw it chewed up in the stampede.[68] Ugly memories of Kernstown surfaced among the Confederates racing to the rear.

The Port Republic road was wide open to the enemy, but Dick Ewell suddenly drew them off. He had neared the field with Steuart's brigade (again temporarily under command of Colonel Scott after Steuart was wounded at Cross Keys) prior to Winder's retreat, and Jackson had sent him toward the coaling with the 44th and 58th Virginia to reinforce Taylor. Seeing Winder's line fracture, Ewell changed his route of march to hit the Union flank from the east. He slowed the Federals, but was roughly handled for his valor. Blue regiments pounded him back toward the Blue Ridge with heavy losses.[69] Another of Scott's (Steuart's) regiments, the 52nd Virginia, had been sent straight forward to aid Winder and was also brushed aside.[70] Chew's battery entered the fight, and George Neese remembered: "The musketry right in front of us raged fearfully. . . . The shells from the battery on the coaling were ripping the ground open all around us, the air was full of screaming fragments of exploding shells, and I thought I was a goner."[71]

More anxious minutes passed, then three fresh regiments under

Colonel Walker appeared. Winder was struggling to rally five tattered regiments from four different brigades and urgently needed
help. Ewell's attack had just bounced off the enemy flank, and the
Federals were massing to resume their assault on Winder. Yet the
coaling remained the key to victory, and Jackson ordered Walker
to follow Taylor's course and attack the Federal guns. Walker
requested a guide. Jackson had none. The colonel took a long
look at the Federal battery, tried to grasp a landmark or two and
plunged into the laurel thickets.[72]

As if they sensed Jackson's resolve, Taylor and Hotchkiss were,
by this time, smashing away some underbrush to get a clearer
view. Taylor's brigade had been groping through a maze of low-
branched laurel for more than an hour. It had reached a point on
the flank of the enemy guns at the coaling but separated from
them by a ravine. Textbook tactics dictated that Taylor should
complete his circuit to the rear of the position, but the fading echo
of Winder's battle demanded immediate action. Taylor waved his
regiments toward the Union guns, and the rebels surged forward
instinctively. Breaking into little groups, unable to see or hear
their officers, Louisianians rolled out of the woods, down, then up
the ravine and onto the coaling before the Federals could fire a
shot. The Union guns were taken, and the gunners were driven
off.

But these were Shields's troops, men who had seen the Valley
Army's back at Kernstown. Federal regiments stationed to support the guns counterattacked savagely and caught the Confederates in a throng before they could form to resist. Fearing to lose
the guns, rebels began to shoot the battery horses; Major Wheat
pulled out a bowie knife and slit the throats of animals near him.[73]
Despite tenacious individual fighting, the rebels were battered
back to their original positions. Here they rallied and blasted
Union gunners who tried to drag away the cannons. Only one was
removed.

Taylor brought his brigade raging out of the forest again within
a few minutes. It was not a storybook charge as at Winchester.
The dense undergrowth made it impossible to deploy. Rebels
tripped on roots and vines; the leaf-caked ground slipped away
under their feet; branches snapped back in their faces as those
ahead pushed on. Federals met them at the ravine edge with

ramrods and rifle butts. They yielded a little, and the battle swirled over the bodies of a hundred dead battery horses, then the rebels were thrown back across the gorge a second time.

Officers screamed commands no one could hear. Drummer boys threw aside drums for muskets they could not use. Eyes glazed with rage, uniforms black from powder and sweat, the rebels looked like crazy men, and they responded wildly as Taylor led a third charge. A Union mob met it. Rebels lunged in with bayonets to spit the Yankees to their artillery. Squirming, writhing wounded piled hub high around the guns. The fighting splintered into little groups of frantic men, and this time the defenders fled.

Taylor's men had won 5 cannons, but now they faced a terrible sight: their charge had arrested the onslaught against Winder, but Northern regiments in the wheatfields were shifting to attack them. Nor was there any sign of help from any quarter. "With colors advanced," recalled Taylor, "like a solid wall [the enemy] marched straight upon us. There seemed nothing left but to set our backs to the mountain and die hard."[74]

This thought had barely cleared Taylor's mind when a ragged line of infantry burst from a stand of pine trees on his left. It was Ewell, flinging profanities at the enemy and waving on the survivors of the 44th and 58th Virginia. Ewell pulled those men together after the repulse of their attack below and resumed the ascent to the coaling. Though the units were hardly regiments any longer—the 44th numbered less than 80 men[75]—they came on like fiends. Ewell brought them into position near Taylor and gave the enemy a volley. Almost simultaneously, Colonel Walker reached Taylor with his three regiments. Winder saw the enemy shifting toward the coaling and gathered his shattered companies to harass their attack; Taliaferro's brigade was arriving from Port Republic to help him. Even Colonel Neff finally had gotten a messenger to Winder, learned the situation, and was actually passing some regiments in his hurry to reach the front.[76] The enemy buckled beneath this long-delayed concentration.

The day now wound down swiftly. Winder's and Taliaferro's brigades, supported by Munford's cavalrymen, began the pursuit, even as Taylor's men dragged corpses aside to turn their captured guns on the enemy. Jackson rode into the coaling, clasped Taylor's hand and promised the guns to him.[77] Additional good

news came from General Trimble: the bottleneck around Port
Republic was broken; all Southern units were now east of the
South River; the bridges at the Port were destroyed; and Frémont
was not yet in sight. Jackson thanked God for his hardest victory
yet: "General," he exclaimed when he met Ewell, "he who does
not see the hand of God in this is blind, sir, blind."[78] Then the
pious Stonewall pushed his infantry after the Yanks for five miles
and sent Munford on for three more. Approximately 450 prisoners,
800 rifles and another fine Union cannon were his reward.[79]

Late that afternoon, the Valley Army returned toward Port
Republic to find Frémont's artillery bristling on the heights across
the South Fork. Now that the Pathfinder enjoyed every possible
advantage, he was eager to fight. Jackson, however, ignored him.
He moved his troops to the Brown's Gap road by a path beyond
range of Frémont's cannons and headed for the summit of the
Blue Ridge under a cold rain.[80]

The stench of death hung over the Army during that climb, but
such a thing had become familiar. Ed Moore of the Rockbridge
Artillery remembered trailing a caisson to which was strapped a
headless corpse. A white handkerchief was tied where the neck
had been, and Moore thought it served as an excellent guide
through the rainy darkness.[81] Men found the ground at the summit so steep that it was necessary to pile rocks into little retaining
walls to keep from rolling away during the night.[82] Working
swiftly, they made their bulwarks, the last act of a long soldier's
day, and fell asleep beneath the rain.

III

Dr. McGuire reported by the morning of June 10 that the Battle
of Port Republic had cost more than 800 Southern casualties,[83]
an appalling number since only three already weak brigades,
Winder's, Taylor's, and Scott's (Steuart's) were engaged for any
length of time. And Federal prisoners revealed that the Federal
force had not been Shields's entire division. Shields himself was at
Luray; he had advanced only two brigades, about 3,000 men with
16 guns, to seize the North River bridge. The battle was a tribute
to the valor of these Union soldiers and proof of what could be

accomplished with well-directed troops. Federal killed and wounded totaled less than 500, although an equal number were captured.[84] These statistics did not speak well for Jackson. It took him four hours to drive away a heavily outnumbered enemy, and the work cost an inordinate number of Southern dead and wounded.

Many of these Confederate casualties can be traced to one factor—Jackson's reckless tactical decision to fight when there simply was not time to prepare the battle. As a result, the vital bridge over the South River was hastily cobbled together and rebel batteries were given insufficient time to resupply. Jackson clearly was unrealistic to expect that his wagon trains (which were already disorganized by the Union raid of June 8) could resupply the Army and then get completely out of the way before the Southern infantry was scheduled to cross the North and South rivers. As Henry Douglas asserted: "The fact is, Jackson went into the fight impetuously and was disappointed."[85]

One of Jackson's familiar problems, poor tactical co-ordination of the Army, was aggravated by haste. The breakfast halt of the Louisiana Brigade was an example. A man like Richard Taylor would not have allowed his troops to break ranks and cook after crossing the South River had Jackson gotten word to him that a battle was brewing one mile downstream. Jackson has been credited with brilliance in bringing superior numbers to his Valley battlefields[86] (except Kernstown and Cross Keys), and he merits this praise. Unfortunately, at Port Republic he left himself unable to employ superior force from the very beginning. Though he had at least 8,000 men within two miles of the enemy by 7 A.M., Jackson did not attack with anything like that number for several more hours. Of course, he did not foresee the collapse of the wagon bridge, and he left Major Dabney at Port Republic to expedite the river crossings, but he then seemed to forget about his rear units. He plunged into an attack without insuring that his brigades were up or that he had sufficient batteries on hand to quell the Union artillery. Jackson swung into battle piecemeal, and his units were strewn over the field in jumbled fragments by the struggle's end. Port Republic can only be described as an action wherein Stonewall displayed afresh an inability to handle his army as a single weapon.

But Jackson was more than impetuous or clumsy at Port Republic; he was also extravagantly ambitious. This battle and the battle intended to follow it were too hazardous for the rewards Jackson could have expected to gain by fighting them. Defense of the Virginia Central Railroad or a continuing need to keep Northern forces from leaving the Shenandoah to reassemble at Fredericksburg justified hitting the enemy if a reasonable opportunity arose, but these reasons did not warrant the risks Jackson assumed on June 9. He contemplated pushing his emaciated brigades through four river crossings (at each of which bottlenecks were probable) and two battles during a single day. Both encounters had to be victories; a loss in either battle would have gravely jeopardized the Army. Had the Confederates lost against Shields, there could have been no meeting with Frémont, only an extremely dangerous retreat before two enemy columns. Shields's strength was unknown,[87] and to chance running headlong into an entire division of his rough fighters—and to allow only four hours to beat them—was rash indeed. Had Jackson defeated Shields and then lost against Frémont, he would have had to get beaten troops over two rivers before superior numbers, another dangerous operation. At this stage of the Campaign there was nothing more crucial than to preserve the Valley Army for Richmond's relief or other maneuvers, possibilities Jackson unduly risked with his battle plan. Boundless ambition, an ambition that was one of Jackson's major faults, is a prime explanation for the Battle of Port Republic.

Another, and heretofore unnoted, explanation for the blunder of Port Republic was that Jackson was too exhausted for his common sense to resist ambition and too tired to properly muster his forces for the attack. It is evident from those close to Stonewall during the period June 6–9 that he was averaging little more than four hours sleep per night, and this came on top of the draining retreat from Harper's Ferry.‡ Jackson probably had had no more than an hour's sleep on the night before the battle itself.[88] Stonewall's weariness, which was certainly also a large factor in his careless location of the Confederate wagon trains on the morning of June 8, seriously marred the Valley Army's last days in the

---

‡ See Appendix C.

Shenandoah. It also foreshadowed the trancelike state into which Stonewall would lapse on the Peninsula.

Weariness also aggravated Stonewall's third major fault, his abrasive manner of dealing with subordinates. After the Battle of Port Republic he sent Major Harman to collect small arms left on the field. Harman later remarked that many of the weapons looked like Confederate arms, a reasonable enough statement considering the number of Southern casualties. Jackson instantly was shouting that Shields's men had arms similar to the Southerners and that he would hear no more talk of weapons being abandoned by his troops. Tough John Harman glared back at the General and snarled that he would not be spoken to in such a manner. He stomped out of Headquarters, threatening to resign. As before, Jackson apologized to mollify this invaluable worker.[89]

It was Winder's turn two days later. He politely requested a short furlough to Richmond for urgent personal business. Jackson had plans afoot and curtly rejected the request. Had he merely bothered to say the situation would not permit it, all might have been well, but the blunt refusal climaxed a host of other irritants, and Winder resigned.[90] Taylor had to untie this knot. He rode to see Stonewall and dwelt at length on the fame Jackson had earned by his brilliant efforts, then appealed to his "magnanimity" on Winder's behalf. The strategy worked, and the matter was smoothed over.[91]

The Harman and Winder incidents lengthened a distressingly long list. Since February, Jackson had brought court-martial charges against two brigadier generals, Loring and Garnett, and two colonels, Gilham and Conner. His actions had prompted threats of or actual resignations from Winder, Ashby, Funsten, and Harman, the latter twice. He had protested Taliaferro's reassignment to the Valley and had insulted Elzey. It was a poor record, and this clumsiness with subordinates, together with his difficulty in wielding the Army on the battlefield and a sometimes unreasonable ambition, had emerged as Jackson's principal defects as a commander.

Jackson's greatest strength remained the bulldog resolve with which he attacked his work. He showed this unyielding determination at Port Republic; realizing that victory hinged on capture of the Federal battery at the coaling, he moved to take it and

clung to his goal throughout the morning. The initial attack by
two regiments of the Stonewall Brigade was repulsed and
Winder's regiments in the wheatfields were left heavily outnumbered, but Jackson resolved to attack the coaling again and again.
In succession, Taylor's, Scott's (Steuart's), and Walker's (Elzey's) brigades were sent to strike the Federal guns, even though
this risked opening the road to Port Republic by Winder's rout.
These orders displayed true mental stamina on Jackson's part, and
without such determination there might have been no victory at
Port Republic.

Jackson's resolve, his "go-aheaditiveness," was his enduring
strength. It outweighed his weaknesses, and it did not falter as he
camped with his army at Brown's Gap. He promptly began to
consider new maneuvers. A dash to Warrenton was conceivable,
or to Fredericksburg, or to Front Royal again. Jackson was not
slow to pull out his maps.

15

WHAT NEXT?

*We are being heavily reinforced
and I suppose will soon be on
the march again after the enemy.*

—JEDEDIAH HOTCHKISS

By June 12 both Frémont and Shields were retreating into the
northern Shenandoah, and Jackson had left Brown's Gap to return to the Valley. Munford occupied Harrisonburg with his cavalry, capturing several hundred wounded abandoned by Frémont.[1]
Jackson moved the infantry through Port Republic and several
miles to the southwest along the Staunton road. Near the lip of a
beautiful grotto called Weyer's Cave he pitched his camps and ordered a general cleanup.[2] The boys soaked away a chalky com-
pound of sweat and mud, and the strain of the past weeks eased.
They basked beneath a warm Valley sun and fished or played
cards or prowled the nearby cavern, "the most beautiful hole in
the ground I ever was in," thought George Neese.[3]

Two days of this unaccustomed repose fortified even the
weariest Confederate for further adventure. Captain Campbell
Brown obtained a short furlough to Staunton with his friend John
Jones. They met some comrades from the Louisiana Brigade at
the hotel and decided to toast their victories; a few hours later one
of the Louisiana men was dead drunk on a lobby bench, while
Jones was tottering toward his room in a "perfectly limp state."[4]

Never willing to permit time for such frolics, Jackson resumed
daily infantry drills.[5] He instructed his staff to help Munford organize Ashby's cavalry.[6] In an order which highlighted Jackson's

zealous devotion to duty, religious as well as military duty, the General both announced new courts-martial and invited his soldiers to join him at divine worship.[7] Major Dabney administered the sacrament before Taliaferro's brigade, and Old Jack was there, standing unobtrusively at the rear.[8]

News from beyond the Shenandoah also occupied Jackson's attention. Alexander Boteler, whom Jackson had dispatched to Richmond from Harper's Ferry, returned after Port Republic with much to tell.[9] He had seen something of the rejoicing excited by the Valley Army's triumphs, rejoicing typified by the diary of one Richmonder who wrote: "[Jackson] has swept [the Federals] out of the valley, scattering their hosts like quails before the fowler. They fly in every direction; and the powers at Washington are trembling for the safety of their own capital. Glorious Jackson!"[10] The Richmond *Whig* outdid itself: "Glorious Old Stonewall is fast becoming the HERO OF THE WAR," it trumpeted.[11] Upon learning of Cross Keys and Port Republic, the *Whig* proclaimed: "[Jackson] is a game cock and he does wheel with a vengeance. He 'cuts and comes again,' and reminds us of that queer and terrible Australian implement which deals death and destruction by the unexpected and unward-off-able process of the circumbendibus. Let Jackson be called the Great Gyrator or the Confederate Boomerang."[12]

News of the Valley Campaign spread beyond Richmond. The Macon, Georgia, *Daily Telegraph* hurrahed for the Valley Army: "The men have little baggage, and [Jackson] moves, as nearly as he can, without encumbrance. He keeps so constantly in motion that he has no need of hospitals. In these habits, and in a will as determined as that of Julius Caesar, are read the secret of his great success. His men adore him . . . because he constantly leads them to victory, and because they see he is a great soldier."[13] The news spread through the rural regions of the South, and from far-off Walthourville, Georgia, a country parson rejoiced: "We have cause of gratitude to God for the manifest indications of his returning favor. Great has been His blessing upon his servant General Stonewall Jackson. That pious man and able commander has executed one of the most brilliant passages at arms during the war."[14] An army nurse at Mobile, Alabama, wrote in her diary: ". . . a star has arisen: his name ('Stonewall') the haughty foe has found, to his cost, has been given prophetically, as he has proved a wall of granite to them. For four weeks he has kept at bay more than one of their boasted armies."[15]

A South parched for victory eagerly drank in news of the Valley Army. Some of these reports were fantastic—the Army was reported to be north of the Potomac[16] or even outside Washington[17] —but the reports were believed. After a springtime of little hope, the Valley Campaign revived confidence across the South, and many of the myths and misconceptions which attached themselves to the Campaign doubtless sprang from this sudden, unrestrained outpouring of much-needed relief. The Confederacy had found its talisman, and from then on, the headline "Stonewall is behind them" would comfort a nation.[18]

This was the commendation Jackson had written about to his wife after the First Battle of Manassas, but he had no time to relish it now. Before Boteler could describe much of it, Jackson cut him off and pressed for war news.[19] There was much to tell of that also. Boteler related the story of Johnston's intended battle of May 29, the battle canceled when McDowell's supposed advance toward Richmond suddenly reversed on May 28. On May 31, the same day Jackson's men were panting through the Northern pincers around Strasburg, Johnston struck McClellan south of the Chickahominy River. In a battle of many blunders and heavy losses Johnston rammed portions of the Union line back a mile, then lost the ground to fresh Federal divisions. Johnston himself fell late in the action with a serious chest wound.

Johnston's wounding particularly saddened Jackson, for the Valley Army owed much to irascible Old Joe. Johnston had supported Jackson during the Romney winter, and he had courted President Davis's ire by allowing the Valley Army to retain the Virginia regiments and batteries of Loring's command. There would have been no Valley Army in the spring of 1862 without those units. Johnston had allowed Ewell's division to shift to the Valley, and though he had almost recalled it, he had corrected his own error. Johnston had fashioned the idea of employing the Valley as a dead end to keep Union forces away from his own command. He displayed shrewd insight in this, but his vision had faltered and he had restricted Jackson's diversionary efforts to Union forces in or near the Valley proper. He had kept the Valley Army a sideshow, never imagining that it might immobilize Union forces far beyond the Blue Ridge.

The man who supplied this vision, Robert E. Lee, had succeeded Johnston. This officially made Lee what he had been in fact for weeks, Jackson's commander, which gratified them both. Boteler had conferred with Lee, and the latter had expressed his hope to make good the Valley Army's losses.[20] On June 11 Lee pledged more: three brigades—8,000 men—under Brigadier General William Whiting. Lee bled his own army to provide some of those men and sent the last units he could peel from the Atlantic seaboard as well.[21]

These reinforcements passed through Richmond amid the best publicity Lee could arrange, because, more than just bolstering the Valley Army for new battles, he also was engaged in a handsome piece of psychological warfare. At virtually the last moment, the North had abandoned what Lee believed to be McDowell's march on Richmond in obvious answer to the Valley Army's attack against Banks. The conclusion Lee drew, if not based on a perfect understanding of Lincoln's actual reason for diverting McDowell, was still useful: the North might be inordinately sensitive about the security of Washington. Lee moved immediately to act on this conclusion. After his latest victories, Jackson had sent two Northern forces fleeing down the Valley. The Union therefore should be doubly apprehensive that he might reappear near Washington. This fear ought to be exploited with new victories in the Shenandoah. And the enemy should be made aware that Jackson was being strengthened; the result could only be more Union divisions kept away from McClellan.

Reinforcements for the Shenandoah accordingly paraded through Richmond to be seen by enemy informers. Lee arranged for Union prisoners about to be repatriated to witness the show "accidently."[22] He sent his aide-de-camp to the Virginia Central station to spread tales that Jackson was only awaiting these reinforcements before advancing again.[23] So that the stratagem would not be too obvious, Lee sought to restrain the Richmond newspapers from any mention of the transfer.[24]

Lee had high expectations about what Jackson might accomplish with fresh men. As early as June 5, inspired by his initial interview with Boteler, Lee wrote President Davis: "After much reflection I think if it was possible to reinforce Jackson strongly, it would change the character of the war. This can only be done by the troops in Georgia, South Carolina and North Carolina. Jackson could in that event cross Maryland into Pennsylvania. It would call all the enemy from our Southern coast and liberate those states."[25] Lee harbored no illusions that the 8,000 men he had provided Jackson so far could get the Valley Army into Pennsylvania, but they could take it close enough to Washington to keep significant Union forces immobilized far from Richmond.

Misled as fully as the Federals by Lee's well-thought-out deceptions, and by the subsequent return of Jackson's entire army to Richmond, early historians concluded Whiting's march was simply a ruse to cover Jackson's eventual descent on McClellan.[26] This explanation has become wedded to the Campaign, but it does not coincide with the facts. Lee explained the real purpose of Whiting's march to Jackson on June 11 when he wrote that Whiting's men were to be employed "to crush the forces opposed to you."[27] Whiting's journey to the Valley was not merely a ruse to facilitate the Valley Army's return to Richmond; it was a means of another strike, preying, *for the first time,* on a newly suspected enemy sensitivity about Washington. When Jackson had scraped that nerve raw, he would come to Richmond.[28]

These were the sort of orders upon which Jackson thrived, yet now he balked. The Federal host which had nearly bagged the Army at Strasburg was scattered from New Market to Martinsburg, raising the possibility that Richmond might be further relieved through action in the Shenandoah. On June 13 Jackson sent Boteler back once more to the capital to urge that the Army be enlarged to 40,000 men and to explain an updated version of the plan he had outlined at Harper's Ferry. As soon as the Army had sufficient strength, it would leave the Valley, push northward through the forests on the eastern slope of the Blue Ridge, then smash back over the first convenient gap to Winchester. The enemy would be crushed piecemeal and the rebels would cross the Potomac. Jackson told Boteler: "By these means, Richmond can be relieved and the campaign transferred to Pennsylvania."[29]

Boteler returned to the capital and forcefully presented Jackson's invasion proposal to Davis and to Lee.[30] The latter listened with particular interest; the plan was remarkably similar to what he had expressed to Davis on June 5. What Jackson proposed was electrifying: his veterans refreshed and his numbers tripled with men clamoring to follow him; his army again exploding into the lower Valley, confronting skittish enemies with superior forces, knifing across the Potomac . . . into Maryland . . . into Pennsylvania . . .

The Confederacy faced a major strategic decision in mid-June, and the alternatives have been debated ever since. The Union's spring offensive was at a halt, and the South possessed both means and momentum to counterattack. But where? On one hand was Jackson's invasion, on the other, Lee's shorter thrust in the Valley and redeployment to Richmond. Jackson's plan was definitely the more intriguing. It might well have transferred the war from Virginia to Pennsylvania, recalled McClellan from the Peninsula, and inflicted serious damage on the Northern heartland. Yet, in the end, the invasion would have only prolonged the war. To force McClellan's recall, to maneuver him off the Peninsula, was not to beat him, and for this reason Lee's resolve to settle accounts on the Peninsula seems wise. McClellan was before him in positions that Lee thought permitted his annihilation, and annihilation of the Army of the Potomac was the only way to Southern independence. Jackson's plan postponed that test; Lee's demanded it now on terms as favorable as he could expect. Further, there were no more troops realistically available for the Valley, not from the Atlantic or the deep South or anywhere, though Richmond tried hard to find them.[31]

Jackson had anticipated there would be no additional reinforcements. In this event, in a letter he sent with Boteler, he frowned on Lee's quick Shenandoah offense prior to moving on McClellan: "So far as I am concerned, my opinion is that we should not attempt another march down the Valley to Winchester, until we are in a condition under the blessing of Providence to hold the country."[32] These words capped Lee's thoughts. Stonewall believed an attack without occupation of the lower Valley was futile, and his judgment must be respected. The needed men were unavailable, so the Valley Campaign must end. Lee recommended to President Davis: "I think the sooner Jackson can move this way the better—The object now is to defeat McClellan. The enemy in the Valley seems at a pause—We must strike them here

21. *above:* Private John Casler.
(Courtesy of the Museum of the Confederacy)

23. *below:* Captain William Poague.
U. S. Signal Corps Photo No. 111-BA-1253,
Brady Collection, in the National Archives.
(Courtesy of the National Archives)

22. *above:* Brigadier General Richard Taylor.
(Courtesy of the Library of Congress)

24. *below:* Colonel Bradley T. Johnson.
(Courtesy of the Library of Congress)

No single group of soldiers left as significant a body of postwar recollections as did those who fought with the Valley Army. Here are only a few of the Army's many authors.

25. Ashby's dying fight. This sketch by Confederate artist William L. Sheppard portrays the charge of the 1st Maryland Infantry during the brief but savage action at close quarters near Harrisonburg on June 6, 1862. (Courtesy of the Library of Congress)

26. *opposite, above:* The Valley Army's June retreat. This sketch depicts Confederate troops destroying the bridge at Mount Jackson, June 3, 1862. (From July 5, 1862, issue of *Frank Leslie's Illustrated Newspaper,* reproduced courtesy of the Virginia State Library)

27. *opposite, below:* Union Major General John C. Frémont attacking at Cross Keys, June 8, 1862. Contemporary drawing. (Courtesy of the Virginia State Library)

28. Typical Valley Army volunteer, Private Thomas Taylor, 8th Louisiana Infantry. (Courtesy of the Museum of the Confederacy)

before they are ready there to move up the Valley. They will naturally be cautious and we must be secret and quick."[33]

"Secret and quick": those words were as much a portent of things to come as a signal of decision reached. Davis concurred with Lee's recommendation. On June 16 Lee sent Jackson a historic assignment. On the seventeenth the Valley Army broke its camps for Richmond.

II

The men Lee called to Richmond were ready for battles that would soon be fought there. As one of them wrote: "We have come to be veterans—have no tents, carry our knapsacks and blankets, never ride on caissons . . . and, in the case of necessity, can live on half rations and not think it anything remarkable. When expecting a fight, our rations are six hard crackers and a quarter pound of pork a day."[34]

No longer did these veterans even talk about going home until the war was won. ". . . I mean to keep at it as long as there is any necessity for it, if it should be the rest of my life," wrote Private Dick Waldrop, who, with his entire company, had refused to re-enlist in February.[35] Captain S. G. Pryor of the 12th Georgia was equally blunt, writing that he was determined to stay with his company "as long as I can raise one foot before the other . . ."[36] Captain Hugh White, who had regarded much of army life as "irksome" in April, now told his family: "I sometimes fear I shall not only become contented, but even pleased with this mode of life. I used to wonder how one could choose the life of a soldier. I thought its dangers and hardships would make it irksome in the extreme. . . . I feel now that if taken back to my former quiet life, it would be, at least for some time, somewhat irksome."[37]

In battle too these men now bore themselves like veterans. At Port Republic the 44th and 58th Virginia earned Ewell's special praise. Double-timing from a difficult river crossing onto a desperate battlefield, those regiments were started toward the coaling, countermarched to assault the Union advance on Winder, thrown back with severe loss, and then reformed to reinforce Taylor. Ewell wrote: "It would be difficult to find another instance of volunteer troops after a severe check rallying and again attacking the enemy."[38] Ewell's enthusiasm led him to overlook another instance of unusual courage during the same battle: the several regiments under Winder also rallied after an extraordinary pounding to join the pursuit.

Even death somehow seemed less awesome. Private Ed Moore, whose stomach had been so weakened at Kernstown, followed a headless corpse to Brown's Gap after Port Republic and looked on it merely as a guide. Corporal George Neese, who had pancaked beneath harmless Union fire at Dam No. 5, had a similar experience. When Chew's battery pulled out of Harrisonburg on June 6, Neese spotted one of Frémont's cavalrymen far in advance of the main Union column: "A [Confederate] rifleman was near me, and I saw that he was deeply interested in the Yankee's bold deportment. . . . The rifleman watched him a while and then I saw him take aim at the Yankee. When he fired I saw the Yankee's horse walk leisurely away, and from all appearances the cavalryman had received a clear pass to that silent land from whose mystery-veiled fields no soldier ever returns. It was a first class shot, as the distance was about six hundred yards."[39] Death had become a subject for praise when skillfully dealt. General Taylor found himself munching from a haversack he picked off a dead Federal after the final shots of Port Republic. "War," he had learned, "is a little hardening."[40]

These were not, however, cruel men, but veteran soldiers, and like all veterans they made their harsh life tolerable with laughter. If they were caught with stolen chickens, they protested that the birds had run out to bite them and they had merely defended themselves.[41] The entire Army was soon grinning as some wag circulated the following spoof:

FOOT CAVALRY CHRONICLE

1. Man that is born of woman and enlisteth in Jackson's army is of few days and short rations.

2. He cometh forth at reveille, is present also at retreat, apparently, at taps.

3. He draweth his rations from the commissary, and devoureth the same; he striketh his teeth against much hard bread, and is

satisfied; he filleth his canteen with water, and clappeth the mouth thereof upon the bung of a whiskey barrel, and after a little while goeth away rejoicing at the strategy.

4. Much soldiering hath made him sharp, yea, even the sole of his shoe is in danger of being cut through.

5. He fireth his Minié rifle in the dead hour of night, and the camp is aroused and formed in line, when to his mess he cometh bearing a fine porker, which he declareth so resembled a Yankee that he was compelled to pull the trigger.

6. The grunt of a pig or crowing of a cock waketh him from the soundest sleep, and he sauntereth forth in search of the quadruped or biped that dared to make night hideous, and many other marvelous things doeth he; and lo! are they not already recorded in the morning reports of Jackson's "Foot Cavalry."[42]

These men could find humor in the misery through which they lived. They also found pride in what they had accomplished. They were coming to think themselves invincible, a belief more valuable to the South than several new divisions. Success brought unity and comradeship, vital elements of morale. Loyalties were no longer exclusively to a regiment or a brigade, but to Jackson's "Foot Cavalry." These men were adopting that curious sobriquet, boasting, with John Casler: ". . . we could break down any cavalry brigade on a long march."[43] And there was fully as much truth as bluster in what Casler said. Those who followed Stonewall from Swift Run Gap on April 30 had trudged almost four hundred miles during six weeks; Ewell's division had marched almost two hundred miles in three weeks. In terms of physical endurance, few campaigns have equaled that pace, and of those that have, fewer still were completed by a force so modestly equipped and fed as was the Valley Army.

Such achievements loom even larger when it is recalled of what material the Army was composed at the beginning of the Campaign. Colonel G. F. R. Henderson, Jackson's classic military biographer at the turn of the century, has written on this point:

[T]here were not more than half a dozen regular officers in the whole Army of the Valley. Not one of the staff had more than a year's service. Twelve months previous, several of the brigadiers had been civilians. The regimental officers were as green as the men. . . . When the march to McDowell was begun, which was to end six weeks later at Port Republic, a considerable number of the so-called "effectives" had only been drilled for a few hours. The cavalry on parade was little better than a mob; on the line of march they kept or left the ranks as the humour took them.[44]

And yet, within just six months, those same men had written history. Men who had quit in the snows of January had learned to push on, if only at a straggler's pace, to abide hunger, to rebound from defeat, and even to regard the soldier's life as normal and the civilian's way as "irksome." In six months of ceaseless striving, men of the Valley Army had grown from a civilian horde into a veteran host, a human triumph as worthy of remembering as that of the campaign they waged.

III

In concluding, what may be said of the Valley Campaign itself? Without question it was a strategic masterpiece. Henry Douglas forecast: "The more it is studied and its difficulties comprehended, the greater will be its rank among military successes"[45]— and this has proven true. Succeeding generations of military thinkers have studied it approvingly,[46] although on two points their approval has been forthcoming for the wrong reasons.

Misguided by Jackson's early biographers, the analysts have maintained that Lee and Jackson intended to immobilize McClellan by arousing Lincoln's fears for Washington and that fear of the Valley Army had precisely this effect. Henderson was particularly guilty of this dual error. He wrote of Lee: "He knew McClellan and he knew Lincoln. He knew the former was over-cautious; he knew the latter was over-anxious. [He also knew] a threat against Washington was certain to have great results."[47] But Lee could have known nothing of the kind. He never met Lincoln and had no way to guess the extent to which the President actually controlled Union armies. And even if Lee had guessed this, there was no way he could have realized Lincoln's "over-anxiety" for

Washington before the Battle of Winchester and McDowell's subsequent rerouting. Lee spent the war's first year in the Alleghenies and plugging holes on the Atlantic seaboard, places where Lincoln's strategic influence was peripheral and diluted through several layers of commanders.

Nevertheless, the idea took hold that Lee and Jackson planned to cause and did cause panic in Washington. Field Marshal Viscount Wolseley, Queen Victoria's able commander-in-chief, considered that Jackson's assigned mission in early 1862 was "to prevent any reinforcements from being sent to McClellan, and, above all things, to create an alarm at Washington for the safety of the capital."[48] Major General J. F. C. Fuller, the foremost military thinker of the twentieth century, implied just such a result: "Jackson's activity . . . ever since November, 1861 . . . perturbed the Federal Government by offering a standing threat to the capital."[49] Such assessments ignore the facts that by late April Washington believed Jackson had abandoned the Valley; that throughout May Secretary Stanton permitted the weakening of Washington's garrison; that on the afternoon of May 24 Lincoln and Stanton weakened Washington further to bolster Banks; and that neither Lincoln nor Stanton betrayed anxiety for their capital until May 25, when McDowell was already committed to the Shenandoah.

Confederate sources reveal no designs for creating panic in Washington during the early spring of 1862. It defies the facts to assert that Jackson intended to frighten Washington with his 3,300 soldiers on March 23, when his latest intelligence told him McClellan's 150,000 men were still packed around the Union capital. (Recall that McClellan's embarkation had begun only a few days before Kernstown and that Jackson was not apprised of developments on the Peninsula until the second week of April.) Jackson's dispatches show that he intended only to prevent Banks's divisions from leaving the Valley to swell the odds against Johnston; he said nothing about Washington prior to or after Kernstown. It again defies the facts to assert that Lee and Jackson intended to stop McClellan with a stampede at Washington when neither Confederate mentioned the city during their month-long correspondence preceding the Battle of Winchester. It is more realistic to read the words they did write and to see that they expected a Southern offensive in central Virginia or the Valley to strip the flank of Union troops at Fredericksburg (on which city both Lee and Jackson kept a worried vigil) and prevent McDowell from crossing the Rappahannock. Lincoln's brief concern for Washington on May 25 and 26 was an unlooked-for bonus of the Valley Campaign and not its goal.

Likewise, Union sources make it clear that the specter of the Valley Army rampaging into Washington did not keep McDowell from McClellan throughout the spring of 1862. Lincoln's general fear for Washington led him to require that McClellan's Peninsula effort be prefaced by a large garrison at Manassas. This general fear indirectly sponsored McDowell's detachment from McClellan after Banks was unable to reach Manassas because of the battle at Kernstown. But it must be remembered that after Kernstown Lincoln was attempting to establish the conditions under which the Peninsula Campaign was supposed to have begun; it is not plausible to think he detached McDowell out of concern for Jackson when, on April 3, the Valley Army was at Rude's Hill confronted by greatly superior forces. Lincoln's rerouting of McDowell from Richmond to the Valley in May was an offensive move ordered prior to any evidence of fear that the Valley Army might approach Washington. To summarize, Lincoln admittedly was concerned throughout the spring of 1862 that some rebel force might attack Washington in McClellan's absence, but the Valley Army at Kernstown and at 5 P.M., May 24, was not the "some force" Lincoln dreaded. The brief fear he felt for Washington's safety after May 24 was a footnote that did no more than make McDowell's march to the Shenandoah irrevocable.

The analysts have been more accurate on other points. They have detailed the problems overcome by the Valley Army, and merely to reiterate these obstacles is to highlight much that is remarkable about the Campaign. The Army was required by Confederate draft laws to hold elections for officers and noncommissioned officers midway through the Campaign, and the ensuing reorganization was so sweeping that the decisive weeks of the Campaign were fought with hundreds of new and inexperienced leaders. There were other adverse effects of this reorganization as well, as the mutiny in the Stonewall Brigade and the situation with the 1st Maryland before Front Royal reveal. More than half the Army reached the Shenandoah after Jackson left Swift Run Gap on April 30, forcing him to learn the capabilities of new units on the march. As he did that, he was harassed by conflicting orders from Lee and from Johnston; as late as May 20 Jackson lacked clear authority to launch the attack he had been preparing for a month. The odds against which the rebels operated were incredible. From early March until mid-May the Army lay within easy striking distance of three to five times its own strength. Only when Banks was struck in late May were these odds reversed, and this was within a net capable of swiftly drawing 50,000 troops around the lower Shenandoah. During the June retreat the Confederates were outnumbered two to one, although the Federals predictably squandered this preponderance.

The analysts have emphasized that, by rising to the challenge of adverse odds, the Valley Army achieved something of immense strategic difficulty, confronted a stronger enemy at four of six encounters with superior forces. There were 30,000 Federals within range of the field at McDowell on May 8, but only 2,200 fought there, as against 17,000 Confederates within range and 6,000 engaged. On May 23, 70,000 Union troops (including McDowell, Shields, Frémont, Banks, and the details along the B & O and Manassas Gap Railroads) might have been concentrated against Jackson; instead, Jackson fought 1,000 Federals at Front Royal (May 23) and 7,000 at Winchester (May 25) with 17,000 men. Frémont did muster odds against Ewell at Cross Keys on June 8, but it is well to note that those odds would have been worse had Jackson's forethought in burning several strategic bridges not left Shields cut off by river from Frémont. Finally, by the end of the battle at Port Republic on June 9, the Valley Army marshaled perhaps 8,000 men (of roughly 12,000 available) against 3,000 Federals, though there were approximately 20,000 enemy troops within a day's march.

Adherence to two fundamentals of good soldiering made possible these remarkable achievements. First, the Valley Army threw its whole strength against enemy fragments. Its battles were small affairs; Winchester, the largest battle, matched less than 25,000 men on both sides. The actions at McDowell, Front Royal, and Cross Keys were hardly more than long skirmishes. Though it lost heavily in material, the Union suffered less than 7,000 casualties in the Valley, half of them prisoners. Confederate losses were under

3,500, light losses indeed compared to the ghastly casualty lists which were later to stain this war. Of course, there could have been larger fights with bigger body counts. Jackson might have attacked Banks at Harrisonburg when Ewell reached the Valley in April, and 40,000 men would have been engaged. He might have marched with Ewell to attack McDowell at Fredericksburg, and 60,000 men would have been engaged. That the Army did not have to resort to such battles was a measure of its success. It beat isolated fractions of the enemy host one at a time.

Second, when it fought, the Valley Army chose the right time (with the exception of Port Republic). Though Stonewall was misinformed about enemy intentions prior to Kernstown, he knew a major redeployment from the Valley was underway. An opponent in the midst of a troop shift signals his vulnerability, and Jackson was well rewarded at Kernstown for alertly reading those signals. That battle locked Banks in the Shenandoah for many weeks. Likewise, Winchester was a well-timed battle. As quickly as Jackson realized Shields's exit from the Valley, which suggested some major Federal move was about to be launched from Fredericksburg, he swarmed over Banks. Had the rebels delayed only three days, their thrust would have come too late. But the Valley Army did not delay, and McDowell was diverted from the Peninsula.

It is in the events surrounding McDowell's diversion that the Valley Campaign's true significance rests. By May 23 the life of the Confederacy literally had trickled down to a handful of days. Only the Valley Army was positioned to retrieve the situation, and it is possible to project with unusual certainty the course of events if the Army had not struck. First, McDowell would have lumbered south from Fredericksburg. Orders for this march had been given by Lincoln himself, and abundant men and material were available to execute those orders. Second, because the South mistook McDowell's feint for a real march on Richmond, we know what the Southern response would have been if McDowell's feint had been real: Johnston's desperate battle of May 29 against McClellan's right flank. Only the melodramatic reversal of McDowell's supposed approach prevented Johnston's attack; Generals Johnston, Smith, Longstreet, and others left ample evidence of Confederate determination to strike if McDowell approached. Given the chaotic Southern preparations and the formidable Federal positions to be assaulted, a result similar to the stalemate following the battle of May 31 would have been inevitable. Further, this would have been a stalemate without the way cleared for Lee to assume command of Johnston's army and complicated by the arrival of 40,000 fresh Northern soldiers. This "if" scenario leads to the inescapable conclusion that without the Valley Army's intrusion, McClellan would have clawed his way into Richmond, probably delivering the mortal blow he set out to deliver. Whatever opportunity the South possessed to win its independence during the battles it would wage against McClellan on the Peninsula, and thereafter, sprang in large measure from the Valley Campaign.

This Campaign, then, was a realistic use of limited Confederate strength at the right place and at the right time. The Valley Campaign bought time, time in which McClellan was stalled, time in which the South finished a reorganization that sustained it for three more years, time in which the Confederacy massed its strength for a deadly counterattack on the Peninsula.

EPILOGUE

On June 18 the Valley Army crossed the Blue Ridge, bound for Richmond. Only Munford's cavalrymen held the Shenandoah, and they were swarming after Frémont as if every rebel within fifty miles were with them. The infantry, including General Whiting's 8,000 men just off the trains from Richmond, were bewildered by their new march, for Jackson shrouded the goal with impenetrable silence. He deserted his own staff in his quest for secrecy.[1] The aides attached themselves to Ewell, who had orders only to move toward Charlottesville.[2] The troops guessed eagerly at their destination—at least, until a covey of stills was discovered along the way and hundreds of canteens were brimming with applejack.[3]

The mood in Mr. Lincoln's Washington, meanwhile, was anything but tranquil. During early June, Lincoln had lost interest in the Valley and concentrated again on the stalled drive for Richmond. He shipped McDowell's last units at Fredericksburg to McClellan by sea. He transferred General Burnside's large command from the North Carolina coast to the Peninsula. The President extended Frémont's Mountain Department to the Massanutten, extended Banks's command to a line twenty miles east of the Blue Ridge, and ordered the two men to co-operate. Frémont would plug the Valley at Mount Jackson, while Banks held the line at Front Royal. These two Federal fronts, so long encased within unrealistic, arbitrary departmental boundaries, were at last unified to guard the Potomac, liberating McDowell, with Shields, to resume his overland march on Richmond from Fredericksburg.[4] Frémont questioned this design, but Lincoln's response indicated he had learned something: "I think Jackson's game—his assigned work—now is to magnify the accounts of his numbers and reports of his movements, and thus by constant alarms keep three or four times as many of our troops away from Richmond as his own force amounts to. Thus he helps his friends at Richmond three or four times as much as if he were there. Our game is not to allow this."[5]

This came on June 15. Had Lincoln "not allowed this" three weeks earlier, when McDowell had offered him essentially the same reason for not redeploying to the Valley, Richmond might already have fallen. By June 15 many factors combined to sap Lincoln's resolve. Frémont and Banks were terrified of the Valley Army. On June 19, with the rebels seventy miles away, Banks fretted that they were upon him.[6] Both generals were inexcusably slow reaching their assigned positions, which delayed Shields's and McDowell's return to Fredericksburg.[7] Rumors persisted of a new Valley Army offensive: the Army was reported moving on Richmond, Charlottesville, Fredericksburg, Luray, Front Royal, and into the Alleghenies.[8]

So it went. Lincoln's generals fretted, demanded more troops, and accomplished nothing. The President grew weary of this travesty and sought a final solution, but he also forgot his recent insight and abandoned his best course, which was to push McDowell on to Richmond and a link-up with McClellan. On June 26 Lincoln lumped Frémont's, Banks's, and McDowell's detachments into a unified command under Major General John Pope. Pope was to do three things: ". . . attack and overcome the rebel forces under Jackson and Ewell, threaten the enemy in the direction of Charlottesville, and render the most effective aid to relieve General McClellan and capture Richmond."[9]

Largely because of a Valley Army phobia, McDowell's march on Richmond was scrapped anew, and the South won the Valley Campaign a second time. A Federal army was created in central Virginia, where it could not aid McClellan as it might have at

Richmond. Pope's army deployed where it was needed least, eighty miles northwest of the Confederate capital, while McClellan was left dangling. McClellan anticipated McDowell would join him and waited with his right wing extended northward toward Fredericksburg until June 26. That flank was isolated and exposed, and as word of Pope's new army reached McClellan, Jackson's divisions, not McDowell's, were descending on McClellan's isolated wing.

The Valley Army swept over McClellan's right, but during a week of unparalleled carnage the South bungled its opportunity to annihilate the Army of the Potomac. Jackson, who strove as mightily as any man to isolate McClellan, did as much as any to permit his escape. Ambition elicited a promise from Old Jack that his column would begin the battle before it was humanly possible, and the rebels never recovered the time lost waiting for Stonewall. As in the Valley, the General was plagued by fatigue at a crucial hour.* Jackson once fell asleep before Federal positions he should have stormed. When he awoke, he sat on a stump gaping at the ground. Officers requested orders. He had none.[10] He called for dinner but could hardly eat because of fatigue.[11] The Army of the Potomac, hurled back from Richmond, its grasp on the city smashed, survived to fight again.

In the broadest sense, the Valley Campaign and the Peninsula Campaign were phases of one immense struggle that raged across Virginia in the spring of 1862, and there was a sequel. The Valley Campaign halted McClellan and created Pope's army; while Pope was organizing, the rebels drove McClellan away from Richmond. Now the Valley Army was free to turn against Pope. Its new theater of operations was within sight of the Blue Ridge but eastward from it, in the rolling countryside north of Charlottesville. At the furious Battle of Cedar Mountain on August 9 the Army bested Pope's vanguard under Banks. Three weeks later the Army tore into Pope's rear via Thoroughfare Gap, the same route by which some of those rebels had journeyed to the Valley so long ago in November 1861. At the ensuing Second Battle of Manassas on August 29–30 Pope was crushed completely enough to satisfy even Jackson.

---

* See Appendix C.

With the climax of this summer's fighting the generals who had contended in the Valley Campaign began to disappear from Virginia. Refusing service under Pope, Frémont was relieved of his command on June 28, 1862, and spent the remainder of the war "awaiting orders." He later caught the public eye when convicted for complicity in a railroad swindle. Banks was shunted off to Louisiana. In 1864 he mismanaged a drive up the Red River against an old antagonist, Richard Taylor, and was routed as badly as in the Valley Campaign. He was relieved of command and suffered congressional censure, but he redeemed himself after being elected to the House of Representatives. There Banks enjoyed far greater success than he had known as a warrior. Shields left the army in March 1863 and pursued a political career in Missouri. Damned because of blunders he was ordered to make and by McClellan's undying enmity, McDowell was court-martialed during the winter of 1862. He was exonerated, but was never trusted against the rebels again. He finished the war commanding Union forces on the Pacific coast.

Valley Army officers disappeared from Virginia more swiftly than the Federals. Richard Taylor departed to rally Confederate strength in western Louisiana. He never saw his splendid brigade thereafter, but he did have the pleasure of thrashing Banks once again. During Reconstruction he energetically advocated fair treatment of the South to his personal friends Presidents Johnson and Grant. The Battle of Cedar Mountain saw the death of Winder, perhaps the Army's best brigade commander. Both Generals Trimble and Taliaferro were wounded at Second Manassas. Feisty old Trimble mended in time to lose a leg and be made prisoner at Gettysburg. After the war he resumed his work as a railroad executive headquartered in Baltimore. Taliaferro later commanded Confederate defenses at Charleston, South Carolina, and passed the balance of his years on his Virginia estate.

Ewell was also among the wounded at Second Manassas, and his was the hardest fate of all Valley Army officers. He was an unmatched division commander when he fell. When he recovered, after Jackson's death, leadership of Stonewall's troops went to him. Without time to master duties three times greater than those he had known, Ewell marched northward to Gettysburg; the dragoon who once had worried lest anyone beat him into battle hesitated to strike. He failed the South at Gettysburg and other places, until Lee gently eased him into less arduous garrison duty. He met death quietly in 1872 as a gentleman farmer and, in this respect he had taken up Jackson's mantle, as a devout Christian.

The summer of 1862 was significant in yet another respect, for it witnessed the last battles of the Valley Army. Jackson continued as the district's titular head until December, and he sometimes prefixed his orders "Headquarters, Valley District." Nevertheless, the Army became an integral element of Lee's command, and only local infantry and cavalry formations defended the Shenandoah after the Army left in June. Veterans of the Valley Campaign became Lee's II Corps. As though to consecrate the occasion, Jackson donned an elegant uniform one autumn day and apprised his staff: "Young gentlemen, this is no longer the headquarters of the Army of the Valley, but of the Second Corps of the Army of Northern Virginia."[12]

Six months later Jackson was dead. Reconnoitering in advance of Confederate lines at Chancellorsville with his staff on May 2, 1863, he was mistaken for a Federal cavalryman and shot down by his own men. His death, on May 10, ended ten months of the war which can only be termed remarkable: those months saw Southern victories at Cedar Mountain and Second Manassas, the capture of 11,000 Federals at Harper's Ferry, a magnificent defense at Sharpsburg, and more victories at Fredericksburg and Chancellorsville. After the Valley Campaign Stonewall wielded a degree of moral ascendancy over his enemies that no American, of any era, has ever equaled. It was not the Army of Northern Virginia the North dreaded, but Jackson, and his death at Chancellorsville, more than Pickett's Charge at Gettysburg, was the point at which the war turned unalterably against the South.

The staff Jackson had assembled so carefully and which had implemented his judgment in the Valley began to dissolve after the General fell. Henry Douglas noted that before Chancellorsville this staff never lost a man, but "after the protection of his presence and his prayers had been withdrawn, death played havoc with them."[13] Some, like Crutchfield and Sandie Pendleton, died facing Northern guns. Pendleton's fall was particularly tragic. He had become, in the opinion of his friend Douglas, "the most brilliant staff officer in the Army of Northern Virginia and the most popular with officers and men . . ,"[14] and he was not twenty-five when he died. Douglas himself carried a Union bullet from Gettysburg to Appomattox. Thereafter, until 1903, he was a respected member of the Maryland bar. Dabney had left the staff because of ill health following the battles around Richmond; after the war he pursued a distinguished teaching career at the University of Texas. Dr. McGuire became medical director of Lee's army and later joined the Virginia Medical College faculty. In peace, as in war, he proved an innovative healer, and his term as president of the American Medical Association was a credit to his profession. John Harman returned to his Valley stage line. The invaluable Hotchkiss served Lee, Ewell, Early, and others throughout the war, then settled in Staunton and promoted Virginia's postwar industrial development. He also undertook meticulous research into the war, particularly Jackson's operations. His studies brought him into contact with the British military theorist Colonel Henderson, and Hotchkiss' efforts contributed much to Henderson's classic biography of Jackson.

Shielded only by local forces, including the reorganized companies that had been Ashby's cavalry, the Shenandoah Valley beat back continued incursions until August 1864. Then Major General Philip Sheridan came with orders from General Ulysses Grant to scorch it. Lee bled his army to dispatch to the Valley the remnant of those who had followed Jackson to stop Sheridan; Lee's instructions—". . . maneuver so . . . as to keep the enemy in check until you can strike him with all of your strength"[15]—might have been written during the dark days when the Valley Army bivouacked at Swift Run Gap wondering "What next?" But there was no Confederate reprieve this time. Sheridan trounced the rebels and devastated the Valley so that the rebels would never be able to draw rations from it again. Sheridan captured or destroyed 71 flour mills, 1,200 barns, 435,000 bushels of wheat, 75,000 bushels of corn, 25,000 cattle and sheep, and 4,000 horses and mules.[16] The Valley was lost, and, as Jackson had augured, Virginia was also lost. Within weeks of Sheridan's onslaught Lee's men were subsisting on a pint of corn meal and an ounce of bacon per day. Within months, Lee surrendered at Appomattox.

Of the 17,000 men who were the Valley Army, few were still in the field at Appomattox. Units like Taylor's Louisiana Brigade had shriveled to a handful by then. The Liberty Hall Volunteers had suffered a staggering 125 per cent casualties. Hundreds of the Army's finest, men like Bull Paxton, soldier of fortune Chatham Wheat, and devout Hugh White, had died in battle. Others, like Jim Edmondson, were crippled and waited out the war in painful frustration.

A small number of men passed through the full agony that stretched from Port Republic to Appomattox and journeyed back home to a ravaged Shenandoah. They found railroads and canals, bridges, highways, industry, orchards, and fields, even schools, all desolated. Students such as Ed Moore resumed their studies in gutted classrooms. George Neese, like most, came back to tend a wasted farm. John Casler began a contracting business around Winchester; William Poague opened a law office in Lexington. These few survivors, who had gone to war as boys and returned as sunken-eyed men, were the Valley's stoutest defenders through a bleak and often troubled future.

APPENDIX A

JACKSON'S PLANS AND MARCHES, MAY 24, 1862

Jackson's intentions and actual movements on May 24, 1862, have been a persistent source of confusion, and the major recountings of this day have compounded the uncertainty. The account offered in Chapter 11 disputes all previous accounts and therefore requires detailed explanation.

Previous Accounts

Jackson's report of the Valley Campaign was prepared during the winter of 1862–63, and it reflected the long lapse between the events and their chronicling. The preliminary draft was written for Jackson by Colonel Charles J. Faulkner, who was not with the General during the Campaign, and recollections conflicted among those Faulkner interviewed even at this comparatively early date.[1] Jackson edited out many of Faulkner's clarifying explanations, lest the enemy "learn [our] mode of doing."[2] The report, therefore, was not intended to be a completely reliable history, but it can be read as if Jackson planned, during the night of May 23–24, to proceed directly from Front Royal to Middletown the following morning. The report stated:

> . . . I determined, with the main body of the army, to strike the turnpike near Middletown, a village 5 miles north of Strasburg and 13 miles south of Winchester.
>
> Accordingly, the following morning General Ashby advanced from Cedarville toward Middletown, supported by skirmishers from Taylor's brigade. . . .[3]

Dabney in 1866, William Allan in 1880, and Colonel G. F. R. Henderson in 1898 each accepted the report on its face and asserted that Jackson moved directly from Front Royal to Middle-town. By doing so, these authors were compelled to provide ex-cuses for the fact that the Army did not reach the village until afternoon, though the distance from Front Royal was only ten miles. Henderson, for example, stressed rough terrain and enemy delaying tactics as reasons for the Army's supposed slowness.[4] But such factors, while certainly to be considered, fail to justify a pace of barely a mile and a half per hour.

In an incisive appendix to his 1942 *Lee's Lieutenants,* D. S. Freeman probed this matter and challenged the view that Jackson initially planned to advance toward the Valley Pike at Middle-town. In essence, Freeman's argument was as follows: The initial Confederate march of May 24 led north from Front Royal, past the road from Cedarville to Middletown, and on to Ninevah; this is known from Hotchkiss' reliable diary and from Ewell's report. Such a march was pointless and a serious waste of time, if Stone-wall intended to strike Banks at Middletown. What was more likely, according to Freeman, was that Jackson contemplated a move to Winchester along the Front Royal road, but, as he neared Ninevah still without word of Banks's location, he grew fearful the enemy would dash for Front Royal. This fear was such that, with-out additional information, Jackson halted and soon counter-marched to Middletown.[5] (The present account suggests Jackson began the day without a definite plan but with a preference to fol-low the Front Royal road to Winchester—perhaps only a difference in degree from Freeman—and that Jackson began his Middletown thrust *after* locating Banks—a major difference from Freeman.[6])

Freeman's analysis was an important step away from the idea that Jackson lunged directly at Middletown on the twenty-fourth. It also helped to explain why the Army took so long to reach the Valley Pike. But Freeman relied almost exclusively upon Hotch-kiss' diary for his account, and this perhaps led him to over-look other evidence which, if analyzed in conjunction with the Hotchkiss diary, would have brought the operations of May 24 into even sharper focus. This evidence concerns the Valley Army's mid-morning halt between Ninevah and Cedarville. When the duration of this halt is understood, a detailed timetable of the day's events becomes possible.

The Halt North of Cedarville

This halt is well documented. In his report (dated June 4, 1862) Ewell wrote that the head of his column was stopped by Jackson eight miles north of Front Royal; this placed it around Ninevah.[7] Colonel Ronald of the 4th Virginia wrote (June 4, 1862): ". . . arriving at the Forks of the road [Cedarville] the brigade was halted for several hours."[8] Colonel Neff of the 33d Virginia implied a lengthy halt, writing (June 4, 1862): ". . . moved from bivouac at 8 A.M. and marched with the brigade on the Winchester road about three miles, where we were halted. About 12 n. we again moved, taking the Middletown road."[9] Hotchkiss noted in his diary that he accompanied the van of the Army to Ninevah, then returned with Jackson to Cedarville, "going by the troops which were halted." Hotchkiss then recorded that Jackson sent him to reconnoiter the Cedarville–Middletown road.[10] A letter dated May 26, 1862, from Hotchkiss to his wife has also survived, and by relating it to the diary it is possible to time the beginning of Hotchkiss' reconnaissance at after 11 A.M. In the letter Hotchkiss wrote that, "shortly after 11 A.M.," he was sent on the reconnaissance, found the enemy, and alerted Jackson, who thereupon started the Army westward.[11] The time occupied by these events could hardly have been under an hour. Thus the Hotchkiss material also demonstrates that the Army started toward Middletown about noon and after a halt.

John Apperson, a careful diarist with the Stonewall Brigade, recorded on May 24 that the Brigade was detained three miles from Front Royal for three or four hours.[12] "W.W.H.," an otherwise unidentified soldier whose generally accurate narrative of the Campaign was written on May 25 and published in the Lynchburg *Republican* of May 31, described a halt lasting several hours before moving on Middletown.[13] Jim Hall of the 31st Virginia, Elzey's brigade, noted in his diary: ". . . marched a mile or two along the road and halted to await orders. . . . About 2 o'clock we started at a brisk pace for Middletown. . . ."[14] (Hall's estimate of the hour at which Elzey marched west was too early, but a lengthy halt is clear from this diary.)

General Trimble, who led Ewell's division to Ninevah, left additional documentation of the mid-morning halt. In a postwar letter to author William Allan, Trimble noted that his advance was halted, on Jackson's orders, at 8 A.M.[15] With Trimble breaking ranks at 8 A.M., units marching behind him, some of which only departed Front Royal at that hour, would have been catching up and halting at 10 A.M., just as many rebels affirm.

To recapitulate: seven individuals ranging in rank from brigadier general to private (six of them writing either on or shortly after May 24) agree that a halt of one to four hours, depending upon the writer's position in the column, occurred north of Cedarville. These reports accepted, it is reasonable to accept further that the halt was made in order to ascertain Banks's whereabouts; Jackson hardly would have been sitting still had he known where Banks was fleeing. Finally, allowing for the hours lost at Cedarville makes possible the following timetable of the events of May 24:

6 A.M.	Ewell moved north from Front Royal on the road to Winchester (Ewell's report).
8 A.M.	Ewell's van, Trimble's brigade, reached a point eight miles from Front Royal and halted (Ewell's report; Trimble's letter).
	The brigades of Jackson's division began to follow Ewell's rear brigades out of Front Royal (Winder's, Campbell's, and Fulkerson's reports).
9 A.M.	Ewell's rear brigades began to halt behind Trimble. (Hall's diary). Winder's brigade neared Cedarville; Campbell's and Taliaferro's brigades were behind it (positions computed by allowing a conservative march rate of two miles per hour over the known distances).
9–10 A.M.	Banks began to evacuate Strasburg for Winchester (Banks's report).
10 A.M.	Jackson, still lacking word of Banks's movements, ordered the brigades of his division to halt as they reached Cedar-

ville (Ronald's and Neff's reports; Apperson's diary).

10–12 A.M. The Army closed up, until the rear was at Cedarville and the entire force was halted (Hotchkiss' diary).

10–11 A.M. Steuart intercepted the Valley Pike around Newtown, swept south, threw enemy trains into a panic and sent word of this to Jackson. (Captain Samuel Zulich, 29th Pennsylvania, who was stationed at Middletown that morning, reported: "At 11 A.M. an excitement was created among the teamsters by an advance of enemy cavalry from Newtown."[16] For the effect of Steuart's raid to have spread the four miles from Newtown to Middletown by 11 A.M., Steuart obviously had to arrive at the former point sometime before 11 A.M.; 10 A.M. was the earliest reasonable time of Steuart's arrival).

11–11:30 A.M. Jackson received word of Steuart's attack and sent Hotchkiss toward Middletown to search for enemy pickets (Hotchkiss' letter).

11:30 A.M.–12:30 P.M. Hotchkiss found enemy pickets one and a half miles west of Cedarville and informed Jackson, who started the Army westward (Hotchkiss' letter; Neff's report).

Federal vedettes on the Cedarville–Middletown road began skirmishing with advancing rebels. (In his report Colonel C. S. Douty, 1st Maine Cavalry, wrote: ". . . at about 12 o'clock . . . the most advanced vedettes came in and reported the enemy's cavalry and infantry advancing. . . . After a delay of half an hour the enemy opened on us with artillery, throwing shell into my

column. I drew off my force and proceeded slowly to Middletown. . . ."[17]).

12:00 or 12:30 P.M.–   The Valley Army marched to Middle-
3:00 or 3:30 P.M.   town.

3:30–4:00 P.M.   The Confederates attacked at Middletown (Jackson's message to Ewell in
OR vol. 51, pt. 2, p. 562).

Considering the countermarch of some units to Cedarville, rain,
a poor road, enemy delaying tactics—which caused frequent halts
—and exhaustion in the ranks, the Valley Army's march of six or
seven miles from Cedarville to Middletown in roughly three hours
was a respectable feat, and, given the timetable offered above,
there is no reason to fault the Army for slowness in reaching
Middletown.

Contrary Evidence

Two Union officers reported that the main Confederate attack
at Middletown occurred between noon and 2 P.M. An attack at
this time would refute the timetable offered here; however, there
are serious inconsistencies in both of these officers' reports.

Colonel G. H. Gordon, who commanded one of Banks's brigades on the trek from Strasburg, stated that soon after passing
Newtown, at approximately 2 P.M., he heard artillery rumbling
behind him and learned that the Union column had been pierced
at Middletown. Gordon immediately countermarched to aid the
rear guard.[18] To have been even one mile beyond Newtown at 2
P.M. Gordon, who evacuated Strasburg at 10 A.M.,[19] would have
had to cover ten miles in four hours. This was possible on the
Valley Pike, but it was unlikely Gordon maintained such a pace,
since his brigade trailed an immense train of wagons. Gordon also
halted for reconnaissance around Middletown, which cost more
time. Further, Gordon certainly was more than only one mile beyond Newtown when he heard the Middletown news. One of Gordon's regimental commanders, Colonel George Andrews, reported
that he was within five miles of Winchester when Gordon ordered
him to countermarch.[20] Gordon's brigade probably traveled as a
unit, so Andrews' report located it thirteen miles north of Stras-

burg, or four miles north of Newtown, when it about-faced. In an 1863 monograph Gordon corroborated Andrews' statement,[21] and it can confidently be asserted that the brigade was roughly thirteen miles north of Strasburg when news of trouble at Middletown was received. If that news was received at 2 P.M., Gordon had hurdled thirteen miles in four hours, an almost impossible feat given the conditions under which the Federals were retreating. (One Union regiment, the 29th Pennsylvania, required eight hours to cover thirteen miles from Middletown to Winchester on May 24.[22]) It thus is doubtful that Gordon had reached the point where he learned of the Middletown attack by 2 P.M., although he could have reached it about 4 P.M.

Gordon's report is suspect in another way, for it leaves several hours unaccounted for. Assume Gordon did learn of the Middletown struggle at 2 P.M. and took two hours to reoccupy Newtown,[23] arriving about 4 P.M. Upon arrival Gordon reported sighting rebel artillery south of town and attacking at once. A skirmish of one "hour or more" followed. But at the conclusion of this combat, Gordon gave the time as 8 P.M.[24] His report thus contains a major gap, a gap eliminated with the assumption Gordon received word of the Middletown trouble at 4 P.M., if not later.

In a personal letter dated May 29, 1862, Lieutenant C. F. Morse of Gordon's brigade supported the contention that the brigade was ordered back toward Newtown after 4 P.M. Morse wrote that the time from the first shots of the brigade's skirmish at Newtown until a point "just as it began to get dark"[25] was about two hours. Assume Morse's regiment countermarched at 2 P.M., took even two hours to complete the march to Newtown and fought there for two more hours. This narrated the day until only 6 P.M., hardly twilight time in late May. The problem, however, is resolved by beginning Morse's countermarch at 4 P.M.

Gordon was not at Middletown when the main Confederate attack surged over it. Major William P. Collins, 1st Vermont Cavalry, was and, in his report, timed this attack as between noon and 1 P.M.[26] In fact, there was a skirmish near Middletown during the late morning or early afternoon; on this fact most Federal sources concur. Three lines of evidence, however, refute Collins' assertion that this attack was delivered by the main Southern column.

First, if the main Confederate attack came during the early afternoon, we would be compelled to believe the tussle at Middletown lasted two or three hours, until 4 P.M., when Jackson informed Ewell that the enemy had begun to retreat northward. Given Federal panic and superior Confederate numbers, a contest of more than thirty minutes is inconceivable. Nor is it logical to think Jackson shattered the enemy column in the early afternoon and waited until 4 P.M. to inform Ewell that the enemy was retreating northward in his direction.

Second, the report of Colonel Douty, Collins' commanding officer, contradicts Collins. Collins reported that he spent the day with or near Douty's command. Douty, in his official statement, positioned his command at least four miles *east* of Middletown between noon and 1 P.M. and wrote that he fell back slowly from this position as the rebels advanced.[27] To have been with Douty at noon, Collins could not have been around Middletown.

Third, the weight of Federal evidence denies a determined attack on the Pike at noon. No other Union officer suggested that the raid which did occur then was serious. None reported Confederate artillery present at this time, and all agreed the rebels were brushed aside easily. Finally, no report credited this early foray with the great destruction and panic known to have accompanied the main attack.[28]

In summary, sources which accelerate to 2 P.M., or earlier, the hour of the principal fight at Middletown must be ruled in error and the brief fight which did occur then must be attributed to some portion of Steuart's cavalry as it swept south from Newtown. To do otherwise ignores a larger body of evidence, from both armies, which sets the attack between 3 and 4 P.M. To ignore such evidence merely returns the operations of May 24 to a state of confusion.

Lenoir Chambers, in his excellent biography of Jackson, suggested that Freeman's appendix study of Confederate movements on May 24, persuasive as it was, failed to explain (1) why Jackson did not mention the crucial events of the day's early hours in his official report; (2) why Jackson, who wished to "deal effectively" with Banks, "changed his mind" (Chambers' words)

after reaching Front Royal and decided to march for Winchester
instead of Strasburg; and (3) how he would have dared to march
toward Winchester on the morning of May 24 knowing that it exposed his flank and rear to Banks at Strasburg.[29]

The present account is subject to the same questions and cannot
offer definitive answers. Such answers, resting with a man long
dead, probably will never be known. Of the first question, it can
only be repeated that Jackson's report was drafted for him by an
aide who did not witness the Campaign. Further, this report was
purposely edited to conceal reasons for major maneuvers. The im-
plication of the second question (that by marching on Winchester
instead of Strasburg Jackson had somehow abandoned his intention to deal effectively with Banks) may be argued: nothing indicates Jackson thought that moving directly on Winchester from
Front Royal would not deal effectively with Banks, and thus nothing establishes that he changed his mind. Vast stores had accumu-
lated at Winchester, and Banks was known to be cautious. It was
reasonable for Jackson to believe that by descending on Winchester directly he could flush Banks into the open and deal effectively with him. Concerning Chambers' third question, it should
be noted that no matter what he did, Jackson could hardly avoid
offering Banks his flank on May 24. If the Valley Army had
closed on Strasburg by a route north of the Shenandoah's North
Fork while Banks was retreating toward Winchester, the Confederates would have been inviting Banks to about-face and strike
their right. Jackson could have countered this threat by moving on
Strasburg south of the North Fork, via the main Front Royal–
Strasburg road, but this route would have required him to cross
that stream near Strasburg, seriously hampering the Army if
Banks were found there. By the same token, an advance from
Cedarville to Middletown potentially opened the Southern left
flank to a stab from Strasburg or, if Banks had passed Middletown, opened the right flank to a stab from the north. It can be
argued that Banks probably would not have interrupted his retreat
from Strasburg to attack the rebels, but this was equally true in
the case of Confederates moving directly on Winchester from
Front Royal. Finally, it should be recalled that Jackson knew
Banks was well entrenched at Strasburg, and Jackson may have

calculated that any risk he took of exposing his flank to Banks was preferable to attacking those fortifications.

Steuart's Raid and
Jackson's Start for Middletown

A final disagreement with Freeman, who suggested that Jackson started to Middletown without positive knowledge of Banks's location because of a growing fear that Banks would dash from Strasburg to Front Royal. According to Freeman, by hurrying to Middletown Jackson achieved the best position to deal with this possibility, as well as with the possibility that Banks would flee to Winchester.[80] This was a strange contention. Had he ventured to Middletown "blind" and discovered there that Banks had made a dash for Front Royal, Jackson would have confronted three unfavorable courses. First, he could have trekked back to Cedarville, united with the brigades under Ewell, moved south to Front Royal, and possibly not been able to cross the North Fork because Banks already had occupied the area and burned the highway bridge (a possibility Freeman admitted). Second, Jackson could have marched sixteen miles via Strasburg to Front Royal with less than half his army. Third, he could have waited for Ewell to reinforce him at Middletown and then marched via Strasburg after losing much time. The two latter choices avoided the necessity of crossing the North Fork near Front Royal. However, the South Fork remained to be crossed at Front Royal, as it would in the first alternative (upon which Freeman made no comment). If Banks destroyed the bridges over this stream, and it was logical to assume he would, Jackson would have had to cross by fords. Valley streams were high from recent heavy rains, and fording them would have consumed many hours. Additionally, the Federals could have taken superb positions from which to retard the rebels once they entered Manassas Gap. Jackson doubtless considered these contingencies. Given the importance of preventing Banks's escape to the east (and the danger such an escape posed to Confederate wagon trains packed around Front Royal on May 24), it was unlikely that Jackson burdened himself with the unfavorable options he might have faced by starting to Middletown without word of Banks's direction of march.

With the present timetable, it seems probable that the information Stonewall needed so desperately reached him about 11 A.M. Assume that General Steuart, in execution of the mission Jackson gave him to cut the Pike at Newtown, moved from Front Royal at 6 A.M. Steuart would have needed to move only approximately three miles per hour to sight Newtown at 10 A.M., not a strenuous pace for cavalry on an important reconnaissance. Steuart's courier, dispatched about 10 A.M., could have reached Jackson by 11 A.M. and no later than noon, early enough to prompt, and certainly to confirm, Hotchkiss' discovery that enemy pickets lay west of Cedarville. Jackson's report cited a dispatch from Steuart which indicated Banks was preparing to evacuate Strasburg.[31] As only this dispatch was recalled many months after the event, its information was doubtless significant.

Hotchkiss bolstered the view that Steuart's news was the decisive factor of the start to Middletown when he wrote, in a postwar journal: ". . . after the position of the enemy had been ascertained by an advance of cavalry on the Newtown road . . . General Jackson sent Col. Ashby with some artillery and cavalry to aid the small force [presumably Hotchkiss' initial scouting party] that went toward Middletown. . . ."[32] Jackson very much desired the intelligence this passage asserted he had received. Jackson took risks, but not the kind of risk inherent in throwing less than half his army toward Middletown without a strong indication Banks would be found there.

APPENDIX B

THREE DAYS OF RUNNING BATTLE: THE UNION RESPONSE

This study has stressed, by design, the Southern viewpoint, a more compelling story than that of the fumbling campaign mounted by the Valley Army's opponents. For this very reason, the Army's deliverance through Strasburg on June 1 has a leaden, an unsatisfying ring. Viewed from rebel ranks, Federal divisions remained strangely passive during the critical period from May 30–June 1. This inactivity cannot be fully explained by anything the rebels did. Jackson pushed his marchers hard; Ashby executed a brilliant diversion on the thirty-first; Ewell handled Frémont well on June 1. Yet these efforts could not retrieve the fact that, at noon on May 30, the Valley Army was demonstrating before Harper's Ferry, while Shields was mopping up Front Royal and Frémont was barely thirty miles west of the Valley Pike at Strasburg. Umpires judging such a situation during peacetime maneuvers would have declared the Army eliminated—yet it escaped. How? The answer requires investigation into the details of Union movements not attempted by those who have studied the Valley Campaign from the Northern viewpoint.[1]

Lincoln's Plan: May 24–May 27

In its most important respect, Lincoln's decision to hurl McDowell into the Valley was a colossal blunder. Even total success there would have been purchased at the prohibitive price of delaying a final battle at Richmond, of stranding McClellan in an awkward position on the Peninsula, and of granting Johnston much-needed time to concentrate additional strength against the Army of the Potomac. Johnston did, in fact, use the time allowed him by McDowell's diversion to effect such a concentration. He massed the bulk of his army against McClellan's southern wing and very nearly overpowered it on May 31.

But in other respects Lincoln evidenced much ability with his plan to trap the Valley Army. His basic strategy was shrewdly workable. Frémont was to plug the principal Confederate escape route by occupying the Harrisonburg area. McDowell was to reach the Valley by a march along the Manassas Gap Railroad or in "advance" (presumably Lincoln meant south) of it.[2] What became a pincer movement began as something much simpler. Frémont was to harass the deep Southern rear; McDowell was to deliver the knockout blow as opportunity offered.

Nor was Lincoln's plan based upon Jackson's tarrying in the lower Valley. Lincoln could read a map and see that if Jackson retired from Winchester on May 25 or 26, neither Frémont nor McDowell could be there to follow him, but this made little difference. Frémont was closer to Harrisonburg than Jackson. Had the rebels begun a withdrawal into the upper Valley on May 26, Frémont still should have been able to beat them there and fight a delaying action until McDowell arrived. Further, the plan had the advantage that every day Jackson lingered around Winchester brought McDowell closer, swelled Banks's forces on the Potomac and gave Frémont additional opportunity to do serious damage in Jackson's rear. Every day Jackson remained in the lower Valley made Lincoln's plan a better one. By dawn of May 31, had others not meddled with it, this plan would have borne excellent results: compact Northern forces would have held Front Royal, while Frémont would have stood solidly athwart the Valley Pike.

Unfortunately, Frémont meddled with the plan, deciding on his own initiative to ignore Lincoln's directive to operate against Jackson at Harrisonburg and to proceed instead through the Alleghenies to Strasburg. This decision was based on four factors: (1) Jackson had blocked the passes between Franklin and Harrisonburg, except one which necessitated a long detour; (2) occupation of Harrisonburg would open an escape corridor through the Alleghenies along the road from Moorefield to McDowell; (3) Frémont's communications were vulnerable if Jackson entered that corridor; and (4) only by moving through the Alleghenies could he secure adequate rations for his army.[3] These reasons provide a controversy in themselves. Beyond the question of whether Frémont was correct to enter the Valley via Strasburg, his decision had one sure result: it eliminated the flexibility Lincoln originally provided.

Frémont, however, was not the only culprit. Apparently writing without Lincoln's knowledge, Secretary of War Stanton advised Frémont on May 25 that he was to fall "upon the enemy at whatever place you can find him with all speed."[4] Without a genuine Union chain of command, Frémont could accept Stanton's message as clarification of the President's order, clarification which allowed him discretion to select his road into the Valley. Frémont read it that way and trudged northward as one arm of a pincer no one at Washington knew was underway.

Next, Stanton shackled what would become the pincer's other arm. On May 25 he required two of the three brigades of Ord's division, which McDowell had scheduled to march for the Valley on May 26, to forgo the direct road through Manassas and to come first to Alexandria by steamer.[5] His idea was to give Washington extra protection by funneling Shenandoah-bound troops through its environs, but the result was to interfere seriously with Lincoln's plan. (Ultimately, the lack of a single commander directing all Union efforts did more than anything else to defeat those efforts.) Stanton had compelled improvisation of a land-sea-rail movement, and the Union lacked logistical talent to carry that off without notice. An unexpected night march from Fredericksburg to the docks at Aquia broke up some of Ord's regiments, which wandered onto the wharfs in groups of three or four.[6] The Union Navy was caught unprepared. The steamers it had available could not reach Aquia's shallow wharfs, so precious hours were lost lightering the soldiers aboard.[7] Debarked at Alexandria, Ord's brigades faced a lurching trip over clogged railroads to Manassas. Like the Navy, the recently captured Confederate rails were overwhelmed by the freshet of blue-clad soldiers; McDowell experienced something of the problem when he journeyed from Alexandria to Manassas and lost valuable time while bleary-eyed dispatchers tried to clear the track for him.[8] Worse, the Navy scrambled Ord's supply and baggage wagons, which left him completely dependent on the jammed railroads.[9] As late as May 28 Ord was assembling his regiments at Manassas.[10]

In contrast, by moving directly from Fredericksburg through Manassas, Shields cleared the latter point and was probing westward along the Manassas Gap Railroad by May 28. His advance was west of Thoroughfare Gap that afternoon, and he had three brigades in supporting range of it.[11] Had Ord, whose men initially were fresher than Shields's, not been detoured through Alexandria, he could have stayed up with Shields. As it was, his division lagged many hours behind Shields. Those hours, lost to pacify Stanton, were among the most costly ever sacrificed by the Union and completed the disruption of Lincoln's plan by deranging McDowell's orderly redeployment to the Shenandoah.

A New Plan: May 28–May 29

With Frémont moving on Strasburg there was need for someone to co-ordinate his operations with those of McDowell, a need not immediately recognized. Before May 29 Frémont and McDowell were each given one sentence on the other's progress. On May 27 Frémont was informed: "General McDowell has a strong force concentrated at Manassas to pursue the enemy and cut off his retreat, if he can be overtaken."[12] Lincoln casually wrote to McDowell on May 28: "By the way, I suppose you know Frémont has got up to Moorefield, instead of going to Harrisonburg."[13] Each commander was briefed only that the other was on the march, hardly adequate orchestration for a pincer movement involving 40,000 men.

These minimal communications are explainable in part by the fact that Lincoln and Stanton knew little of Frémont's whereabouts. Lincoln did not learn until May 27 that Frémont was en route to Strasburg.[14] At 1 P.M. the next day the President instructed him to stop at Moorefield and await orders.[15] It happened that Frémont was ten miles east of Moorefield when this order was received, and, stung by an implied Presidential rebuke for bypassing Harrisonburg, he responded literally. He promised to turn around and march back to Moorefield the next morning.[16] The President then was too disgusted to reply. Stanton relayed Lincoln's instructions: Jackson was somewhere between Winchester and Martinsburg; Frémont was to move against him without delay.[17] Positive though these orders were, they contained no hint of concerted action with McDowell.

Stanton's message of May 28 required Frémont to acknowledge. Not uncharacteristically, Frémont's acknowledgment—"The President's order will be obeyed as promptly as possible"[18]—masked his inaction the next day. His army remained in camp on May 29. To be sure, it needed a rest. Frémont's medical director had made a written plea for one day's halt. Stragglers numbered in the thousands; morale was abysmal; artillery and wagon teams were starving.[19] Nevertheless, Frémont knew the enemy was before him, and he had been enjoined by Stanton as early as May 25: "You must not stop for supplies, but seize what you need and push rapidly forward. . . ."[20] Had Frémont pushed forward even slowly on the twenty-ninth, had he covered only six or seven miles, he probably could have slipped athwart the Valley Pike ahead of Jackson. As with the circuit Stanton arranged for Ord, Frémont's halt on May 29 squandered irretrievable hours.

That halt bordered on insubordination after the receipt of new, urgent, and pre-emptory orders from Lincoln. About noon of May 29 the President grasped the obvious. Shields was moving in the direction of Front Royal, and Frémont supposedly was nearing Strasburg, while Jackson was loitering outside Harper's Ferry. Lincoln suddenly realized that he might close both halves of the Shenandoah under the best possible circumstances, no enemy forces between the tips of his armies. The President moved to accelerate the pincer movement he had discovered. He wrote to Frémont: "General McDowell's advance, if not checked by the enemy, should, and probably will, be at Front Royal at 12 (noon) to-morrow. His force, when up, will be about 20,000. Please have your force at Strasburg, or, if the route you are moving on does not lead to that point, as near Strasburg as the enemy may be by the same time."[21]

As Lincoln indicated, Shields was making excellent progress despite problems similar to Frémont's. His men were tired, forage was scarce, and the Manassas Gap Railroad was blocked,[22] but Shields kept coming with supreme confidence. He half seriously advised McDowell to keep Ord at Manassas, claiming his own division could thrash all the rebels in the Valley.[23] At dawn of May 29 Shields's advance brigades were at Rectortown, twenty miles from Front Royal.[24] During the day a supply train jumped the track in Thoroughfare Gap, and Shields feared he would lose twenty-four hours as a result. But shown a telegram from the President urging speed, Shields promised to march through the night with only what supplies his men could carry.[25]

So Shields kept driving, and the gap between him and Ord kept getting wider. Ord was still in the vicinity of Manassas by sunrise of May 29.[26] To complicate matters, McDowell had received intelligence on May 28 that the rebels who had confronted him at Fredericksburg had slipped westward to join Jackson.[27] This rumor never quite died during the Valley Army's operations in the lower Shenandoah, and now McDowell who had doubted it a few days earlier, feared it might hold some truth. On the twenty-eighth and twenty-ninth he started Bayard's cavalry brigade and Brigadier General Rufus King's infantry division from Fredericksburg to the Valley.[28] These units were, of course, farther behind Shields than Ord, so that McDowell's column was strung out badly. The position of Bayard's brigade, which only reached Catlett's Station on May 29, was especially bad: Shields was grumbling that very day about his want of cavalry.[29]

Nevertheless, McDowell's forces were approaching the Valley, and Lincoln sent McDowell his pincer plan during the afternoon of May 29: "General Frémont's force should, and probably will, be at or near Strasburg by 12 (noon) to-morrow. Try to have your force or the advance of it at Front Royal as soon."[30] Lincoln dispatched identical information to Banks and Saxton and told them to pursue if Jackson withdrew from the Potomac.[31]

These dispatches were Lincoln's outstanding contribution to the pincer maneuver. He had co-ordinated his forces to the extent that four separate detachments had orders to strike specific targets in the lower Valley. More important, Frémont and McDowell knew (1) approximately where the other was supposed to be; (2) the point toward which the other was moving; and (3) the other's estimated time of arrival. This information was distorted by Frémont's failure to march on May 29, but this was a small matter compared to Jackson's troubles. Throughout May 29 he hammered at Harper's Ferry, farther than Frémont or Shields from his escape route. Stanton gave this news to both Frémont and McDowell at 11:30 P.M. of May 29,[32] supplementing the information of each with the exact enemy location. Despite meddling, despite a disorganized command structure, despite futile delay, Lincoln had thousands of men converging from superior positions. The situation was becoming, in the Commander-in-Chief's oft-quoted phrase, "a question of legs."[33]

Failure: May 30–June 1

May 30

The day began unbelievably well. Shields's advance capped a strenuous night march by storming Front Royal at 11 A.M., one hour ahead of schedule. Thunderstruck rebels abandoned the highway bridges over the North and South Forks and left them intact, throwing the roads to Strasburg and to Winchester open to the enemy. Shields's rear brigades arrived at Front Royal before midnight.

Shields now estimated Jackson's strength at approximately 20,000 and pondered a rumor of powerful Confederate reinforcements from Richmond approaching Front Royal. Forgetting the boast that his division could clear the Valley unaided, Shields telegraphed McDowell to hurry Ord's and King's divisions to him. He added: "Frémont has not yet reached Strasburg, and I fear that he will not reach it in time."[34]

Frémont, in fact had already awarded himself extra time. During the afternoon of May 30 Lincoln received a letter from Frémont dated the twenty-ninth. Frémont attempted to put a good face on his halt of that day with a promise that he would reach Strasburg at 5 P.M. of the thirty-first.[35] This was the worst possible news, and Lincoln pleaded: "You must be up to time you promised, if possible."[36]

Shields read such words and staggered on; Frémont seemed indifferent. His efforts on May 30 are a mystery. It is known that he camped ten miles east of Moorefield on the twenty-ninth. He later reported that only on the thirty-first did he pass "the mountain between Lost River and Cedar Creek,"[37] a point roughly twenty miles east of Moorefield, indicating that he lumbered a mere ten miles on the thirtieth. Frémont offered excuses for this mediocre performance which he fancied novel to his army: rain, mud, and fatigue.[38]

Lincoln, growing worried, noted Frémont's delay to McDowell and authorized him to act accordingly.[39] Unfortunately, the precious discretion the President gave had already been curtailed by the Secretary of War. Ord's division was exhausted by Stanton's worthless detour through Alexandria. McDowell came to herd Ord forward and found chaos. He wrote Stanton: "This place [Rectortown] is filled with stragglers and broken-down men from every brigade." Ord's division was, as McDowell described it, "in much confusion," and its van was only five miles west of Rectortown at noon of May 30. Its rear brigade was still east of Rectortown. Ord had collapsed under the pressure and surrendered command to Brigadier General James Ricketts. Bayard's cavalry also was out of range; it did not reach Rectortown until after dark.[40]

Nevertheless, on balance, the day's events did not augur ill for the Union. Shields had done everything planned and wanted more work. Frémont and Ord had managed less, yet had achieved better positions than Jackson, whose army stretched from Harper's Ferry to Newtown encumbered by eight miles of wagons and 2,300 prisoners. One final heroic effort might bring the kill.

May 31

Frémont was incapable of a final spurt. He plodded along, his army grossly strung out, for another fifteen or so miles on May 31. The effort he reported to Washington, however, was excellent. He announced that his cavalry had the enemy in sight and added: "The army is pushing forward, and I intend to carry out operations proposed."[41] Reading those words, Lincoln could not have guessed that Frémont had halted for the day several miles out of Strasburg without a skirmish.

Shields, on the other hand, was eager for action. He had entered the Shenandoah looking for a fight. As early as May 29 he was considering what to do after he captured Front Royal. Shields had envisioned his command moving from Front Royal to Strasburg, while Ord's division swept from Front Royal to Winchester. Shields saw no way for Jackson to escape such a net.[42] But Ord was not up—Shields's reasonable plan for Ord's deployment illustrates how costly Stanton's detour had been—and other factors conspired to deny Shields the action he craved. Shields left a meager record of his activities during this day, which therefore must be reconstructed according to what Shields can be assumed to have known, the orders he received, and the situation that developed around him.

Shields knew several things on May 31, though the sum was less than the parts. First, he knew Ord and Bayard were nowhere in sight. Second, he knew Frémont was supposed to occupy Strasburg but doubted he would do it. Third, his intelligence from the previous day placed Jackson at Winchester, and Shields had to assume Jackson had moved somewhere since then. Shields did not know where. Lastly, there was the nagging concern that a large enemy column from Richmond or Fredericksburg was approaching Front Royal.[43] When he marshaled these facts, Shields found he knew little of friend or foe.

Shields's bleak prospect was darkened further by orders arriving from McDowell. McDowell stated, among other things, that Frémont had promised to reach Strasburg at 5 P.M. and that Shields must "Get your division well in hand to go forward to his support."[44] This order was ambiguous. Should Shields go forward before 5 P.M., so as to reach Strasburg in concert with Frémont, or was he to go later, after Frémont had arrived? Shields evidently made the latter interpretation, perhaps believing the over-all chance of trapping Jackson was better if he stayed at Front Royal. If he occupied Strasburg with his entire division, he would have to abandon Front Royal, opening it for Jackson. If he moved with a fraction of his division, he risked either that fraction or the fragment left at Front Royal running afoul of superior enemy forces. Certainly it was better to barricade one escape road (Front Royal) than to open it in an effort to block the other (Strasburg) when Frémont was only a few hours away from the latter and enemy reinforcements were believed to be approaching Front Royal.

Shields's decision to remain at Front Royal promptly appeared wise. Ashby came knocking on the Winchester road, and Shields advanced four regiments to meet him. A brisk skirmish ensued. Though Ashby was driven off, Shields, having only a token contingent of cavalry, was unable to pursue effectively and discover what force the rebels possessed.[45] Thus ensnarled, he was compelled to remain at Front Royal. One of his brigades was engaged all afternoon with a force of uncertain size; to send other units west toward Strasburg without Ord near was to scatter McDowell's column in Jackson's immediate presence. Ashby slipped away at dark, having performed the invaluable service of wasting Shields's afternoon.

So ended May 31, a day of lost opportunity. It also proved to be the last day Lincoln might have trapped Jackson in the lower Valley. Still, the advantage held by Lincoln's columns was such that much might have been salvaged on June 1. Rebel wagon trains were within range of determined cavalry and artillery; the Stonewall Brigade was isolated and exhausted. If it was too late to encircle the Valley Army, the Federals could inflict a grievous wound—if only they would act.

June 1

This day was a sad monument to the lack of an over-all Federal commander at the front. Frémont complained: "We hear nothing of McDowell"[46]; McDowell echoed: "General Frémont's forces have not yet made their appearance"[47]; Banks fretted: "Have heard nothing of Frémont."[48] McDowell comprehended so little of Banks's movements that at one point he believed Banks, who actually was at Martinsburg, was battling Jackson around Middletown.[49] Though the President had coached Banks along in pursuit of Jackson for several days, McDowell was denied news of Banks's progress until the early hours of June 1.[50] Then, however, it was too late for anyone to co-ordinate the Federal thrust.

Ewell jumped Frémont's van before dawn and kept it five miles from Strasburg. It was 10 A.M. before Frémont's main strength reached the front and began to skirmish with Ewell. Frémont then told Washington that there would probably be a battle that afternoon. Later, he reported that the morning skirmish had ended with Ewell's retreat after only two hours, yet it was 6 P.M. before Frémont advanced again.[51] That he should cling to the retiring Ewell with every man capable of holding a rifle apparently escaped Frémont's consideration. At any rate, he failed to account for the unfilled hours cited in his own report.

Frémont did serve one useful function by squatting west of Strasburg. Ewell had to pull off the Valley Pike to get at him, which exposed his rear to Shields—and this was an opportunity for which Shields was at last free. The problems which had trussed him the day before were unraveling. The van of Ord's division entered Front Royal on the morning of June 1. These troops were in poor condition but were reviving with the prospect of action. Bayard's cavalry also was present. McDowell had come in on May 31 and huddled long with Shields planning for this day. They decided to implement the dragnet originally envisioned by Shields, with his division sweeping to Strasburg and Ord's infantry and Bayard's cavalry marching on Winchester.[52]

Shields actually began this sweep. His division marched. His 10,000 doughty Midwesterners, men who had seen the Valley Army's back, were unleashed. And yet, with everything at last arranged, Shields never crossed the South Fork of the Shenandoah. Why? The answer was a mistake which altered many events of this war: somehow, Shields wandered onto the wrong road.

The blunder apparently happened this way: as the march commenced, two officers dispatched by Shields to scout Jackson's movements galloped up with a false report that the Valley Army had cleared Strasburg. This report was accepted, and it was hastily decided to hurl Bayard upon the rebels before they moved too far south of Strasburg. The cavalry therefore was redeployed from the Winchester to the Strasburg road.[53] The shift entailed considerable confusion, and in starting out again, Shields wandered off the Strasburg and onto the Winchester road.

When Shields's division had initally left the Valley for Fredericksburg in mid-May, it had marched via Front Royal; it had spent the previous two days picketing the area; Shields was an alert commander who knew where he went. Though it hardly seems credible that such soldiers took the wrong road, the evidence is supplied by men who were there. George L. Wood, an intelligent member of the 7th Ohio, recorded: ". . . Shields, with his entire division, was ordered out on the road to Strasburg, for the purpose of intercepting the retreat of the enemy. But instead of taking the road which he was ordered to take, he crossed over the north branch of the Shenandoah River on the road to Winchester."[54] Private William Kepler of the 4th Ohio agreed: "Our division must again rush forward, this time to intercept the enemy by way of the Strasburg road. For some reason, Shields, having taken the wrong road, was permitted to continue up the Luray Valley."[55] Major James Huntington of Shields's 1st Ohio Artillery also concurred: "It was late in the afternoon before Shields got ready to move, and then, owing to some blunder never clearly explained, he took the road to Winchester."[56] McDowell reported the error in testimony before the infamous Committee on the Conduct of the War: "I then went to see where Gen. Shields was, and found him over on the road towards Winchester. He had sent his troops on that road, instead of on the one I had ordered him to send them on."[57]

Whatever the cause of this mistake, it is certain that Shields started out on the wrong road, and by the time he could have been set right, it was too late. Bayard advanced to Strasburg unsupported and could do nothing against "heavy masses of [rebel] infantry, artillery and cavalry all plainly discernible, drawn up on commanding positions around [Strasburg]—a force so largely exceeding my own that an attack was utterly out of the question. The enemy threw a couple of shells at us, and just before dark I withdrew my forces. . . ."[58]

Conclusion

The Valley Army escaped from the lower Shenandoah for many reasons. Some were the product of its own effort. Swelling with notions of their invincibility as they cleared Strasburg, the rebels would have resented the suggestion that deliverance was also the result of Federal misjudgments and bad luck. Nevertheless, five discernible Union blunders helped to open the gates for the Valley Army.

First, Frémont altered Lincoln's flexible plan into a pincer operation with little margin for delay. He then proceeded to make an unpardonably slow march. His delay on May 29 proved especially damaging and made it almost certain that he would be halted just far enough from Strasburg to be little more than a nuisance.

Second, and most telling, the Federal operation was never synchronized. This was the inevitable concomitant of Lincoln's compartmentalized command structure, a system totally unsuited for the operation thrust upon it. Three of Lincoln's independent com-

manders, Frémont, Banks, and McDowell, were involved, and
none of them could do more than suggest deployment of the others.
Only Lincoln and Stanton, who were too far away during the critical hours, could co-ordinate this drive, and they failed, as illustrated by the absurd oversight which left McDowell without word
of Banks's location until June 1. The entire operation should have
been delegated to one general officer rather than kept in the hands
of two civilians who were necessarily distracted during the crucial
period of May 31–June 1 by the great battle before Richmond.

Another failure of co-ordination was Stanton's decision to route
two thirds of Ord's division through Alexandria. In this instance
the Secretary was even out of touch with the President. Lincoln
was trying to shuttle 20,000 men from Fredericksburg to the Valley with all speed; Stanton wanted additional protection for Washington. These objectives were incompatible. Required to do two
things at once, Ord accomplished neither fully and was rendered a
negative factor until June 1. Stanton's detour was the third
blunder.

The fourth mistake was the oversight which kept Bayard's cavalry from reaching the Shenandoah before June 1. The necessity
to have Bayard at the van of Shields's division should have been
manifest. Even a cursory knowledge of the Valley Army should
have warned McDowell that he would require mounted reconnaissance to find the elusive rebels when he entered the Valley.
McDowell's inexcusably late marching order for Bayard was the
former's principal miscalculation of the drive.

Finally, on one of the few occasions of his military career,
Shields followed the wrong road on June 1.

And yet, until Shields took that wrong turn, the Union might
have smashed at least part of the Valley Army. The North had no
monopoly on mistakes or bad luck in the Shenandoah. If Frémont
lost precious time by pausing on May 29, Jackson did the same by
ignoring signals of Shields's approach on May 28. If Shields was
unlucky in taking the wrong road, Jackson was unfortunate in garrisoning Front Royal with a colonel who lost his nerve, the town,
and its vital bridges to a surprise enemy attack. If Shields was
harassed by reports of rebel reinforcements entering the Shenandoah, Jackson's scouts made mighty columns of Banks's and

Geary's regimental-sized reconnaissances. Where the Federals were slowed by want of supplies, Jackson was handicapped by miles of captured booty and several thousand prisoners. The Union had its opportunities to destroy the Valley Army; it simply missed them.

APPENDIX C

JACKSON'S STATE OF MIND
AT THE CLOSE OF THE CAMPAIGN

In his *R. E. Lee,* Douglas Southall Freeman chronicles Jackson's strenuous activities during the period preceding and including his strange failures on the Peninsula (June 22–30). Freeman examined Jackson's activities both during the daylight and nighttime hours of this crucial eight-day period and wrote:

> In summary, during the eight days from noon, June 22, to noon, June 30, Jackson rode approximately 100 miles with no rest intervening except while in conference at Lee's headquarters; he lost all of four nights' sleep or else had no sleep after midnight; he was probably up at dawn on the four mornings following a night of sleep; two of these four nights were spent on or close to fields where battles had been fought the preceding day; finally, on six of the eight days, he was either making his hurried ride to Richmond or else was on the march with his troops, under the most exacting conditions.[1]

This activity, which Freeman believed denied Jackson sleep upon which he was very dependent, was, in Freeman's opinion, a significant cause of Jackson's poor performance on the Peninsula. Later, in *Lee's Lieutenants,* Freeman modified this opinion only somewhat,[2] and more recent authors have tended to emphasize even more strongly than did Freeman the debilitating effect of Jackson's want of sleep.[3]

The final days of the Valley Campaign saw Jackson endure a similar period of concentrated effort allowing little sleep. This was the ten-day retreat beginning with the Valley Army's withdrawal from Harper's Ferry and ending with the Battle of Port Republic. During these days and nights of alternating severe summer heat and hard rain, the Valley Army retreated approximately one hundred miles, fighting numerous skirmishes against a numerically superior foe while encumbered with enormous trains. It is the author's contention that the rigors of this retreat impaired Jackson almost as greatly, if not just as greatly, in the fighting around Port Republic as the strain of the march to Richmond impaired him on the Peninsula, and that this impairment is reflected in the poorly fought battle at Port Republic. In support of these contentions Jackson's daily activities from noon, May 30, to noon, June 9, are chronicled below:

Day of May 30:	Napping and riding train from Charlestown to Winchester.
Night of May 30–31:	Conferring late with Boteler; conferring with Hotchkiss at 3 A.M.
Day of May 31:	Marching to Strasburg.
Night of May 31–June 1:	Talking and praying for "some time"[4] at Taylor's campfire.
Day of June 1:	Observing day-long skirmish against Frémont's army.
Night of June 1–2:	Marching from Strasburg to Woodstock in a heavy rain and hail storm; arriving at Woodstock "late"[5]; eating about midnight and marching again soon thereafter.
Day of June 2:	Marching and observing skirmishing of the Army's rear guard; heavy rainstorm in the afternoon.
Night of June 2–3:	Riding six or more miles through a heavy rainstorm in response to a false alarm attributable to Ashby's cavalry; rising "very early."[6]
Day of June 3:	Marching to Rude's Hill under a heavy rainstorm; "having lost much sleep,"[7] Jackson retires early.
Night of June 3–4:	Sleeping in the mud beneath a torrential downpour; rising after a "very unpleasant night,"[8] Jackson appears "wet and wearied."[9]
Day of June 4:	Studying Valley geography and being interviewed by a Union war correspondent.[10]

Night of June 4–5:	Marching during early hours of the night; conferring with Hotchkiss as late as 10 P.M.[11]
Day of June 5:	Marching beyond Harrisonburg beneath light to moderate rainstorms.
Night of June 5–6:	Conferring with Hotchkiss "quite late."[12]
Day of June 6:	Marching along "very, very muddy"[13] roads to Port Republic.
Night of June 6–7:	Interviewing Sir Percy Wyndham until "late"[14]; meditating about Ashby for "some time"[15] thereafter.
Day of June 7:	Maneuvering throughout the day to tempt Frémont into an attack near Cross Keys.
Night of June 7–8:	No record; probably sleeping; rising by at least 7 A.M.
Day of June 8:	Skirmishing in and around Port Republic.
Night of June 8–9:	Planning battle as late as 2 A.M.; conferring with Colonel John Imboden thereafter[16]; rising in time to meet Winder in Port Republic at approximately 5 A.M.
Day of June 9:	Battle of Port Republic.

Descriptions of the terrible physical punishment suffered by the Valley Army during its retreat from Harper's Ferry to Port Republic are legion. Strong men such as John Harman admitted to "knocking under" from fatigue,[17] and they carried fewer burdens than Jackson. It is little wonder, then, that as the Army stumbled toward Port Republic its General was hardly as alert as he had been earlier in the Campaign. Lieutenant McHenry Howard spent several hours near Jackson on June 8 and recalled that most of the time the General stood gazing at the ground with his cap pulled tightly over his eyes—a description strikingly similar to some of those of Jackson on the Peninsula.[18] Sandie Pendleton's June 7 description of Jackson can well serve as a conclusion regarding his physical and mental condition at the Campaign's close: "General Jackson is completely broken down."[19]

APPENDIX D

Valley Army Tables of Organization, January to June 1862[1]

Army organization 1 January 1862

Maj. Gen. T. J. Jackson, ———————— Lt. Col. Turner Ashby
Commander, Valley District   Commander, Valley Cavalry

Headquarters staff ———

7th Virginia Cavalry

10 (approximately) companies of cavalry

Chew's battery of mounted artillery

1st Brigade (Stonewall)
Brig. Gen. R. B. Garnett

2d Virginia Infantry
4th Virginia Infantry
5th Virginia Infantry
27th Virginia Infantry
33d Virginia Infantry

Army artillery

Carpenter's (Allegheny)
  battery
Cutshaw's section (lost
  7 January 1862)
McLaughlin's battery
  (Rockbridge Artillery)
Waters' (West Augusta)
  battery

Army of the Northwest
Brig. Gen. W. W. Loring

Brig. Gen. S. R. Anderson's
  brigade.

1st Tennessee Infantry
7th Tennessee Infantry
14th Tennessee Infantry

Col. William Gilham's brigade

21st Virginia Infantry
42d Virginia Infantry
48th Virginia Infantry
  1st Regular (Irish) battalion

Col. William B. Taliaferro's
  brigade

3d Arkansas Infantry
1st Georgia Infantry
23d Virginia Infantry
37th Virginia Infantry

Army of the Northwest
  artillery

Marye's (Hampden) battery
Shumaker's (Danville) battery

Valley District Militia

Brig. Gen. Boggs's brigade
Brig. Gen. J. H. Carson's brigade
Brig. Gen. G. S. Meem's brigade

Army organization at Kernstown, 23 March 1862

Maj. Gen. T. J. Jackson, ———————————— Col. Turner Ashby
Commander, Valley District   Commander, Valley Cavalry

                                                                 7th Virginia Cavalry

Headquarters staff ———   18 (approximately) companies of
                                                                    cavalry
                                                                 Chew's battery of mounted
                                                                    artillery

1st Brigade (Stonewall)   Remaining detachments of
   Brig. Gen. R. B. Garnett   Valley militia (not present
                                                                 at battle)
  2d Virginia Infantry
  4th Virginia Infantry
  5th Virgnia Infantry
27th Virginia Infantry
33d Virginia Infantry
Carpenter's (Allegheny) battery
McLaughlin's battery
   (Rockbridge Artillery)

2d Brigade
   Col. Jesse Burks

21st Virginia Infantry
42d Virginia Infantry
48th Virginia Infantry
      1st Regular (Irish) battalion
      Marye's (Hampden) battery
      Waters' (West Augusta) battery

3d Brigade
   Col. S. V. Fulkerson

23d Virginia Infantry
37th Virginia Infantry
Shumaker's (Danville) battery

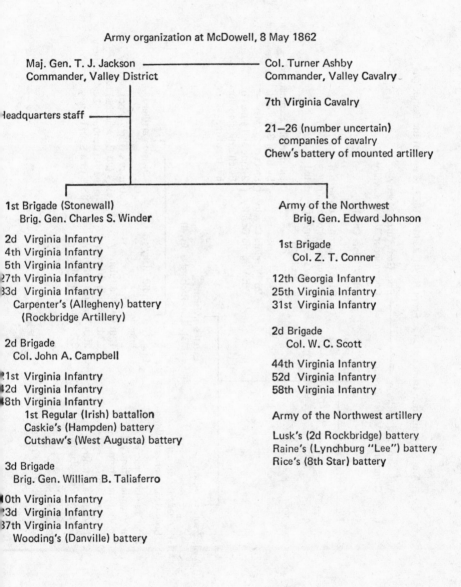

Army organization at McDowell, 8 May 1862

Maj. Gen. T. J. Jackson ──────────── Col. Turner Ashby
Commander, Valley District   Commander, Valley Cavalry

                                 7th Virginia Cavalry

Headquarters staff ──────

                                 21–26 (number uncertain)
                                    companies of cavalry
                                 Chew's battery of mounted artillery

| 1st Brigade (Stonewall) | Army of the Northwest |
| Brig. Gen. Charles S. Winder | Brig. Gen. Edward Johnson |

1st Brigade (Stonewall)
  Brig. Gen. Charles S. Winder

2d Virginia Infantry
4th Virginia Infantry
5th Virginia Infantry
27th Virginia Infantry
33d Virginia Infantry
  Carpenter's (Allegheny) battery
  (Rockbridge Artillery)

2d Brigade
  Col. John A. Campbell

21st Virginia Infantry
42d Virginia Infantry
48th Virginia Infantry
  1st Regular (Irish) battalion
  Caskie's (Hampden) battery
  Cutshaw's (West Augusta) battery

3d Brigade
  Brig. Gen. William B. Taliaferro

10th Virginia Infantry
23d Virginia Infantry
37th Virginia Infantry
  Wooding's (Danville) battery

Army of the Northwest
  Brig. Gen. Edward Johnson

1st Brigade
  Col. Z. T. Conner

12th Georgia Infantry
25th Virginia Infantry
31st Virginia Infantry

2d Brigade
  Col. W. C. Scott

44th Virginia Infantry
52d Virginia Infantry
58th Virginia Infantry

Army of the Northwest artillery

Lusk's (2d Rockbridge) battery
Raine's (Lynchburg "Lee") battery
Rice's (8th Star) battery

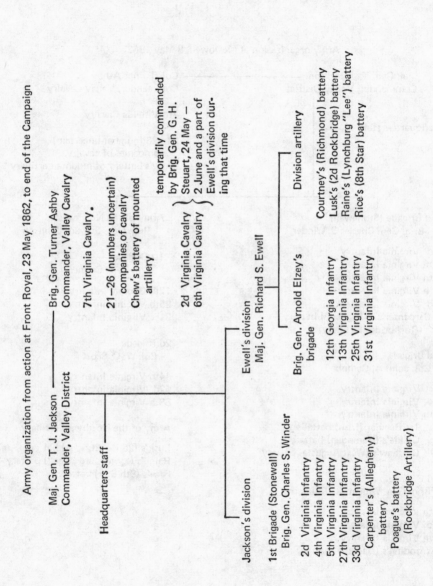

Army organization from action at Front Royal, 23 May 1862, to end of the Campaign

Maj. Gen. T. J. Jackson ——— Brig. Gen. Turner Ashby
Commander, Valley District   Commander, Valley Cavalry

7th Virginia Cavalry.

21–26 (numbers uncertain)
companies of cavalry
Chew's battery of mounted
artillery

temporarily commanded
by Brig. Gen. G. H.
Steuart, 24 May –
2 June and a part of
Ewell's division dur-
ing that time

2d Virginia Cavalry
6th Virginia Cavalry

Headquarters staff

Jackson's division

1st Brigade (Stonewall)
Brig. Gen. Charles S. Winder

2d Virginia Infantry
4th Virginia Infantry
5th Virginia Infantry
27th Virginia Infantry
33d Virginia Infantry
Carpenter's (Allegheny)
battery
Poague's battery
(Rockbridge Artillery)

Ewell's division
Maj. Gen. Richard S. Ewell

Brig. Gen. Arnold Elzey's
brigade

12th Georgia Infantry
13th Virginia Infantry
25th Virginia Infantry
31st Virginia Infantry

Division artillery

Courtney's (Richmond) battery
Lusk's (2d Rockbridge) battery
Raine's (Lynchburg "Lee") battery
Rice's (8th Star) battery

2d Brigade
Col. John M. Patton (as of 25 May)

21st Virginia Infantry
42d Virginia Infantry
48th Virginia Infantry
1st Regular (Irish) battalion
Caskie's (Hampden) battery
Cutshaw's (West Augusta) battery

3d Brigade
Brig. Gen. William B. Taliaferro

10th Virginia Infantry
23d Virginia Infantry
37th Virginia Infantry
Wooding's (Danville) battery

Carrington's (Charlottesville) battery
(present as of 7 June)

Col. W. C. Scott's brigade
(after 2 June commanded by Brig. Gen. G. H. Steuart)

44th Virginia Infantry
52d Virginia Infantry
58th Virginia Infantry

Brig. Gen. Richard Taylor's brigade

6th Louisiana Infantry
7th Louisiana Infantry
8th Louisiana Infantry
9th Louisiana Infantry
Maj. R. C. Wheat's battalion
(Louisiana Tigers)

Brig. Gen. Isaac Trimble's brigade

15th Alabama Infantry
21st Georgia Infantry
16th Mississippi Infantry
21st North Carolina Infantry

Maryland Line
Brig. Gen. George H. Steuart
(Steuart temporarily assigned to command of 2d and 6th Virginia Cavalry, 24 May–2 June, then to command of Scott's brigade; Maryland Line acted as a part of Steuart's brigade after 6 June)

1st Maryland Infantry
Brockenbrough's battery
(Baltimore Light Artillery)

NOTES

Introduction

1. Walter Lord, ed., *The James A. L. Fremantle Diary* (Boston: Little, Brown and Co., 1954), p. 179.
2. G. F. R. Henderson, *Stonewall Jackson and the American Civil War,* (New York: Longmans Green and Co., 1936).
3. William Allan, *History of the Campaign of General T. J. (Stonewall) Jackson in the Shenandoah Valley of Virginia* (Philadelphia) J. B. Lippincott, 1880; reprint ed., Dayton, Ohio: Morningside, 1974), p. 5. (Cited hereafter as Allan, *Valley Campaign.*)
4. Allan, *Valley Campaign,* p. 56.
5. R. L. Dabney, *Life and Campaigns of Lieutenant General Thomas J. Jackson* (New York: Blelock and Co., 1866), p. 394.
6. Allan, *Valley Campaign,* pp. 122–23.
7. Ibid., p. 5.

Prologue

1. James K. Edmondson to his wife, 11 November 1861, Edmondson Letters, Rockbridge Historical Society, Lexington, Va.
2. Sam R. Watkins, *Co. Aytch* (Nashville, Tenn.: Cumberland Presbyterian Publishing House, 1882; reprint ed., Jackson, Tenn. McCowart-Mercer Press, 1952), p. 52.
3. John N. Opie, *A Rebel Cavalryman with Lee, Stuart and Jackson* (Chicago: W. B. Conkey Co., 1899), pp. 48–50.
4. Henry K. Douglas to "Miss Tippie," 16 November 1861, Douglas Letters, Duke University Library, Durham, N.C.
5. Opie, *Rebel Calvaryman,* p. 50.
6. John O. Casler, *Four Years in the Stonewall Brigade* (Girard, Kans.: Appeal Publishing Co., 1906; reprint ed. Marietta, Ga.: Continental Book Co., 1951), p. 60
7. George Baylor, *Bull Run to Bull Run* (Richmond: B. F. Johnson Publishing Co., 1900), pp. 29–30.

CHAPTER 1

1. J. Lewis Peyton, *History of Augusta County* (Staunton, Va.: Yost and Son 1882), pp. 5–6.
2. Samuel Kercheval, *A History of the Valley of Virginia*, 4th ed. (Strasburg, Va.: Shenandoah Publishing House, 1925), pp. 36–37.
3. John W. Wayland, *The German Element of the Shenandoah Valley of Virginia* (Charlottesville, Va.: Michie Co., 1907), pp. 11–14.
4. Ibid., p. 9.
5. Ann Maury, ed., *Memoirs of a Huguenot Family* (New York: G. P. Putnam's Sons, 1901), pp. 288–89.
6. Hermann Schuricht, *History of the German Element in Virginia* (Baltimore: Theo. Kroh & Sons, 1898), pp. 86–88.
7. Wayland, *German Element of the Shenandoah*, pp. 24–26.
8. Kercheval, *History of the Valley*, p. 178.
9. Ibid., p. 80.
10. John C. Fitzpatrick, ed., *The Writings of George Washington*, 39 vols. (Washington, D.C., 1931–44), vol. 1, p. 144.
11. Ibid., pp. 203–206.
12. Louis K. Koontz, *The Virginia Frontier: 1754–1763* (Baltimore: Johns Hopkins Press, 1925), p. 99.
13. Fitzpatrick, ed., *Writings of Washington*, vol. 1, p. 494.
14. Ibid., vol. 2, p. 153.
15. Stanislaus Hamilton, ed., *Letters to Washington and Accompanying Papers*, 5 vols. (Boston: Houghton Mifflin and Co., 1898–1902), pp. 398–400.
16. Schuricht, *German Element in Virginia*, p. 109.
17. Charles Campbell, *History of the Colony and Ancient Dominion of Virginia* (Philadelphia: J. B. Lippincott, 1860), p. 585.
18. Ibid., pp. 585–86.
19. Wayland, *German Element of the Shenandoah*, pp. 143–44.
20. Quoted in Harry M. Strickler, *A Short History of Page County* (Richmond: Dietz Press, 1952), p. 86.
21. Kercheval, *History of the Valley*, p. 147.
22. Frederic Morton, *The Story of Winchester* (Strasburg, Va.: Shenandoah Publishing House, 1925), p. 136.
23. Ibid., p. 53.
24. T. K. Cartmell, *Shenandoah Valley Pioneers* (Winchester, Va.: Eddy Press, 1909), p. 162; Morton, *Winchester*, p. 124.
25. Cartmell, *Valley Pioneers*, p. 149.
26. Ibid., p. 143.
27. Morton, *Winchester*, pp. 123–25.
28. Ibid., pp. 233; Cartmell, *Valley Pioneers*, p. 158.

29. Freeman H. Hart, *The Valley of Virginia in the American Revolution* (Chapel Hill: University of North Carolina Press, 1942), p. 99.

30. Thomas A. Ashby, *Life of Turner Ashby* (New York: Neale Publishing Co., 1914), p. 75.

31. *War of the Rebellion: A Compilation of the Official Records of the Union and Confederate Armies,* 70 vols. in 127 and index (Washington, D.C., 1880–1901), ser. IV, vol. 1, p. 385. (Cited hereafter as *OR.* Unless otherwise specified, all references are to Series I.)

32. Ibid., p. 382.

33. Virginia Militia Laws (Richmond, Va., 1855), p. 24.

34. See Jean Gottman, *Virginia at Mid-Century* (New York: Henry Holt and Co., 1955), pp. 99–104.

35. John W. Wayland, *History of Rockingham County* (Dayton, Va.: Ruebush-Elkins Co., 1912), pp. 376–77; John W. Wayland, *History of Shenandoah County* (Strasburg, Va.: Shenandoah Publishing House, 1927), pp. 207, 291.

36. Wayland, *Rockingham County,* pp. 418, 423.

37. Cartmell, *Valley Pioneers,* p. 54; Wayland, *Shenandoah County,* pp. 262–66.

38. "Thirty-Sixth Annual Report of the Baltimore and Ohio Railroad Company, 1862," Baltimore, Md., 1864.

39. Wayland, *Shenandoah County,* p. 293.

40. "Twenty-Sixth Annual Report of the Virginia Central Railroad Company," Richmond, Va., 1861, p. 17.

41. Peyton, *Augusta County,* pp. 227–29.

42. Winchester *Virginian,* 21 November 1860.

43. Thomas Jefferson, *Notes on the State of Virginia,* ed. by William Peden (Chapel Hill: University of North Carolina Press for the Institute of Early American History and Culture, 1955), p. 24.

44. Samuel V. Leech, *The Raid of John Brown at Harper's Ferry* (Washington, D.C.: De Soto Press, 1909), p. 5.

45. Ibid., pp. 7–8; "Report of Colonel Robert E. Lee, Report of the Select Committee of the Senate appointed to inquire into the Late Invasion and Seizure of the Public Property at Harper's Ferry" (Senate Com. Report No. 279, 1st Sess., 36th Congress Washington, D.C., 1866), pp. 40–43.

46. Leech, *Raid of John Brown,* p. 13.

47. Mary Anna Jackson, *Life and Letters of General Thomas J. Jackson,* (New York: Harper & Brothers, 1892), pp. 130–32.

CHAPTER 2

1. R. U. Johnson and C. C. Buel, eds., *Battles and Leaders of the*

Civil War, 4 vols. (New York: Century, 1887–1888; reprint ed., New York: Thomas Yoseloff, 1956), vol. 1, pp. 115–17. (Cited hereafter as *B & L.*)

2. Casler, *Four Years,* p. 19.

3. Opie, *Rebel Cavalryman,* p. 19.

4. James B. Avirett, *The Memoirs of General Turner Ashby and his Compeers* (Baltimore: Selby and Dulany, 1867), p. 62.

5. J. K. Edmondson to his wife, 3 and 17 May 1861, Edmondson Letters.

6. George W. Booth, *Personal Reminiscences of a Maryland Soldier in the War Between the States* (Baltimore: Fleet, McGinley and Co., 1898), p. 10.

7. *B & L,* vol. 1, p. 118.

8. John Esten Cooke, *Stonewall Jackson and the Old Stonewall Brigade,* ed. by Richard Harwell (Charlottesville: University of Virginia Press, 1954), p. 10.

9. Baylor, *Bull Run,* p. 14.

10. Henry D. Monier, *Military Annals of Louisiana* (New Orleans, 1875), p. 89.

11. *B & L,* vol. 1, p. 121.

12. Thomas J. Jackson Order Book, 1861, 12 April–30 May 1861, Hotchkiss Papers, Library of Congress, Washington, D.C.

13. *B & L,* vol. 1, p. 118.

14. *OR,* vol. 2, pp. 832–33.

15. Ibid., pp. 809–10.

16. *B & L,* vol. 1, p. 122.

17. Ibid., pp. 121–22.

18. Ibid., p. 123.

19. Hunter McGuire, "General Thomas J. Jackson," *Southern Historical Society Papers,* XIX, p. 302. (Cited hereafter as *S.H.S.P.*)

20. *OR,* vol. 2, p. 183.

21. Jackson, *Life of Jackson,* p. 168.

22. Edward Hungerford, *The Story of the Baltimore and Ohio Railroad,* 2 vols. (New York: G. P. Putnam's Sons, 1928), vol. 2, p. 28; "Annual Report of the Baltimore and Ohio Railroad, 1861," p. 7.

23. Mrs. Cornelia McDonald, *A Diary of Reminiscences of the War and Refugee Life in the Shenandoah Valley* (Nashville: Cullom and Ghertner Co., 1934), p. 77.

24. Origins of the name "Stonewall" are traced in Douglas Southall Freeman, *Lee's Lieutenants,* 3 vols. (New York: Charles Scribner's Sons, 1942–44), vol. 1, Appendix V.

25. See Chapter 3, notes 23–25 and accompanying text, infra.

26. Roy Bird Cook, *The Family and Early Life of General Thomas J. Jackson,* 3rd ed. (Charles Town, W. Va., 1948), pp. 160–62.

27. Jackson, *Life of Jackson,* pp. 179–80.
28. Casler, *Four Years,* p. 47.
29. Ibid., p. 41, 51.
30. *OR,* vol. 5, p. 904.
31. Marcus B. Toney, *The Privations of a Private* (Nashville, Tenn., 1905), p. 20.
32. John H. Worsham, *One of Jackson's Foot Cavalry* (New York: Neale Publishing Co., 1912), p. 43.
33. James E. Hall, *The Diary of a Confederate Soldier,* ed. by Ruth Woods Dayton (Philippi, W. Va.: 1961), 25 and 27 November 1861.
34. *OR,* vol. 5, pp. 942–43.
35. Ibid., pp. 889, 943.
36. Ibid., p. 936.
37. Ibid., p. 937.
38. Ibid., pp. 378–80.
39. Ibid., pp. 239–48, 898–99, 920; Avirett, *Ashby,* p. 127.
40. *OR,* vol. 5, p. 899.
41. Ibid., p. 919.
42. Ibid., p. 890.
43. Henry Kyd Douglas, *I Rode with Stonewall* (Chapel Hill: University of North Carolina Press, 1940), p. 28.
44. A. S. Pendleton to his mother, 21 March 1862, William G. Bean, ed., "The Valley Campaign of 1862 as Revealed in Letters of Sandie Pendleton," *Virginia Magazine of History and Biography,* vol. 78, no. 3, July 1970, p. 340. (Cited hereafter as Bean, ed., "Pendleton Letters.")
45. *OR,* vol. 5, p. 913.
46. Ibid., p. 909.
47. Ibid., p. 913.
48. Jackson, *Life of Jackson,* pp. 183–84.
49. *OR,* vol. 2, p. 863.
50. Ibid., vol. 5, p. 942.
51. Ibid., pp. 936–37.
52. Ibid., p. 937.
53. Ibid., p. 938.
54. Ibid., p. 939.
55. Ibid., p. 940.
56. Casler, *Four Years,* p. 49.
57. John H. Graybill, *Diary of a Soldier of the Stonewall Brigade* (Woodstock, Va., n.d.), 10 November 1861.

CHAPTER 3

1. McDonald, *Diary,* p. 37.
2. John G. Paxton, ed., *Elisha F. Paxton: Memoir and Memorials*

(New York, 1907), p. 38. J. H. Langhorne to his father, 21 November 1861, Langhorne Letters, Virginia Historical Society, Richmond; H. K. Douglas to "Miss Tippie," 16 November 1861, Douglas Letters.

3. MS. Diary of John S. Apperson, Rockbridge Historical Society, Lexington, Va., 23 and 30 November 1861.

4. J. H. Langhorne to his mother, 12 November 1861, Langhorne Letters.

5. *OR*, vol. 5, pp. 976–77.

6. H. K. Douglas to "Miss Tippie," 16 November 1861, Douglas Letters.

7. Opie, *Rebel Cavalryman*, p. 56.

8. Baylor, *Bull Run*, p. 31.

9. Judith W. McGuire, *Diary of a Southern Refugee* (Richmond: E. J. Hale and Son, 1867), p. 72.

10. Recollections of John N. Lyle (unpublished typescript entitled "Stonewall Jackson's Campguard"), Rockbridge Historical Society, Lexington, Va., p. 300.

11. L. Minor Blackford, ed., *Mine Eyes Have Seen the Glory* (Cambridge, Mass: Harvard University Press, 1954), p. 181.

12. Abraham S. Miller to his wife, 24 February 1862; letters in possession of Dr. James A. Miller, Winchester, Va.

13. Opie, *Rebel Cavalryman*, p. 57.

14. Lyle Recollections, p. 313.

15. Opie, *Rebel Cavalryman*, pp. 57–58.

16. Gen. D. H. Hill, "Address," *S.H.S.P.* XIII, p. 261.

17. Opie, *Rebel Cavalryman*, p. 15

18. Randolph H. McKim, *A Soldier's Recollection* (New York: Longmans, Green and Co., 1910), p. 99.

19. William Couper, *One Hundred Years at V.M.I.*, 4 vols. (Richmond: Carrett and Massie, 1939), vol. 3, p. 178.

20. Couper, *V.M.I.*, vol. 1, p. 313.

21. Richard Taylor, *Destruction and Reconstruction* (New York: D. Appleton and Co., 1879; reprint ed., New York: Longmans Green and Company, 1955).

22. *B & L*, vol. 2, p. 297.

23. Taylor, *Destruction and Reconstruction*, p. 37.

24. Jackson Letter Book, 1862, 31 July 1862, Hotchkiss Papers, Library of Congress, Washington, D.C.

25. Jackson Letter Book, 1862, 11 February 1862, Hotchkiss Papers.

26. Couper, *V.M.I.*, vol. 4, p. 76.

27. Elizabeth P. Allan, *The Life and Letters of Margaret Junkin Preston* (Boston: Houghton Mifflin and Co., 1903), p. 72.

28. Taylor, *Destruction and Reconstruction*, pp. 89–91.

29. *OR*, vol. 12, pt. 3, pp. 841–42.

30. John Esten Cooke, *Wearing of the Gray* (New York, 1867; reprint ed., Bloomington: Indiana University Press, 1959), p. 45.

31. Jackson Letter Book, 1862, 25 February 1862, Hotchkiss Papers.

32. Allan, *Valley Campaign,* p. 16.

33. Apperson Diary, 26 November 1861.

34. Carlton McCarthy, *Detailed Minutiae of Soldier Life in the Army of Northern Virginia* (Richmond, 1882; reprinted in *Soldier Life of the Union and Confederate Armies,* ed. by Philip Van Doren Stern, Bloomington: Indiana University Press, 1961), p. 305.

35. *OR,* vol. 5, pp. 942, 965.

36. Jackson to Alexander R. Boteler, 6 May 1862, Boteler Papers, Duke University, Durham N.C.; Allan, *Preston,* p. 125; J. H. Langhorne to "Aunt Nannie," 12 December 1861, Langhorne Letters. There is no known evidence of favoritism in the selection of Garnett to command the Stonewall Brigade.

37. *OR,* vol. 5, p. 977.

38. Ibid., p. 976.

39. Ibid., pp. 390, 976.

40. Jackson, *Life of Jackson,* p. 160.

41. William T. Poague, *Gunner with Stonewall* (Jackson, Tenn.: McCowart-Mercer Press, 1957), p. 12.

42. Jennings C. Wise, *The Long Arm of Lee,* 2 vols. (Lynchburg, Va.: J. P. Bell Co., Inc., 1915), vol. 1, pp. 163–64.

43. William N. McDonald, *A History of the Laurel Brigade* (Baltimore: Sun Job Printing, 1907), pp. 22–24.

44. *OR,* vol. 2, p. 881.

45. *B & L,* vol. 1, p. 124.

46. *OR,* vol. 2, pp. 861–62.

47. Ibid., p. 868.

48. Ibid., pp. 832–33.

49. Ibid., p. 954.

50. Avirett, *Ashby,* p. 190.

51. Ibid., p. 173.

52. Thomas Clarence, *General Turner Ashby* (Winchester, Va.: Eddy Press Corp., 1907), p. 193.

53. *OR,* vol. 5, p. 919.

54. Douglas, *I Rode with Stonewall,* pp. 81–82.

55. *OR,* vol. 2, p. 954.

56. Baylor, *Bull Run,* p. 37.

57. Ibid., p. 48.

58. *OR,* vol. 5, p. 892; vol. 12, pt. 3, p. 880; vol. 51, pt. 2, p. 336; Turner Ashby to J. P. Benjamin, 7 November 1861, Ashby Letters, Chicago Historical Society, Chicago, Ill.

59. *OR,* vol. 5, p. 974.

60. Ibid., p. 969.

61. Jackson, *Life of Jackson,* p. 209.

62. *OR,* vol. 2, pp. 832–33.

63. McGuire, "General Jackson," *S.H.S.P.* XIX, p. 314.
64. Richmond *Dispatch,* 20 September 1900; "Sketch of the Life and Career of Hunter Holmes McGuire," *S.H.S.P.* XXVIII, p. 273.
65. Lyle Recollections, p. 313.
66. Ibid., p. 315.
67. *OR,* vol. 5, p. 965.
68. Ibid., p. 966. By late December, however, Johnston was more in favor of the drive. *OR,* vol. 5, p. 1007.
69. *OR,* vol. 5, p. 968.
70. Ibid., p. 983.
71. J. H. Langhorne to his father, 15 December 1861, Langhorne Letters.
72. *OR,* vol. 5, pp. 988–89.
73. J. H. Langhorne to his father, 15 December 1861, Langhorne Letters. Italics his.
74. Theodore ("Ted") Barclay to his sister, 23 December 1861, Barclay Letters, Rockbridge Historical Society, Lexington, Va.
75. Apperson Diary, 16 December 1861.
76. J. H. Langhorne to his mother, 23 December 1861, Langhorne Letters.
77. *OR,* vol. 5, p. 395.
78. Apperson Diary, 17 December 1861; Neese, George M., *Three Years in the Confederate Horse Artillery* (New York: Neale Publishing Co., 1911), p. 8.
79. J. H. Langhorne to his mother, 23 December 1861, Langhorne Letters.
80. Neese, *Horse Artillery,* pp. 9–10.
81. Poague, *Gunner with Stonewall,* pp. 13–14.
82. Apperson Diary, 18 December 1861.
83. Ted Barclay to his sister, 23 December 1861, Barclay Letters.
84. Ibid.
85. J. H. Langhorne to his mother, 23 December 1861, Langhorne Letters.
86. *OR,* vol. 5, p. 390; Jackson Order Book, 1861, 24 December 1861, Hotchkiss Papers.
87. Douglas, *I Rode with Stonewall,* p. 19.
88. *OR,* vol. 5, pp. 1003–4.
89. Paxton, *Elisha Paxton,* p. 37.
90. J. H. Langhorne to his mother, 31 December 1861, Langhorne Letters.
91. *OR,* vol. 5, p. 1004.
92. Ibid.
93. Lavender R. Ray to his father, 7 December 1861. Ray Letters, Georgia Department of Archives and History, Atlanta, Ga.
94. Jackson Order Book, 1861, 26 December 1861, Hotchkiss Papers.
95. L. R. Ray to his father, 7 December 1861, Ray Letters.

96. J. H. Chamberlayne, *Ham Chamberlayne—Virginian*, ed. C. G. Chamberlayne (Richmond: Dietz Printing Co., 1932), p. 55.
97. R. W. Waldrop to his father, 26 December 1861, Waldrop Letters, Southern Historical Collection, University of North Carolina, Chapel Hill, N.C.
98. L. R. Ray to his sister, 13 December 1861, Ray Letters.
99. Toney, *Privations*, pp. 25–26.
100. Jackson Order Book, 1861, 26 December 1861, Hotchkiss Papers.
101. J. H. Langhorne to his mother, 31 December 1861. Langhorne Letters.
102. A. S. Miller to his wife, 1 January 1862, Miller Letters.
103. Apperson Diary, 31 December 1861.
104. J. H. Langhorne to his mother, 31 December 1861, Langhorne Letters.
105. Graybill, *Diary*, 31 December 1861.

CHAPTER 4

1. A. S. Miller to his wife, 6 January 1862, Miller Letters; L. R. Ray to his brother, 12 January 1862, Ray Letters.
2. Toney, *Privations*, p. 27; Baylor, *Bull Run*, p. 31.
3. Unpublished manuscript recollections of William Allan, Allan Papers, Southern Historical Collection, University of North Carolina, Chapel Hill, N.C., p. 96.
4. Casler, *Four Years*, p. 73.
5. Unpublished manuscript journal of Clement D. Fishburne, Fishburne Journal, University of Virginia, Charlottesville, Va., p. 23.
6. Douglas, *I Rode with Stonewall*, p. 20.
7. Apperson Diary, 3 January 1862; William S. White, *Sketches of the Life of Captain Hugh A. White* (Columbia, S.C.: Columbia Steam Press, 1864), p. 71.
8. L. R. Ray to his brother, 12 January 1862, Ray Letters.
9. A. K. Kelley to his mother, 19 January 1862, Kelley-Williamson Papers, Duke University, Durham, N.C.; R. W. Waldrop to his father, 12 January 1862, Waldrop Letters.
10. MS Journal of Jedediah Hotchkiss, Hotchkiss Papers, Library of Congress, Washington, D.C., p. 2.
11. Ibid.
12. L. R. Ray to his brother, 12 January 1862, Ray Letters.
13. Henderson, *Stonewall Jackson*, p. 144.
14. A. S. Miller to his wife, 6 January 1862, Miller Letters.
15. MS Journal of J. Hotchkiss, Hotchkiss Papers, p. 2.
16. George A. Porterfield, "A Narrative of the Service of Colonel

George A. Porterfield in Northwestern Virginia in 1861–1862,"
S.H.S.P. XVI, p. 90.

17. *OR*, vol. 5, p. 1066. Loring later denied making such a comment. *OR*, vol. 5, p. 1070.
18. L. R. Ray to his brother, 12 January 1862, Ray Letters.
19. A. S. Miller to his wife, 6 January 1862, Miller Letters.
20. *OR*, vol. 5, p. 391. Loring wrote later that this inactivity was a consequence of Jackson's direct orders, *OR*, vol 5, p. 1070, but Jackson never reported any such orders.
21. Worsham, *Foot Cavalry*, pp. 58–59; William Gilham to Jedediah Hotchkiss, 25 November 1866, Hotchkiss Papers, Library of Congress, Washington, D.C.
22. MS Journal of J. Hotchkiss, Hotchkiss Papers, p. 3.
23. *OR*, vol. 5, p. 391; William Gilham to Jedediah Hotchkiss, 25 November 1866, Hotchkiss Papers.
24. MS Journal of J. Hotchkiss, Hotchkiss Papers, p. 3.
25. H. K. Douglas to his mother, 12 January 1862, Douglas Letters.
26. Frank Moore, ed., *Rebellion Record*, 12 vols. (New York, 1862–71), vol. 4, p. 16.
27. Winchester *Daily Republican*, 18 January 1862.
28. Harry Gilmor, *Four Years in the Saddle* (New York: Harper & Brothers, 1866), p. 28.
29. MS Journal of J. Hotchkiss, Hotchkiss Papers, p. 3.
30. Watkins, *Co. Aytch*, p. 56.
31. Neese, *Three Years*, pp. 5, 17.
32. MS Journal of J. Hotchkiss, Hotchkiss Papers, p. 3.
33. Toney, *Privations*, p. 31; C. A. Fonerden, *A Brief History of the Military Career of Carpenter's Battery* (New Market, Va.: Henkel & Co., 1911), pp. 17–18.
34. *OR*, vol. 5, p. 392.
35. MS Memoirs of Edward H. MacDonald, MacDonald Memoirs, Southern Historical Collection, University of North Carolina, Chapel Hill, N.C. p. 34.
36. H. K. Douglas to his mother, 12 January 1862, Douglas Letters.
37. Lyle Recollections, p. 327.
38. H. K. Douglas to his mother, 12 January 1862, Douglas Letters; Douglas, *I Rode with Stonewall*, p. 24; Worsham, *Foot Cavalry*, p. 59.
39. Moore, *Rebellion Record*, vol. 4, p. 17.
40. Casler, *Four Years*, p. 63.
41. Fishburne Journal, p. 33.
42. Fonerden, *Carpenter's Battery*, pp. 17–18.
43. Lyle Recollections, p. 328; J. H. Langhorne to his mother, 12 January 1862, Langhorne Letters.
44. Watkins, *Co. Aytch*, p. 57.
45. MS Journal of J. Hotchkiss, Hotchkiss Papers, p. 4.

46. Fishburne Journal, pp. 31–32; Worsham, *Foot Cavalry*, p. 63.
47. Paxton, *Elisha Paxton*, p. 43.
48. *OR*, vol. 5, p. 392.
49. Ibid., p. 1018.
50. Ibid., p. 1026.
51. Ibid.
52. Ibid.; here Jackson reviewed the disposition of his forces, including the fact that 2,300 men were spread over the lower Shenandoah in small detachments. Such a deployment clearly suggests a defensive posture.
53. Apperson Diary, 10 January 1862.
54. Moore, *Rebellion Record*, vol. 4, p. 16.
55. *OR*, vol. 51, pt. 1, p. 461.
56. Diary of Julia Chase, typescript in Handley Library, Winchester, Va., 12 January 1862.
57. William Gilham to J. Hotchkiss, 25 November 1866, Hotchkiss Papers, supports the view that Jackson had abandoned the attempt to take Romney prior to learning the enemy had evacuated it.
58. H. K. Douglas to his mother, 12 January 1862, Douglas Letters; Fishburne Journal, p. 33.
59. MS Journal of J. Hotchkiss, Hotchkiss Papers, p. 4.
60. *OR*, vol. 5, p. 636.
61. Ibid., pp. 631, 678.
62. Ibid., p. 404.
63. Ibid., pp. 676, 697.
64. Ibid., p. 696.
65. William Gilham to J. Hotchkiss, 25 November 1866, Hotchkiss Papers.
66. MS Journal of J. Hotchkiss, Hotchkiss Papers, p. 5; Jackson Order Book, 1862, 12 January 1862, Hotchkiss Papers.
67. Allan Recollections, p. 102.
68. Fishburne Journal, p. 35.
69. Allan Recollections, p. 102.
70. R. W. Waldrop to his father, 19 January 1862, Waldrop Letters.
71. Ibid.
72. J. H. Langhorne to his father, 19 January 1862, Langhorne Letters.
73. Worsham, *Foot Cavalry*, p. 60.
74. J. H. Langhorne to his father 19 January 1862, Langhorne Letters.
75. Watkins, *Co. Aytch*, p. 57; Fishburne Journal, p. 37.
76. *OR*, vol. 5, p. 1036.
77. Ibid., p. 1035.
78. Ibid., p. 1039; Apperson Diary, 17 January 1862.
79. *OR*, vol. 5, p. 1034.
80. Apperson Diary, 21 January 1862.

81. J. H. Langhorne to his father, 19 January 1862, Langhorne Letters.

82. William F. Harrison to his wife, 23 January 1862, Harrison Letters, Duke University, Durham, N.C.

83. *OR*, vol. 5, p. 1039.

84. Ibid., p. 1034.

85. Ibid.

86. Ibid., pp. 1043–44.

87. S. M. Barton, Loring's chief engineer, evaluated the possibility of defending the Romney area much less favorably. *OR*, vol. 5, pp. 1055–56. Other views are found in *OR*, vol. 5, pp. 201–4, pp. 378–79.

88. Ted Barclay to his sister, 22 and 25 January 1862, Barclay Letters.

89. Apperson Diary, 15 January 1862.

90. Poague, *Gunner*, p. 17.

91. R. W. Waldrop to his father, 28 January 1862, Waldrop Letters.

92. Baylor, *Bull Run*, p. 33.

93. Fishburne Journal, p. 37.

94. Apperson Diary, 25 January 1862.

95. Paxton, *Elisha Paxton*, p. 47.

96. Although the Union had planned no pincer movement toward Martinsburg prior to 1 January 1862, plans had been made for a strike from the Alleghenies to Winchester. Allan, *Valley Campaign*, pp. 19–20.

97. *OR*, vol. 51, pt. 1, pp. 461–62.

98. W. H. Harrison to his wife, 31 January 1862, Harrison Letters.

99. Dabney, *Jackson*, pp. 274, 275.

100. *OR*, vol. 5, pp. 1046–48.

101. Ibid., pp. 1040–41.

102. Ibid., p. 1042.

103. William H. Taliaferro to "Conrad," 11 July 1877, Taliaferro Papers College of William and Mary, Williamsburg, Va. Davis never verified this interview.

104. *OR*, vol. 5, p. 1040.

105. Ibid., p. 1050.

106. Ibid., p. 1044.

107. Ibid., p. 1049.

108. Ibid., p. 1051.

109. Ibid., pp. 1071, 1050.

110. Ibid., p. 1059.

111. Ibid., p. 1050.

112. Ibid., p. 1053.

113. Ibid., p. 1044.

114. Ibid., p. 1053.

115. Ibid., p. 1056.

116. Ibid., p. 1063.

117. Ibid., pp. 1059–60.
118. Ibid., pp. 1071–72, 1062.
119. Ibid., pp. 1053, 1063; Douglas, *I Rode with Stonewall,* p. 26.
120. J. H. Harman to his brother, 6 February 1862, Hotchkiss Papers, Library of Congress, Washington, D.C.
121. R. W. Waldrop to his father, 7 and 14 February 1862, Waldrop Letters.
122. *OR,* vol. 5, pp. 1065–66.
123. Ibid., p. 1068.
124. Ibid., p. 1076.
125. A. S. Miller to his wife, 22 December 1862, Miller Letters.
126. In his answers to Jackson's court-martial specifications, Loring blamed this delay entirely upon Jackson, *OR,* vol. 5, p. 1070.
127. Poague, *Gunner,* p. 18.
128. Jonathan Green to "Miss Sallie," 1 February 1862, Green Letters, Duke University, Durham, N.C.
129. George K. Harlow to his family, 8 and 17 February 1862, Harlow Letters, Duke University, Durham, N.C.
130. H. K. Douglas to his mother, 12 January 1862, Douglas Letters.
131. J. H. Langhorne to his mother, 12 January 1862, Langhorne Letters.
132. G. K. Harlow to his family, 23 January 1862, Harlow Letters.
133. John Garibaldi to his wife, 25 January 1862, Garibaldi Letters, Virginia Military Institute, Lexington, Va.
134. A. S. Miller to his wife, 24 February 1862, Miller Letters.
135. *OR,* ser. IV, vol. 1, pp. 1114–15, 1011.
136. Ibid., vol. 5, p. 1016.
137. Graybill, *Diary,* 28 February and 7 March 1862.
138. Ted Barclay to his sister, 10 February and 3 March 1862, Barclay Letters.
139. Baylor, *Bull Run,* p. 34.
140. *OR,* vol. 12, pt. 3, p. 880.
141. Turner Ashby to J. P. Benjamin, 17 March 1862, Ashby Letters.
142. McDonald, *Laurel Brigade,* p. 21.
143. Chamberlayne, *Chamberlayne,* p. 67; R. W. Waldrop to his father, 14 February 1862, Waldrop Letters.
144. Jackson Letter Book, 1862, 25 February 1862, Hotchkiss Papers.
145. Robert W. Hooke to his family, 9 March 1862, Hooke Letters, Duke University, Durham, N.C.
146. *OR,* vol. 5, p. 1086.
147. Apperson Diary, 19 February 1862.

CHAPTER 5

1. Rowland Dunbar, ed., *Jefferson Davis, Constitutionalist:* Mississippi Department of Archives and History, (Jackson, Miss. 1923), vol. 5, pp. 198–203.

2. *OR,* vol. 5, pp. 525–26; vol. 51, pt. 2, p. 497.

3. *OR,* vol. 5, p. 1074.

4. Ibid., p. 1081.

5. Testimony of General Irwin McDowell before the Committee on the Conduct of the War, Senate Documents, 37th Cong., 1863, vol. 2, p. 139.

6. *OR,* vol. 5, pp. 41, 56, 57; *B & L,* vol. 2, p. 163.

7. *OR,* vol. 5, pp. 50, 56; vol. 12, pt. 1, p. 223.

8. *OR,* vol. 5, pp. 55–56; *OR,* vol. 12, pt. 1, pp. 228–29.

9. *OR,* vol. 12, pt. 1, p. 224.

10. Ibid., vol. 5, pp. 19–22.

11. *OR,* vol. 11, pt. 3, p. 15.

12. The original copy of these orders has been lost, but the essence can be found in *OR,* vol. 5, p. 1087, and Joseph E. Johnston, *Narrative of Military Operations* (New York: D. Appleton and Co., 1874; reprint ed., Bloomington: Indiana University Press, 1959), p. 106.

13. *OR,* vol. 5, pp. 1072–73.

14. Ibid., p. 1086; Allan, *Valley Campaign,* p. 39.

15. *OR,* vol. 5, p. 735.

16. J. H. Langhorne to his father, 8 March 1862, Langhorne Letters.

17. Chase Diary, 9 March 1862.

18. Jonathan Green to "My dear Friend," 3 March 1862, Green Letters.

19. R. W. Waldrop to his mother, 21 February 1862, Waldrop Letters.

20. White, *Hugh White,* pp. 73–74.

21. Jonathan Green to "My dear Friend," 3 March 1862, Green Letters.

22. T. J. Jackson to General D. H. Hill, 25 February 1862, Jackson Papers (b), Virginia Military Institute, Lexington, Va.

23. White, *Hugh White,* p. 75.

24. *OR,* vol. 5, p. 1095.

25. Douglas, *I Rode with Stonewall,* p. 27.

26. J. K. Edmondson to his wife, 8 March 1862, Edmondson Letters.

27. J. H. Langhorne to his father, 8 March 1862, Langhorne Letters.

28. Diary Apperson, 9 March 1862.

29. MS Diary of Harry R. Morrison, Rockbridge Historical Society, Lexington, Va., 8–10 March 1862.

30. John Harman to his brother, 7–10 March 1862, Hotchkiss Papers.

31. J. Se Cheverell, *Journal History of the 29th Ohio* (Privately printed, Cleveland, 1883), pp. 36–37.

32. Paxton, *Elisha Paxton,* p. 51.

33. Apperson Diary, 11 March 1862; Morrison Diary, 11 March 1862.

34. Morrison Diary, 11 March 1862.

35. Actually, it was never documented whether Jackson called this

meeting to debate his plan or simply to issue orders. Jackson's reported use of the term "council of war" later that evening (note 37, infra) suggests the former.

36. Henderson, *Stonewall Jackson*, p. 174, attributed this error to the staff.
37. Ibid., pp. 174–75.

CHAPTER 6

1. Douglas, *I Rode with Stonewall*, p. 82; Cooke, *Wearing of the Gray*, p. 60.
2. Cooke, *Jackson*, pp. 106–7. Dabney, *Jackson*, p. 311, gives a more realistic account of this episode.
3. Henderson, *Stonewall Jackson*, p. 170.
4. *OR*, vol. 5, p. 395.
5. Jackson to Turner Ashby, 14 March 1862, Jackson Letters (b).
6. Commissary General L. B. Northrop noted approvingly on 12 April 1862 that "no stores whatsoever were lost" in the evacuation of Winchester. *OR*, vol. 51, pt. 2, p. 534.
7. A. S. Pendleton to his mother, 16 March 1862, Bean ed., "Pendleton Letters," p. 339.
8. *OR*, vol. 51, pt. 2, p. 495.
9. Ibid., vol. 5, p. 1097.
10. J. A. Waddell, *Annals of Augusta County* (Richmond: William Ellis Jones, 1886), p. 44.
11. Jedediah Hotchkiss, *Make Me a Map of the Valley: The Civil War Journal of Stonewall Jackson's Topographer*, ed. by Archie P. McDonald (Dallas: Southern Methodist University Press, 1973) 26 March 1862. (Cited hereafter as Hotchkiss, *Diary*.)
12. *OR*, vol. 5, p. 1088.
13. Ibid., p. 1092.
14. Ibid., vol. 12, pt. 1, p. 380.
15. Ibid., p. 385; Dabney, *Jackson*, p. 312; Testimony of T. J. Jackson at Court-Martial of General R. B. Garnett, 6 August 1862, Garnett Court-Martial Papers, Museum of the Confederacy, Richmond, Va.
16. *OR*, vol. 12, pt. 1, p. 381.
17. Ibid., p. 389.
18. Ibid., p. 383.
19. Ibid., pp. 379, 381.
20. Ibid., pp. 381–84; Testimony of T. J. Jackson, 6 August 1862, Garnett Court-Martial Papers.
21. Fonerden, *Carpenter's Battery*, p. 20.
22. Edward Moore, *Story of a Cannoneer under Stonewall* (New

York: Neale Publishing Co., 1907), pp. 24–26, 30; Clement Fishburne, "Historical Sketch of the Rockbridge Artillery," *S.H.S.P.* XXIII, p. 130.

23. J. Echols to R. B. Garnett, 30 July 1862, and Garnett's report of the battle (dated March 30, 1862) both stress the confusion resulting from this breakdown in the chain of command. Both sources are in the Garnett Court-Martial Papers.

24. Testimony of T. J. Jackson, 6 August 1862, and R. B. Garnett to Samuel Cooper, 20 June 1862, Garnett Court-Martial Papers.

25. *OR,* vol. 12, pt. 1, pp. 405–7. This aspect of the battle is noted again in Chapter 12, infra, notes 83–85 and accompanying text.

26. Ibid., p. 382.

27. Moore, *Cannoneer,* p. 31; Fishburne Journal, p. 41.

28. *OR,* vol. 12, pt. 1, pp. 393, 402.

29. Worsham, *Foot Cavalry,* pp. 67–68.

30. *OR,* vol. 12, pt. 1, pp. 381–82.

31. R. B. Garnett to Samuel Cooper, 20 June 1862, Garnett Court-Martial Papers.

32. Casler, *Four Years,* p. 69.

33. A. S. Pendleton to his father, 29 March 1862, Pendleton Papers, Duke University, Durham, N.C.

34. This assumes that Jackson came to this realization at roughly 5:30 P.M.

35. Fishburne Journal, p. 43.

36. A. S. Pendleton to his father, 29 March 1862, Pendleton Papers; *OR,* vol. 12, pt. 1, p. 388.

37. Cooke, *Jackson,* p. 114.

38. Worsham, *Foot Cavalry,* p. 68.

39. *OR,* vol. 12, pt. 1, pp. 374, 376.

40. Ibid., p. 397.

41. Ibid., p. 382.

42. R. B. Garnett to Samuel Cooper, 20 June 1862, Garnett Court-Martial Papers.

43. William H. Harman to unidentified correspondent, 20 June 1862, Garnett Court-Martial Papers.

44. Henderson, *Stonewall Jackson,* p. 186.

45. Worsham, *Foot Cavalry,* p. 68.

46. Testimony of T. J. Jackson, 6 August 1862, Garnett Court-Martial Papers.

47. Lyle Recollections, p. 398.

48. Fishburne Journal, p. 45.

49. *OR,* vol. 12, pt. 1, p. 398.

50. Ibid., p. 392.

51. Ibid., pp. 391–93, 404–5.

52. Neese, *Three Years,* p. 36.

53. A. S. Pendleton to his father, 29 March 1862, Pendleton Papers.
54. G. K. Harlow to his family, 26 March 1862, Harlow Letters.
55. J. K. Edmondson to his wife, 25 March 1862, Edmondson Letters.
56. *OR,* vol. 12, pt. 1, p. 383.
57. Paxton, *Elisha Paxton,* p. 54.
58. Henderson, *Stonewall Jackson,* pp. 188–89.
59. *OR,* vol. 12, pt. 1, p. 379. Jackson maintained this opinion for some time. Jackson, *Life of Jackson,* p. 248.
60. *OR,* vol. 5, p. 750.
61. Ibid., vol. 12, pt. 1, pp. 346–47.
62. Ibid., pp. 335, 336.
63. Ibid., p. 341.
64. Ibid., pt. 3, p. 16.
65. Ibid., pt. 1, pp. 234–35.
66. Ibid., pp. 226–27.
67. Ibid., pp. 224–25.
68. Ibid., pp. 112–15, 228–29.
69. Ibid., pp. 228–29.
70. Ibid., pp. 230–31.
71. Ibid., pt. 3, p. 43.
72. Ibid., vol. 8, p. 605.
73. Ibid., vol. 12, pt. 1, p. 5.
74. A. S. Pendleton to his mother, 3 April 1862, Bean, ed., "Pendleton Letters," p. 344.
75. Mrs. W. N. Pendleton to W. N. Pendleton, 13 April 1862, Pendleton Papers.
76. R. B. Garnett to Samuel Cooper, 20 June 1862, Garnett Court-Martial Papers.
77. See Chapter 12, infra, notes 83–85 and accompanying text.
78. *OR,* vol. 12, pt. 1, p. 392.
79. Henderson, *Stonewall Jackson,* p. 193; Poague, *Gunner,* p. 20.
80. Jackson Letter Book, 1862, 29 April 1862, Hotchkiss Papers. About this same time, Jackson wrote privately to Alexander Boteler that Garnett had been nothing but an obstacle to his defense of the Valley; T. J. Jackson to A. R. Boteler, 6 May 1862, Boteler Papers. Garnett heard rumors in April 1862 that Jackson had made a written complaint about him to the War Department the previous January; R. B. Garnett to R. M. Hunter, April 1862, Garnett Court-Martial Papers. No record of these charges exists today, but such a complaint is not unlikely, especially in view of Jackson's letter to Boteler.
81. Douglas, *I Rode with Stonewall,* p. 37.
82. Ibid., p. 38.
83. Jackson, *Life of Jackson,* pp. 246–47.

CHAPTER 7

1. Neese, *Horse Artillery,* p. 37.
2. Moore, *Cannoneer,* p. 34.
3. Ibid.; Paxton, *Elisha Paxton,* p. 54.
4. *OR,* vol. 12, pt. 1, p. 385.
5. T. J. Jackson Testimony, 6 August 1862, Garnett Court-Martial Papers.
6. *OR,* vol. 12, pt. 1, pp. 386–87.
7. Turner Ashby to J. P. Benjamin, 17 March 1862, Ashby Letters.
8. *OR,* vol. 12, pt. 1, p. 386.
9. Turner Ashby to J. P. Benjamin, 17 March 1862, Ashby Letters.
10. *OR,* vol. 12, pt. 3, p. 844.
11. Ibid., pt. 1, p. 383.
12. Ibid., p. 384.
13. Ibid., pt. 3, p. 838.
14. Ibid., p. 841.
15. Neese, *Horse Artillery,* pp. 37–38; *OR,* vol. 12, pt. 3, p. 420.
16. Hotchkiss, *Diary,* 31 March 1862.
17. Hungerford, *Baltimore and Ohio Railroad,* vol. 2, pp. 7–14.
18. A. S. Pendleton to his sister, 12 April 1862, Bean, ed., "Pendleton Letters," p. 347.
19. Jackson Letter Book, 14 April 1862, Hotchkiss Papers.
20. Ibid., 4 April 1862.
21. Casler, *Four Years,* p. 73.
22. McHenry Howard, *Recollections of a Maryland Staff Officer* (Baltimore: Williams and Wilkins Co., 1914), p. 83.
23. Poague, *Gunner,* pp. 19, 21.
24. Paxton, *Elisha Paxton,* p. 53.
25. Graybill, *Diary,* 28 April.
26. Neese, *Horse Artillery,* pp. 41, 43; Moore, *Cannoneer,* p. 37.
27. Worsham, *Foot Cavalry,* p. 71.
28. Douglas, *I Rode with Stonewall,* p. 75.
29. *OR,* vol. 12, pt. 3, p. 843.
30. Ibid., pp. 843–844.
31. These instructions can be inferred from same reference, ibid., pp. 845, 848, 863.
32. Ibid., p. 848.
33. Ibid., pp. 845, 850.
34. Ibid., pt. 1, p. 426.
35. Avirett, *Ashby,* pp. 401–2.
36. *OR,* vol. 12, pt. 3, p. 426.
37. Neese, *Horse Artillery,* pp. 44–45; Averitt, *Ashby,* p. 173; John

W. Wayland, *Virginia Valley Records* (Strasburg, Va.: Shenandoah Publishing House, 1930), pp. 280–82.

38. Neese, *Horse Artillery*, pp. 44–46.
39. Avirett, *Ashby*, p. 174.
40. Neese, *Horse Artillery*, p. 46; Wayland, *Virginia Valley Records*, pp. 278–80.
41. Douglas, *I Rode with Stonewall*, p. 41; Howard, *Staff Officer*, p. 84.
42. Neese, *Horse Artillery*, p. 46.
43. *OR*, vol. 12, pt. 3, p. 855.
44. Hotchkiss, *Diary*, 18 April 1862.
45. *OR*, vol. 12, pt. 3, p. 848.
46. Jackson Letter Book, 1862, 16 April 1862, Hotchkiss Papers.
47. J. Hotchkiss to his wife, 19 April 1862, Hotchkiss Papers; Hotchkiss, *Diary*, 19 April 1862.
48. Avirett, *Ashby*, p. 176.
49. Hotchkiss, *Diary*, 24 April 1862.
50. Ibid.
51. Clarence, *General Ashby*, p. 209.
52. John Harman to his brother, 25 April 1862, Hotchkiss Papers.
53. Clarence, *General Ashby*, p. 204.
54. Dabney, *Jackson*, p. 397.
55. John Harman to his brother, 26 April 1862, Hotchkiss Papers.
56. *OR*, vol. 51, pt. 2, p. 543.
57. Ibid., ser. IV, vol. 1, pp. 1045 ff.
58. Ted Barclay to his sister, 15 April 1862, Barclay Letters.
59. White, *Hugh White*, p. 87.
60. Hotchkiss, *Diary*, 24 April 1862.
61. Poague, *Gunner*, p. 21.
62. Baylor, *Bull Run*, p. 37.
63. Jackson reported that Ashby had given him a total of 21 companies, *OR*, vol. 12, pt. 3, p. 880; Avirett, *Ashby*, p. 169 and Clarence, *General Ashby*, p. 72, reported 26 companies; McDonald, *Laurel Brigade*, p. 49, reported 20 companies.
64. Neese, *Horse Artillery*, p. 54.
65. White, *Hugh White*, p. 81; Paxton, *Elisha Paxton*, p. 55.
66. Jennings C. Wise, *The Military History of the Virginia Military Institute* (Lynchburg, Va.: J. P. Bell, 1915), p. 188.
67. Casler, *Four Years*, p. 72.
68. *OR*, vol. 12, pt. 3, p. 879.
69. Hotchkiss, *Diary*, 14 April 1862.
70. Douglas, *I Rode with Stonewall*, p. 56.
71. Robert L. Dabney, "Stonewall Jackson," *S.H.S.P.* XI, p. 129. (Cited hereafter as Dabney, "Stonewall Jackson.")
72. Thomas C. Johnson, *Life and Letters of Robert Lewis Dabney* (Richmond: Whittet and Shepperson, 1903), p. 244.
73. *OR*, vol. 12, pt. 1, p. 725, 728.

74. Douglas, *I Rode with Stonewall,* p. 27.
75. Moore, *Cannoneer,* p. 41.
76. Hotchkiss, *Diary,* 20 April 1862.
77. *OR,* vol. 12, pt. 1, pp. 7, 470.
78. Ibid., pt. 3, pp. 458, 859–60.
79. Ibid., vol. 5, p. 1099.
80. Ibid., vol. 12, pt. 3, p. 852.
81. See ibid., pp. 878, 884, 885, and 887 for Lee's repeated references to this mission.
82. Ibid., pp. 859–60.
83. Ibid., pp. 862–63.
84. Ibid., pp. 863–64.
85. Ibid., p. 861.
86. Ibid., pp. 865–66.
87. Douglas Southall Freeman, *R. E. Lee,* 4 vols. (New York: Charles Scribner's Sons, 1934), vol. 2, p. 31, noted that Lee's authority over the Valley District was based on an informal, oral working arrangement with President Davis.
88. So far as he had authority to grant it, Lee gave permission to strike beyond the Valley on 1 May 1862. *OR,* vol. 12, pt. 3, p. 878.
89. Ibid., pp. 865–66.
90. Hotchkiss, *Diary,* 24 April 1862.
91. *OR,* vol. 12, pt. 3, p. 875.
92. Ibid., pt. 1, p. 466.
93. Ibid.
94. Ibid., pp. 446–47.
95. Ibid., pt. 3, p. 118.
96. Ibid., p. 122.
97. Ibid., p. 872.

Chapter 8

1. MS Diary of Joe Kaufman, Southern Historical Collection, University of North Carolina, Chapel Hill, N.C., 30 April 1862.
2. Howard, *Staff Officer,* p. 92.
3. Fishburne Journal, p. 51.
4. Neese, *Horse Artillery,* p. 51.
5. Apperson Diary, 1 and 2 May 1862.
6. White, *Hugh White,* p. 82.
7. Apperson Diary, 2 May 1862; Douglas, *I Rode with Stonewall,* pp. 47–48.
8. J. Hotchkiss to his wife, 3 May 1862, Hotchkiss Papers.
9. Hotchkiss, *Diary,* 1 May 1862.
10. Kaufman Diary, 2 May 1862.

11. Moore, *Cannoneer,* p. 45.
12. Apperson Diary, 4 May 1862.
13. James Huffman, *Ups and Downs of a Confederate Soldier* (New York: William E. Rudge's Sons, 1940), p. 46.
14. Waddell, *Augusta County,* pp. 296–97.
15. Ibid., p. 297; *B & L,* vol. 2, p. 286.
16. Wise, *Military History of V.M.I.,* pp. 192–93.
17. Douglas, *I Rode with Stonewall,* p. 48; Moore, *Cannoneer,* p. 46.
18. Hotchkiss, *Diary,* 5 May 1862.
19. Wise, *Military History of V.M.I.,* p. 205.
20. Hungerford, *Baltimore and Ohio Railroad,* vol. 2, pp. 7–14.
21. Hotchkiss, *Diary,* 6 May 1862.
22. *OR,* vol. 12, pt. 3, p. 135.
23. Hotchkiss, *Diary,* 6 and 7 May 1862.
24. Ibid., 7 May 1862.
25. Toney, *Privations,* p. 19.
26. Wise, *Military History of V.M.I.,* pp. 205–6.
27. R. W. Waldrop to his mother, 6 April 1862, Waldrop Letters; McCarthy, *Soldier Life,* p. 295.
28. Wise, *Military History of V.M.I.,* p. 206.
29. Moore, *Cannoneer,* p. 47.
30. McCarthy, *Soldier Life,* pp. 312, 328.
31. Lyle Recollections, pp. 402–3.
32. McCarthy, *Soldier Life,* p. 321.
33. Moore, *Cannoneer,* pp. 49–50.
34. McCarthy, *Soldier Life,* p. 309.
35. *OR,* vol. 12, pt. 3, p. 884.
36. Ibid.
37. Hotchkiss, *Diary,* 8 May 1862.
38. Allan, *Valley Campaign,* pp. 73–74.
39. Henderson, *Stonewall Jackson,* p. 226; *OR,* vol. 12, pt. 1, pp. 471, 485.
40. *OR,* vol. 12, pt. 1, p. 483.
41. Worsham, *Foot Cavalry,* pp. 29–30.
42. *OR,* vol. 12, pt. 1, p. 483.
43. Ibid., pp. 466, 476.
44. Ibid., p. 481.
45. Dabney, *Jackson,* p. 345; Allan, *Valley Campaign,* p. 76.
46. *OR,* vol. 12, pt. 1, p. 486.
47. Ibid.
48. Ibid., pp. 483, 486.
49. Ibid., p. 481; Hotchkiss, *Diary,* 8 May 1862.
50. *OR,* vol. 12, pt. 1, pp. 467, 472.
51. MS Recollections of Charles C. Wright, Virginia Historical Society, Richmond, Va., p. 8.
52. *OR,* vol. 12, pt. 1, pp. 462, 476.
53. Ibid., p. 470.

54. Ibid., pt. 3, p. 886.
55. J. Hotchkiss, undated, 3-page MS "Account," Hotchkiss Papers; Hotchkiss, *Diary,* 10 May 1862.
56. Ibid.
57. *B & L.*, vol. 2, p. 287.
58. Kaufman Diary, 10 May 1862.
59. John Harman to his brother, 15 May 1862, Hotchkiss Papers.
60. John Harman to his brother, 18 May 1862, Hotchkiss Papers.
61. Worsham, *Foot Cavalry,* p. 80.
62. Apperson Diary, 12 May 1862; Howard, *Staff Officer,* p. 103.
63. Philip Slaughter, *A Sketch of the Life of Randolph Fairfax* (Baltimore: Innen and Co., 1878), pp. 25–26.
64. *OR*, vol. 12, pt. 3, p. 883.
65. Ibid., p. 126.
66. Ibid., pp. 126–217.
67. Ibid., pt. 1, p. 465.
68. Ibid., pt. 3, p. 878.
69. Ibid., p. 888.
70. Ibid., p. 878.
71. Ibid., pp. 180, 143.
72. Kauffman Diary, 14 May 1862.
73. Hall, *Diary,* 14 May 1862.
74. Wise, *Military History of V.M.I.,* p. 209.
75. McCarthy, *Soldier Life,* pp. 308–9.
76. Apperson Diary, 14 May 1862.
77. Jackson Letter Book, 1862, 13 May 1862, Hotchkiss Papers. Emphasis added.
78. Dabney, *Jackson,* p. 354.
79. Hall, *Diary,* 15 May 1862.
80. Kaufman Diary, 15 May 1862.
81. Wise, *Military History of V.M.I.* p. 203.
82. Apperson Diary, 16 May 1862.
83. H. W. Wingfield, "Diary," ed. by W. W. Scott, *Virginia State Library Bulletin* (July 1927), 16 May 1862.
84. Ted Barclay to his sister, 16 May 1862, Barclay Letters.
85. Jackson Letter Book, 1862, 16 May 1862, Hotchkiss Papers.
86. Avirett, *Ashby,* p. 180; *OR,* vol. 12, pt. 3, p. 880.
87. William L. Wilson, *A Borderland Confederate* (Pittsburgh: University of Pittsburgh Press, 1962).
88. Frank M. Myers, *The Comanches: A History of White's Battalion* (Baltimore: Kelley Piet and Co., 1871), p. 48.

Chapter 9

1. William C. Oates, *The War Between the Union and the Confederacy* (New York: Neale Publishing Co., 1905), p. 93.

2. James C. Nisbet, *Four Years on the Firing Line,* ed. by Bill I, *Wiley* (Jackson, Tenn.: McCowart-Mercer Press, 1963), p. 33.
3. Oates, *The War,* p. 93.
4. R. H. Peck, *Reminiscences of a Confederate Soldier* (Privately printed, Fincastle, Va., 1913), p. 13; J. William Jones, "Reminiscences of the Army of Northern Virginia," *S.H.S.P.* IX, p. 187. (Cited hereafter as Jones, "Reminiscences.")
5. Taylor, *Destruction and Reconstruction,* pp. 33–38; Peck, *Reminiscences,* p. 13; T. T. Munford, "Reminiscences of Jackson's Valley Campaign," *S.H.S.P.* VII, p. 523. (Cited hereafter as Munford, "Jackson's Valley Campaign.")
6. MS Memoirs of Campbell H. Brown, Brown Memoirs, Manuscript Unit, Tennessee State Library and Archives, Nashville Tenn., p. 39.
7. Clement A. Evans, gen. ed., *Confederate Military History,* 13 vols. (Atlanta: Confederate Publishing Co., 1899), vol. 2 *Maryland* by Bradley Johnson, p. 683.
8. Tayor, *Destruction and Reconstruction,* pp. 48–49, 68, 87.
9. Ibid.; New Orleans *Daily True Delta,* 15 August 1861; Brown Memoirs, p. 31.
10. Taylor, *Destruction and Reconstruction,* pp. 21–22.
11. Ibid., pp. 35, 40.
12. Jennings C. Wise, *The Long Arm of Lee,* 2 vols. (Lynchburg, Va.: J. P. Bell, 1915), vol. 1, p. 170.
13. *OR,* vol. 12, pt. 3, pp. 876, 881; Hotchkiss, *Diary,* 30 April 1862.
14. Brown Memoirs, p. 33.
15. *OR,* vol. 12, pt. 3, pp. 878, 882, 887.
16. Ibid., p. 878.
17. Ibid., p. 879.
18. Ibid., p. 881.
19. Ibid.
20. Ibid., p. 882.
21. Ibid., p. 884.
22. Ibid., p. 886.
23. Munford, "Jackson's Valley Campaign," *S.H.S.P.* VII, p. 527.
24. *OR,* vol. 12, pt. 3, pp. 880–81.
25. Ibid., p. 135.
26. Ibid., p. 885.
27. Ibid., p. 888.
28. Munford, "Jackson's Valley Campaign," *S.H.S.P.* VII, p. 527.
29. Cooper, *One Hundred Years at V.M.I.,* vol. 3, p. 179.
30. Jones, "Reminiscences," *S.H.S.P.* IX, pp. 364–65.
31. *OR,* vol. 12, pt. 3, pp. 888–89.
32. Ibid., vol. 11, pt. 3, pp. 499–500.
33. Ibid., vol. 12, pt. 3, p. 888.
34. Ibid., p. 891.
35. Ibid., pp. 889, 892.

36. Percy G. Hamlin, *The Making of a Soldier: Letters of General R. S. Ewell* (Richmond, Va.: Whittet & Shepperson, 1935), p. 108.

37. R. S. Ewell to T. J. Jackson, 16 May 1862, Jackson Papers (d), Confederate Memorial Institute, Richmond, Va.

38. *OR,* vol. 12, pt. 3, pp. 888–89.

39. Ibid., pp. 891–92.

40. Ibid., p. 893.

41. Ibid.

42. Ibid., pt. 1, p. 502.

43. Charles Camper, *Historical Record of the First Maryland Infantry (Union)* (Washington: Gibson Brothers, 1871), p. 31.

44. J. E. Johnston to R. S. Ewell, 2 letters, 18 May 1862, Jackson Papers (b).

45. *OR,* vol. 12, pt. 3, p. 894.

46. Ibid., p. 895.

CHAPTER 10

1. Moore, *Cannoneer,* p. 50.

2. Ibid.

3. Shephard G. Pryor to his wife, 18 May 1862, Pryor Letters, Georgia Department of Archives and History, Atlanta, Ga.

4. John W. Wayland, *Stonewall Jackson's Way* (Staunton, Va.: The McClure Co., 1940), p. 102.

5. McGuire, *Diary,* p. 112.

6. *OR,* vol. 12, pt. 3, pp. 892–93.

7. Ibid., p. 894.

8. Dabney, *Jackson,* p. 359.

9. *OR,* vol. 12, pt. 3, p. 897.

10. MS Record Book of William B. Taliaferro, 19 May 1862, Taliaferro Papers, National Archives, Washington, D.C.

11. *OR,* vol. 12, pt. 3, p. 202.

12. Moore, *Cannoneer,* p. 53; Worsham, *Foot Cavalry,* p. 80.

13. *OR,* vol. 12, pt. 1, p. 70.

14. Ibid., pt. 3, p. 898. See note 30, infra, and accompanying text.

15. Casler, *Four Years,* p. 76.

16. Worsham, *Foot Cavalry,* p. 81.

17. Taylor, *Destruction and Reconstruction,* p. 50.

18. Ibid., p. 52.

19. *OR,* vol. 12, pt. 3, pp. 896–97.

20. Ibid., p. 898.

21. This assumes that Jackson continued to believe Banks had between 21,000 and 22,000 men (*OR,* vol. 12, pt. 3, p. 870) before Shields moved to Fredericksburg with a reported 6,000 men

(ibid., p. 894). Banks's actual strength at Strasburg was closer to 7,000 (ibid., pt. 1, p. 524).

22. Ibid., pt. 3, p. 898.

23. J. E. Johnston to R. S. Ewell, 18 May 1862, 2 P.M., Jackson Papers (b).

24. J. E. Johnston to R. S. Ewell, 18 May 1862, no time given, Jackson Papers (b).

25. Douglas Southall Freeman apparently discovered Johnston's dispatches of 18 May 1862 (*Lee's Lieutenants*, vol. 1, p. 371). He had previously noted (*R. E. Lee*, vol. 2 p. 57), that Lee's response to Jackson's plea could not be known, but that there doubtless was a response. In *Lee's Lieutenants* Freeman failed to link Johnston's dispatches of 18 May with the absence of any known reply by Lee to Jackson. Lenoir Chambers, in his *Stonewall Jackson* (New York: William Morrow and Co., 1959), p. 521, was the first to suggest this link.

26. Taylor, *Destruction and Reconstruction*, p. 52.

27. Howard, *Staff Officer*, p. 103.

28. McCarthy, *Soldier Life*, p. 312.

29. Hall, *Diary*, 20 May 1862.

30. Taylor, *Destruction and Reconstruction*, p. 53. Jackson never explained the purpose of Taylor's march to join the Army near New Market. Probably the best supposition is that the detour, like Ashby's demonstrations before Strasburg, was intended to confuse Banks about the Southern objective. Jackson may have reasoned that part of Ewell's division coming to the west of the Massanutten would distract attention from movement in the Luray Valley.

31. *OR*, vol. 12, pt. 3, p. 895; Allan, *Valley Campaign*, p. 92.

32. Hall, *Diary*, 22 May 1862.

33. Avirett, *Ashby*, p. 198; Baylor, *Bull Run*, p. 40 each reported 4 companies left opposite Strasburg; McDonald, *Laurel Brigade*, p. 59, gave the total as 3.

34. Harry Gilmore, *Four Years in the Saddle*, pp. 30–40; T. J. Jackson to R. E. Lee, 15 May 1862, Jackson Papers (a), Southern Historical Collection, University of North Carolina, Chapel Hill, N.C. In this letter, Jackson specifically confirmed to Lee that he had left only one company at McDowell and had returned to the Valley with "all my other force."

35. W. W. Goldsborough, *The Maryland Line in the Confederate States Army* (Baltimore: Kelly Piet and Co., 1869), pp. 46–47.

36. *OR*, vol. 12, pt. 3, p. 898.

37. Kaufman Diary, 22 May 1862.

38. *OR*, vol. 12, pt. 1, p. 702.

39. Hall, *Diary*, 22 May 1862.

40. Apperson Diary, 22 May 1862.

41. David Strother, *A Virginia Yankee in the Civil War: Diaries of David Strother*, ed. by Cecil Eby (Chapel Hill, N.C.: University

of North Carolina Press, 1961), 22 May 1862. (Cited hereafter as Strother, *Diary*.)

42. George H. Gordon, *Brook Farm to Cedar Mountain* (Boston: Osgood and Co., 1863), pp. 191–92.
43. *OR*, vol. 12, pt. 1, p. 524.
44. Ibid., pp. 523–24.
45. Ibid., p. 524.
46. Ibid., pt. 3, p. 213.
47. Ibid., pt. 1, pp. 278, 281.
48. Ibid., pt. 3, p. 214.
49. Ibid., pt. 1, p. 282.
50. Ibid., vol. 11, pt. 3, p. 504.
51. Ibid., pp. 508, 536.
52. Richmond *Daily Dispatch*, 16 May 1862.
53. Memphis *Daily Appeal*, 22 May 1862.
54. Mobile *Daily Advertiser and Register* 22 May 1862; Richmond *Daily Dispatch*, 19 May 1862.
55. E. A. Pollard, *Southern History of the War* (New York: Charles B. Richards, 1866), p. 382.
56. W. A. Christian, *Richmond* (Richmond: L. H. Jenkins, 1912), pp. 230–32.
57. J. B. Jones, *A Rebel War Clerk's Diary*, ed. by Earl Schneck Miers (New York: Sagamore Press, 1958), 20 and 23 May 1862.
58. *OR*, vol. 11, pt. 1, p. 651.
59. Johnston, *Military Narrative*, p. 130.
60. Jones, *Diary*, 24 and 25 May 1862.
61. Johnston, *Military Narrative*, p. 130.
62. Gustavus Smith, *Confederate War Papers* (New York: Atlantic Publishing and Engraving Co., 1884), pp. 146–47.

CHAPTER 11

1. Apperson Diary, 23 May 1862.
2. *OR*, vol. 12, pt. 1, p. 560.
3. Avirett, *Ashby*, pp. 187–88; Wayland, *Valley Records*, p. 287.
4. *OR*, vol. 12, pt. 1, p. 702.
5. MacDonald Memoirs, p. 42; McDonald, *Laurel Brigade*, p. 53.
6. Bradley T. Johnson, "Memoir of the First Maryland Regiment," *S.H.S.P.* X, p. 53. (Cited hereafter as Johnson, "First Maryland.")
7. Goldsborough, *Maryland Line*, pp. 47–48.
8. *OR*, vol. 12, pt. 1, p. 702.
9. Johnson, "First Maryland, *S.H.S.P.* X, p. 53.
10. Ibid.
11. *OR*, vol. 12, pt. 1, p. 725.

12. MS Diary of John Griffin, Emory University, Atlanta, Ga., 23 May 1862; Apperson Diary, 23 May 1862; and Hotchkiss, *Diary*, 23 May 1862, all reported the capture of two trains.
13. Dabney, *Jackson* p. 365.
14. *OR*, vol. 12, pt. 1, pp. 702, 557; Taylor, *Destruction and Reconstruction*, p. 56; Goldsborough, *Maryland Line*, p. 52.
15. Taylor, *Destruction and Reconstruction*, pp. 56–57.
16. Dabney, *Jackson*, p. 366.
17. Ibid.
18. *OR*, vol. 12, pt. 1, p. 734; John C. Donohoe, "Fight at Front Royal," *S.H.S.P.* XXIV, p. 134.
19. Dabney, *Jackson*, p. 368.
20. *OR*, vol. 12, pt. 1, p. 779.
21. Ibid., p. 526.
22. Ibid., p. 558.
23. Apperson Diary, 24 May 1862.
24. Taylor, *Destruction and Reconstruction*, p. 58.
25. *OR*, vol. 12, pt. 3, pp. 870, 894. See note 21, Chapter 10, supra, and accompanying text. Henderson, *Stonewall Jackson*, p. 249, concurred with this estimate of Jackson's knowledge.
26. *OR*, vol. 12, pt. 1, p. 703.
27. Ibid., pt. 770; Hotchkiss, *Diary*, 24 May 1862.
28. Neese, *Horse Artillery*, p. 56.
29. Only Taylor's brigade is reported with any reliability to have crossed both forks of the Shenandoah on May 23. MS Diary of George P. Ring, Tulane University, New Orleans, La., 23 May 1862.
30. *OR*, vol. 12, pt. 1, pp. 732, 754.
31. Ibid., p. 764.
32. Ibid., p. 772.
33. Ibid., p. 703.
34. Avirett, *Ashby*, p. 193.
35. *OR*, vol. 12, pt. 1, p. 546.
36. Ibid., pp. 546–47.
37. Allan, *Valley Campaign*, p. 128.
38. Hotchkiss, *Diary*, 24 May 1862.
39. *OR*, vol. 12, pt. 1, p. 703.
40. J. Hotchkiss to his wife, 26 May 1862, Hotchkiss Papers.
41. *OR*, vol. 12, pt. 1, p. 754.
42. Taylor, *Destruction and Reconstruction*, p. 58.
43. Dabney, *Jackson*, p. 371.
44. Neese, *Horse Artillery*, p. 56.
45. Douglas, *I Rode with Stonewall*, p. 54; Neese, *Horse Artillery*, pp. 56–57; Avirett, *Ashby*, p. 194.
46. *OR*, vol. 12, pt. 1, pp. 703, 726.

47. Taylor, *Destruction and Reconstruction*, p. 58.
48. Dabney, *Jackson*, p. 372.
49. *OR*, vol. 12, pt. 3, p. 899. This dispatch mentioned only Elzey's brigade; however, Scott's brigade was attached to Elzey's during the day. Brown Memoirs, p. 40.
50. *OR*, vol. 12, pt. 1, pp. 703, 726.
51. MS Recollections of Robert T. Barton, Barton Family Papers, Virginia Historical Society, Richmond, Va., p. 5.
52. Taylor, *Destruction and Reconstruction*, pp. 59–60.
53. *OR*, vol. 12, pt. 3, p. 899.
54. Taylor, *Destruction and Reconstruction*, p. 38.
55. *OR*, vol. 12, pt. 1, p. 779.
56. Poague, *Gunner*, p. 22; Dabney, *Jackson*, p. 373.
57. Douglas, *I Rode with Stonewall*, p. 55; Oates, *The War*, p. 30.
58. Douglas, *I Rode with Stonewall*, p. 55.
59. Dabney, *Jackson*, p. 373.
60. Neese, *Horse Artillery*, pp. 59–60.
61. MacDonald Memoirs, p. 43.
62. *OR*, vol. 12, pt. 1, p. 726.
63. Neese, *Horse Artillery*, p. 60.
64. Ibid.
65. *OR*, vol. 12, pt. 1, p. 704.
66. Barton Recollections, p. 7.
67. Moore, *Cannoneer*, pp. 54–55.
68. Apperson Diary, 24 May 1862.
69. Dabney, *Jackson*, p. 374.
70. Poague, *Gunner*, p. 23.
71. *OR*, vol. 12, pt. 1, p. 754.
72. Ibid., p. 735.
73. Apperson Diary, 24 May 1862.
74. *OR*, vol. 12, pt. 1, p. 735.
75. Hall, *Diary*, 24 May 1862; James H. Wood, *The War* (Cumberland, Md.,: Eddy Press, 1910), p. 52.
76. Apperson Diary, 24 May 1862.
77. Douglas, *I Rode with Stonewall*, p. 56.
78. *OR*, vol. 12, pt. 1, p. 704.
79. See, e.g., Ring Diary, 24 May 1862.
80. Avirett, *Ashby*, pp. 196–97; Douglas, *I Rode with Stonewall*, p. 57; *OR*, vol. 12, pt. 1, p. 776.
81. *OR* vol. 12, pt. 1, p. 751; White, *Hugh White*, p. 83; Apperson Diary, 24 May 1862.
82. Douglas, *I Rode with Stonewall*, pp. 56–57.
83. Ibid., p. 57.
84. Howard, *Staff Officer*, p. 108.
85. *OR*, vol. 12, pt. 1, p. 736.
86. Including reinforcements rushed to Winchester on 24 May,

Banks's force probably numbered between 6,000 and 7,000 men. *OR*, vol. 12, pt. 1, p. 528; Allan, *Valley Campaign*, p. 109.

87. Probably between 5:30 and 6:00 A.M. Worsham, *Foot Cavalry*, p. 85; Hall, *Diary*, 25 May 1862.
88. Myers, *White's Battalion*, p. 52. Colonel Crutchfield carried similar orders to Ewell; *OR*, vol. 12, pt. 1, p. 726.
89. Booth, *Maryland Soldier*, p. 34; Goldsborough, *Maryland Line*, p. 55.
90. *OR*, vol. 12, pt. 1, pp. 779, 794.
91. Ibid., p. 761.
92. Barton Recollections, p. 9; Poague *Gunner*, p. 24.
93. *OR*, vol. 12, pt. 1, pp. 736, 758.
94. Ibid., p. 761.
95. Blackford, *The Glory*, p. 189.
96. Moore, *Cannoneer*, p. 56.
97. Worsham, *Foot Cavalry*, p. 86; *OR*, vol. 12, pt. 1, p. 764.
98. Howard, *Staff Officer*, p. 110.
99. Taylor, *Destruction and Reconstruction*, p. 61. Douglas reported this interchange somewhat differently (*I Rode with Stonewall*, p. 58).
100. Taylor, *Destruction and Reconstruction*, p. 63.
101. Ibid., *OR*, vol. 12, pt. 1, p. 801.
102. Worsham, *Foot Cavalry*, pp. 87–88.
103. Taylor, *Destruction and Reconstruction*, pp. 63–64; Worsham, *Foot Cavalry*, pp. 86–87.
104. *OR*, vol. 12, pt. 1, pp. 779, 794.
105. Douglas, *I Rode with Stonewall*, p. 59; Worsham, *Foot Cavalry*, p. 87; Evans, gen. ed. *Confederate Military History*, vol. 3: *Virginia* by Jedediah Hotchkiss, p. 242.
106. Worsham, *Foot Cavalry*, p. 87.
107. J. K. Edmondson to his wife, 26 May 1862, Edmondson Letters.
108. *OR*, vol. 12, pt. 1, pp. 748–49.
109. Ibid., p. 706.
110. Avirett, *Ashby*, p. 293.
111. *OR*, vol. 12, pt. 1, p. 722; Dabney, *Jackson*, p. 381.
112. Fonerden, *Carpenter's Battery*, p. 47.
113. *OR*, vol. 12, pt. 1, pp. 709–10; Brown Memoirs, p. 43.
114. Dabney, *Jackson*, p. 382.
115. *OR*, vol. 12, pt. 1, pp. 706–7.
116. Ibid. See Chapter 12, note 97, infra, and accompanying text.
117. White, *Hugh White*, p. 85.
118. *OR*, vol. 12, pt. 1, p. 708.
119. Ibid. Banks reported total casualties of 2,019, including 1,663 prisoners, ibid., p. 554.
120. Jackson Letter Book 1862, 27 May 1862. Hotchkiss Papers.
121. *OR*, vol. 12, pt. 1, pp. 707, 720–24.
122. Richmond *Daily Dispatch*, 26 May 1862.

CHAPTER 12

1. *OR*, vol. 12, pt. 1, p. 706.
2. Douglas, *I Rode with Stonewall*, p. 65.
3. Smith, *Confederate War Papers*, pp. 146–47.
4. *OR*, vol. 12, pt. 3, p. 555; *B & L.*, vol. 2, p. 322.
5. Richmond *Daily Dispatch*, 29 May 1862; 30 May 1862.
6. *B & L*, vol. 2, p. 223.
7. *OR*, vol. 11, pt. 3, p. 557.
8. Gustavus W. Smith, *The Battle of Seven Pines*, (New York: G. Crawford, 1891), p. 14.
9. Johnston, *Military Narrative*, p. 131.
10. Ibid., pp. 131–32; *B & L.*, vol. 2, p. 224.
11. James Longstreet, *From Bull Run to Appomattox* (Philadelphia: J. B. Lippincott Co., 1896; reprint ed., Bloomington: Indiana University Press, 1960), p. 86.
12. Jefferson Davis, *Rise and Fall of the Confederate Government* (New York: D. Appleton and Co., 1881), vol. 2, p. 121.
13. Longstreet, *Bull Run to Appomattox*, p. 86.
14. Washington *Daily National Intelligencer*, 16 June 1862.
15. *OR*, vol. 12, pt. 1, p. 701.
16. Ibid., p. 525.
17. Ibid.
18. Ibid., p. 526.
19. Ibid., p. 626.
20. Ibid., pt. 3, pp. 233, 323; pt. 1, p. 626.
21. Ibid., pt. 1, p. 528.
22. Ibid., p. 643.
23. Ibid., pt. 3, pp. 219, 220.
24. Ibid., pt. 1, p. 626.
25. Ibid., vol. 11, pt. 1, p. 20.
26. Ibid., vol. 12, pt. 1, p. 527.
27. Ibid., pt. 3, p. 222.
28. In his outstanding *Lincoln Finds a General*, 5 vols. (New York: Macmillan, 1949), vol. 1, p. 175, K. P. Williams is one of the few historians to note this distinction.
29. *OR*, vol. 12, pt. 1, pp. 528, 529.
30. Ibid., pt. 3, pp. 230–31.
31. Ibid., p. 241.
32. Ibid., pp. 232, 234.
33. Ibid., p. 242.
34. Ibid., p. 247.
35. Ibid.
36. Ibid., p. 248.
37. Ibid., pt. 1, pp. 729–30.

38. Avirett, *Ashby*, p. 198.
39. This work was evidently quite successful. See *OR*, vol. 12, pt. 3, p. 273.
40. *OR*, vol. 12, pt. 1, pp. 225–26.
41. Ibid., pt. 3, p. 150.
42. Ibid., pp. 109, 185.
43. Ibid., pp. 160, 185.
44. Abram P. Smith, *History of the 76th New York Infantry* (Syracuse: Smith & Miles, 1867), p. 55.
45. *OR*, vol. 12, pt. 3, pp. 109, 160, 185.
46. The fluctuating strength of the Washington garrison during the spring of 1862 will provide a fascinating study for the scholar attuned to detail. In outline, the following can be asserted (only infantry regiments, the backbone of the garrison, are considered here): In 1863 McClellan prepared a roster of Wadsworth's command as of April 1, 1862 (*OR*, vol. 5, pp. 22–23). This roster appears generally accurate, but it nevertheless was part of McClellan's effort to justify his command of the Army of the Potomac and cannot be accepted uncritically. At least one discrepancy is immediately evident. McClellan reported that the entire 26th Penn. was assigned to Washington, yet in the same roster he listed that regiment as part of Hooker's division (ibid., p. 17), which moved to the Peninsula with McClellan. Other sources indicate that only one company of this regiment was left in Washington (ibid., vol. 12, pt. 3, p. 313). Still, since there is little else available, we must begin with McClellan's totals. Subtracting the 26th Penn. from the 21 full infantry regiments claimed for Washington's garrison leaves 20 regiments, a generous estimate of the infantry actually provided.

Of these 20 regiments, 10 are known to have transferred to points some distance from Washington during April and May of 1862. The 95th N.Y. was stationed ten miles north of Fredericksburg as of April 27 (ibid., pt. 3, p. 109). The 97th and 104th N.Y. and 105th and 107th Penn. moved to Catlett's Station on May 11 and passed from Wadsworth's control (ibid., pp. 160, 185, 241). The 26th and 94th N.Y. and 88th Penn. became part of Rickett's brigade, which reached the Fredericksburg area on May 14 (ibid., p. 144, 313). The 54th Penn. was not in or near Washington on April 1 and thereafter became part of a special brigade guarding the B & O; it was in the Shenandoah when the Valley Army struck at Winchester (ibid., p. 211). The 76th N.Y. moved to Fredericksburg on May 22 (Smith, *History of 76th N.Y.*, p. 55).

Of the remaining 10 regiments, 8 were in Washington in May, according to Wadsworth's end of the month report. These were the 2d D.C., 59th, 86th, and 101st N.Y., 10th N.J., and 91st and 99th Penn. One regiment, the 112th Penn., had been con-

verted into a heavy artillery unit and was present as such. Of
the remaining two units, the 91st N.Y. redeployed to Florida
(*OR*, vol. 14, p. 363) and the 12th W.Va. returned to its native
state (ibid., vol. 12, p. 338); both transfers must have been
completed before May 24, 1862, as neither unit is rostered in
the weekly report of the Army of the Rappahannock for that
date (see note 48, infra).

These detachments were only very partially made good. The
Army of the Rappahannock's weekly report of 24 May rostered
only 2 infantry regiments not with the Washington garrison in
April—78th N.Y. and 109th Penn. (see note 48, infra). Thus
2 regiments had been made available to supply the place of 10
taken from Wadsworth's command.

Because McClellan clearly lacked authority over this com-
mand after April 4, only Stanton and McDowell—and, ultimately,
Lincoln—can be responsible for the steady drain on it. Stanton
and McDowell clearly left Washington weakly garrisoned in
May 1862, and this weakness made Lincoln's redeployment of
McDowell irrevocable.

47. *OR*, vol. 12, pt. 3, p. 241.
48. "Morning Report of 24 May 1862," Record Group 94, Record
    of the Adjutant General's Office, Civil War Organization Re-
    turns, Army of the Rappahannock, National Archives, Wash-
    ington, D.C.
49. *OR*, vol. 12, pt. 3, p. 267.
50. Newel Cheney, *History of the 9th Regiment of New York
    Cavalry* (Privately printed, Jamestown, N.Y., 1901), pp. 44–45.
51. *OR*, vol. 12, pt. 3, p. 231.
52. Allan, *Valley Campaign*, footnotes pp. 121–22.
53. *OR*, ser. III, vol. 2, pp. 69–70.
54. See, e.g., Davis, *Rise and Fall of the Confederate Government*,
    vol. 2, pp. 107–9; Henderson, *Stonewall Jackson*, p. 263.
55. Allan, *Valley Campaign*, footnotes pp. 121–22.
56. Ibid.
57. Boston *Daily Advertiser*, 28 May 1862.
58. New York *Herald*, 26, 27 and 29 May 1862.
59. New York *Times*, 26 and 27 May 1862.
60. Philadelphia *Inquirer*, 27 May 1862. A similar account is found
    in the Harrisburg (Pa.) *Daily Telegraph*, 27 and 28 May 1862.
    Freeman collected a number of such accounts in *Lee's Lieuten-
    ants*, vol. 1, p. 410, note 94.
61. Washington *Sunday Morning Chronicle*, 25 May 1862.
62. Washington *Daily National Intelligencer*, 27 May 1862. Equally
    low-key coverage is found in the Washington *National Republi-
    can*, 26 May 1862. The Washington *Evening Star*, 26 May 1862,
    is the only major city paper to refer to any alarm, and, interest-

ingly, it noted that this alarm was confined to excitable abolitionists.

63. New York *Times,* 27 May 1862.

64. Allan, *Valley Campaign,* p. 120.

65. Ibid., p. 121.

66. See chapter 15, notes 47–49, infra, and accompanying text for
an analysis of this view.

67. *OR,* vol. 12, pt. 3, pp. 22–23.

68. Ibid., p. 221.

69. Ibid., pp. 230, 235.

70. Ibid., pp. 232, 233.

71. Ibid., p. 872.

72. Ibid., p. 894.

73. Ibid., p. 866. Johnston's letter to Ewell of May 18, 1862, reveals an equally sound grasp of this basic principle: "I cannot
provide for modification of the case. But, having full confidence
in the judgment and courage of both the division commanders,
rely upon them to conform to circumstances without fear of the
result." Jackson Papers, Virginia Historical Society.

74. Carl von Clausewitz, *Principles of War,* trans. and ed. by Hans
W. Gatzke (Harrisburg, Pa.: Stackpole Company, 1942), p. 46.

75. *OR,* vol. 12, pt. 1, p. 14.

76. Ibid., p. 10.

77. Ibid., pt. 3, pp. 146, 171, 184, 192.

78. Ibid., pp. 162, 180; pt. 1, p. 458.

79. Ibid., pt. 3, p. 202.

80. Ibid., p. 160.

81. Ibid., p. 865.

82. Ibid., vol. 5, p. 1004.

83. R. B. Garnett to Samuel Cooper, 20 June 1862, Garnett Court-
Martial Papers. Col. Fulkerson supported this claim; *OR,* vol.
12, pt. 1, p. 408. Major F. B. Jones, who relayed the initial oral
order from Jackson to Garnett (ibid., p. 388), died after the
Seven Days' fighting without giving his testimony, so exactly
what was told to Garnett can never be known.

84. Testimony of T. J. Jackson, 6 August 1862, Garnett Court-
Martial Papers.

85. R. B. Garnett to Samuel Cooper, 20 June 1862, Garnett Court-
Martial Papers.

86. See, e.g. Freeman, *Lee's Lieutenants,* vol. 1, pp. 481, 484, and
Chambers, *Stonewall Jackson,* vol. 1, p. 595.

87. Donohoe, "Fight at Front Royal," *S.H.S.P.* XXIV, p. 133.

88. *OR,* vol. 12, pt. 1, p. 724.

89. Avirett, *Ashby,* p. 270.

90. Ibid., p. 198.

91. Gilmor, *Four Years in the Saddle,* pp. 39–40; see also Chapter
10, note 34, supra.

92. Wilson, *Diary*, 22 May 1862.

93. Avirett, *Ashby*, p. 198, and Baylor, *Bull Run*, p. 40, concur that 4 companies were deployed above Strasburg.

94. Avirett, *Ashby*, p. 270.

95. *OR*, vol. 12, pt. 1, p. 726; Douglas, *I Rode with Stonewall*, p. 53.

96. Authorized strength of a cavalry company was 80 men; Jackson Letter Book, 1862, 19 April 1862, Hotchkiss Papers.

97. *OR*, vol. 12, pt. 1, pp. 706–7.

98. Brown Memoirs, p. 43.

99. *OR*, vol. 12, pt. 3, p. 900.

100. Moore, *Cannoneer*, p. 59.

101. McKim, *Soldier's Recollections*, p. 106.

102. Ibid.

103. Booth, *Maryland Soldier*, p. 37.

104. Ibid.

105. *OR*, vol. 12, pt. 3, p. 900.

106. John Harman to his brother, 27 May 1862, Hotchkiss Papers.

107. Jackson Letter Book, 1862, 26 May 1862, Hotchkiss Papers.

108. Casler, *Four Years*, p. 78.

CHAPTER 13

1. *OR*, vol. 12, pt. 1, pp. 730, 634.

2. Ibid., p. 738.

3. Ibid.

4. Douglas, *I Rode with Stonewall*, p. 63; John Harman to his brother, 29 May 1862, Hotchkiss Papers.

5. *OR*, vol. 12, pt. 1, p. 730; Wilson, *Diary*, 29 May 1862.

6. Hotchkiss, *Diary*, 30 May 1862.

7. Howard, *Staff Officer*, p. 114.

8. Hotchkiss, *Diary*, 30 May 1862.

9. Gilmor, *Four Years in the Saddle*, p. 40; MacDonald Memoirs, pp. 44–45.

10. A. R. Boteler, "Stonewall Jackson in the Campaign of 1862," *S.H.S.P.* XL, pp. 164–66. (Cited hereafter as Boteler, "Campaign of 1862.")

11. *OR*, vol. 12, pt. 1, pp. 682, 707–8, 727; Allan, *Valley Campaign*, pp. 130–31; Boteler, "Campaign of 1862," pp. 165–66.

12. Hotchkiss, *Diary*, 30 May 1862.

13. Hall, *Diary*, 31 May 1862.

14. Hotchkiss, *Diary*, 31 May 1862.

15. *OR*, vol. 12, pt. 1, p. 13.

16. Ibid., p. 535.

17. Ibid.

18. Ibid., p. 636.

19. Ibid., p. 14.

20. Neese, *Horse Artillery*, p. 62, and Shields in *OR*, vol. 12, pt. 1, p. 682, mention the presence of Confederate infantry on this diversion, but do not indicate which units were involved.

21. Hotchkiss, *Diary*, 31 May 1862.

22. John Harman to his brother, 2 June 1862, Hotchkiss Papers.

23. Hotchkiss, *Diary*, 1 June 1862.

24. John Harman to his brother, 31 May 1862, Hotchkiss Papers.

25. Worsham, *Foot Cavalry*, p. 94.

26. Douglas, *I Rode with Stonewall*, p. 162.

27. Henry Douglas to "My Dear Cousin," 24 July 1862, Douglas Letters.

28. Hall, *Diary*, 31 May 1862.

29. Thomas Munford, untitled recollections, Munford Papers, Duke University, Durham, N.C.

30. Douglas, *I Rode with Stonewall*, p. 69.

31. Howard, *Staff Officer*, p. 115.

32. Casler, *Four Years*, pp. 80–81.

33. J. K. Edmondson to his wife, 3 June 1862, Edmondson Letters; Hotchkiss, *Diary*, 31 May 1862.

34. Taylor, *Destruction and Reconstruction*, p. 72; *OR*, vol. 12, pt. 3, p. 904.

35. *OR*, vol. 12, pt. 1, pp. 718, 677.

36. McKim, *Soldier's Recollections*, pp. 107–8

37. Ibid.; Johnson, "First Maryland," *S.H.S.P.* X, p. 101; Booth, *Maryland Soldier*, p. 38.

38. Howard, *Staff Officer*, p. 38.

39. Johnson, "First Maryland," *S.H.S.P.* X, p. 102.

40. Casler, *Four Years*, pp. 80–81.

41. Allan, *Valley Campaign*, p. 135.

42. Howard, *Staff Officer*, p. 130; Goldsborough, *Maryland Line*, p. 62.

43. Jackson discussed this possibility with Taylor as early as the evening of 31 May 1862. Taylor, *Destruction and Reconstruction*, p. 67.

44. *OR*, vol. 12, pt. 1, p. 711; Brown Memoirs, p. 46.

45. Hotchkiss, *Diary*, 2 June 1862.

46. John Harman to his brother, 1 June 1862, Hotchkiss Papers.

47. *OR*, vol. 12, pt. 1, p. 712; Taylor, *Destruction and Reconstruction*, pp. 75–76.

48. *OR*, vol. 12, pt. 1, pp. 712, 731.

49. Oates, *The War*, p. 101; Douglas, *I Rode with Stonewall*, p. 71.

50. Oates, *The War*, p. 101.

51. Allan Recollections, p. 132.

52. Wayland, *Valley Records*, p. 289.

53. Wright Recollections, p. 20.

54. J. K. Edmondson to his wife, 2 June 1862, Edmondson Letters; *OR*, vol. 12, pt. 1, p. 756, and pt. 3, p. 879.

55. *OR*, vol. 12, pt. 1, p. 765.
56. John Harman to his brother, 5 June 1862, Hotchkiss Papers.
57. Hotchkiss, *Diary*, 1–5 June 1862.
58. MacDonald Memoirs, p. 48.
59. Hotchkiss, *Diary*, 3 June 1862.
60. *OR*, vol. 12, pt. 1, p. 16.
61. Ibid., p. 719.
62. Wilson, *Diary*, 6 June 1862.
63. MacDonald Memoirs, pp. 47–48. Charles T. O'Ferrall, *Forty Years of Active Service* (New York: Neale Publishing Co., 1909), p. 40.
64. MacDonald Memoirs, p. 51.
65. W. A. McClendon, *Recollections of War Times* (Montgomery, Ala.: Paragon Press, 1909), p. 40.
66. Johnson, "First Maryland," p. 103.
67. Ibid.; MacDonald Memoirs, pp. 51–52; T. T. Munford to Jedediah Hotchkiss, 19 August 1896, Hotchkiss Papers; Goldsborough, *Maryland Line*, p. 70.
68. Douglas, *I Rode with Stonewall*, p. 87.
69. Hotchkiss, *Diary*, 6 June 1862.
70. Avirett, *Ashby*, p. 223.
71. Wilson, *Diary*, 6 June 1862.
72. O'Ferrall, *Active Service*, p. 38; Avirett, *Ashby*, p. 226.
73. Hotchkiss, *Diary*, 6 June 1862.
74. *OR*, vol. 12, pt. 1, p. 712.
75. T. J. Jackson to A. R. Boteler, 6 May 1862, Boteler Papers.
76. Ashby's very formidable problems are discussed in McDonald, *Laurel Brigade*, pp. 51–52; Ashby, *Life of Ashby*, pp. 185–86; Clarence, *General Ashby*, p. 85, and Munford, "Jackson's Valley Campaign," *S.H.S.P.* VII, pp. 323–24.
77. Hotchkiss, *Diary*, 24 April 1862.
78. Douglas, *I Rode with Stonewall*, p. 75.
79. Taylor, *Destruction and Reconstruction*, p. 81.
80. McDonald, *Laurel Brigade*, p. 51.
81. Douglas, *I Rode with Stonewall*, p. 82.

CHAPTER 14

1. Wilson, *Diary*, 7 June 1862; Douglas, *I Rode with Stonewall*, p. 82; Avirett, *Ashby*, pp. 234–35.
2. *OR*, vol. 12, pt. 1, p. 732.
3. Ibid., pt. 3, p. 907.
4. Taylor, *Destruction and Reconstruction*, p. 88.
5. *OR*, vol. 12, pt. 1, p. 712.
6. Ibid., p. 713.

7. J. C. Moore to Jedediah Hotchkiss, 18 June 1896, Hotchkiss Papers.
8. *OR,* vol. 12, pt. 1, p. 732.
9. Ibid., p. 712; Douglas, *I Rode with Stonewall,* p. 85.
10. A. S. Pendleton to his mother, 7 June 1862, Bean, ed., "Pendleton Letters," p. 364.
11. Douglas, *I Rode with Stonewall,* p. 85; Wilson, *Diary,* 8 June 1862; Allan Recollections, p. 137; Griffin Diary, 8 June 1862.
12. *OR,* vol. 12, pt. 3, p. 908.
13. Ibid., pp. 907–8.
14. Robert L. Dabney to G. F. R. Henderson, undated, Hotchkiss Papers.
15. *OR,* vol. 12, pt. 1, pp. 712–13; Allan Recollections, p. 137.
16. Robert L. Dabney to G. F. R. Henderson, undated, Hotchkiss Papers.
17. L. W. Cox to Jedediah Hotchkiss, 17 August 1896, Hotchkiss Papers.
18. For some unknown reason, Hotchkiss became interested in this skirmish during 1896 and sought details from surviving participants. Considering the passage of time, the responses are remarkably consistent. J. C. Moore to Hotchkiss, 18 June 1896; L. W. Cox to Hotchkiss, 17 August 1896; James Carrington to Hotchkiss, undated; Robert L. Dabney to G. F. R. Henderson, undated; all in Hotchkiss Papers.
19. Poague, *Gunner,* p. 26.
20. *OR,* vol. 12, pt. 1, p. 739.
21. Taylor, *Destruction and Reconstruction,* p. 81.
22. Allan, *Valley Campaign,* p. 150; Moore, *Cannoneer,* pp. 68–69.
23. Wood, *The War,* p. 59.
24. Ibid. The Federals had been ordered to secure the North River bridge and probably did not realize what might have been achieved by destroying it; *OR,* vol. 12, pt. 3, p. 335.
25. Allan Recollections, p. 137.
26. *OR,* vol. 12, pt. 1, p. 712.
27. Ibid., pp. 781, 728.
28. Ibid., p. 20.
29. Ibid., p. 783.
30. Ibid., p. 795.
31. Ibid., p. 782.
32. Ibid., p. 789.
33. Ibid., p. 818.
34. Ibid., pp. 796, 783; McClendon, *War Times,* p. 66; Oates, *The War,* pp. 102–3.
35. *OR,* vol. 12, pt. 1, p. 782.
36. Ibid., p. 714.
37. Ewell arrived at Headquarters at dusk. Dabney, *Jackson,* p. 419.
38. *OR,* vol. 12, pt. 1, pp. 664–65, 782–84.

39. Ibid., p. 798.

40. Jackson revealed the essence of his reasoning in 1863 during a private conversation, which Hotchkiss recorded. Hotchkiss, *Diary*, 4 April 1863.

41. Dabney, *Jackson*, p. 419.

42. *OR*, vol. 12, pt. 1, pp. 714–15.

43. Douglas, *I Rode with Stonewall*, p. 89.

44. It seems incredible that Jackson delayed until midnight the construction of this vital span. Nevertheless, Dabney, whose account of this phase of the Campaign is reliable, is clear that construction began "about midnight." Dabney, *Jackson*, p. 419.

45. Ibid., pp. 420–21.

46. *B & L.*, vol. 2, p. 293.

47. *OR*, vol. 12, pt. 1, p. 728.

48. Ibid., p. 785.

49. Ibid., pp. 785–86.

50. Ibid., p. 740, 757.

51. An unusually large number of those who crossed this bridge recalled its deficiencies. Fonerden, *Carpenter's Battery*, p. 26; Munford, "Jackson's Valley Campaign," *S.H.S.P.* VII, pp. 529–30; Worsham, *Foot Cavalry*, pp. 92–93; Howard recalled that the bridge was still under construction when Winder's brigade arrived to cross it, but this is not supported by any other source (*Staff Officer*, p. 126.).

52. *OR*, vol. 12, pt. 1, p. 747.

53. Ibid., p. 728.

54. Ibid., p. 740.

55. Ibid., p. 757.

56. Allan Recollections, p. 137.

57. Dabney, "Stonewall Jackson," *S.H.S.P.* XI pp. 151–52.

58. Taylor, *Destruction and Reconstruction*, p. 83; Henry B. Kelly, *Port Republic* (Philadelphia: J. B. Lippincott Co., 1886), pp. 15–16.

59. *OR*, vol. 12, pt. 1, pp. 745, 747.

60. Ibid., p. 745.

61. Ibid., p. 757.

62. Ibid., p. 760.

63. Ibid., p. 728. One piece even arrived at the front minus gunners; ibid., p. 741.

64. Taylor, *Destruction and Reconstruction*, p. 84.

65. Hotchkiss, *Diary*, 9 June 1862.

66. *OR*, vol. 12, pt. 1, p. 753.

67. Ibid., p. 741.

68. Ibid., pp. 741, 763.

69. Ibid., pp. 715, 786.

70. Ibid., p. 790.

71. Neese, *Horse Artillery*, p. 74.

72. *OR,* vol. 12, pt. 1, p. 792.
73. Samuel D. Buck, *With the Old Confeds* (Baltimore: H. E. Houck and Co., 1925), p. 38; Moore, *Cannoneer,* p. 75.
74. Taylor, *Destruction and Reconstruction,* p. 86.
75. *OR,* vol. 12, pt. 1, p. 791.
76. Ibid., p. 758.
77. Taylor, *Destruction and Reconstruction,* p. 86.
78. Douglas, *I Rode with Stonewall,* p. 91.
79. *OR,* vol. 12, pt. 1, p. 715.
80. Dabney, *Jackson,* p. 425.
81. Moore, *Cannoneer,* p. 78.
82. Buck, *With the Old Confeds,* p. 39.
83. *OR,* vol. 12, pt. 1, pp. 717–18.
84. Ibid., p. 690.
85. Douglas, *I Rode with Stonewall,* p. 90.
86. See Chapter 15, infra.
87. As late as April 1863, Jackson seems not to have realized the relatively small numbers he faced at Port Republic. *OR,* vol. 12, pt. 1, p. 716.
88. Dabney, *Jackson,* p. 420–22; *B & L,* vol. 2, p. 293.
89. Hotchkiss, *Diary,* 15 April 1863.
90. Howard, *Staff Officer,* p. 92.
91. Taylor, *Destruction and Reconstruction,* pp. 89–90.

CHAPTER 15

1. *OR,* vol. 12, pt. 1, p. 716.
2. Hotchkiss, *Diary,* 12 June 1862.
3. Neese, *Horse Artillery,* p. 56.
4. Brown Memoirs, p. 56.
5. Kaufman Diary, 16 June 1862.
6. *OR,* vol. 12, pt. 3, p. 911.
7. Jackson Letter Book, 1862, 13 June 1862, Hotchkiss Papers.
8. Dabney, *Jackson,* p. 430.
9. Boteler, in "Campaign of 1862," *S.H.S.P.* XL, does not state when he returned. However, as he does not narrate the battles of June 8 and 9, it must be assumed that he returned after those dates.
10. Jones, *War Clerk's Diary,* 22 May 1862.
11. Richmond *Whig,* 27 May 1862.
12. Richmond *Whig,* 11 June 1862.
13. Macon *Daily Telegraph,* 3 June 1862. The same sort of praise could be found throughout the South. See, e.g., Augusta (Ga.) *Daily Constitutionalist,* 8 June 1862, and Charlotte *Whig,* 17 June 1862.
14. Robert E. Myers, ed., *The Children of Pride* (New Haven: Yale University Press, 1972), p. 908.

15. Richard B. Harwell, ed., *Kate: The Journal of a Confederate Nurse* (Baton Rouge: Louisiana State University Press, 1959), pp. 53–54.
16. Atlanta *Intelligencer*, 3 June 1862; Americus (Ga.) *Sumter Republican*, 30 May 1862.
17. Jones, *War Clerk's Diary*, 22 May 1862.
18. Sally Putnam, *In Richmond During the Confederacy* (New York: G. W. Carleton and Co., 1867), p. 146.
19. Johnston, *Military Narrative*, pp. 138–39.
20. *OR*, vol. 12, pt. 3, p. 906.
21. Ibid., vol. 11, pt. 3, p. 854, 894; vol. 12, pt. 3, pp. 908, 910.
22. Henderson, *Stonewall Jackson*, p. 298.
23. Charles Marshal, *An Aide-de-Camp to General Lee* (Boston: Little, Brown and Co., 1927), p. 84.
24. *OR*, vol. 11, pt. 3, p. 590.
25. Douglas Southall Freeman, *Lee's Dispatches to Jefferson Davis* (New York: G. P. Putnam's Sons, 1957), pp. 5–6.
26. The traditional view of Lee's efforts to reinforce the Valley has been that the operation was simply a ruse in preparation for the Army's march on Richmond; Allan, *Valley Campaign*, p. 169. Freeman, in *R. E. Lee*, vol. 2, pp. 95–96, disputed this view and offered the explantion which is also advanced here. Read carefully, Lee's dispatch to Jackson of June 11, 1862, and his letter to Davis of June 5, 1862, both indicate that the Valley Army was to strike another blow in the Shenandoah. In this regard, Jackson's letter to Lee of June 6, 1862 (predicting little further activity in the Valley), is significant, for Lee endorsed it: "If General Jackson cannot undertake offensive operations, which seems to be the case, re-enforcement would be lost upon him"; *OR*, vol. 12, pt. 3, p. 907.
27. *OR*, vol. 12, pt. 3, p. 910.
28. Ibid.
29. Boteler, "Campaign of 1862," *S.H.S.P.* XL, pp. 172–73.
30. Ibid., pp. 173–74.
31. *OR*, vol. 14, p. 558; vol. 51, pt. 2, p. 569.
32. Jackson to R. E. Lee, 13 June 1862. R. E. Lee Papers, Duke University, Durham, N.C.
33. Ibid.
34. Slaughter, *Randolph Fairfax*, p. 26.
35. R. W. Waldrop to his mother, 27 May 1862, Waldrop Letters.
36. S. G. Pryor to his wife, 12 June 1862, Pryor Letters.
37. White, *Hugh White*, pp. 94–95.
38. *OR*, vol. 12, pt. 1, p. 786.
39. Neese, *Horse Artillery*, p. 67.
40. Taylor, *Destruction and Reconstruction*, p. 87.
41. Casler, *Four Years*, p. 78.
42. Wayland, *Jackson's Way*, p. 134.
43. Casler, *Four Years*, pp. 86–87.

44. Henderson, *Stonewall Jackson,* p. 322.
45. Douglas, *I Rode with Stonewall,* p. 92.
46. An interesting summary of subsequent military analysis of the Campaign is contained in Jay Luvass, *Military Legacy of the Civil War* (Chicago: University of Chicago Press, 1959).
47. Henderson, *Stonewall Jackson,* p. 312.
48. General Viscount Wolseley, "An English View of the Civil War," *North American Review,* vol. 149, p. 166.
49. J. F. C. Fuller, *Grant and Lee* (Bloomington: Indiana University Press, 1957), p. 154. See also Introduction, notes 2–6, supra.

Epilogue

1. Douglas, *I Rode with Stonewall,* p. 97.
2. Jones, "Reminiscences," *S.H.S.P.* IX, p. 363.
3. J. B. Powley, *A Soldier's Letters to Charming Nellie* (New York: Neale Publishing Co., 1908), p. 46.
4. *OR,* vol. 12, pt. 3, p. 354; pt. 1, pp. 542–43.
5. Ibid., pt. 1, p. 661.
6. Ibid., pt. 3, p. 411.
7. McDowell would later assert that, had he been able to leave the Valley on the day he was ordered to depart (June 8, 1862), he could have joined McClellan by June 26, 1862, the opening day of the Seven Days. Ibid., pt. 1, p. 288.
8. Ibid., pt. 3, pp. 382, 384, 392, 395, 407, 434.
9. Ibid., p. 435.
10. Ibid., vol. 11, pt. 2, p. 810.
11. Dabney, *Jackson,* p. 467.
12. James P. Smith, "With Stonewall Jackson in the Army of Northern Virginia," *S.H.S.P.* XLIII, p. 24.
13. Douglas, *I Rode with Stonewall,* p. 111.
14. Ibid., p. 313.
15. *OR,* vol. 43, pt. 2, p. 880.
16. Ibid., pt. 1, p. 37.

Appendix A

1. Hotchkiss, *Diary,* 4 April 1862.
2. Ibid., 31 March 1863.
3. *OR,* vol. 12, pt. 1, p. 703.
4. Henderson, *Stonewall Jackson,* pp. 251, 252.
5. Freeman, *Lee's Lieutenants,* vol. 1, pp. 735–39.
6. See notes 30–32 and accompanying text, infra, for a detailed discussion of this point.
7. *OR,* vol. 12, pt. 1, p. 779.

8. Ibid., p. 746.
9. Ibid., p. 754.
10. Hotchkiss, *Diary*, 24 May 1862.
11. J. Hotchkiss to his wife, 26 May 1862, Hotchkiss Papers.
12. Apperson Diary, 24 May 1862.
13. Lynchburg (Va.) *Daily Republican*, 31 May 1862.
14. Hall, *Diary*, 24 May 1862.
15. Allan, *Valley Campaign*, p. 128
16. *OR*, vol. 12, pt. 1, p. 623.
17. Ibid., p. 576.
18. Ibid., p. 614.
19. Ibid.
20. Ibid., p. 620.
21. Gordon, *Brook Farm to Cedar Mountain*, p. 215.
22. *OR*, vol. 12, pt. 1, p. 623.
23. Gordon, *Brook Farm to Cedar Mountain*, p. 215, indicated that it in fact took two hours to countermarch to Newtown.
24. *OR*, vol. 12, pt. 1, p. 615.
25. C. F. Morse, *Letters Written During the Civil War* (privately printed, 1898), pp. 58–60.
26. *OR*, vol. 12, pt. 1, p. 587.
27. Ibid., p. 576.
28. Ibid., pp. 567, 579, 605, 612. It should be noted further that the other Federal sources fixing a time for the main Confederate attack place it at or after 3:30 P.M. Ibid., pp. 568, 586.
29. Chambers, *Stonewall Jackson*, vol. 1, pp. 530–31.
30. Freeman, *Lee's Lieutenants*, vol. 1, pp. 386, 737–38.
31. *OR*, vol. 12, pt. 1, p. 703.
32. MS Journal of J. Hotchkiss, Hotchkiss Papers, p. 19.

Appendix B

1. The most readable and best researched study of Lincoln's May counterthrust is found in Williams, *Lincoln Finds a General*, vol. 1, chapter VII.
2. *OR*, vol. 12, pt. 3, p. 219.
3. Ibid., pt. 1, p. 11.
4. Ibid., p. 644.
5. Ibid., pt. 3, p. 235.
6. Ibid., p. 244.
7. Ibid., pp. 244–45.
8. Ibid., p. 258.
9. Ibid., pt. 1, p. 283.
10. Ibid., pt. 3, p. 260.
11. Ibid., p. 266.
12. Ibid., pt. 1, p. 644.

13. Ibid., pt. 3, p. 267.
14. Ibid., pt. 1, p. 644.
15. Ibid., p. 645.
16. Ibid..
17. Ibid., p. 646.
18. Ibid., p. 647.
19. Ibid., p. 11.
20. Ibid., p. 644.
21. Ibid., p. 647.
22. Ibid., pt. 3, p. 259.
23. Ibid.
24. Ibid., p. 276.
25. Ibid., pp. 277, 278–79.
26. Ibid., p. 285.
27. Ibid., p. 269.
28. Ibid., pp. 265, 284.
29. Ibid., p. 282.
30. Ibid., p. 277.
31. Ibid., pt. 1, p. 533.
32. Ibid., pt. 3, p. 278.
33. Ibid., p. 267.
34. Ibid., pp. 293–94.
35. Ibid., pt. 1, p. 647.
36. Ibid., p. 648.
37. Ibid., p. 13.
38. Ibid.
39. Ibid., pt. 3, pp. 290–91.
40. Ibid., p. 291.
41. Ibid., pt. 1, p. 649.
42. Ibid., pt. 3, p. 281.
43. Ibid., pp. 293–94.
44. Ibid., p. 302.
45. Ibid., pt. 1, pp. 682–83.
46. Ibid., p. 649.
47. Ibid., pt. 3, p. 314.
48. Ibid., pt. 1, p. 538.
49. Ibid., pt. 3, p. 315.
50. Ibid., pp. 299–300.
51. Ibid., pt. 1, pp. 649–50.
52. Ibid., p. 283.
53. Ibid. This explanation is that of McDowell. Shields left no known explanation of his false start.
54. George L. Wood, *History of the 7th Ohio* (New York: J. Miller, 1865; reprint ed., Louisville, Ky.: Lost Cause Press, 1958), p. 114.
55. William Kepler, *History of the 4th Regiment of Ohio Volunteers* (Privately printed, Cleveland, Ohio, 1886), p. 67.

56. Military Historical Society of Massachusetts, *Papers of the Military Historical Society of Massachusetts,* vol. 6, *The Shenandoah Campaigns of 1862 and 1864* (Boston, 1907), p. 19.
57. Allan, *Valley Campaign,* p. 135.
58. *OR,* vol. 12, pt. 1, p. 677.

Appendix C

1. Freeman, *R. E. Lee,* vol. 2, p. 580.
2. Freeman, *Lee's Lieutenants,* vol. 1, p. 659.
3. See, e.g., Clifford Dowdey, *The Seven Days,* (Boston: Little, Brown and Co., 1964), pp. 196–205.
4. Taylor, *Destruction and Reconstruction,* p. 61.
5. Hotchkiss, *Diary,* 1 June 1862.
6. Douglas, *I Rode with Stonewall,* p. 74.
7. Ibid.
8. Hotchkiss, *Diary,* 4 June 1862.
9. Douglas, *I Rode with Stonewall,* p. 75.
10. Ibid.
11. Hotchkiss, *Diary,* 4 June 1862.
12. Ibid., 5 June 1862.
13. Ibid., 6 June 1862.
14. Ibid.
15. Ibid.
16. *B & L,* vol. 2, p. 293.
17. John Harman to his brother, 6 June 1862, Hotchkiss Papers.
18. Howard, *Staff Officer,* p. 124.
19. A. S. Pendleton to his mother, 7 June 1862, Bean, ed., "Pendleton Letters," p. 364.

Appendix D

1. Compiled from Allan, *Valley Campaign; B & L,* vol. 12, pp. 300–1; and *OR,* vol. 12, pt. 1.

BIBLIOGRAPHY

Manuscript Material

Allan Papers. Unpublished manuscript written by William Allan, an officer in the Valley Army Quartermaster Department, after the war. Southern Historical Collection, University of North Carolina, Chapel Hill, North Carolina.

Apperson Diary. Unpublished diary of John Apperson, a hospital orderly with the 4th Va. Inf., covering the years 1861 and 1862. Rockbridge Historical Society, Lexington, Virginia.

Army of the Rappahannock, Morning Reports, April–May, 1862. Record Group 94, Record of the Adjutant General's Office, Civil War Organizations Returns, National Archives, Washington, D.C.

Ashby Letters. Unpublished wartime letters of Turner Ashby, written during 1862. Chicago Historical Society, Chicago, Illinois.

Barclay Letters. Unpublished wartime letters of Theodore Barclay, a member of the 4th Va. Inf.; scattered dates. Rockbridge Historical Society, Lexington, Virginia.

Barton Recollections. Unpublished "Recollection of Robert Thomas Barton of the Rockbridge Artillery of the Battle of Winchester," written after the war. Typescript in the Virginia Historical Society, Richmond, Virginia.

Boteler Papers. Unpublished letters and papers of Alexander R. Boteler, who served briefly as a member of the Valley Army Staff during 1862. Duke University Manuscript Collection, Durham, North Carolina.

Brown Memoirs. Papers of Campbell Brown and Richard S. Ewell. Military reminiscences of Captain Campbell Brown, Chief of Staff, R. S. Ewell's division. Manuscript Unit, Tennessee State Library and Archives. (These papers were the gift of Campbell Brown, 203 Meadowgreen Drive, Franklin, Tennessee 37064, grandson of Captain Campbell Brown. Colonel Brown still lives at that address.)

Chase Diary. Unpublished wartime diary of Miss Julia Chase, a resident of Winchester. Typescript in Handley Library, Winchester, Virginia.

Douglas Letters. Unpublished wartime Letters of Henry Kyd Douglas, a member of the Valley Army Staff, written during 1861 and 1862. Duke University Manuscript Collection, Durham, North Carolina.

Edmondson Letters. Unpublished wartime letters of James K. Edmondson, a member of the 27th Va. Inf., written for the most part during 1861 and 1862. Rockbridge Historical Society, Lexington, Virginia.

Fishburne Journal. Unpublished manuscript journal of Clement D. Fishburne, a member of the Rockbridge Artillery, written after the war. (This journal formed the basis of Fishburne's "Historical Sketch of the Rockbridge Artillery," XXIII *Southern Historical Society Papers.*) University of Virginia Manuscript Collection, Charlottesville, Virginia.

Garibaldi Letters. Unpublished wartime letters of John Garibaldi, a member of the 4th Va. Inf., written for the most part in 1861 and 1863. Virginia Military Institute Manuscript Collection, Lexington, Virginia.

Garnett Court-Martial Papers. Typed transcript of testimony and various supporting documents collected for court-martial of Brigadier General Richard B. Garnett during August 1862. Museum of the Confederacy, Richmond, Virginia.

Green Letters. Unpublished wartime letters of Jonathan Green, a member of the 21st. Va. Inf. and later of the Rockbridge Artillery; scattered dates. Duke University Manuscript Collection, Durham, North Carolina.

Griffin Diary. Unpublished diary of John Levi Griffin, a member of the 12th Ga. Inf., 1861–62. Typescript in Emory University Library, Atlanta, Georgia.

Harlow Letters. Unpublished wartime letters of George K. Harlow, a member of the 23d Va. Inf.; scattered dates. Virginia Historical Society, Richmond, Virginia.

Harper Diary. Unpublished diary of W. P. Harper, a member of the 7th La. Inf. Typescript in the Tulane University Library, New Orleans, Louisiana.

Harrison Letters. Unpublished wartime letters of William F. Harrison, a member of the 23d Va. Inf.; scattered dates. Duke University Manuscript Collection, Durham, North Carolina.

Hawks Papers. A vast collection of receipts, rosters, and various documents relating to the work of Major W. J. Hawks, Valley Army Commissary Officer, throughout the war. Duke University Manuscript Collection, Durham, North Carolina.

Hightower Letters. Unpublished wartime letters of Thomas M. Hightower, a member of the 21st Ga. Inf.; scattered dates. Georgia Department of Archives and History, Atlanta, Georgia.

Hooke Letters. Wartime letters of Robert W. Hooke, a member of the 5th Va. Inf.; scattered dates. Duke University Manuscript Collection, Durham, North Carolina.

Hotchkiss Papers. The essential source on the Valley Campaign. This vast collection contains the complete wartime letters of Jedediah Hotchkiss, a member of the Valley Army Staff. Also included are Hotchkiss' diary, postwar unpublished journal, and various short recollections. The wartime letters of John Harman, Valley Army Quartermaster, are contained herein, as are copies of T. J. Jackson's Order and Letter Books covering the entire war. Finally, these papers contain the fruits of Hotchkiss' postwar research, including dozens of letters to and from surviving participants of various battles. This postwar correspondence extends to 1896. Manuscript Division, Library of Congress, Washington, D.C.

Jackson Papers (a). Wartime letters of T. J. Jackson; scattered dates. Southern Historical Collection, University of North Carolina, Chapel Hill, North Carolina.

Jackson Papers (b). Wartime letters of T. J. Jackson; scattered dates. Virginia Historical Society, Richmond, Virginia.

Jackson Papers (c). Wartime letters of T. J. Jackson; scattered dates. Virginia Military Institute Manuscript Collection, Lexington, Virginia.

Jackson Papers (d). Wartime correspondence to and from T. J. Jackson; scattered dates. Confederate Memorial Institute, Richmond, Virginia.

Kaufman Diary. Unpublished diary of Joseph Kaufman, a member of the 10th Va. Inf., written during 1862. Typescript in Southern Historical Collection, University of North Carolina, Chapel Hill, North Carolina.

Kelly Letters. Unpublished wartime letters of A. K. Kelly, a member of the 21st Va. Inf.; scattered dates. Kelly-Williamson Papers, Duke University Manuscript Collection, Durham, North Carolina.

Langhorne Letters. Wartime letters of James Langhorne, a member of the 4th Va. Inf., primarily written during 1861 and 1862. Virginia Historical Society, Richmond, Virginia.

Lyle Recollections. Unpublished recollections (entitled "Stonewall Jackson's Campguard") of John N. Lyle, a member of the 4th Va. Inf., written during or shortly after the war. Typescript in Rockbridge Historical Society, Lexington, Virginia.

MacDonald Memoirs. Unpublished manuscript of Edward H. MacDonald, a member of Ashby's cavalry, written in 1866. Southern Historical Collection, University of North Carolina, Chapel Hill, North Carolina.

Miller Letters. Wartime letters of Abraham S. Miller, a Virginia Militia surgeon, written primarily during 1861 and 1862. In possession of Dr. James A. Miller, Winchester, Virginia.

Morrison Diary. Unpublished diary of Harry R. Morrison, a member of the 4th Va. Inf., covering the month of March 1862. Rockbridge Historical Society, Lexington, Virginia.

Munford Papers. Unpublished reminiscences of Thomas Munford, commander of the 2d Va. Cav. and subsequently of the entire Valley Cavalry, written after the war, and numerous letters, papers, etc. Duke University Manuscript Collection, Durham, North Carolina.

Nadenbousch Papers. Scattered wartime orders, letters, etc., of J. Q. A. Nadenbousch, a member of the 2d Va. Inf. Duke University Manuscript Collection. Durham, North Carolina.

Pendleton Papers. Family letters and papers of the William N. Pendleton family, including wartime letters of A. S. Pendleton, a member of the Valley Army Staff, written until his death in 1864. Duke University Manuscript Collection, Durham, North Carolina.

Penn Letters. Unpublished wartime letters of Thomas G. Penn, a member of the 48th Va.; scattered dates. Duke University Manuscript Collection, Durham, North Carolina.

Pryor Letters. Unpublished wartime letters of Shephard G. Pryor, a member of 12th Ga. Inf., written 1861–63. Typescript in Georgia Department of Archives and History, Atlanta, Georgia.

Ray Letters. Unpublished wartime letters of Lavender R. Ray, a member of the 1st Ga. Inf., 1861–65. Typescript in Georgia Department of Archives and History, Atlanta, Georgia.

Richardson Letters. Unpublished wartime letters of Sidney J. Richardson, a member of the 21st Ga.; scattered dates. Georgia Department of Archives and History, Atlanta, Georgia.

Ring Diary. Unpublished wartime diary of George P. Ring, a member of Taylor's Louisiana Brigade. Tulane University Library, New Orleans, Louisiana.

Taliaferro Papers. Scattered wartime papers, letters, orders, etc., of William B. Taliaferro, commander of the 3d Brigade, Jackson's division, Army of the Valley. National Archives, Washington, D.C.

————. A large collection of scattered papers, including much on the expedition to Romney in January 1862. William and Mary College Library, Williamsburg, Virginia.

Waldrop Letters. Wartime letters of Richard W. Waldrop, a member of the 21st Va. Inf., written throughout the war. Southern Historical Collection, University of North Carolina, Chapel Hill, North Carolina.

Wright Recollections. Unpublished manuscript of Charles C. Wright, a V.M.I. cadet, written after the war. Virginia Historical Society, Richmond, Virginia.

PERSONAL REMINISCENCES AND UNIT HISTORIES

Avirett, James B. *The Memoirs of General Turner Ashby and His Compeers.* Baltimore: Selby and Dulany, 1867.

Baylor, George. *Bull Run to Bull Run.* Richmond: B. F. Johnson Publishing Co., 1900.

Booth, George W. *Personal Reminiscences of a Maryland Soldier in the War Between the States*. Baltimore: Fleet, McGinley and Co., 1898.

Bosang, J. N. *Memoirs of a Pulaski Veteran*. Privately printed. Pulaski, Virginia, 1912.

Buck, Samuel D. *With the Old Confeds*. Baltimore: H. E. Houch & Co., 1925.

Casler, John O. *Four Years in the Stonewall Brigade*. Girard, Kans: Appeal Publishing Co., 1906; reprint ed., Marietta, Ga.: Continental Book Co., 1951.

Chamberlayne, John Hampden. *Ham Chamberlayne—Virginian*, ed. by C. G. Chamberlayne. Richmond: Dietz Printing Co., 1932.

Cooke, John Esten. *Wearing of the Gray*. New York, 1878; reprint ed., Bloomington: Indiana University Press, 1959.

Douglas, Henry Kyd. *I Rode with Stonewall*. Chapel Hill: University of North Carolina Press, 1940.

Fonerden, C. A. *A Brief History of the Military Career of Carpenter's Battery*. New Market, Va.: Henkel & Company, 1911.

Gill, John. *Reminiscences of Four Years as a Private Soldier in the Confederate Army*. Baltimore: Sun Printing Office, 1904.

Gilmor, Harry. *Four Years in the Saddle*. New York: Harper & Brothers, 1866.

Goldsborough, W. W. *The Maryland Line in the Confederate States Army*. Baltimore: Kelly Piet & Co., 1869.

Graybill, John H. *Diary of a Soldier of the Stonewall Brigade*. Privately printed. Woodstock, Va., no date.

Hall, James E. *Diary of a Confederate Soldier,* ed. by Ruth Woods Dayton. Privately printed. Philippi, W. Va., 1961.

Hamlin, Percy G., ed. *The Making of a Soldier: Letters of General R. S. Ewell*. Richmond: Whittet and Shepperson, 1935.

Houghton, W. R. *Two Boys in the Civil War and After*. Montgomery, Ala.: Paragon Press, 1912.

Howard, McHenry. *Recollections of a Maryland Staff Officer Under Johnston, Jackson and Lee*. Baltimore: Williams and Wilkins, 1914.

Huffman, James. *Ups and Downs of a Confederate Soldier*. New York: William E. Rudge's Sons, 1940.

Jones, J. B. *A Rebel War Clerk's Diary,* ed. by Earl Schenck Miers. New York: Sagamore Press, 1958.

Johnston, Joseph E. *Narrative of Military Operations*. New York: D. Appleton and Co., 1874; reprint ed., Bloomington: Indiana University Press, 1959.

Kelly, Henry B. *Port Republic*. Philiadelphia: J. B. Lippincott Co., 1886.

Longstreet, James. *From Manassas to Appomattox*. Philadelphia: J. B. Lippincott Co., 1896; reprint ed., Bloomington: Indiana University Press, 1960.

McCarthy, Carlton. *Detailed Minutiae of Soldier Life in the Army of*

Northern Virginia. Privately printed. Richmond, Virginia, 1882; reprinted in *Soldier Life of the Union and Confederate Armies*, ed. by Philip Van Doren Stern, Bloomington: Indiana University Press, 1961.

McClendon, W. A. *Recollections of War Times*. Montgomery, Ala.: Paragon Press, 1909.

McDonald, Archie P., ed. *Make Me a Map of the Valley: The Civil War Journal of Stonewall Jackson's Topographer* [Jedediah Hotchkiss]. Dallas: Southern Methodist University Press, 1973.

McDonald, Mrs. Cornelia. *A Diary with the Reminiscences of the War and Refugee Life in the Shenandoah Valley*. Nashville: Cullom and Ghertner Co., 1934.

McDonald, William N. *A History of the Laurel Brigade*. Baltimore: Sun Job Printing Office, 1907.

McGuire, Judith W. *Diary of a Southern Refugee*. Richmond: E. J. Hale and Son, 1867.

McKim, Randolph H. *A Soldier's Recollections*. New York: Longmans, Green and Co., 1910.

Moore, Edward A. *The Story of a Cannoneer Under Stonewall Jackson*. New York: Neale Publishing Co., 1907.

Myers, Frank M. *The Comanches: A History of White's Battalion*. Baltimore: Kelly Piet & Co., 1871.

Neese, George M. *Three Years in the Confederate Horse Artillery*. New York: Neale Publishing Co., 1911.

Nisbet, James C. *Four Years on the Firing Line*, ed. by Bill Irvin Wiley. Jackson, Tenn.: McCowart-Mercer Press, 1963.

Oates, William C. *The War Between the Union and the Confederacy: A History of the 15th Alabama Regiment*. New York: Neale Publishing Co., 1905.

O'Ferrall, Charles T. *Forty Years of Active Service*. New York: Neale Publishing Co., 1904.

Opie, John N. *A Rebel Cavalryman with Lee, Stuart and Jackson*. Chicago: W. B. Conkey Co., 1899.

Peck, R. H. *Reminiscences of a Confederate Soldier*. Privately printed. Fincastle, Va. 1913.

Poague, William T. *Gunner with Stonewall*. Jackson, Tenn.: McCowart-Mercer Press, 1957.

Powley, J. B. *A Soldier's Letters to Charming Nellie*. New York: Neale Publishing Co., 1908.

Smith, Gustavus W. *Confederate War Papers*. New York: Atlantic Publishing and Engraving Co., 1884.

———. *The Battle of Seven Pines*. New York: G. Crawford, 1891.

Taylor, Richard. *Destruction and Reconstruction*. New York: D. Appleton and Co., 1879; reprint ed., New York: Longmans, Green and Co., 1955.

Toney, Marcus B. *The Privations of a Private*. Privately printed. Nashville, Tenn., 1905.

Watkins, Samuel R. *Company Aytch*. Nashville, Tenn.: Cumberland Presbyterian Publishing House, 1882; reprint ed., Jackson, Tenn.: McCowart-Mercer Press, 1952.

Wilson, William L. *A Borderland Confederate*, ed. by Festus P. Summers. Pittsburgh: University of Pittsburgh Press, 1962.

Wood, James H. *The War*. Cumberland, Md.: Eddy Press, 1910.

Worsham, John H. *One of Jackson's Foot Cavalry*. New York: Neale Publishing Co., 1912.

OTHER PRIMARY SOURCES

Allan, William. *History of the Campaign of Gen. T. J. (Stonewall) Jackson in the Shenandoah Valley of Virginia*. Philadelphia: J. B. Lippincott, 1880; reprint ed., Dayton, Ohio: Morningside, 1974.

Ashby, Thomas A. *The Valley Campaigns*. New York: Neale Publishing Co., 1914.

Blackford, L. Minor, ed. *Mine Eyes Have Seen the Glory*. Cambridge, Mass.: Harvard University Press, 1954.

Davis, Jefferson. *Rise and Fall of the Confederate Government*. 2 vols. New York: D. Appleton and Co., 1881.

Evans, Clement A., gen. ed. *Confederate Military History*. 13 vols. Atlanta: Confederate Publishing Co., 1899.

Johnson, Robert U., and C. C. Buel, eds. *Battles and Leaders of the Civil War*. 4 vols. New York: Century, 1887–88; reprint ed., New York: Thomas Yoseloff, 1956.

Marshal, Charles. *An Aide-de-Camp to General Lee*. Boston: Little, Brown & Co., 1927.

Paxton, John G., ed. *Elisha F. Paxton: Memoir and Memorials*. Privately printed. New York, 1907.

Pollard, E. A. *Southern History of the War*. New York: Charles B. Richmond, 1866.

Slaughter, Philip. *A Sketch of the Life of Randolph Fairfax*. Baltimore: Innen and Co., 1878.

Southern Historical Society. *Southern Historical Society Papers*. 52 vols. Richmond, 1876–1959.

U. S. War Department. *War of the Rebellion: A Compilation of the Official Records of the Union and Confederate Armies*. 128 vols. Washington, D.C.: Government Printing Office, 1880–1901.

Waddell, Joseph A. *Annals of Augusta*. Richmond: William E. Jones, 1886.

White, Henry A. *Sketches of the Life of Captain Hugh A. White*. Columbia, S.C.: South Carolina Steam Press, 1864.

Wise, Jennings C. *The Long Arm of Lee*. 2 vols. Lynchburg, Va.: J. P. Bell, 1915.

Wise, Jennings C. *The Military History of the Virginia Military Institute from 1839–1875.* Lynchburg, Va.: J. P. Bell, 1915.

Biographical Works

Allan, Elizabeth P. *The Life and Letters of Margaret Junkin Preston.* Boston: Houghton Mifflin and Co., 1903.

Arnold, Thomas J. *Early Life and Letters of General Thomas J. Jackson.* New York: Fleming H. Revell Co., 1916.

Ashby, Thomas A. *Life of Turner Ashby.* New York: Neale Publishing Co., 1914.

Bean, W. G. *Stonewall's Man: Sandie Pendleton.* Chapel Hill: University of North Carolina Press, 1959.

Chambers, Lenoir. *Stonewall Jackson.* 2 vols. New York: William Morrow and Co., 1959.

Clarence, Thomas. *General Turner Ashby.* Winchester, Va.: Eddy Press Corp., 1907.

Cook, Roy Bird. *The Family and Early Life of Stonewall Jackson.* Charles Town, W.Va., 1948.

Cooke, John Esten. *Stonewall Jackson.* New York: D. Appleton and Co., 1876.

Dabney, Robert L. *Life and Campaigns of Lieutenant General Thomas J. Jackson.* New York: Blelock and Co., 1866.

DuFour, Charles L. *Gentle Tiger.* Baton Rouge: Louisiana State University Press, 1957.

Freeman, Douglas Southall. *R. E. Lee.* 4 vols. New York: Charles Scribner's Sons, 1934.

Hamlin, Percy G. *Old Bald Head.* Strasburg, Va.: Shenandoah Publishing House, 1940.

Henderson, Col. G. F. R. *Stonewall Jackson and the American Civil War.* New York: Longmans, Green and Co., 1936.

Jackson, Mary Anna. *Life and Letters of General Thomas J. Jackson.* New York: Harper & Brothers, 1892.

Johnson, Thomas C. *The Life and Letters of Robert Lewis Dabney.* Richmond: Whittet and Shepperson, 1903.

Vandiver, Frank E. *Mighty Stonewall.* New York: McGraw-Hill Book Company, 1957.

GENERAL SOURCES

Bean, W. G. *The Liberty Hall Volunteers.* Charlottesville: University of Virginia Press, 1964.

Bill, Alfred Hoyt. *The Beleaguered City.* New York: Alfred A. Knopf, 1946.

Black, Robert C., III. *The Railroads of the Confederacy*. Chapel Hill: University of North Carolina Press, 1952.

Brice, Marshall. *The Stonewall Brigade Band*. Verona, Va.: McClure Printing Co., 1967.

Campbell, Charles. *History of the Colony and Ancient Dominion of Virginia*. Philadelphia: J. B. Lippincott, 1860.

Camper, Charles. *Historical Record of the First Maryland Infantry (Union)* Washington, D.C.: Gibson Brothers, 1871.

Cartmell, T. K. *Shenandoah Valley Pioneers*. Winchester, Va.: Eddy Press Corp., 1909.

Cheney, Newel. *History of the 9th Regiment of New York Cavalry*. Privately printed. Jamestown, N.Y., 1901.

Christian, W. A. *Richmond*. Richmond: L. H. Jenkins, 1912.

Clausewitz, Carl von. *Principles of War*, trans. and ed. by Hans W. Gatzke. Harrisburg, Pa.: Stackpole Co., 1942.

Cooke, John Esten. *Stonewall Jackson and the Old Stonewall Brigade*. Charlottesville: University of Virginia Press, 1954.

Couper, William. *One Hundred Years at V.M.I.* 4 vols. Richmond: Garrett and Massie, 1939.

Cummings, Kate. *The Journal of a Confederate Nurse*, ed. by Richard B. Harwell. Baton Rouge: Louisiana State University Press, 1959.

Dowdey, Clifford. *The Seven Days*. Boston: Little, Brown and Co., 1964.

Fitzpatrick, John C., ed. *The Writings of George Washington*. 39 vols. Washington, D.C.: Government Printing Office, 1931–44.

Freeman, Douglas Southall. *Lee's Dispatches to Jefferson Davis*. New York: G. P. Putnam's Sons, 1957.

————. *Lee's Lieutenants*. 3 vols. New York: Charles Scribner's Sons, 1942–44.

Fuller, J. F. C. *Grant and Lee*. Bloomington: Indiana University Press, 1957.

Gordon, George H. *Brook Farm to Cedar Mountain*. Boston: Osgood and Co., 1863.

Gottman, Jean. *Virginia at Mid-Century*. New York: Henry Holt and Co., 1955.

Hamilton, Stanislaus, ed. *Letters to Washington and Accompanying Papers*. 5 vols. Boston: Houghton Mifflin and Co., 1898–1902.

Hart, Freeman H. *The Valley of Virginia in the American Revolution*. Chapel Hill: University of North Carolina Press, 1942.

Hungerford, Edward. *The Story of the Baltimore and Ohio Railroad*. 2 vols. New York: G. P. Putnam's Sons, 1928.

Jefferson, Thomas. *Notes on the State of Virginia*, ed. by William Peden. Chapel Hill: University of North Carolina Press for the Institute of Early American History and Culture, 1955.

Johnston, Angus J., II. *Virginia Railroads in the Civil War*. Chapel Hill: University of North Carolina Press, 1961.

Kellogg, Sanford C. *The Shenandoah Valley and Virginia, 1861–1865*. New York: Neale Publishing Co., 1903.

Kepler, William. *History of the 4th Regiment of Ohio Volunteers*. Privately printed. Cleveland, Ohio, 1886.

Kercheval, Samuel. *A History of the Valley of Virginia*. Strasburg, Va.: Shenandoah Publishing House, 1925.

Koontz, Louis K. *The Virginia Frontier: 1754–1763*. Baltimore: Johns Hopkins University Press, 1925.

Leech, Samuel V. *The Raid of John Brown at Harper's Ferry*. Washington, D.C.: DeSoto Press, 1909.

Luvass, Jay. *Military Legacy of the Civil War*. Chicago: University Chicago Press, 1959.

Manarin, L. H., ed. *Richmond at War: The Minutes of the City Council, 1861–1865*. Chapel Hill: University of North Carolina Press, 1966.

Maury, Ann, ed. *Memoirs of a Huguenot Family*. New York: G. P. Putnam's Sons, 1901.

Monier, Henry D. *Military Annals of Louisiana*. New Orleans, 1875.

Moore, Frank, ed. *The Rebellion Record*. 12 vols. New York, 1862–71.

Morse, C. F. *Letters Written During the Civil War*. Privately printed, 1898.

Morton, Frederic. *The Story of Winchester in Virginia*. Strasburg, Va.: Shenandoah Publishing House, 1925.

Myers, Robert M., ed. *The Children of Pride*. New Haven: Yale University Press, 1972.

Peyton, J. Lewis. *History of Augusta County*. Staunton, Va.: Yost and Son, 1882.

Pollard, E. A. *Life of Jefferson Davis*. Philadelphia: National Publishing Co., 1896.

Pollard, E. A. *The Lost Cause*. New York: E. B. Treat & Co., 1866.

Putnam, Sally. *In Richmond During the Confederacy*. New York: G. W. Carleton and Co., 1963.

Robertson, James I., Jr. *The Stonewall Brigade*. Baton Rouge: Louisiana State University Press, 1963.

Rowland, Dunbar, ed. *Jefferson Davis: Constitutionalist*. Jackson, Miss.: Mississippi Department of Archives and History, 1923.

Schuricht, Hermann. *History of the German Element in Virginia*. Baltimore: Theo. Kroh & Sons, 1898.

Se Cheverall, J. *Journal History of the 29th Ohio*. Privately printed. Cleveland, 1883.

Smith, Abram P. *History of the 76th New York Infantry*. Syracuse: Smith & Miles, 1867.

Strickler, Harry M. *A Short History of Page County*. Richmond: Dietz Press, 1952.

Strother, David. *A Virginia Yankee in the Civil War: Diaries of David*

Strother, ed. by Cecil D. Eby. Chapel Hill: University of North Carolina Press, 1961.

Summers, Festus P. *The Baltimore and Ohio in the Civil War.* New York: G. P. Putnam's Sons, 1939.

Thomas, Emory M. *The Confederate State of Richmond.* Austin: University of Texas Press, 1971.

Warner, Ezra. *Generals in Gray.* Baton Rouge: Louisiana State University Press, 1959.

Wayland, John W. *German Element of the Shenandoah Valley of Virginia.* Charlottesville, Va.: Michie Co., 1907.

————. *History of Rockingham County.* Dayton, Va.: Ruebush-Elkins Co., 1912.

————. *History of Shenandoah County.* Strasburg, Va.: Shenandoah Publishing House, 1927.

————. *Stonewall Jackson's Way.* Staunton, Va.: McClure Co., 1940.

————. *Twenty-five Chapters on the Shenandoah Valley.* Strasburg, Va.: Shenandoah Publishing House, Inc., 1957.

————. *Virginia Valley Records.* Strasburg, Va.: Shenandoah Publishing House, 1930.

Williams, Kenneth P. *Lincoln Finds a General.* 5 vols. New York: Macmillan, 1949.

Wood, George L. *History of the 7th Ohio.* New York: J. Miller, 1865; reprint ed., Louisville, Ky.: Lost Cause Press, 1958.

NEWSPAPERS

(The newspapers listed below are in the Newspaper Collection, Duke University Library, Durham, North Carolina.)

Americus, Georgia, *Sumter Republican,* 1862.
Atlanta, Georgia, *Intelligencer,* 1862.
Augusta, Georgia, *Daily Constitutionalist,* 1862.
Boston, Massachusetts, *Daily Advertiser,* 1862.
Charlotte, North Carolina, *Whig,* 1862.
Harrisburg, Pennsylvania, *Daily Telegraph,* 1862.
Harrisonburg, Virginia, *Rockingham Register,* 1862.
Lynchburg, Virginia, *Daily Republican,* 1862.
Macon, Georgia, *Daily Telegraph,* 1862.
Memphis, Tennessee, *Daily Appeal,* 1862.
Mobile, Alabama, *Daily Advertiser and Register,* 1862.
New Orleans, Louisiana, *Daily True Delta,* 1861.
New York, New York, *Herald,* 1862.
New York, New York, *Times,* 1862.
Philadelphia, Pennsylvania, *Inquirer,* 1862.
Richmond, Virginia, *Daily Dispatch,* 1861 and 1862.
Richmond, Virginia, *Enquirer,* 1862.

Richmond, Virginia, *Whig*, 1861 and 1862.
Washington, D.C., *Daily National Intelligencer*, 1862.
Washington, D.C., *Evening Star*, 1862.
Washington, D.C., *National Republican*, 1862.
Washington, D.C., *Sunday Morning Chronicle*, 1862.
Winchester, Virginia, *Virginian*, 1860.
Winchester, Virginia, *Daily Republican*, 1861–62.

PERIODICAL ARTICLES

Anderson, Carter. "Train Running for the Confederacy," *Locomotive Engineering*, July 1892.

Bean, William G. "The Valley Campaign of 1862 as Revealed in Letters of Sandie Pendleton," *Virginia Magazine of History and Biography*, 78, No. 3 (July 1970).

Beirne, R. R., ed. "Three War Letters" [including letter of John Eager Howard Post of the 1st Md. Inf.], *Maryland Historical Magazine*, 40, No. 4 (December 1945).

Davis, Jackson Beauregard. "The Life of Richard Taylor," *Louisiana Historical Quarterly*, 29, No. 1 (January 1941).

Hopkins, C. A. Porter, ed. "An Extract from the Journal of Mrs. Hugh H. Lee of Winchester, Va." *Maryland Historical Magazine*, 53, No. 4 (December 1958).

Montague, Ludwell Lee. "Subsistence of the Army of the Valley," *Military Affairs*, 12, No. 4, (Winter 1948).

Osterhout, Charles Hotchkiss. "A Johnny Reb from Windsor, New York," *Courier Magazine* (January 1955).

Wingfield, H. W. "Diary," *Bulletin of the Virginia State Library*, 16 Nos. 2 and 3 (July 1927).

Wolseley, General Viscount. "An English View of the Civil War," *North American Review*, 149 (July 1889).

INDEX

Abraham's Creek, 230

Allan, Col. William, xvi, xvii, 333

Allegheny Mountains, 7, 43, 44
  Jackson's offensive in, 60–62,
    65–66, 68–91
  Lee's offensive in, 36–37, 45,
    113
  map of, 39
  Washington's defense of,
    12–15, 61, 80, 81

Allen, Col. J. W., 265, 300

American Medical Association,
  331

Anderson, Brig. Gen. Joseph R.,
  208, 234, 238, 240

Anderson, Brig. Gen. S. R., 67

Andrew, John, 243

Apperson, Hospital Orderly John,
  24, 68, 77, 80, 93, 97, 163,
  180, 209
  at Battle of Winchester, 225,
    335

Army of Tennessee
  (Confederate), 87

Army of the Northwest
  (Confederate), 45, 62,
  66–68, 165
  end of, 103
  See also Loring, Brig. Gen.
    William W.

Army of the Potomac, U.S.,
  98–103, 127–32
  March, 1862, strength of, 103

Arnell, Sgt. Charles, 125

Artillery
  Edward's, 165
  Ewell's, 185
  infantry and, 168
  Jackson's 45, 55–56, 59, 68,
    104, 152–53, 255
  See also Rockbridge Artillery;
    specific commanders

Ashby, Brig. Gen. Turner, 38, 42,
  56–59, 63–64, 92, 104–6,
  117, 143–45, 165, 241
  in Battle of Front Royal,
    209–10, 214, 253, 255–58
  in Battle of Kernstown, 117–19
  in Battle of Winchester, 218,
    220–25, 232, 233, 256–58
  brash heroics of, 141–42,
    284–85
  death of, 279–82
  evaluation of, 282–86
  follows Bank's retreat, 190
  growth of command of, 151,
    152
  illness of, 180
  romanticism of, 110–11
  in Romney compaign, 70, 75,
    78, 80
  in second retreat from
    Winchester, 270, 274, 276,
    278
  stripped of command and
    restored, 146–49, 256

S